The Gothic and Theory

Edinburgh Companions to the Gothic

Series Editors
Andrew Smith, University of Sheffield
William Hughes, Bath Spa University

This series provides a comprehensive overview of the Gothic from the eighteenth century to the present day. Each volume takes either a period, place, or theme and explores their diverse attributes, contexts and texts via completely original essays. The volumes provide an authoritative critical tool for both scholars and students of the Gothic.

Volumes in the series are edited by leading scholars in their field and make a cutting-edge contribution to the field of Gothic studies.

Each volume:
- Presents an innovative and critically challenging exploration of the historical, thematic and theoretical understandings of the Gothic from the eighteenth century to the present day
- Provides a critical forum in which ideas about Gothic history and established Gothic themes are challenged
- Supports the teaching of the Gothic at an advanced undergraduate level and at masters level
- Helps readers to rethink ideas concerning periodisation and to question the critical approaches which have been taken to the Gothic

Published Titles
The Victorian Gothic: An Edinburgh Companion
    Andrew Smith and William Hughes
Romantic Gothic: An Edinburgh Companion
    Angela Wright and Dale Townshend
American Gothic Culture: An Edinburgh Companion
    Joel Faflak and Jason Haslam
Women and the Gothic: An Edinburgh Companion
    Avril Horner and Sue Zlosnik
Scottish Gothic: An Edinburgh Companion
    Carol Margaret Davison and Monica Germanà
The Gothic and Theory: An Edinburgh Companion
    Jerrold E. Hogle and Robert Miles
Twenty-First-Century Gothic: An Edinburgh Companion
    Maisha Wester and Xavier Aldana Reyes

Visit the Edinburgh Companions to the Gothic website at:
www.edinburghuniversitypress.com/series/EDCG

The Gothic and Theory

An Edinburgh Companion

Edited by
Jerrold E. Hogle and
Robert Miles

EDINBURGH
University Press

Edinburgh University Press is one of the leading university presses in the UK. We publish academic books and journals in our selected subject areas across the humanities and social sciences, combining cutting-edge scholarship with high editorial and production values to produce academic works of lasting importance. For more information visit our website: edinburghuniversitypress.com

© editorial matter and organisation Jerrold E. Hogle and
  Robert Miles, 2019, 2020
© the chapters their several authors, 2019, 2020

Edinburgh University Press Ltd
The Tun – Holyrood Road
12(2f) Jackson's Entry
Edinburgh EH8 8PJ

First published in hardback by Edinburgh University Press 2019

Typeset in 11/13 Adobe Sabon by
IDSUK (DataConnection) Ltd, and
printed and bound by CPI Group (UK) Ltd,
Croydon, CR0 4YY

A CIP record for this book is available from the British Library

ISBN 978 1 4744 2777 7 (hardback)
ISBN 978 1 4744 2778 4 (paperback)
ISBN 978 1 4744 2779 1 (webready PDF)
ISBN 978 1 4744 2780 7 (epub)

The right of Jerrold E. Hogle and Robert Miles to be identified as the editors of this work has been asserted in accordance with the Copyright, Designs and Patents Act 1988, and the Copyright and Related Rights Regulations 2003 (SI No. 2498).

Contents

Acknowledgements	vii
1. The Gothic–Theory Conversation: An Introduction *Jerrold E. Hogle*	1

Part I: The Gothic, Theory and History

2. History/Genealogy/Gothic: Godwin, Scott and their Progeny *Robert Miles*	33
3. The Gothic in and as Race Theory *Maisha Wester*	53
4. Postcolonial Gothic in and as Theory *Alison Rudd*	71

Part II: The Gothic of Psychoanalysis and its Progeny

5. The Gothic Body before and after Freud *Steven Bruhm*	91
6. Abjection as Gothic and the Gothic as Abjection *Jerrold E. Hogle*	108

Part III: Feminism, Gender Theory, Sexuality and the Gothic

7. Unsettling Feminism: The Savagery of Gothic *Catherine Spooner*	129
8. Gothic Fiction and Queer Theory *George E. Haggerty*	147

Part IV: Theorising the Gothic in Modern Media

  9. The Gothic at the Heart of Film and Film Theory   165
     Elisabeth Bronfen

10. Techno-Terrors and the Emergence of Cyber-Gothic   182
     Anya Heise-von der Lippe

Part V: The Gothic before and after Post-structuralism

11. The Gothic as a Theory of Symbolic Exchange   203
     David Collings

12. Incorporations: The Gothic and Deconstruction   220
     Tilottama Rajan

13. Dark Materialism: Gothic Objects, Commodities and Things   240
     Fred Botting

14. Thinking the Thing: The Outer Reaches of Knowledge in Lovecraft and Deleuze   260
     Anna Powell

15. Gothic and the Question of Ethics: Otherness, Alterity, Violence   279
     Dale Townshend

Part VI: The Gothic–Theory Relationship in Retrospect and Prospect

16. On the Threshold of Gothic: A Reflection   301
     David Punter

Notes on Contributors   320
Index   325

Acknowledgements

The editors are deeply grateful, first, to Professors William Hughes and Andrew Smith, the General Editors of the Edinburgh Companions to the Gothic, for inviting us to put this collection together and for supporting us in, and counselling with us on, this effort in every way they could. We are immensely appreciative, too, of all our contributors, every one of whom seized insightfully on our approach to the Gothic-and-theory conversation and provided expert analyses in their areas of greatest knowledge in ways well suited to the readership anticipated for Edinburgh Companions. We know that these scholars, world-class Gothicists and theoreticians all, often had to carve out time from busy and demanding lives to write these essays, and we thank them all for working back-and-forth with us, and even giving us some good ideas that we had not considered at first, to achieve the results that we are happy and proud to present to our readers. Both we and our contributors, in addition, are grateful to our universities, and often to key staff members within them, for their steady support of our work on the Gothic and theory. We also happily acknowledge, all of us, the indispensable help offered to us by our families – and our spouses or most significant others in particular. Finally – after saluting and appreciating each other, to be sure – we send our thanks to Edinburgh University Press, and especially to our main editorial facilitator, Ersev Ersoy, for all their encouragement, special consideration and professional expertise. We feel privileged to have been asked to envision and to have brought together this *Gothic and Theory* volume in the Edinburgh Companions to the Gothic series.

To all our colleagues in

THE INTERNATIONAL GOTHIC ASSOCIATION

and *in memoriam*

ALLAN LLOYD SMITH

great theoretical analyst of the Gothic and first president of the IGA

Chapter 1

The Gothic–Theory Conversation: An Introduction
Jerrold E. Hogle

Gothic fiction-making and theory – philosophical, aesthetic, psychological and cultural – have been in a sustained dialogue with each other from the start of the Gothic as a genre (really a *mixture* of genres, or a *mode*, as we will see), and they have recently been in close conversation again, despite a long intervening period of distance from each other. The very first work of fiction to call itself 'A Gothic Story', Horace Walpole's *The Castle of Otranto* (1764), added that label to its second edition of 1765 and simultaneously explained it with a second Preface that theoretically defined what this new, mixed mode was and remains: 'an attempt to blend the two kinds of romance, the ancient and the modern', by interspersing the 'imagination and improbability' of medieval, supernatural and chivalric tales, assuming that audiences no longer believed in all their premises, with elements of the then-rising novel of Samuel Richardson, Henry Fielding and Tobias Smollett, in which 'nature' as it is empirically perceived 'is always intended to be, and sometimes has been, copied with success' (Walpole 1996: 9). This flagrant cross-breeding, demanding definition as much as the emergent novel did, thereby entered an active theoretical conversation of the mid-eighteenth century, in prefaces to new fictions as well as reviews in critical journals, about where 'Romance' rooted in 'the dark ages' leaves off and where 'undisguised', natural 'humors and passions' break free of Romance in the kind of extended Enlightenment narrative that 'brings every incident home to life' (Smollett, Preface to *Roderick Random*, 1748, in Williams 1970: 119–20). Walpole's transformation of 'Gothic', itself a term floating at the time between quite discordant meanings from 'barbaric' and 'grotesque' to 'imaginative in a medieval manner' (see Tucker 1967: 149–55) – for which Walpole theorised yet another definition (the ancient–modern 'blend') – also extended Richard Hurd's

1762 attempt in his *Letters on Chivalry and Romance* to re-establish the 'Gothic' as a 'fine fabling' that could lead England back to its literary, if not its 'feudal', roots, and thus to a scheme wedded to spatial 'unity of *design*', as in Spenser's *Faerie Queene* (1595), rather than the causal (and classical) unity of 'action' demanded in Aristotle's ancient *Poetics* (Clery and Miles 2000: 70–7). At the same time, Walpole was surely responding to his fellow Whig Edmund Burke's theory of the sublime in the latter's *Philosophical Enquiry* on *the Sublime and Beautiful* of 1757. There, for the first time in the history of theory, the 'highest', most expansive aesthetic affect is linked primarily with 'terror' in audience responses to depictions or descriptions that range from the 'obscurity' of old ruins to 'vastness' to 'notions of ghosts'; all these are *Otranto* ingredients and all of them for Burke arouse the observer's mental associations with the fear of death, which is transmogrified into 'delightful terror' because its representation in paintings or words distances the threat from what is 'actually noxious' (Clery and Miles 2000: 113–21).

This link between the Walpolean Gothic and the Burkean sublime, to be sure, was not made explicit until they were connected by name in a 1773 essay joined to an incomplete story: 'On the Pleasure Derived from the Objects of Terror; with Sir Bertrand, A Fragment' by John Aiken and his sister Anna Laetitia (later Mrs Barbauld). Whereas Walpole had offered a fiction and then theorised it in a second edition (while also responding to theories that preceded his tale), this effort starts by calling *Otranto* a quintessential 'modern' instance of 'our imagination . . . rejoic[ing] in [an] expansion of its powers' where 'the pain of terror is lost in amazement' (Clery and Miles 2000: 129). This celebration of Burke via Walpole is then exemplified by 'Sir Bertrand', in which the title character is led by a 'dead cold hand' through 'an intricate widening passage', on 'both sides' of which are 'gigantic statues of black marble, attired in the Moorish habit' (Clery and Miles 2000: 131). The back story of these statues is never revealed because this fragment admittedly exists, not to stand alone as a completed fiction, but to exemplify a theory of sublime affect – even as it here appeals to *race*-based fear, which Walpole does not emphasise directly (though the setting of *Otranto* is during the Crusades) and which the Aikens' theory never mentions, thus opening up more questions that call for further explanations. The Gothic–theory interplay, then, is distinctively established after the first nine years of its existence. The Gothic is so mixed and unstable, based as it is in conflicting theories, that it must itself be theorised at once, and the resulting theories must be tested, perhaps even altered or extended, by further experimentations – including more theorising – within Gothic fictions themselves, which then almost beg to be re-theorised yet again.

Such an oscillation did continue, with slight variations, as Gothic prose fiction and drama exfoliated across the rest of the eighteenth century and from England outwards to western Europe and across the Atlantic to the emerging United States. Clara Reeve must theorise, before it opens, how her novel *The Old English Baron* (1777–8) works to keep the supernatural 'within limits of credibility' that she thinks Walpole oversteps (Clery and Miles 2000: 134). Accordingly, her tale proceeds, with its spectres appearing only in dreams, to keep strictly on the 'modern' side of the Romance dichotomy, in the wake of which Reeve is able to declare the firm difference between Romance as 'fabulous' and novel as 'natural' in her theoretical treatise, *The Progress of Romance* (1785; Clery and Miles 2000: 179–80). Ann Radcliffe's influential Gothic romances of the 1790s keep stopping their action to theorise their scenes in terms of Burke's sublime and/or William Gilpin's and Uvedale Price's notions of the picturesque, as well as her Walpolean sense of 'modern' beliefs inclining away from, yet still longing for, aspects of 'ancient' symbolic orders (see Radcliffe 1998: 5–6, 30–1, 225–7, 248–9, for examples). It is thus not surprising that she looks back on her own writing career in her posthumously published dialogue, 'On the Supernatural in Poetry' (1826), by defending her preference for the 'terror' kept removed from gross physicality that 'awakens the faculties to a high degree of life', as in Burke, over against the 'horror' that 'contracts, freezes, and annihilates them', a contrast she supports by using Shakespeare as her exemplar, appropriately by way of *Hamlet* and *Macbeth* rather than *Titus Andronicus* (Clery and Miles 2000: 168). In helping to launch American Gothic fiction, Charles Brockden Brown meanwhile prefaced his *Edgar Huntly* (1799) with this theoretical claim: that the same symbolic mechanisms that have underwritten 'Gothic castles and chimeras' in Europe after the belief-systems behind them have been 'exploded' (echoing Walpole's word for those systems in his first *Otranto* Preface [1996: 6]) can be repurposed for 'incidents of Indian hostility' and 'the perils of the western wilderness', all 'growing out of the condition of our country' (Brown 1988: 3). This assertion is grounded, in part, on how the terrifying 'sublime' in Burke's words 'comes upon us in the gloomy forest' (Clery and Miles 2000: 117), yet it also leaves as an open question the nature of specifically *Gothic* symbol-making: what is it about the symbolic capacities of the Walpolean 'blend' that they can be transferred from 'castles and chimeras' emptied of their ideological grounds to the fears of Indian uprisings and the untamed wild in the undercurrents of the Anglo-American consciousness?

That question, however, has remained unanswered for a long time because the same era, often called 'Romantic', that saw Gothic fictions proliferate from the eighteenth into the nineteenth century also witnessed an increase in anti-Gothic critiques that used theoretical reasons to declare this mode's mixture of contradictory ingredients to be beneath respectable critical attention. Samuel Taylor Coleridge, reviewing Matthew Lewis's horror-Gothic *The Monk* in 1797, finds that the organic unity of subject matter and style that appeals to the best levels of 'taste' in his eyes is violated by this 'species of composition'; in Gothic of this kind, he writes, 'the most awfully true in religion' is placed alongside the 'ridiculously absurd in superstition', because of which Coleridge relegates most Gothic to what is 'low and vulgar' by comparison to 'exalted' literature (Clery and Miles 2000: 187–8). He consequently helps inaugurate a long debate over how 'high culture' or 'low culture' Gothic fiction can be – and what it might mean if it were both at once. We can hardly be surprised that the Gothic after 1800 soon became 'in both periodical review and literary essay [widely] blamed for various [undesirable] changes in literary production and consumption', as Michael Gamer reminds us, to such an extent that many respectable writers had 'to appropriate gothic using duplicitous strategies' (Gamer 2000: 67).

Granted, there remained occasional theoretical forays that accounted for the Gothic, as in Sir Walter Scott's gradations of 'romantic narrative' in his 1823 essay on Walpole for Ballantyne's Novelists Library (Scott 1968: 89–90), gradations filled out in his longer treatise 'On Romance' (1824) and quite visible in the inclusion of Gothic in Scott's own historical novels before and after the mid-1820s (see Gamer 2000: 163–200). Mostly, though, the Gothic-and-theory dialogue nearly vanished the more the nineteenth century unfolded and the more the Gothic proliferated into various formats from magazine stories and chapbooks to plays and operas, as well as many novels, including portions of 'realistic' ones. As William Hughes accurately puts it, 'Gothic criticism became the preserve of the more minor monthly magazines', and most Gothic in the nineteenth century 'bec[a]me subcultural, beneath the critical notice of the literary intelligentsia', many of whom, 'paradoxically [and like the earlier English Romantics], continue[d] to exploit the genre's conventions' in their own fictions (Hughes 2006: 13–14). Except in the case of an author-critic such as Edgar Allan Poe in the 1830s–1840s in America, that suspension of the Gothic–theory dialogue continued throughout the most of nineteenth and well into the twentieth century in England, Europe and the United States.

One primary reason was the rise in academia, starting in the late 1920s with T. S. Eliot and I. A. Richards, of the so-called 'New Criticism', in which tightly crafted interactions among different words that crystallised into a unity formed out of contraries, à la Coleridge, became such a standard for judging literary quality that the Gothic, glad to exploit its contradictory elements while still being considered 'low culture', remained outside the realm of literature worthy of study, keeping itself subcultural and rarely theorised for decades (see Hogle 2006: 29–30). Only two major counter-views interrupted this long-lasting suppression in ways that have gradually led the Gothic and theory back towards something like their initial dialogue. One of these, highlighted by Edith Birkhead's *The Tale of Terror* in 1921, manifested what we now call 'old historicism', for which the conflicts on the surface of Gothic texts reflect a deep unity of thought in Western culture of the later eighteenth and nineteenth centuries (Hogle 2006: 30–1). As this kind of theory-based criticism developed, the Gothic as a historical phenomenon became one product of an Enlightenment rationalism that so hollowed out the meaning in medieval Catholic symbols, as Walpole did, that there needed to be a substitute access in fiction to the 'numinous' level of being. That level now became a projection from an internal, psychological depth, perhaps even – with phenomenological theory added in later to this sense of history – a mental 'intending' of a 'deep space' of 'sublime terror' whereby archaic spaces or looming shadows drew forth the most primordial and feared drives in what were increasingly thought of as the depths in Western psyches (see Varma 1957; Lévy 1968).

This last added element, in turn, points to the second counter-discourse of the early twentieth century that also helped restart the Gothic–theory dialogue: the rise of psychoanalysis based on the published works of Sigmund Freud and his disciples. Freud, after all, announces the Gothic–psychoanalysis connection outright in his 1919 essay 'The Uncanny', aptly recalled by some of the essays in this volume, where he famously interprets E. T. A. Hoffman's thoroughly Gothic tale 'The Sandman' (1817). That story, for Freud, it turns out, is a pre-theorising over a century earlier of his own scheme of primal impulses and fears, repressed into the unconscious, that are called up by seemingly strange, unfamiliar, 'other' beings (such as ghosts or what appear to be monsters); these actually resurrect the most repressed drives and phobias (the all-too-deeply familiar) both in individuals and, since Freud was influenced by Charles Darwin, in the pre-evolved stages of the human race that are still harboured within us all (Freud 1959: 387–94). It is not simply that psychoanalysis turned out to be useful for analysing Gothic fiction, but rather that the Gothic produced figurations of haunting surfaces and their concealed, archaic depths that helped to form the assumptions and articulation of psychoanalysis itself. Such an admission of Gothic literature as theorising before theory echoes Freud's and his students' earlier dialogues with Shakespeare's *Hamlet*, a principal influence on Walpole's inaugural 'Gothic Story' (see Walpole 1996: 10–12) and especially prominent in Freud's own *Interpretation of Dreams* (1900). There he flatly claims that *Hamlet*, in its Oedipal triangle of Hamlet/his mother/his usurping stepfather, announces 'the secular advance of repression in the emotional life of mankind' and thus thoroughly prefigures his own theories. For Freud, Prince Hamlet's famous delay in executing the usurper who murdered his father reveals his avoidance of his own unconscious drives precisely because that stepfather, having killed the father to marry the mother, 'shows [Hamlet] the repressed wishes of his own childhood realized' (Freud 1965: 298–9). The initial stage of Gothic leading to theory that then reappears in Gothic works and theories about them is thus re-established, if a little differently, and this revival continued both before and after 'The Uncanny' of 1919. Even H. P. Lovecraft, despite his off-and-on disavowal of formulaic Freudianism in his American horror stories of the 1910s–1930s – often with gigantic and species-crossing demons emerging into Gothicised spaces from deep beneath the earth – admits in 'Supernatural Horror in Literature' (his theory essay first published in 1927) that the best Gothic horror arouses the most basic of the 'inner instincts' embedded in our 'subconscious minds' from the most primal and bestial stages of human evolution (Lovecraft 1967: 141–3).

As psychoanalytic theory continued to both interpret and prompt Gothic fiction well into the twentieth century, however, a different theoretical scheme – Marxism – began to assert itself alongside it. Its progenitor, Karl Marx, was plainly influenced by earlier Gothic when he wrote in the 1860s that capitalism was 'vampire-like' because it 'lives only by sucking living labor' (Marx 1976: 342). Marxist theory sees aesthetic constructions as being like that simile: as being part of the 'superstructure' of belief-systems that arises out of and purports to explain, while it also obscures, the deeply conflicted 'base' of cultural and economic production that is material human life. As such, these constructs manifest, albeit in disguises (the vampire being just one of them), conflicts between contending ideologies. These, in turn, point to the deeper contestations between owners and workers *and* between newer inventions and established ways of organising production (including capitalism) at particular historical moments, contestations that put the unified *Zeitgeist* of old historicism into question. This scheme has therefore proven just as well suited as psychoanalysis to interpreting Gothic writings, since they are pulled, as Walpole said, between antiquated, once-aristocratic and largely Catholic world-views and modes of discourse, on the one hand, and rising, middle-class and usually Protestant alternatives, on the other. By 1960, then, in just this vein, Leslie Fiedler can argue that large stretches of American literature are Gothic from the 1790s on, in that they keep articulating this very tug-of-war. An ongoing focus, he writes, is 'the guilt of the revolutionary' in a 'world of [almost] collapsed ego ideals' because he finds himself 'haunted by the (paternal) past that he has been trying to destroy', as was the case with rising bourgeois readers in eighteenth- and nineteenth-century England (Fiedler 1966: 129–31). At the same time, though, in referring to the Freudian 'ego-ideal', Fiedler finds Marxism, as others have since, entirely compatible with psychoanalysis. Consequently, for him the 'levels of the ruined castle or abbey', or whatever takes their place in more recent Gothic, 'represent the contradictory fears at the heart of gothic terror: the dread of the super-ego' held over from older, God-centred belief-systems 'whose splendid battlements have been battered but not quite cast down', combined with the deeper apprehension that, 'beneath the crumbling shell of paternal authority, lies the maternal blackness', the horrifying birthplace to which the psyche desires to return and yet from which it continues to flee so as not to be reabsorbed and dead (1966: 132).

As a result, Gothic fiction since 1960 has explicitly absorbed this combination of Freudian and Marxist theory, even in the case of bestselling authors who then re-theorise what they have demonstrated in Gothic novels. As anti-hero Jack Torrence, the writer who becomes the temporary caretaker of the Overlook Hotel, puts it to his wife when they anxiously discuss their son's prophetic dreams in Stephen King's *The Shining* (1977), 'Freud says that the subconscious never speaks to us in a literal language. Only in symbols' (King 1977: 264). Here Jack is asserting a twentieth-century ideology to help explain what is undeniably supernatural in a much older belief-system, leaving King's readers hovering, like Walpole's, between the ancient and the modern. Jack is similarly suspended himself, struggling as he is through a transitional combination of jobs that leave him caught between fading and emerging roles for men in an ever-shifting material economy. Steven Bruhm, a contributor to this volume, has therefore noted in King's wake 'how contemporary Gothic' is 'intensely *aware* of this Freudian rhetoric and self-consciously *about* the longings and fears it describes' (Bruhm 2002: 262). All of this occurs, Bruhm adds, at a time of deep ideological conflicts in the West manifested in the fears aroused by burgeoning 'foreign otherness . . . technological explosion . . . feminism, gay liberation, and African American civil rights', alongside 'the powerful threat (and attraction) posed by our culture's increased secularity' in the face of backward-looking, but still-prevalent, religious values (2002: 260–1). King himself follows up on his novels of the 1970s by theorising the kind of fiction he writes as coming from and calling up the 'uneasy dreams of the mass subconscious' that themselves 'arise from a pervasive sense of disestablishment' in a modern era careening between 'periods of fairly serious economic and/or political strain' (King 1981: 20, 22, 40). Such Freudian-Marxist assumptions, in fact, became so persistent from the 1960s to the early 1980s in Gothic scholarship that they together form the theoretical foundations of *The Literature of Terror* (1980, expanded in 1996) by David Punter, another contributor to this collection, the book that most helped to launch the world-wide acceleration in the study of the Gothic over the last four decades that has led to this volume and all the Edinburgh Companions to the Gothic (see especially Punter 1996: II, 210–30).

Yet as these theoretical 'schools' increasingly interacted, another one forcefully arose to contend with and dialogue with them. It was so effective, in fact, that it revised our sense of the whole Gothic (indeed, the entire literary) canon and eventually led to offshoots that also affected the Gothic and theory quite profoundly. This approach appeared in criticism based in feminist theory that came to academic prominence in the 1970s–1980s, which may have been inspired by the Women's Movement of the 1960s but was also prefigured long before in Gothic writing itself, as much as it then fed into Gothic fictions from the late 1970s onwards. When Elaine Showalter, for example, points to the subjugation of women by patriarchal control that forces women to articulate themselves in a 'double-voiced discourse' where their self-articulation must be filtered through a male-dominated language (Showalter 1985: 266), she is providing a theoretical term for numerous Gothic fictions ranging from *The Mysteries of Udolpho*, in which Radcliffe's heroine keeps evaluating her feelings by the standards of her father's teachings (Radcliffe 1998: 671–2), to Charlotte Brontë's *Jane Eyre* (1847), in which the title character's outburst that women 'suffer from too rigid a restraint' occurs only when she is already engulfed by the patriarchally Gothic Thornfield Hall and first hears the suppressed voice of the Bertha Rochester imprisoned there (Brontë 1996: 116–17), all in a novel initially published as 'by Currer Bell'. Even when feminist theory counters such male dominance by asserting the special capacity of women authors to listen to their bodies and to assert strictly feminine feelings and experiences in ways that unhinge masculine norms, such a pioneer of feminist criticism as Ellen Moers in 1974 must admit that Mary Shelley made that very case a century-and-a-half earlier. In the male-narrated *Frankenstein* (1818), now the most famous and influential of Gothic novels, Shelley injects, even in the making of a creature ostensibly without a mother, the 'revulsion against newborn life ... the drama of guilt, dread, and flight surrounding birth' and 'the trauma of afterbirth' that only a woman can know (Moers 2012: 320–1). By the end of the 1970s, then, when feminist theory had made clear that 'women should not allow traditional configurations of gender to limit their potential for change' (Horner and Zlosnik 2014: 62), this revision of cultural norms could be reinvested in new versions of the Gothic mode that had so long prefigured it. In 'The Bloody Chamber', the title work in a 1979 collection of pointedly Gothic stories, Angela Carter has her heroine-narrator first submit, double-voiced, to the old 'female subject position' within male-dominated discourse in a recasting of the Bluebeard story in which a masculine predator seduces, then murders, his wives in an old house, only for her to embrace a rebellious shattering of those confines when she accepts being 'rescued by her gun-wielding mother on horseback'; this shift affirms, as feminist theory and Gothic texts have gone on to show in and between each other, that 'the fantastic' can allow 'women writers and readers to go beyond a reality that [has been] both oppressive and depressing', sometimes by hyperbolically exposing it, as in Margaret Atwood's *The Handmaid's Tale* (1985, more recently adapted for television), and sometimes by forcefully resisting it (Horner and Zlosnik 2014: 57; see Chapter 7 below).

Since feminism has thereby joined, while also critiquing, Marxist historicism and psychoanalysis in re-establishing the Gothic–theory conversation, moreover, each of these approaches has also proliferated, from the 1970s onwards, into variations that have expanded their horizons *and* altered the reach of Gothic fiction too. In that process, earlier Gothic has still been revealed to be a precursor repeatedly, and more recent Gothic has arisen, in several forms of media, to further enact these unfoldings of theory. On the one hand, feminist theory has helped instigate and then given way, first, to a broader gender theory that explains the cultural fabrication of 'masculinity' as much as 'femininity' around the world and, more recently, to a growing range of 'queer theory' that has started by critiquing strictures on same-sex orientations and come to examine the cultural positioning of *all* 'non-normative' forms of sexuality outside the narrow realm of a man and a woman having sex to reproduce. With Teresa de Lauretis revealing every gender-distinction as the 'product of various social technologies' and Judith Butler suggesting that the 'construct called "sex" is as socially constructed as gender' (de Lauretis 1987: 2–3; Butler 1990: 7), 'masculine' as well as 'feminine' has come to be seen as a deployment of learned postures that both obscure and intimate far more fluid depths where such boundaries blur in both individuals and groups. Anticipating and extrapolating such theories have been such 'new Gothic' fictions as Iain Banks's *The Wasp Factory* (1984). Here a growing boy, born a girl, is subject, in an echo of *Frankenstein*, to a 'gender experiment' of 'hormone treatments' so persistently linked to the 'cultural expectation that masculinity is founded on misogyny and brutality' that this new monstrosity produces a predatory 'identity' that is 'validated through extreme acts of violence' (Horner and Zlosnik 2014: 61). As Eve Kosofsky Sedgwick theorised in 1985, however, the forced staging of masculinity is actually among the subtexts haunting the Gothic as early as *The Castle of Otranto* by Walpole, now known to be a self-masking 'queer' when he launched his 'Gothic Story' (Sedgwick 1985: 162–8). His two principal male contenders for the throne of Otranto try to dramatise their traditional manhood by exchanging daughters between them, even when Prince Manfred, 'flushed by wine and love', deliberately 'had come to seek' the Marquis Frederic instead of the latter's daughter (Walpole 1996: 108). For George Haggerty, another contributor here, this conundrum has opened out the many instances of non-normative sexual behaviour, homosexual or otherwise, in the founding Gothic text and many of its successors. Hence the Gothic as a mode turns out to be fundamentally, rather than occasionally, 'queer' from the outset, 'a testing ground for many unauthorized genders and sexualities', and thereby 'transgressive, sexually coded, and resistant to dominant ideology' even in its most conservative manifestations, such as the ultimate restoration of the true heir in *Otranto* (Haggerty 2006: 2; see Chapter 8 below). No wonder there has come to be a post-1985 explosion of 'queer' postmodern Gothic, as in Randall Kenan's *A Visitation of Spirits* (1989) about 'a black, gay teen' contending with 'a conservative Baptist family', a work of revisionist southern Gothic, or in Rebecca Brown's collection *The Terrible Girls* (1992), where, in each tale, several of which echo older Gothic texts, 'one seeks a lover for their sameness to one and the goal of [such a] union is [inherently] self-shattering' (see McCallum 2014: 79–83).

On the other hand, historicist theory and criticism, most of it with a Marxist cast, has extended itself since the late 1970s into even more various directions than gender-based theory has. It has reappeared as what we now call 'New Historicism', which itself has dovetailed with 'cultural studies' descended from both the Frankfurt School of Critical Theory in 1930s Germany and the Birmingham Centre for Contemporary Cultural Studies in 1960s England, which in turn has been transmogrified more recently into postcolonial theory and race studies, among other variations. All of these branchings have uncovered hitherto-unseen dynamics in the many forms of Gothic, alternately revealing how such discoveries have already been made in older Gothic works and proceeding to inspire new Gothic fictions that recast the discovered tendencies. New Historicism, starting with the criticism of Stephen Greenblatt and his UC Berkeley colleagues in 1979–80, has further upended the consistent *Zeitgeist* of 'old' historicism by joining Marxism to linguistic anthropology, including the theory of all words referring 'dialogically' advanced by Mikhail Bakhtin (in which all parts of a text really refer out to their uses in more than one context). The result, most of the time, has revealed particular works as teeming crossroads where many other contemporary and earlier texts, not all of them literary, are drawn in to play out their conflicts with each other and thereby to dramatise the ideological tugs-of-war over the best modes of human self-representation at definite historical moments (Hogle 2006: 37–40). This approach is what allows E. J. Clery to analyse *The Castle of Otranto* as symbolising the 'contradiction' in the 1760s 'between the traditional [aristocratic] claims of landed property and the new [more middle-class] claims of the private family: a conflict between two versions of economic "personality"' (Clery 1995: 77). At the same time, that very revelation shows that the 'Gothic Story' was established, more than almost any other literary mode, as precisely the kind of crucible for contending discourses that the New Historicism has theorised, anticipating this effective way of explaining it. Cultural studies, meanwhile, even more Marxist yet just as language-based, has added an emphasis explicitly on the tension at specific times between purportedly 'high'-culture and supposedly 'low'-culture forms of discourse (as in the study of the Gothic in Brantlinger 1998). That perspective, too, is forecast by

Walpole's *Otranto* in its juxtaposing of 'high' old romance with what had been the 'lower' middle-class novel – hence the claim of Coleridge by 1800 that Gothic is more 'low' than 'high' culture – and so the Gothic since, long before Birmingham and Frankfurt, has often been about this exact conflict, particularly in Robert Louis Stevenson's *Strange Case of Dr Jekyll and Mr Hyde* (1886), Bram Stoker's *Dracula* (1897) and Gaston Leroux's *The Phantom of the Opera* (1910; see Hogle 2002: 67–76).

It is also a relatively small step from bringing out the construction of the 'high' versus the 'low' in centres of Western culture from London to Paris to describing encounters, actual or fictionalised, between the coloniser/conqueror and the colonised/'subaltern' in the postcolonial theory that has emerged out of cultural studies, mostly in the wake of Edward Said's *Orientalism* (1978). The Gothic, as it happens, can take real credit for getting this theorising started because of how Jean Rhys's *Wide Sargasso Sea* (1966) rewrites and undercuts Brontë's *Jane Eyre*. Rhys allows both the 'madwoman in the attic', 'Bertha' renamed from Antoinette, and her husband/coloniser/captor, Edward Rochester, to tell their own haunted back stories so as to reveal their forced 'marriage' as the expropriation of a mixed-race West Indian creole, who brings with her the 'ghosts' of her complex culture, by an English estate-builder ultimately determined to take what he has colonised back to England and to keep his world's dependence on colonisation Gothically concealed (see Rhys 1982: 56–173). This novel draws readers back through the history of the Gothic in and before *Jane Eyre* to recover the sub-texts of colonisation or conquest in many of them, even to the point of leading me to point up the 'Moorish' statues in the Aikens' 'Sir Bertrand'. Yet it has also set the stage for a postcolonial Gothic criticism that has since revealed how many texts, such as Joseph Conrad's *Heart of Darkness* (1899, now viewed as more Gothic than it used to seem), 'dramatize the "relations of domination" buried within them' and 'focus . . . on the possession of the "civilized" by the local characteristics of those once-unknown but now-colonized places' even after official colonisation has ceased to apply (Gelder 2014: 192; see Chapter 4 below). One result has been post-1980 Gothic fiction that has revealed the haunting conflicts within colonial and postcolonial conditions, not just in the Caribbean, but in the histories of South Africa (J. M. Coetzee's *Waiting for the Barbarians* [1980]), postcolonial India (Salmon Rushdie's *Midnight's Children* [1981]), Canada (Eden Robinson's *Monkey Beach* [2000]) and Australia and New Zealand (Andrew McGahan's *The White Earth* [2004]; see Gelder 2014: 198–204).

Another result, of course, has been a post-1985 attention to constructions of *racial* 'otherness', sadly the 'colored' 'low' in relation to the white 'high'. This critical lens has brought that long-suppressed dimension forward in *Frankenstein* and *Dracula* (see Malchow 1996) and particularly in the American Gothic, including and beyond the Faulknerian southern Gothic. In an American literature that turns out to be pervasively Gothic, as D. H. Lawrence suggested in 1923 and Fielder pointedly argued in 1960, we can recently see anew 'the haunted, the uncanny, and the return of the repressed' in the covered-over decimation of Native Americans from Brockden Brown's *Edgar Huntly* (1799) to Nathaniel Hawthorne's *House of the Seven Gables* (1851) and in the 'evil perpetrated by the white on the body of the black', as well as 'the return of the black as a revenant to exact revenge', as much in Poe's 'The Black Cat' (1843) and 'The Raven' (1845) as in Harriet Beecher Stowe's occasionally Gothic *Uncle Tom's Cabin* (1852; see Savoy 2002: 168–82). These very texts thus emerge as among the progenitors of race-based theorising about them and about the pervasive racial under- *and* over-tones of the Gothic since Walpole. Even so, it is just as true, as Maisha Wester (another of our contributors) has shown, that African-American writers themselves produced equally prescient Gothic works prior to the current race-theory revival, such as Richard Wright's *Native Son* (1940, revisionist of both 'The Black Cat' and *Frankenstein*), *and* have gone on since to take their own possession of the dialogue between fiction and theory swirling around the Gothic, 'revising this very genre's features' while also employing and reanalysing them (Wester 2014: 168–9; see Chapter 3 below). The supreme case in point has been Toni Morrison, who has radically re-theorised American literature and the Gothic in the lectures published as *Playing in the Dark* (1992), yet only after combining a specifically African type of the living dead with the Walpolean-Radcliffean ghosting of memories in her Pulitzer Prize-winning Gothic novel, *Beloved* (1987). Here, in fact, as in her *Dark* lectures, she brings together suggestions from New Historicism (alluding to real newspaper articles from the 1850s), cultural studies (offering an oral-illiterate 'low' alternative to 'high' abolitionist writing), postcolonial theory (letting her ghost recall the capitalisation of Africa in collective-unconscious memories of the Middle Passage) and inevitably race theory (Morrison 1988: 162–6, 272–6, 221–4), so much so that the Gothic here 'becomes a way of both mystifying and symbolizing the living nightmare of racial oppression' even as the Gothic itself is recast and reconceptualised (Wester 2014: 171).

All this while, however, cultural studies, persistently forming more offshoots, has also turned the attention of theorists to the multiplication of media forms in the twentieth and twenty-first centuries through which the Gothic has been transmitted beyond the realms of print. Since film has been brought forward, from the Frankfurt School onwards, as a once-'lesser' form now equally indicative of culture as written literature, theorists of the Gothic have done much more than notice how many Gothic-based films and television programmes there have come to be. They have also seen that even Walpole's 'Gothic' is rooted in the pre-cinematic 'magic lantern' projection of moving spectres in earlier eighteenth-century 'phantasmagoria shows' (Jones 2014: 7–14); that the earliest Gothic narratives are visual and stagey on purpose – and thus also pre-cinematic – modelled as they are on Shakespeare and opera (see Walpole 1996: 10–14; Hogle 2002: 30–2); and that early cinema was not only receptive to the Gothic, quite understandably, but highly dependent on it from the start, as we can see in the Edison Company's 1910 *Frankenstein* and in the pioneering films of Georges Méliès from 1896 to 1913, with their 'penchant for fairies, demons, and other marvels' (Bronfen 2014: 107). Hence Elisabeth Bronfen, another of our contributors, theorises that there is a 'special relation' that 'film art has to the Gothic', not only because of this history, but because cinema itself often 'confronts us', as Gothic does, 'with uncomfortable realities but also makes them ghostly'; film gives us 'images imprinted on celluloid' that appear to come alive, though they are only transparent spectres, and so 'render palpable an immaterial world' suspended, like the Gothic as Walpole defined it, 'between the actual and the imaginary, the present and the past' (Bronfen 2014: 107–8). To probe to the heart of film-making and film-projection, then, is to probe into much of what makes the Gothic possible – and vice versa (see Chapter 9 below). By 'telling stories based on blurring the boundary between life and death, human and animal, flesh and machine', Gothic 'films speak to the uncanniness of their own mode of communication' to such a degree that each such picture 'self-consciously speaks to its own apparatus' (Bronfen 2014: 108), enacting a theory of film, as much as Walpole's ghosts walking out of pictures bespeak the technology of phantasmagorias.

Film's reference to its own technology also brings up the Gothic's relation to changing technologies in general, which we can see, not just in the very recent Gothic of cybernetics and cyberspace and present-day theories about these, but in the unfolding of early Gothic fiction too. Of course the most influential example is the original 1818 *Frankenstein*, which helped found science fiction while also advancing the Gothic. As much as current theory and fairly recent Gothic, such as David Cronenberg's film *Videodrome* (1983), arouses our fears about the 'morphing of the human into . . . the machine . . . the digital, the automated', Shelley's *Frankenstein* confronted us with that very movement towards 'the posthuman' two hundred years ago, showing that 'the condition of being ordinarily human and wanting to exceed that condition are thoroughly intertwined' – and full of ideological conflicts – in the mechanical production of a near-automaton out of once-natural ingredients artificially stitched together (Mousley 2016: 158–61). Moreover, Mary Shelley herself admitted in 1831 that a major influence on her creature-figure was 'a gigantic, shadowy form' of a castle's dead ruler walking out of the frame of his portrait (Shelley 2012: 166–7; Hogle 2017: 18) in a German-French imitation of the spectre from a picture in Walpole's *Castle of Otranto* (Walpole 1996: 26); and Walpole himself – especially when his first *Otranto* Preface urges readers not to believe in his antiquated tale's 'preternatural' causalities (1996: 6) – raised the question of what technology permits a portrait-figure to float out into the air from its base surface, if not the projection-machines and mobile slides of phantasmagorias or some other process by which psychological projections appear outside of the projector. Hence, when William Gibson coins the word 'cyberspace' in his cyberpunk Gothic novel *Neuromancer* (1984), naming 'a virtual world designed through a combination of direct neural interfaces and simulated reality' enabled by computer-based technology, he thereby theorises yet another 'of those transdialectical places [like the magic-lantern shows] that the Gothic occupies and challenges'; consequently there needs to be only some 'retheorization of the Gothic' in the face of cybertechnology, since 'cyberspace' in theory and fiction 'appears as a new deserted and uncanny place', like so many Gothic settings before it, 'simultaneously arousing enthusiasm and fright for the potencies of technology' given 'the uncanniness and spectres' of the newly created 'spaces'; these are as 'in-between' in their spectral fashions, albeit because of more recent technology, as Walpole's and Mary Shelley's Gothic figures were in the eighteenth and nineteenth centuries (Van Elferen 2009: 99–101; see Chapter 10 below).

Theorising the cyber-Gothic, after all, considering its many avatar-signifiers disconnected in techno-media from the bodies that they are presumed to reflect, has been aided immensely over the last several decades by the rise of post-structuralism since the late 1960s in several forms, ones that have even attached themselves to other theoretical schemes in ways that have unsettled those theories as much as the Gothic has unsettled a great deal of Western (and, more recently, Eastern) literature and film. 'Structuralism' in the late 1950s through the early 1970s, based heavily on the linguistics of Ferdinand de Saussure (1857–1913), analysed language-systems, myths, written works and whole genres of writing down to the underlying dynamics determining the relationships among their word-patterns. Many of these dynamics turned out to be fundamental tensions between binary oppositions, particularly in structuralism's most lasting contribution to Gothic studies, Tzvetan Todorov's book *The Fantastic* (1970). Here the unstable genre of the title, anchored in many classic Gothic examples, is rooted in an unresolved hesitation between verbalisations of the truly marvellous and the strictly realistic (see Todorov 1973), much as Walpole suggested in his 1765 Preface to *Otranto*. Post-structuralism, by contrast, has used Saussurean assumptions to undermine structuralism's sense of unities formed from contraries. It argues that Saussure's sense of the 'signifer' (the visible or audible figure viewed as separate from any meaning) relates first to other signifiers by differing from and deferring to them. As signifiers therefore float over (being only temporarily anchored by) various 'signifieds', their relationships become inherently intertextual, in that they refer widely outside, as well as across, any particular construct (to uses of the same or related signifiers in other contexts), far more than they are intratextual and devoted to unifying binaries in clearly bounded compositions. The most influential post-structuralist, Jacques Derrida, thus argues that the process of living, since it involves self-articulation across signifiers-leading-to-signifiers that always leave their reference-points at least somewhat behind (becoming epitaphs for the potential or actual 'death' of those signifieds that are 'never present as such'), means that we must always 'live with ghosts' in a *'non-contemporaneity with itself of the living present'* in which we accept 'the principle of some *responsibility* . . . before the ghosts of those who are not yet born or who are already dead' (Derrida 1994: xvii–xviii). 'As in *Hamlet*', Derrida even writes, 'everything begins by the apparition of a specter' (1994: 2). Allan Lloyd Smith therefore claims that the Gothic from the start, more than most discourses, has always been pre-post-structuralist, as well as pre-postmodern. First there is the Gothic's use of Shakespearean spectres that are really spectres of the already spectral – whether they are revenants of older effigies in Walpole, projections of ghost-like memories in Radcliffe, or flickering images of avatars in films or cyberspace – but then too there is the consequent opening out of 'the uncertainty of signs by [the Gothic] locating each of them within more than one interpretive framework' (Lloyd Smith 1996: 12), between 'ancient' and 'modern romance' to start with, per the principle of dialogism in Bakhtin. If there has been a flurry of post-structuralist readings of the Gothic such as Lloyd Smith's since Derrida's early writings of the late 1960s, which is only to be expected (we now see), that onslaught has now been exposed as reacting to the extremes of 'floating signifers' and intertexual references that are as endemic to, and thus as foretold by, the Gothic as cinematic spectres or 'posthuman' self-projections. Postmodern Gothic has consequently continued to exploit these proclivities even more, as we can see in the endless, ever-branching intertextually that both deepens and opens out a very current interior space in Mark Z. Danielewski's *House of Leaves* (2000).

This interplay of the Gothic and the post-structural, consequently, was bound to infect other theorisings of the Gothic that it has already prefigured just as much. The immediate attraction of New Historicism towards the Gothic, for example, is intimately connected with how much New Historicism assumes Derridean, and hence Gothic, intertextuality as well as Marxist conflicts among the ideological schemes of different classes. In articulating the dependence of Marx on signifying spectres, after all, Derrida began with Marx's own statement, another one reflective of earlier Gothic: 'A specter is haunting Europe – the specter of communism' (a quotation from *The Communist Manifesto* [1848] in Derrida 1994: 2), which itself refers to an underground movement of social antagonism reflected and half-distorted through a kind of 'glass darkly' that re-symbolises and names it. New Historicist analyses of Gothic, like the Gothic itself, as a result, can show *both* the multidirectional outreach of any text to myriad, conflicting documents of the past or immediate present – including conflicting theories of history itself (see Chapter 2 below) – *and* the ways in which such texts create schemes of symbolic exchange, composed from intertextual references, that seem to provide textual solutions, from a post-structural perspective, to otherwise insoluble historical antagonisms (see Chapter 11 below).

Meanwhile, though, post-structuralism has been just as transformative with psychoanalysis in crafting lenses of interpretation from a Freudian base that explain the Gothic exceptionally well even as they have been anticipated by the Gothic for some time. Julia Kristeva, the Bulgarian-French psychoanalyst, has been known since the 1970s for post-structurally explaining the subject-in-the-process-of-composing-itself as it emerges out of a primordial body-language or 'semiotic' level and enters a public symbolic order of already floating signifiers where the subject is subjected to conventional discourses. The 'semiotic' language-before-language is a chaotic shifting of signifiers/sensations between and across each other without any anchorings in public reference points, and it is in further elaborating this pre-symbolic level that she has advanced a theory of what we commonly call the Gothic in her *Powers of Horror* (1980). There she posits her sense of 'abjection' as the psychological throwing of what 'disturbs [the] identity, system, order' of the public symbolic from deep in our infancy (including the semiotic as she sees it) over into what the psyche projects as an 'abject' otherness on the margins of the symbolic, an uncanny monstrosity almost inadmissible there, which both conceals and contains the otherness-from-itself in the archaic roots of the subject-in-process (Kristeva 1982: 4). Kristeva's apt literary examples are from modern French writers, such as Jean Genet, but her sense of the abject is inconceivable without the much earlier castings-off in Gothic fictions of what is chaotic and anomalous inside every human being, usually on to figures ranging from the uncanny ghosts of effigies in Walpole and Frankenstein's creature to Dr Jekyll's Mr Hyde, the vampire Dracula, and the dead-but-still haunting title character in Daphne du Maurier's *Rebecca* (1938), adapted into a fully Gothic film by Alfred Hitchcock in 1940 (see Horner and Zlosnik 1998: 99–127 and Chapter 6 below).

Yet theories such as abjection, developed out of the Gothic that they are so helpful for interpreting, contain within them a threat to their own consistency and coherence, as well as to the explanatory completeness of psychoanalysis and post-structuralism, whether they work together or separately. Kristeva's view of the subject-in-process, we should remember, is indebted to (among others) the neo-Freudian theorist Jacques Lacan (1901–81), who, much earlier, theorises the 'thrown-ness' of the human subject (à la Martin Heidegger) into language as a journey of desire from signifier to signifier in a quest, across one substitute after another, for the lost/unattainable Mother. In this quest all signs point to, yet remain removed from, the ultimate *and* 'intimate exteriority or "extimacy"' that he calls the 'Real' (Lacan 1992: 139). This Real is the never-fully-knowable, yet always near, location where all boundaries blur that Gary Farnell has helpfully defined for students of the Gothic as 'that amorphous, chaotic, meaningless physical level beyond all reference that both resists and provokes [the] symbolization' that can never – and would never consciously want to – reach it (Farnell 2009: 113). Based on Immanuel Kant's *Ding an sich*, or 'Thing in itself', that lies in and beyond the tangled Manifold of Sense that is hurled at the mind from outside and for which only the mind for Kant can provide any organisation (which misrepresents the Thing while leaving it threateningly close *and* distant), such a therefore 'impossible reality', that 'senseless – and centerless – welter' (Farnell 2009: 113–14), is one locus for Kristeva for what 'disturbs identity, system, order'. After all, the Real includes the dimly remembered, and always desired and avoided, state of being born, 'the immemorial violence with which a body becomes separated from another body in order to be' yet is also still partly inside the birth-canal, half-dead and half-alive (Kristeva 1982: 10). All forms of self-representation, then, both seek and avoid this level, since to become one with it is to die back into it even as it beckons as a sheer material void beyond all signifiers, subjectivities and symbolisations.

The 'haunted spaces and decaying properties' of the Gothic, Farnell shows, are extraordinarily effective at suggesting this level (Farnell 2009: 113), since they intimate the deathly pulling-backwards of the Real as well as its no-longer-being-present within them. On the one hand, all of this makes the hyperbolic and never conventionally realistic Gothic unusually suggestive of the Real's frightening draw and its ever-threatening absence. On the other hand, by stressing the primacy of a formless, pre-linguistic 'Real', theory undermines itself; that which is beyond or outside language cannot be understood through language, which is theory's medium. This haunting sense *in* theory of theory's limitations is also found in Gothic's foundational text, Walpole's *Otranto* again, given how rooted this first 'Gothic Story' is in Edmund Burke's terrifying 'sublime', as we saw earlier. In Burke's scheme, there is always the suggestion of a beckoning death or dissolution should that reality absorb the observing subject, even as the artistic representation of it keeps such an unintelligible horror removed from immediacy, while never totally denied. This tug-of-war in the Gothic, always added to its pull between the archaic and the modern, however, means that the threat of gross materiality and death remains beckoning, while it also remains out of reach, in every Gothic attempt to keep it at bay by playing aesthetically with it. In the same fashion, this unresolvable tension inevitably invades the psychoanalytic and post-structuralist theories that try to explain and have some of their basis in the Gothic. It raises questions about whether abjection can fully throw off the gross anomalies (such as the birth-state) it monsterises, whether Freudian dream interpretation can ever really arrive at the deepest and most material paradoxes of somatic drives, and whether Derrida's raising of the 'ghosts' in Marx can actually escape from *or* comprehend the base materiality behind the superstructures of ideology in which the spectres of the Real keep haunting society – especially in the Gothic (see both Chapter 12 and Chapter 13 below). Such questions within all these schemes, it turns out, are vividly posed in post-1980s Gothic, as in the novel *Poor Things* (1992) by Alisdair Gray, very much in the way Fred Botting shows in Chapter 13 below.

Meanwhile, the affiliations with additional theories that post-structuralism keeps helping to form have proliferated beyond historicist and psychoanalytic frames in ways that have further illuminated the Gothic and pointed to the foundations of theory in it at the same time. Both echoing and reacting against Freud, Marx and his fellow postmodernists, starting in the 1960s, Gilles Deleuze, writing sometimes with his psychoanalyst partner Félix Guattari, has claimed that any linguistic construct is ultimately 'defined' by 'what causes it to move, to follow, and to explode' both within *and beyond* the mere differing and deferring of words (Deleuze and Guattari 1983: 133). Rather than an amorphous welter such as Lacan's Real, life in general for Deleuze is initially and always an 'intense germinal influx' (1983: 164). It is a 'diverse, mobile, and creative' production of 'differences' from and with other differences that produces 'mind and language', among other entities that temporarily coalesce differing elements; all of these are 'effects of a general and inhuman desire', moving through the individual out to the social and the cosmic realms, that precedes and drives every human being or construct, meaning that 'language' is a 'flow of signs alongside other signs, signs which themselves are effective and productive without being *meaningful*' until they are momentarily linked to particular significations (Colebrook 2015: 200–1). These universal, multiple surges of desire towards further differentiations produce 'affects' felt from one point of difference, or one mind, to another that can seek a 'territorialization of affect' in a 'collection of bodies', such as a nation or smaller group, 'investing in certain repeated affects' to the point of governing them under 'concepts' (Colebrook 2015: 206). At that stage, systems that limit possible meanings are often established by people to control the larger differential movement and even suppress its mobility, which then comes to seem insane, threatening or even unearthly to any would-be-closed system that establishes 'fixed beings and relations' (Colebrook 2015: 202).

This kind of post-structural vision, as it happens, looks back to what Marshall Brown has seen as the most fundamental revelation of Gothic writing: the point where 'absolute, pure consciousness' cast back into the darkness at its base edges towards a chaotic 'secret life' of 'unresolved antinomies' that can be taken to be 'madness' but may also be 'unconditioned drives and desires' operating at a 'level free from the categories and conditions of ordinary existence' (Brown 2005: 14–15, 80, 120–1). This extreme depth of multiplicities is established as quintessentially Gothic in Walpole's *Otranto* when the threatened Isabella flees into the 'subterraneous regions' that form the passage between the castle and the nearby abbey. Here, in a 'labyrinth of [total] darkness', she is buffeted by 'blasts of wind', the 'grating' of 'hinges' and other 'murmurs' that unleash the uncontrollable myriad of 'suggestions' that 'rushed into her mind' (Walpole 1996: 27–8). These raise 'horror' in her because she fears being pursued and/or constrained by a patriarchal system in which a prince may catch her and force her to marry against her will, or a priest (on the church end) may enjoin her to comply with that or some other paternalistic tyranny. The multiple sounds she hears end up meaning neither of these options, at least not immediately, so there is a multifariousness of affects and mobile desires that remains outside her present purview and surpasses the points of reference on which Isabella comes to rest. Yet even she, to avoid insanity, ascribes set meanings to this flow of signs and affects by accepting, even as its victim, a system that constrains what they can signify. The readers of this scene, so influential on future Gothic variations, are therefore left hesitating, like her, between numberless future possibilities and a 'territorialization of affect', which makes this moment as Deleuzean as it is foundationally Gothic. Much later derivations of Gothic, as Anna Powell argues in Chapter 14 of this book, would build more horrifically on Deleuze's connection between 'inhuman desires' and the suppression of them into deep, dark and covered-over spaces. But there can be no question that Deleuze offers an alternative post-structural lens of interpretation – even more influential than Derrida on parts of Danielewski's *House of Leaves* – that both stems from the older Gothic and helps explain or instigate some Gothic of the twentieth and the twenty-first centuries.

Still another affiliate of post-structuralism offers a quite different view indeed, even though it has just as much of a basis in, and is continuing to affect, the Gothic. The French-Lithuanian thinker Emmanuel Levinas, well known to and often in conversation with Derrida from the mid-1960s (both being Jewish and susceptible to 'othering' themselves), developed, in his own way, what has turned out to be an answer to Derrida's call for a writer's – or really anyone's – ethical 'responsibility' towards the 'othered' ghosts of past and future generations. In Levinas's eyes, particularly in *Totality and Infinity* (1961), before even the Heideggerian 'thrownness' of the subject, there is, primordially, the subject encountering the Other and especially 'the face' of the Other (which can take many forms). This 'relation between the Other and me', Levinas writes, 'issues neither in number or concept' at its most foundational, though there can, unfortunately, be later attempts to restrict its significance using such devices; instead, most immediately, the 'Other remains infinitely transcendent, infinitely foreign; his face in which epiphany is produced and appeals to me breaks with the world that can be common to us, whose virtualities are inscribed in our *nature* and absolute difference' (Levinas 1969: 194). At this basic level, until we un-ethically repress it, 'the face speaks to me and thereby invites me to a relation incommensurate with [any kind of] power exercised [including my own], be it enjoyment or knowledge' (1969: 198). That is because the Other's face, at this basic point, is not yet made into an alter ego or ideal self-image or anything in particular, but is an opening on to an infinite possibility of being that can truly carry the subject out of itself to levels of interrelationships and understandings it cannot yet comprehend – and because of which it could be much fuller by letting the Other help to expand it far beyond itself. As Dale Townshend shows in Chapter 15 here, this encounter, as well as its suppression and diminishment by self-serving power-plays, has appeared in the Gothic many times over the years, from the Frederic of Walpole's *Otranto* confronted by the skull-face of the dead Hermit of Joppa (Walpole 1996: 106–7) to Frankenstein seeing the multi-coloured visage of his creature for the first time (Shelley 2012: 35) all the way to the face of Mrs Bates superimposed over that of Norman at the end of Alfred Hitchcock's film (1960) of Robert Bloch's novel *Psycho* (1959).

True, the fear, doubt and revulsion that come with these encounters, Townshend also shows, need the help of Derrida in his *Of Hospitality* seminars, published after Levinas's death in 1995, to more fully explain them (see Derrida 2000). But the revival over the past several decades in the use of Levinas for a resurgent 'ethical criticism' to reinterpret major literary texts (see Womack 2015; Young 2015) is now rooted more clearly in the whole history of the Gothic than it ever has been up to now. Levinasian ethics have also had an effect on the Gothic going forward, as we can see in the film *The Shape of Water* (2017), directed by Guillermo del Toro, co-written by him and Vanessa Taylor, and full of Gothic elements, including reminiscences of *Frankenstein*, continuing the frequent Gothic in earlier del

Toro pictures. Here a humanoid-amphibian water-creature, as multi-coloured as he is apparently cross-bred, especially in his face, has been captured by a secret government laboratory in Baltimore and is reduced by his lead captors, bent as they are on power-plays supported by 'number and concept', to a source of data and organic matter that may provide a boost to the US in its Cold War with Russia in 1962 (del Toro and Taylor 2017). For Elisa Esposito, though, the mute attendant who becomes enamoured of this same creature and works with other 'minorities' to free him, he is an opening on to an unknown and 'infinitely transcendent' new world – a sexual one, yes, but far more than that – one that she refuses to make a means to her or anyone's power, despite her being found originally as a scarred foundling very close to water with some potential/primordial relationship to this new 'creature from the lagoon'. The primal ethic-before-social-ethics of Levinas could not be more Gothically in evidence than it is here. It therefore contributes to the growth of a postmodern Gothic that now seeks to put in question many of the 'otherings' that earlier Gothic has made fearful, whether they are based on racial or species differences or on ecologically damaging constructs that set human beings over against an 'othered' and boundary-blurring natural world.

As my colleague and co-editor Robert Miles has helpfully reminded me, a story or narrative is a first-order of existence. An aesthetic critique is second-order. Theory is third-order in most forms, insofar as it seeks to explain, not just what is being said, including the indirect saying in the form of a discourse, but the grounds that enable what it is that has been said in the first place. Theory engages, as it should, with the discontents of modernity, focusing not just on the ostensible content of a text (which might be the target of an analysis rooted in theory), but on the conditions of textual production more generally, whether linguistic, material, 'psychic', 'cultural' or a mix thereof. Only then are latent assumptions – and sometimes conflicts among assumptions – finally revealed. As we have seen throughout this opening chapter, Gothic texts themselves actually aspire from the beginning to the condition of third-order explanation, while subsuming the other two, even as they probe the problematic foundations of modern identity. Gothic and theory, then, are not mutually explanatory frames of reference; rather they are linked responses to the contest among older, religion-based and increasingly secular ideas ('ancient' vs. 'modern') that have emerged in Western thought over the centuries that have produced what we now find to be 'modernity'. The essays in the rest of this volume argue, therefore, that these two coeval streams of cultural expression have always been in conversation with each other, as the above history has begun to show. By focusing on a particular Gothic–theory interaction, and exploring how each inflects the other, every essay in this volume aims to revitalise both sides of this historic dialogue. As such, this book unabashedly aims to make a substantial, indeed cutting-edge, contribution to both fields.

To that end, each essay in this collection focuses on a particular kind of theory–Gothic relationship, every one of which has a history and each of which is still being explored in enactments of the Gothic and of theory today. Rather than recounting how different schools of theory and criticism have viewed the Gothic (accounts of which are already available elsewhere), these chapters argue how Gothic and theory have defined and affected – and still define and affect – each other in particular aesthetic, intellectual and cultural realms. In each case, the Gothic is revealed as containing and inciting the very theoretical schemes and assumptions that have purported to explain it from a particular perspective. Hence the Gothic, as it has progressed across Western and world history, emerges as both a producer of what a type of theory promulgates and an active Gothic-iser of that type to the point of advancing the development of each theoretical enterprise *in* Gothic works. This approach allows each essayist to reflect from the perspective of 2018 (the 200th anniversary of Shelley's original *Frankenstein*) – starting at the stage that each Gothic-and-theory conversation has reached, or not quite reached, by this time – on how a particular realm of theory has opened up forms of the Gothic to our understandings and to the wider possibilities of Gothic texts (from printed to film to cyberspace versions) as performers of 'cultural work'. At the same time, each approach enlists the realm of theory on which it concentrates to explain how those very openings are incipient in forms of the Gothic and how the Gothic can also question existing theoretical claims, challenge them, and reorient them as this mode unfolds from its largely literary and theatrical development across the eighteenth and nineteenth centuries to its explosion across many more forms of media in the twentieth and twenty-first.

The following essays, too, are ordered according to the broad strands of theory they each develop, beginning with the rise, in the early twentieth century, of historicism, which has since gone through many changes, decades ago and quite recently (all of the essays that are primarily historicist are included in Part I: The Gothic, Theory and History). This first grouping is succeeded by other theoretical developments, roughly in the chronological order in which they came (or reasserted themselves) into prominence – psychoanalysis and its extensions; feminist, gender and 'queer' theories connected to sexuality; modern media studies from film to cyberspace; and forms of post-structuralism as they have linked up with increasingly related strands – each of which has further advanced the relationship of Gothic and theory while each theoretical 'school' has grown in importance and generated offshoots of itself. In Part I, then, are history-oriented arguments that proceed from a post-New Historicist revelation of conflicting theories of history in the Gothic (Chapter 2) to historicist race theory within the growth of cultural studies (Chapter 3) to cultural studies as it has become postcolonial theory and criticism (Chapter 4), each of which discovers pre-statements in the Gothic and has led to Gothic reactions. Part II juxtaposes a retrospection on Freudian psychoanalysis, by the author of the book *Gothic Bodies* (1994), that examines how that movement has revived and re-explained the demonaical possession of the body (Chapter 5), with an account of the very post-Freudian theory of abjection and how its recent importance in the study of the Gothic stems from the very nature of Gothic symbol-making (Chapter 6). Part III places an assessment of how the feminist movement in criticism *and* Gothic fiction has reached a stage where social toleration and accommodation are no longer enough (Chapter 7, a remarkable parallel to current female protests against newly uncovered exploitations of women) alongside the clearest of statements yet that 'queer theory', with all it includes and battles against, has long been inherent in the Gothic and is still partly carried out through it (Chapter 8).

Part IV, which covers the two major realms in which theories of 'new media' interface with the Gothic, starts with an exposition of just how much cinema has always been inherent in the Gothic and thus how film is fundamentally Gothic in its very nature and techniques (Chapter 9) and closes with an account of how the cyber-Gothic, incipient in *Frankenstein*, has become the repository in the postmodern world of all our conflicted feelings about technology and the 'posthuman' conditions it keeps creating (Chapter 10). Part V is our largest section because of all the variations on post-structuralism, itself incipient in the Gothic, that have arisen and progressed from the late 1960s until 2018 and are likely to continue. It begins with a study of how earlier Gothic reacted to quandaries about human history and mortality by developing systems of symbolic exchange that seem to resolve in entirely verbal forms what cannot be as readily resolved in life (Chapter 11). Chapter 12 then shows how Derridean deconstruction, particularly as it has become attenuated after its most radical beginnings, remains haunted by what is most Gothic – and hence what is most radically beyond (or beneath) theorising – in it. Chapter 13 follows, as though responding directly to Derrida's *Specters of Marx*, by displaying how the extreme dark materiality that Gothic keeps pointing to as the ultimate threat to human meanings (like but eluding even what Lacan calls 'the Real') is, to a great extent, generated and projected by the very superstructural textualities that both claim to represent it and keep it forever remote. In Chapter 14, the affinity of Gilles Deleuze's post-structuralism for Gothic configurations is revealed as achieving its most shocking, fearsome interface in the unlikely similarities of Deleuzian affects to the horrors of H. P. Lovecraft's stories of the much earlier twentieth century. Chapter 15 finishes Part V by connecting the primal 'ethics' of Levinas back to the Gothic, both in long-classic novels and recent films, finally suggesting, however, that an accurate post-structural account of what Gothic 'facings' of the primordially Other contain can be produced only by pairing the thinking of Levinas with the very post-structuralism of Derrida with which Levinas himself has long been in dialogue and remains in tension. The Gothic itself, as we have seen, is a kind of conversation among different modes of belief, so it is only fitting that its dialogue with theory, from the 1760s to now, leads to differing schemes interfacing with each other in this very modern world of multiple perspectives that the Gothic *and* theory have increasingly revealed to us in both scary and powerful ways.

Our final essay, the sole piece in our Part VI, consequently looks broadly at this whole Janus-faced quality in the Gothic, as well as in theories within and about it, and offers an appropriate summative response that looks backwards and forwards simultaneously. It reflects back on the fundamental cultural quandaries raised by such a conflicted mode and the theorising in and of it over two-and-a-half centuries, on the one hand, and the questions that still remain unanswered – and haunting us into the future – in the deep uncertainties that the Gothic and theory still make us confront in our own times, on the other. Its author, David Punter, instigated, more than anyone else, the effulgence over the last four decades in the Gothic–theory conversation, so Robert Miles and I asked him 1) to recall the issues that have been raised most prominently in that interplay since the first version of his *Literature of Terror* in 1980 and 2) to draw out the nagging problems that remain the most pressing and unresolved right now because of what the Gothic and theory have brought forward together in the cultural unconscious of the West. Professor Punter has addressed that double charge by focusing on several areas in which the Gothic, as it theorises and has been theorised, acts as a *liminal* aesthetic mode operating at many 'thresholds', leaving its readers at the fulcrum-point between past and present belief-systems, the conscious and the unconscious, dominant and resistant modes of discourse, and attempted stabilities and disturbing instabilities of gender, class, race and nationality, among other equipoises. The result is thus not an argument for or against anything but an apt reflection on where the Gothic-and-theory conversation has gone and where it might go in the years to come. Such a reflection at this juncture is exactly what the Gothic–theory relationship finally calls for, since its contests among ideas are far from over and its many hauntings lead us forward to more theory and Gothic, less to 'get to the bottom' of their mysteries than to open up their possibilities.

References

Atwood, Margaret (1985), *The Handmaid's Tale*, Toronto: McClelland and Stewart.
Birkhead, Edith (1921), *The Tale of Terror: A Study of the Gothic Romance*, London: Constable.
Brantlinger, Patrick (1998), *The Reading Lesson: The Threat of Mass Literacy in Nineteenth-Century Britain*, Bloomington: Indiana University Press.
Bronfen, Elisabeth (2014), 'Cinema of the Gothic Extreme', in Jerrold E. Hogle (ed.), *The Cambridge Companion to the Modern Gothic*, Cambridge: Cambridge University Press, pp. 107–22.
Brontë, Charlotte (1996) [1847], *Jane Eyre*, ed. Beth Newman, Boston: Bedford/St. Martin's.
Brown, Charles Brockden (1988) [1799], *Edgar Huntly, or, Memoirs of a Sleep-Walker*, ed. Norman S. Grabo, New York: Penguin.
Brown, Marshall (2005), *The Gothic Text*, Stanford: Stanford University Press.
Bruhm, Steven (1994), *Gothic Bodies: The Politics of Pain in Romantic Fiction*, Philadelphia: University of Pennsylvania Press.
Bruhm, Steven (2002), 'The Contemporary Gothic: Why We Need It', in Jerrold E. Hogle (ed.), *The Cambridge Companion to Gothic Fiction*, Cambridge: Cambridge University Press, pp. 259–76.
Butler, Judith (1990), *Gender Trouble*, London: Routledge.
Clery, E. J. (1995), *The Rise of Supernatural Fiction, 1762–1800*, Cambridge: Cambridge University Press.
Clery, E. J., and Robert Miles (eds) (2000), *Gothic Documents: A Sourcebook, 1700–1820*, Manchester: Manchester University Press.
Colebrook, Claire (2015), 'Deleuzean Criticism', in Julian Wolfreys (ed.), *Introducing Criticism in the 21st Century*, 2nd edn, Edinburgh: Edinburgh University Press, pp. 195–214.
Cronenberg, David, writer/director (1983), *Videodrome*, Canadian Film Development Corporation/Universal Pictures.

Danielewski, Mark Z. (2000), *House of Leaves*, New York: Pantheon.
De Lauretis, Teresa (1987), *Technologies of Gender*, Bloomington: Indiana University Press.
Deleuze, Gilles, and Félix Guattari (1983) [1972], *Anti-Oedipus: Capitalism and Schizophrenia*, trans. Robert Hurley, Mark Seem and Helen R. Lane, London: Athlone.
del Toro, Guillermo, co-writer/director, and Vanessa Taylor, co-writer (2017), *The Shape of Water*, TSG Entertainment/Double Dare You Productions/Fox Searchlight Pictures.
Derrida, Jacques (1994), *Specters of Marx: The State of the Debt, the Work of Mourning and the New International*, trans. Peggy Kamuf, New York: Routledge.
Derrida, Jacques, with Anne Duformatelle (2000), *Of Hospitality*, trans. Rachel Bowlby, Stanford: Stanford University Press.
du Maurier, Daphne (1938), *Rebecca*, London: Victor Gollancz.
Farnell, Gary (2009), 'The Gothic and the Thing', *Gothic Studies*, 11.1: 113–23.
Fiedler, Leslie (1966) [1960], *Love and Death in the American Novel*, rev. edn, New York: Stein and Day.
Freud, Sigmund (1959) [1919], 'The Uncanny', in *Collected Papers*, ed. and trans. Joan Riviere, New York: Basic Books, IV, pp. 368–407.
Freud, Sigmund (1965) [1900, 1931], *The Interpretation of Dreams*, trans. and ed. James Strachey, New York: Avon Books.
Gamer, Michael (2000), *Romanticism and the Gothic: Genre, Reception, and Canon Formation*, Cambridge: Cambridge University Press.
Gelder, Ken (2014), 'The Postcolonial Gothic', in Jerrold E. Hogle (ed.), *The Cambridge Companion to the Modern Gothic*, Cambridge: Cambridge University Press, pp. 191–207.
Gibson, William (1984), *Neuromancer*, New York: Ace.
Haggerty, George E. (2006), *Queer Gothic*, Urbana: University of Illinois Press.
Hitchcock, Alfred, director (1940), *Rebecca*, Selznick International/United Artists.
Hogle, Jerrold E. (2002), *The Undergrounds of* The Phantom of the Opera: *Sublimation and the Gothic in Leroux and its Progeny*, New York: Palgrave.
Hogle, Jerrold E. (2006), 'Theorizing the Gothic', in Anna Powell and Andrew Smith (eds), *Teaching the Gothic*, New York: Palgrave Macmillan, pp. 29–47.
Hogle, Jerrold E. (ed.) (2014), *The Cambridge Companion to the Modern Gothic*, Cambridge: Cambridge University Press.
Hogle, Jerrold E. (2017), 'The Gothic Image at the Villa Diodati', *The Wordsworth Circle*, 48.1: 16–26.
Horner, Avril, and Sue Zlosnik (1998), *Daphne du Maurier: Writing, Identity and the Gothic Imagination*, London: Macmillan.
Horner, Avril, and Sue Zlosnik (2014), 'Gothic Configurations of Gender', in Jerrold E. Hogle (ed.), *The Cambridge Companion to the Modern Gothic*, Cambridge: Cambridge University Press, pp. 55–70.

Hughes, William (2006), 'Gothic Criticism: A Survey, 1764–2004', in Anna Powell and Andrew Smith (eds), *Teaching the Gothic*, New York: Palgrave Macmillan, pp. 10–28.
Jones, David J. (2014), *Sexuality and the Gothic Magic Lantern: Desire, Eroticism and Literary Visibilities from Byron to Bram Stoker*, New York: Palgrave Macmillan.
King, Stephen (1977), *The Shining*, Garden City, NY: Doubleday.
King, Stephen (1981), *Danse Macabre*, New York: Everest House.
Kristeva, Julia (1982) [1980], *Powers of Horror: An Essay on Abjection*, trans. Leon S. Roudiez, New York: Columbia University Press.
Lacan, Jacques (1992) [1960, 1986], *The Ethics of Psychoanalysis: The Seminar of Jacques Lacan, Book VII*, ed. Jacques-Alain Miller, trans. Dennis Porter, New York: Norton.
Leroux, Gaston (1990) [1910], *The Phantom of the Opera*, trans. Lowell Bair, New York: Bantam Books.
Levinas, Emmanuel (1969) [1961], *Totality and Infinity: An Essay on Exteriority*, trans. Alphonso Lingus, Pittsburgh: Duquesne University Press.
Lévy, Maurice (1968), *Le Roman 'Gothique' Anglais, 1764–1824*, Toulouse: la Faculté des Lettres et Sciences Humaine.
Lloyd Smith, Allan (1996), 'Postmodernism/Gothic', in Victor Sage and Allan Lloyd Smith (eds), *Modern Gothic: A Reader*, Manchester: Manchester University Press, pp. 6–19.
Lovecraft, H. P. (1967) [1916–39], *Dagon and Other Macabre Tales*, London: Victor Gollancz.
Malchow, Howard L. (1996), *Gothic Images of Race in Nineteenth-century Britain*, Stanford: Stanford University Press.
Marx, Karl (1976) [1867], *Capital: A Critique of Political Economy, Volume I*, trans. Ben Fowkes, New York: Penguin.
McCallum, E. L. (2014), 'The "Queer Limits" in Modern Gothic', in Jerrold E. Hogle (ed.), *The Cambridge Companion to the Modern Gothic*, Cambridge: Cambridge University Press, pp. 71–86.
Moers, Ellen (2012) [1974], 'Female Gothic: The Monster's Mother', repr. in Mary Shelley, *Frankenstein*, ed. J. Paul Hunter (2nd edn), New York: Norton, pp. 317–27.
Morrison, Toni (1988) [1987], *Beloved*, New York: Penguin/Plume.
Morrison, Toni (1992), *Playing in the Dark: The William E. Massey Lectures in the History of American Civilization, 1990*, Cambridge, MA: Harvard University Press.
Mousley, Andy (2016), 'The Posthuman', in Andrew Smith (ed.), *The Cambridge Companion to Frankenstein*, Cambridge: Cambridge University Press, pp. 158–72.
Powell, Anna, and Andrew Smith (eds) (2006), *Teaching the Gothic*, New York: Palgrave Macmillan.
Punter, David (1996) [1980], *The Literature of Terror: A History of Gothic Fictions from 1765 to the Present Day*, rev. edn, 2 vols, London: Longman.

Radcliffe, Ann (1998) [1794], *The Mysteries of Udolpho*, ed. Bonamy Dobrée and Terry Castle, Oxford: Oxford University Press.

Rhys, Jean (1982) [1966], *Wide Sargasso Sea*, New York: Norton.

Said, Edward (1978), *Orientalism*, New York: Pantheon.

Savoy, Eric (2002), 'The Rise of American Gothic', in Jerrold E. Hogle (ed.), *The Cambridge Companion to Gothic Fiction*, Cambridge: Cambridge University Press, pp. 167–88.

Scott, Sir Walter (1968) [1805–28], *On Novelists and Fiction*, ed. Ioan Williams, New York: Barnes and Noble.

Sedgwick, Eve Kosofsky (1985), *Between Men: English Literature and Male Homosocial Desire*, New York: Columbia University Press.

Shelley, Mary (2012) [1818], *Frankenstein*, ed. J. Paul Hunter (2nd edn), New York: Norton.

Showalter, Elaine (1985) [1981], 'Feminist Criticism in the Wilderness', in Elaine Showalter (ed.), *The New Feminist Criticism*, New York: Pantheon, pp. 243–70.

Todorov, Tzvetan (1973) [1970], *The Fantastic: A Structural Approach to a Literary Genre*, trans. Richard Howard, Cleveland: Press of Case Western Reserve University.

Tucker, Susie I. (1967), *Protean Shape: A Study in Eighteenth-century Vocabulary*, London: Athlone Press.

Van Elferen, Isabella (2009), 'Dances with Spectres: Theorising the Cybergothic', *Gothic Studies*, 11.1: 99–112.

Varma, Devendra P. (1957), *The Gothic Flame*, London: Arthur Barker.

Walpole, Horace (1996) [1764], *The Castle of Otranto: A Gothic Story*, ed. W. S. Lewis and E. J. Clery, Oxford: Oxford University Press.

Wester, Maisha (2014), 'The Gothic and the Politics of Race', in Jerrold E. Hogle (ed.), *The Cambridge Companion to the Modern Gothic*, Cambridge: Cambridge University Press, pp. 157–73.

Williams, Ioan (ed.) (1970), *Novel and Romance, 1700–1800: A Documentary Record*, New York: Barnes and Noble.

Wolfreys, Julian (ed.) (2015), *Introducing Criticism in the 21st Century*, 2nd edn, Edinburgh: Edinburgh University Press.

Womack, Kenneth (2015), 'Ethical Criticism and the Philosophical Turn', in Julian Wolfreys (ed.), *Introducing Criticism in the 21st Century*, 2nd edn, Edinburgh: Edinburgh University Press, pp. 81–100.

Wright, Richard (1940), *Native Son*, New York: Harper and Brothers.

Young, Frederick (2015), 'Levinas and Criticism: Ethics in the Impossibility of Criticism', in Julian Wolfreys (ed.), *Introducing Criticism in the 21st Century*, 2nd edn, Edinburgh: Edinburgh University Press, pp. 101–21.

Part I

The Gothic, Theory and History

Chapter 2

History/Genealogy/Gothic: Godwin, Scott and their Progeny
Robert Miles

History has always been theoretical. The point becomes apparent if we ask this question: what is it that separates the narrative practices whereby pre-literate societies know themselves from the set of narrative practices whereby literate societies memorialise the past? The answer, arguably, is theory, by which I mean conceptualisations of the function of 'history' as a specific set of practices for recording the past's value. By this measure, all modern history, and certainly any academic practice of history, is founded on theory. But for the purposes of this chapter, I mean something different when I speak of history and theory: I mean the overriding sense that history's customary practices are in fact inadequate for the narration of the motive forces of the cultures in which we live. In the 1980s there was an attempt to corral some diverse expressions of this literary-historical dissatisfaction as 'New Historicism'. Once ubiquitous, the term is not now much heard, for three reasons: fashion has moved on, rendering the 'new' old; those corralled by the term often differed more than they agreed, thus undermining the notion of a school; and finally, and more significantly, 'New Historicism' has done its work. We now take it for granted that the line separating text and context is a permeable one; that the act of narrating the past is itself part of how the past is constituted; that there is no outside vantage point from which the past may be objectively viewed; that the historian is not immune from the distortions of history that the New Historicist seeks to correct; and that it may be in the overlooked detail, in some unassimilated expression or story – an anecdote, say – that an apprehension of the past may be had that helps us break free of our historiographical, mind-forged manacles.

This echo of William Blake takes me to my next point, which is that the impulses behind New Historicism have Gothic-Romantic roots.

As much as Blake himself, Johann Gottfried Herder and Edmund Burke (of terror-sublime fame) argued against the general and for the resonant particular. Indeed, for both Herder and Burke, all meaning, all culture, is local, peculiar, distinct. If one puts the argument in its broadest terms, New Historicism and Herder and Burke join other nay-sayers in opposing those grand narratives, often unconsciously held, that progress is the order of the day, that whatever the circuitous routes of history, all prejudices, class differences, social deference, old-fashioned patriarchy and other pre-modern leftovers are gradually being cleansed from the body politic as secular republics and parliamentary democracies carry on with their inexorable upward march towards the light. Nevertheless, there is a world of difference between the kind of opposition to narratives of progress mounted by the likes of Burke and Herder and the kind mounted by a tradition of sceptical thought traceable from Friedrich Nietzsche and Karl Marx to Michel Foucault and New Historicist thinkers. For Burke and Herder, the local and the peculiar is held up against theory itself, meaning any kind of systematic analysis of power that ends with a schematisation of progress. For Nietzsche and Foucault, on the contrary, scepticism emerges from theory. For Burke and Herder, tradition, custom and even prejudice are the enablers of personal agency, of personhood, identity and, finally, happiness. For Nietzsche as much as for Marx, prejudice, tradition and custom are what lock us into our mind-forged manacles.

In the development of the Gothic across the Anglophone world, William Godwin and Walter Scott parallel Nietzsche/Marx/Foucault and Burke/Herder as key figures for the interplay of theory and history at the moment when the Enlightenment transitions into Romanticism. Their point of contact is their claim to write 'historical romance'. In both cases they mean a theoretical blending of fiction and history. Despite a common beginning, however, their projects pull in opposite directions. As I shall argue, Godwin's practice takes us deep into Gothic territory, into a form of historical enquiry that Nietzsche and Foucault both call 'genealogy', whereas Scott veers in the direction of the kind of historical practice that 'New Historicism' arose to contest. In short, Godwin's form of historical romance is Gothic, whereas Scott's is closer to being antithetical to it. I am not arguing that all Gothic writing is 'genealogical', in a manner anticipatory of New Historicism. On the contrary I contend that some Gothic texts are more genealogical than others, especially in a line of influence that stretches from Friedrich Schiller's *The Ghostseer*, through Radcliffe, Godwin, Charles Brockden Brown, Mary Shelley and their great American heirs, Nathaniel Hawthorne and Herman Melville. I cannot cover this line of influence in detail in the space of a single essay; instead I shall make a sketch of the larger argument, focusing on the Godwin/Brockden Brown connection, as representatives of Gothic 'genealogical' thinking. This line of Gothic writing was sometimes known as 'philosophical romance' (Murray 1805: 145), but as we shall see, its deepest purposes engage history or 'genealogy'. But to understand the distinctiveness of Godwin's thought, we must first look more deeply at the contrast with Scott and how this difference anticipates New Historical concerns.

Scott is the great interpreter of Burke, the writer who puts Burkean thought into narrative form, with incalculable effect. We might not want to go so far as Archibald Alison in the 1840s and embrace Scott as the great figure who saved the world for feudalism, rescuing his age from the delusions of democracy (Alison 1845: 347), but it was certainly possible to believe that, more than any other writer, Scott renewed a love for chivalry, medievalism, hereditary distinction and the honour codes of the aristocratic, warrior class. However, as Eric Hobsbawm argues, Scott's deeper contribution – beyond instantiating the chivalric manners that Burke thought the glory and salvation of Europe – was a historical version of the 'fortunate fall' story: out of historic conflict and bloodshed Scott narrates the slow workings of culture that produce a saving unity and a higher national consciousness (Hobsbawm 1990: 90).

It was this conservative, and Romantic, habit of history-making, surviving into the twentieth century within the belletristic confines of literary history, that the New Historicists in particular set out to disrupt, as we can see in that branch of New Historicism that emerged out of Renaissance studies. A prime target for New Historicists was the (as they saw it) lazy historical thinking that flowed from the too-ready acceptance of a work such as E. M. W. Tillyard's 'old historicist' *The Elizabethan World Picture* (1942). The New Historicists' point of greatest disagreement with Tillyard was the implicit determinism with which he imagined the past. For Tillyard a 'world picture' was indeed a culture-wide, mind-forged manacle from which it was impossible to struggle free, however much a subject might chafe against it. The deep background of cultural assumption lying behind Shakespeare's texts constrained interpretation by modern critics committed to objective knowledge; more to the point, intellectually, it conceived resistance to the dominant, hegemonic assumptions of the 'world picture' as futile, because resistance amounted to the retrospective wish-fulfilment of the modern critic to find his values reflected back in the work of his aesthetic heroes. We might wish to read Shakespeare as an avatar of the class warrior, but such a wish is, scholarly speaking, nugatory, for it was not possible within the Elizabethan world-picture to think such a thing. In a mental world conditioned by belief in a great chain of being, the conditions for modern class-consciousness simply did not exist, and ascribing such thoughts to Shakespeare was a grave historical solecism.

New Historicists begged to differ. In doing so, they fought a rearguard action against a would-be ally, vulgar Marxism. In arguing, against Tillyard, that 'background' was not destiny – was not an all-encompassing intellectual and moral condition – New Historicists struck a blow for political agency, albeit severely conditioned: power may be everywhere, may exert itself on both sides of any question, but the question could always be turned to reveal a contradiction, an incongruity, a logical gap. It was in these curious interstices of discursive expressions of power that the Renaissance subject found a gap in which to plant the point of her or his lever, to move history along. As such, the New Historicist critic simultaneously took issue with the bête noire of the vulgar Marxist: the question of how political resistance was possible if ideology, or false consciousness, was a systematic *camera obscura* inverting appearance and reality. Or, to put it differently, why was the Marxist critic exceptionally outside the totalising power of ideology, right side up, while everyone else was stuck inside it, upside down? Taking their cue from Michel Foucault, who had fought precisely this battle with his Marxist colleagues, New Historicists argued alike against old-fashioned historicists such as Tillyard, and against (as they saw it) the unsophisticated historicism of dogmatic, often highly theoretical, Marxists. To put matters another way, the cultural poetics of the New Historicists – a patient hermeneutical practice in which one sifted text, and context, for scattered clues – resisted grand narratives, whatever their ideological provenance. For the New Historicists, militant Marxist materialism and Romantic constructions of Renaissance cultural difference were alike suspect.

Scott and Godwin work through the same argument. But whereas, for the New Historicists, Marx was the theoretical figure in the background through whom they conducted their debate, for Scott and Godwin it was Aristotle. This is the key passage informing Godwin's and Scott's differences, from Aristotle's *Poetics* (which assumes that by 'poetry' one may understand any kind of fictional work):

> For this reason poetry is a more philosophical and more serious thing than history; poetry tends to speak of universals, history of particulars.

A universal is the sort of thing that a certain kind of person may well say or do in accordance with probability or necessity – this is what poetry aims at, although it assigns names [to the people]. (Leitch 2010: 95)

Aristotle is making two key points: first, that whereas history deals in particulars, poetry represents universals; and second, emerging out of this difference, poetry is more philosophical than history, 'because in order to unfold a plot in a manner that is convincing to the audience, the poet must grasp and represent the internal logic, the necessity, of the outcome of those events' (Zuern 1998: Guide to *Poetics* Book IX).

In his 1821 review of Jane Austen's *Northanger Abbey* and *Persuasion*, Richard Whateley cites the above passage from Aristotle to argue that Austen was the pre-eminent 'philosophical' novelist of her age. Her novels are 'a kind of fictitious biography' and, as such, 'bear the same relation to the real, that epic and tragic poetry . . . bear to history: they present us . . . with the general, instead of the particular, the probable, instead of the true . . .' They are philosophical, because they 'present us with a clear and abstracted view of the general rules themselves' (Whateley 1968: 87). Whateley's article is a kind of theoretical summing up of Walter Scott's review of Austen's *Emma*, six years earlier, also published in the *Quarterly Review*. Although Scott makes more of the importance of manners in his assessment of Austen – of the inductive particular, as Ian Watt would later term it in *The Rise of the Novel* (1957) – he is with Whateley in arguing that Austen's texts are fundamentally, and philosophically, conditioned by a deep sense of the 'probable'. It was the quality Scott himself was looking to instil in his version of the historical romance.

It is precisely here that Godwin differs from Scott. In the analogy I am drawing, Scott stands to Godwin as Tillyard and the vulgar Marxists stand to the New Historicists. The basis for this assertion is that, like Tillyard and the vulgar Marxists, Scott, even at his most Gothic, surrenders to the romance of there being some kind of governing or providential patterning, some kind of grand narrative, at work in history that minimises individual agency. It is the presence of such patterning that constitutes the probable. Godwin, meanwhile, struggles towards what Jerome Christensen calls 'impossible history', this phrase being another iteration of what the New Historicists felt they were groping their way towards: a way of understanding different and conflicting forms of human possibility in history that seem to have been expunged by the upward, linear, inexorable march of the history that Francis Fukuyama in 1992, famously and prematurely, declared to be at an end with the triumph of the capitalist West over the communist East. Christensen's point was that our conventional sense of history, Western history, the history of capitalist modernity, now triumphant, seems so inexorable, so immune to the possibility of negation, that it has become an all-encompassing mentality outside of which it is extremely hard to think. As Slavoj Žižek famously quipped, 'the paradox is, that it's much easier to imagine the end of all life on earth than a much more modest radical change in capitalism' (Žižek 1999: 6). For Christensen, the only alternative to the victorious group-think of Western capitalist modernity, with its hardened sense of the 'probable', is the existential insistence on there being inchoate, unnamed, yet viable popular practices that resist being co-opted into the overarching narratives – the mind-forged manacles – of modernity (in that sense, they remain 'impossible' [Christensen 1994: 475]).

The differences between Godwin and Scott are perfectly captured in this passage from Foucault's essay 'Nietzsche, Genealogy, History':

> Genealogy does not pretend to go back in time to restore an unbroken continuity that operates beyond the dispersion of forgotten things; its duty is not to demonstrate that the past actively exists in the present, having imposed a predetermined form on all its vicissitudes. Genealogy does not resemble the evolution of a species and does not map the destiny of a people. On the contrary, to follow the complex course of descent is to maintain passing events in their proper dispersion . . . it is to discover that truth or being does not lie at the root of what we know and what we are, but the exteriority of accidents. (Foucault 1984: 81)

Here Foucault contrasts conventional history with a more radical kind that he calls, following Nietzsche, 'genealogy'. In one sense, it is a contrast between a history that charts the manifest contours of the past and one that seeks to reveal what Freud would call its 'latent contents'. But, more particularly, it is a polemical call to resist the tendency to romanticise the past by positing clear origins to events, or by identifying some kind of upward, evolutionary trajectory. Instead, the genealogist must be alive to the dispersed, contingent, fragmentary (and fragmenting) play of power. Christensen writes like a genealogist when he contests Fukuyama's implicit reading of the rise of the West as some kind of evolutionary narrative that has completed itself in a new sense of inexorability. More particularly, if we attend closely to this excerpt from Foucault, we can see that the object of his critique fits exactly with the tendencies of nationalist romance, which is what, finally, Scott writes in *Waverley* or *Ivanhoe*. Scott travels back in time to reveal the unbroken continuity between the origins of the nation and its current expression, a continuity that takes the shape of an evolution, the creation of a higher unity out of conflict and difference ('the destiny of a people'), which is the primary burden of national history (Gellner 1983: 120).

By way of contrast, Godwin begins his 1797 essay 'On History and Romance' by drawing a distinction between the history of nations (Scott's métier) and the history of individuals. Godwin argues that the former is customarily held in high, the latter in low, repute. As the essay unfolds, it is evident that Godwin is reworking Aristotle; by the end, we are invited to regard conventional history of nations as a tissue of incoherent particulars: 'What sort of an object is the history of England? Till the extinction of the wars of York and Lancaster, it is one scene of barbarism and cruelty' (Godwin 1797). The conventional history of nations, argues Godwin, is an idiotic tale full of random events, signifying nothing. Such aristocratic history is meaningless because it excludes the 'history of genuine independent man'. Without a full understanding of the human agent and human agency, history is essentially meaningless. 'But let us suppose that the genuine purpose of history, was to enable us to understand the machine of society, and to direct it to its best purposes' (Godwin 1797). Godwin speaks rhetorically; clearly, for him, understanding 'the machine of society' is the real purpose of history, and there is only one kind of history capable of informing us of these deep motive forces, the knowledge of which constitutes true philosophy. By the end of his essay, Godwin's reworking of Aristotle completes itself in this paean to the writer of romance:

> The writer of romance is to be considered as the writer of real history; while he who was formerly called the historian, must be contented to step down into the place of his rival, with this disadvantage, that he is a romance writer, without the arduous, the enthusiastic and the sublime licence of imagination, that belong to that species of composition. True history consists in a delineation of consistent, human character, in a display of the manner in which such a character acts under successive circumstances, in showing how character increases and assimilates new substances to its own, and how it decays, together with the catastrophe into which by its own gravity it naturally declines. (Godwin 1797)

The steps Godwin takes to get to this remarkable conclusion may be summarised as follows: to understand the machine of society, we need to understand the nature of man; man can only be known through the individual; a true political praxis necessarily rests on human psychology; and whereas the conventional writer of history necessarily relies upon supposition of otherwise opaque historical actors when generalising about them, the romance writer has the advantage because she or he writes about creatures of her or his own imagination. When the romance writer is a true historian, his characters will be based, onerously, in

> a genuine praxis upon the nature of man . . . From these considerations it follows that the noblest and most excellent species of history, may be decided to be a composition in which, with a scanty substratum of facts and dates, the writer interweaves a number of happy, ingenious and instructive inventions, blending them into one continuous and indiscernible mass.

Recalling the French writer Prevost, Godwin terms this species of historical writing 'historical romance' (Godwin 1797).

If we want to know what this strenuous exercise of the sympathetic imagination looks like in practice, we need look no further than Godwin's Gothic and historical romance *Caleb Williams* (1794), the work that prompted Hugh Murray's critical phrase 'philosophical romance'. As Godwin makes clear in his preface, this work is a species of history-writing, a means of comprehending, at a deep level, the current 'machine of society', one he typifies as motivated, systematically, by a spirit of tyranny (referring to how, in the immediate aftermath of the French Revolution, the English state forestalled revolution in Britain through draconian laws against assembly and free speech). It is necessarily a history of the individual. While both Scott and Godwin may recur to the same passage in Aristotle, they have very different understandings of the word 'universal', the quality that makes fiction philosophical. For Scott, universality is a matter of manners, of characters behaving in a 'probable' manner, where probability is defined by the interplay of human psychology with national and class differences. For Godwin, universality refers to the probable effects of the power of the 'machine of society' on human psychology. To adapt Foucault's terms, at the 'root of what we know and what we are' we discover, in Godwin's fiction, not the truths of our national being, 'but the exteriority of accidents'. The 'accidents' that shape us are contingent, environmental (exterior to us), but also brutal. Godwin's fictions are, after all, a kind of history; and being historical, they focus on the play of power, where power shapes the individual, leaving its mark. Inevitably this means violence and trauma. In Godwin, but also the Gothic in general (albeit with qualifications that I shall shortly make), trauma is a mark of the genre's 'genealogical' ambition.

The tragic hero of the novel, Falkland, is deep-dyed in the motive forces that Burke ascribes to European society as its best hope of an upward turn towards the light: chivalry. Paradoxically, the internalisation of this ideal proves to be an act of violence, one that begets yet more violence. The false god of 'chivalry' is the origin of a scene of deep and abiding trauma: Falkland's melancholic fixation on the trunk in which he keeps the Gothic secret of his crimes. Falkland's back story is itself a kind of New Historical anecdote, before the fact. Of diminutive stature, the noble Falkland likes to think of himself as the apotheosis of chivalry, of the manners and ethics that justify the hierarchical ordering of society, where obligations balance the privileges of the elite, the gentry, who are the pillars of country life. His neighbour, Barnabas Tyrrel, is Falkland's antithesis, and more like the contemporary reality of a country gentleman, being nasty, brutish and short-tempered. Falkland takes Tyrrell to task for his oppressive treatment of his niece, Emily Melvile, dressing Tyrrell down in public. Tyrrell responds by laughing at the diminutive Falkland, knocking him flat, and kicking him across the floor. The humiliated Falkland retires from the scene, later to murder his neighbour in the most unchivalric manner possible: by ambush. Worse, two of Tyrrell's tenants, father and son, are hanged for Tyrrell's murder while Falkland remains silent.

All three are, so to speak, the victims of Falkland's devotion to chivalry, to Burke's idealised version of Gothicism. The mystery deepens, and the plot advances, with the arrival of Caleb Williams, a young orphan of parts employed by Falkland as his secretary. Caleb becomes gripped by insatiable curiosity after witnessing his master exhibiting signs of deep mental distress after reviewing material kept in a strongbox. Caleb successfully solves the mystery of his master's behaviour, but pays a terrible price: determined to protect his reputation at all costs, Falkland pursues Caleb across the length and breadth of England, not literally, but through his command of media (newspapers, broadsides and wanted posters). He also expertly pulls the levers of an incipient police state, relying on his status as a respected magistrate to ensure that no stone is left unturned in the pursuit of Caleb, who discovers that flight is ultimately useless.

In schematic terms, we can say that Godwin opposes Burke's influential version of the historical process by imagining the reality in individual terms. 'The real essence of every story of human affairs', writes Godwin, 'is character. Without this it is all rottenness and dust. It is by character that I understand a story, and come to feel its reality' (Godwin 2016: 249). Godwin literalises Burke's political theory, where the spirit of chivalry is the glory and salvation of Europe, by imagining a character, Falkland, who has thoroughly internalised it. Against the madness of Revolutionary theory – the abstract rights of man, including equality and fraternity – Burke set custom and cultural practice, or as he puts it, 'manners' (Burke 1791: 115–17). Rather than the slow gyrations of history leading to the realisation of mankind's better nature, as successive generations strive to live up to the lofty ideals of chivalry embedded in their manners (as one might find in Scott's historical romances), Godwin's story quickly founders on trauma. Unprincipled prejudice, no matter how noble its intent, quickly breaks apart on contact with the reality of things as they currently are. In Godwin's genealogy of modernity, there is no happy outcome, no means of a higher synthesis as oppositions work themselves out, in the manner of *Waverley* or *Ivanhoe*. Instead one finds neurosis and repetition; even at the end Caleb is unable to free himself from his own destructive dependency on an ideal Falkland. Having 'introjected' the ideal, just as Falkland had before him, Caleb has no means of moving forward, only in circles, like Blake's mental traveller – or, indeed, like a Nietzschean *untermensch*, who insists on trying to live out the bad faith of contemporary ethics (the point of departure for Nietzsche's *Genealogy of Morals*).

It is in this paralysis, in the live burial of internalised ideals that only leads to splitting, abjection and violence, that Godwin's tale enjoys its Gothic life. Arguably the defining trauma of the tale – its dark Gothic heart – is not Falkland's, but Caleb's. Falkland's trauma is a given in the tale; it happens offstage, as it were, in the time before the story. Caleb's trauma is, so to speak, lived out in front of the reader. Or rather, we read inductively, or hermeneutically, as we scan Caleb's narrative for signs of the trauma that deforms it. Caleb's narrative is a retrospective one; the trauma has happened long before; we deduce its subterranean work by the outcroppings of identification, grief and denial that periodically interrupt Caleb's first-person narrative. Caleb's subject-formation is mental, and is not by precept, but by what Freud eventually calls 'introjection' (Freud 1958: 241, n. 1): as much as Falkland has internalised Burke, Caleb has internalised Falkland. The processes of culture – of identification, sympathy and character formation – are not progressive or elective, but disruptive and unconscious.

At this point we need to be very careful about terminology. So far I have used 'trauma' to denote the genealogical ambition of Gothic writing, by which I mean the Gothic's alternative form of history, which emphasises events in their 'proper dispersion', discontinuity and contradiction. As Godwin instructs us, this 'impossible' form of history (borrowing once again from Christensen) is written at the level of the person. In Godwin's Gothic genealogy the individual (in his or her full, lived, anecdotal detail) is a minute record for how the spirit of tyranny lives on in the contemporary system of government. The history of the individual reveals larger historical forces that are not apprehensible to other modes of investigation and that are certainly beyond the ken of conventional history (as Godwin understood it). In the paralysis of the individual – the live burial, to use an appropriate Gothic trope, of internalised 'ideals' – we encounter Godwin's, and the Gothic's, equivalent to genealogy, to a form of narrative that seeks to expose the hidden prehistory of violence, including violence against oneself. A friable, fragmented subject is not the sturdy material on which one can build a grand narrative or posit evolutionary progress. Instead of Scott's upward gyres, one encounters neurosis and repetition. But here we get ahead of ourselves. In articulating what it is that the Gothic tells us about modernity and the histories it might support, we reach, automatically, for theory. I have already used 'introjection', from psychoanalysis, a notion emerging from Freud's work on mourning and melancholia. One could thus as usefully employ the word 'melancholia' as 'trauma', where both terms are underpinned by Freud's theory of the unconscious. Alternatively one might think of it as an aporia, the site of irresolvable contradiction, in the manner of Derrida.

The history of the Gothic and the history of theory are so intertwined that it is unwise, if not impossible, to consider either in isolation. Still, my purpose here is to keep the two as distinct as one can. For that reason, my preferred term for the kind of radical, subjective, historically inflected paralysis narrated by the Gothic is 'tranced grief'. The phrase comes from Herman Melville's most Gothic tale, *Pierre; or, the Ambiguities* (1851). The narrator comments on Pierre's efforts to move on with life after the double trauma of breaking with his fiancé, Lucy, while losing his mother:

> At last he dismissed his mother's memory into that same profound vault where hitherto had reposed the swooned form of his Lucy. But, as sometimes men are coffined in a trance, being thereby mistaken for dead; so it is possible to bury a tranced grief in the soul, erroneously supposing that it hath no more vitality of suffering. Now, immortal things only can beget immortality. (Melville 2017: 285)

Melville uses this sequence as a means of articulating one of the deepest mysteries of culture: intergenerational haunting and cycles of violence. How is dysfunction handed down from one generation to another, a dead hand on posterity? Melville's phrase, one may say, is a psychological 'riff' on live burial (see Hoeveler 2010). It is also, in advance of Freud, a theory of the unconscious. Melville's self-conscious formulation is enabled by previous generations of Gothic writers; but in particular it emerges from a line of influence that stretches from Godwin, to Charles Brockden Brown, to Godwin again, and thence to Melville. The remainder of this essay will aim to tease out these connections.

From Godwin, then, we move to the American Gothicist Charles Brockden Brown, Godwin's canniest reader. Brown's most influential novel, *Wieland; or, the Transformation* (1798), is both the first American Gothic novel and a reading of Godwin's *Caleb Williams*. Brown turned to Godwin, in part, because only Godwin and the Gothic afforded him a narrative language for writing a form of history adequate to his present task, that of making sense of the pregnant moment in which history had placed him: living through the revolutionary aftermath of the establishment of the world's first modern democracy, when the outcome of this world historical event was not yet clear. Would the experiment succeed, setting a precedent for all mankind, or would it fizzle out, starved by a lack of revolutionary, and republican, virtue? Such was the burning question of Brown's time and place.

Brown based *Wieland* on a true story. An upstate New York farmer, John Yates, suffering from religious mania, in 1781 murdered his wife and four children. Brown sets his tale some time after the French and Indian War, but it is clear that Brown is drawing an analogy between that moment of post-war peace and his post-Revolutionary present. In imagining the circumstances of Yates's unimaginable act, Brown turns his story into a Godwinian historical romance, which is to say, into a genealogy of his present. As with Godwin's tale, Brown's also ends in fracture and paralysis. Like *Caleb Williams*, *Wieland* is told in the first person, by Wieland's sister, Clara, who writes, retrospectively, in a state of tranced grief: as she asks, rhetorically, in an aside to her unspecified reader, 'What but ambiguities, abruptnesses, and dark transitions, can be expected from the historian who is, at the same time, the sufferer of these disasters?' (Brown 1994: 135). Accordingly, as one reads, one constantly has to remind oneself that the narrator is unreliable, that she suffers from, as we would now say, post-traumatic stress disorder.

This point is important as it relates directly to the historical question addressed by Brown. Brown's America was in transition from a predominantly oral to a print culture. Revolutionary consciousness had been mediated through a hyperbolic version of the eighteenth-century Enlightenment republic of letters. Town hall meetings, corresponding societies and committees constituted a 'platform' with both outreach and rapid feedback (Warner 2013: 234). In the post-Revolutionary period, print and print media began its historic rise, to a point of saturation and dominance. The town-hall style still retained the virtues typical of oral cultures, above all else sincerity and authenticity, and the importance of being a known quantity. The favoured rhetorical style of the Revolutionary period was plain speaking, the authentic voice of a sincere actor. One's word was one's bond, but also one's brand: in an oral culture, one's reputation for probity was everything. The recent coming to dominance of 'print culture', on the other hand, was equivalent to the transition from 'analogue' to 'digital': in the latter, all traces of the original speaker are lost, as words circulate independent of their originating sources. To be sure, as the republic developed, complex institutions and norms evolved in order to regulate, and govern, the flows of information, thereby ensuring that the new republic's public sphere functioned reasonably. But in Brown's immediate, post-Revolutionary aftermath, these cultural institutions and norms were still in the making.

This was Brown's question: in this moment of historical uncertainty, where should we place our trust? In Burke or Thomas Paine? Alexander Hamilton or Thomas Jefferson? The Federalists or Jeffersonian Democrats? Congregationalists or free-thinking materialists (see Wood 1982; Stewart 2014)? The conservative answer was that without the customary support of tradition, age-old manners, indeed the whole array of inherited beliefs and practices, including religion, the individual was bound to fall, fail or even float away altogether, born off by windy rhetoric and impossible ideals (Clemit 1993: 128). The progressive response was that liberty would set man free; that self-determination was man's entitled destiny; that once freed from the 'Gothic and unintelligible burden of past institutions' (Godwin 1793: I, 33), with their regressive and imprisoning superstitions, man would ascend the steps of an ever-improving society, one founded on universal, abstract rights.

Brown answers his question by putting it to the test in the manner of a Godwinian historical romance, where history is written at the level of character. As Emory Elliott notes, in beginning his tale with the back story of the Wielands, Brown efficiently sets the scene through an allegory of America's origins (Brown 1994: xvi–xviii). The elder Wieland's story begins where most Gothic stories begin, with a star-crossed love affair between ranks, which results in the elder, aristocratic Wieland's expulsion from the embrace of European feudal culture owing to his desire for a merchant's daughter. Without the customary supports of his class and culture, Wieland comes to create his own version of a do-it-yourself Puritan religion, like an autodidact or bricoleur – or a Horace Walpole assembling the first 'Gothic Story' – putting together a kind of faith *and* a critique of dominant faiths from the odds and sods of his own distracted reading. The American references include the 'errand in the wilderness': understanding himself to be a 'distinguished favourite of the Deity' (see Hume 1754), the elder Wieland believes himself divinely enjoined to bring the light of personal revelation to the natives of the New World. When this hope fails, he establishes his household back near Philadelphia, where he erects a home-made shrine to his personal Protestant deity. By this point his incessant struggles with Calvinist anxiety have left him a burnt-out case, his brain 'scorched to cinders' (Brown 1994: 13), and, apparently, he spontaneously combusts.

The story proper begins with the second generation who emblematically represent, not Brown's America, but representative ideas of what it should be. The second generation are the Wielands and Pleyels: Arthur Wieland and his sister, Clara, the tale's narrator; and Pleyel and his sister, Catherine, who marries the younger Wieland. Clara claims to love Pleyel, but that romance founders along with the rest of the family's fortune after the entrance of the mysterious stranger, Carwin. Like his father, Arthur Wieland is a staunch Calvinist, but unlike his father, he is an educated one. Pleyel is a standard Enlightenment intellectual, a materialist and free-thinker. Together the young people compose the American public sphere in miniature; alternatively, they are the realisation of the Jeffersonian dream of a democratic society, pastoral and patriarchal, built around the family and the land, and devoted to the higher ideals of a democratic society. Into this Eden comes a snake, Carwin, who has a special skill: 'biloquism', the art of throwing, not just his voice, but uncanny imitations of other people's. While enjoying one of their al fresco salons, discussing (as they apparently do) the merits of Roman orators such as Cicero and other matters of public moment, Wieland heads up the hill to the paternal shrine to fetch something for his wife. The skulking Carwin, fearing discovery, throws his voice, imitating Wieland's wife's, calling her husband back down the hill. From that moment on, Wieland begins to hear voices, which he takes to be divine injunctions of ever increasing severity, until they include the sacrifice of his entire family, which he ultimately performs.

As many of Brown's critics have pointed out, the allegory here also represents the perilous moment in America's evolving public sphere, as it transitions from an oral to a print culture, from speech to writing. Carwin is a perilous presence, precisely because his voice is the embodiment of 'analogue' ideals:

> The voice was not only mellifluent and clear, but the emphasis was so just, and the modulation so impassioned, that it seemed as if an heart of stone could not fail of being moved by it. It imparted to me an emotion altogether involuntary and incontroulable. When he uttered the words 'for charity's sweet sake,' I dropped the cloth that I held in my hand, my heart overflowed with sympathy, and my eyes with unbidden tears. (Brown 1994: 48)

If ever there was a voice that embodied the benevolent ideals of sensibility, of honest and sincere plain speaking with its democratic promise, it would be Carwin's. On the other hand, he is an unknown entity: no one really knows who is, where he is from, and whether he is to be trusted. More to the point, his biloquism figures writing, being a pitch-perfect voice without a clear origin, being 'read' when he is not present (Gilmore 1987: 38). At the very least, Brown is suggesting that Jeffersonian ideas of America as an ideal pastoral community are hopelessly idealistic, given the new reality of print and the unregulated circulation of voices without a provenance, without an origin vouchsafing their authenticity. However, Brown's allegory cuts both ways. If Wieland's introspective Calvinism ends in personal delusion and tragedy, Pleyel's Enlightenment beliefs do not fare much better. Convinced that hearing is believing, Pleyel puts his faith in his senses and falsely believes that Clara has been unfaithful with the uncouth Carwin, having overheard Carwin's incriminating performance of an indelicate Clara, which blasts the happiness of them both. America's nascent public sphere – the guarantor of the sovereign public will, the ultimate source of the republic's political legitimacy – is caught in a cleft stick: it requires print – writing – to form the public sphere that underwrites the public will, but without institutions to regulate it, it becomes a chaotic, destructive force.

The narrative is told by Clara Wieland, and like Caleb Williams, she is an unreliable witness. Her stilted language is a language frozen by grief, in which words and subjective referent are forever sundered by unprocessed pain. In such stilted language the process of self-knowledge and republican virtue, without which the republic cannot survive, is not possible. The alternative, a Burkean reliance on custom and tradition, is antithetical to the American project. In the manner of Gothic and genealogy, two epistemic structures collide – not unlike Scott's and Godwin's – without any higher synthesis or resolution.

Wieland, then, is a deep history, in the manner of Godwin's historical (which is to say, Gothic) romance. It internalises two key features of Gothic genealogy: it references a received historical narrative (the allegory of republican becoming that starts the novel) and opposes it with 'trauma', with the repercussions of unresolved violence, 'griefs' that have become 'tranced'. We gain the measure of Brown's ambition from *Wieland*'s sequel, the *Memoirs of Carwin the Biloquist* (1803–5). In providing his back story, Carwin aims to absolve himself. His story is a strange one and is also lifted directly from Godwin. Born in Pennsylvania, the son of a poor farmer like Caleb Williams, Carwin is liberated from a life of drudgery, first by his aunt in Philadelphia, but ultimately by Ludloe, a visiting Irishman of independent means and a strong, philosophic outlook, one strongly reminiscent of Godwin's. His quirky views on marriage, cohabitation, promising and sincerity (Brown 1994: 268, 249, 247, 253), for instance, directly echo Godwin's *An Enquiry Concerning Political Justice* (1793). Ludloe appears to belong to a secret society devoted to the betterment of the world (1994: 258). Its ideals are utopian, guided by 'beneficence and wisdom' (1994: 262). There is only one catch: the secret society requires total transparency on the part of its adherents and complete subordination to its hierarchy. Adepts must confess all and withhold nothing, with breaches being punishable by death. Carwin, already on thin ice with Ludloe owing to his reticence in confessing his voice-throwing gifts, fears he has fallen through altogether when he surmises that Ludloe has been secretly monitoring him, even as Carwin ransacks Ludloe's private library for clues to his benefactor's secret character. It is at this point that the *Carwin* fragment ends.

Carwin's story strongly echoes the relationship between Caleb Williams and Falkland. It is also a reprise of the essential details of the Bavarian Illuminati controversy (Wood 1982: 433), which, at the time of Brown's writing, was convulsing the public sphere of the new republic (Bradshaw 2003: 358–61). According to its leading publicists, John Robison and the Abbé Barruel (aided and abetted by Burke), an international conspiracy by members of the radical Enlightenment, self-styled the Illuminati, was bent on world revolution, the end of religion as we know it, along with the patriarchal family structure: instead, there were to be Masonic lodges, and most disturbing of all, free love. Are 'our daughters' to be made 'concubines of the Illuminati?', asked Timothy Dwight, the president of Yale

(Hofstader 1996: 13). This was an especially forthright rhetorical question hurled about in the press. Carwin's trafficking in the dominant conspiracy theory of the age was not extrinsic to *Wieland*: the elder Wieland's uncle seems to believe that his brother was possibly murdered by the Illuminati and that spontaneous combustion is a red herring (Brown 1994: 17–18). Carwin's memoir provides an important frame for *Wieland*, for it raises this question: in a world mediated by print, and without traditional structures of deference, hierarchy and censorship, how is information to be governed? And how is knowledge possible where there is a media free-for-all of opinion, belief and, indeed, paranoia? Worse, what if reason is not a reliable guide? What if rationality is itself a false god? Here is where Brown's sly intertextual engagement with Godwin enters the picture. Apart from being a member of the Illuminati, Ludloe is an arch rationalist, which is to say, a Godwinian. As many conservative commentators noted, the Enlightenment project exchanged one authority, Church and State in the body of the monarch, for another, reason; hence the glaring contradiction of the Illuminati's founder, Adam Weishaupt, who both proselytised the virtues of reason and demanded blind obedience (as Ludloe does).

It is in this way that Brown's temporal setting, the immediate aftermath of the French and Indian War when the fate of a continent was decided, is a scarcely concealed allegory for his post-Revolutionary moment. By tweaking Godwin, by bringing Godwin into the paradoxes of modern authority (where the will of the people is sovereign, and where that will is often wilful), Brown seems to have been paying Godwin a compliment. Brown counters the customary stories then being told of how the republic would unfold (whether through a modern Hamiltonian state, pastoral Jeffersonianism, or a recourse to the Congregationalists and customary religious authority) with rupture, paralysis and trauma, where irresolution between conflicting beliefs is placed in historical context through an analysis of the contemporary public sphere.

Godwin appears to have taken Brown's Godwinian ironies positively, as we can see from his 1817 novel, *Mandeville*, which returns the favour. Informed by Brown, Godwin now brings trauma front and centre within the historical romance and thereby launches into a far more ambitious genealogy of his present than he had previously essayed. The following Brownian devices reappear in *Mandeville*: traumatic national history told through the fate of a single individual with a proliferation of complicating detail; related to this, intergenerational haunting and violence; a temporal setting where an earlier revolutionary moment mirrors the present (in *Mandeville*'s case, the aftermath of the English Civil War is a mirror for post-Napoleonic Britain); national history told through the dysfunctions of family history; an unreliable narrator, one permanently stunted by his tranced griefs; and a dialogical method that maps, not the linguistic particularities of class and social difference, but differences in ideological outlooks (in *Mandeville*, Cavaliers, radical Puritans, Presbyterians, the merchant class). But the device that he draws upon the most, and most profoundly, is the one the New Historicists were to adapt especially from Jacques Derrida: 'intertextuality'.

Mandeville's allegorical back story begins with Cromwell's invasion of Ireland (the first in a concatenating series of violent acts). Mandeville's aristocratic, Protestant father was the head of an English garrison in Ireland when it was overrun by the local Irish in imagery strongly recalling the Wexford Rebellion of 1798. There members of the loyalist garrison, men, women and children, were reportedly piked and thrown off bridges to drown in the river, or burned alive (Godwin's point being, where there is trauma, there is repetition). While the rest of his family was massacred, Mandeville escaped, protected by his Irish nurse, Judith, with whom he had developed a deep bond. Once the English regain control, Mandeville is wrenched away from his nurse by Hilkiah Bradford, a Presbyterian fanatic sent by Mandeville's uncle Audley to retrieve him. Audley's story is itself a miniature Gothic vignette. Having been stymied in love by his tyrannical father – who boasts of his 'absolute and uncontrollable power' – Audley turns into a melancholic recluse and dreamer, transforming his isolated country estate into a place of mourning and death. Mandeville's education is left to the fanatical Bradford. Foxe's *Acts and Monuments* is a particular favourite of this tutor's, the reading of which

> occasions that sort of tingling and horror, that is particularly inviting to young persons of a serious disposition . . . The representation of all imaginable cruelties, racks, pincers and red-hot irons, cruel mockings and scourgings, flaying alive . . . produced a strange confusion and horror in my modes of thinking, that kept me awake whole nights, that drove the colour from my cheeks, and made me wander like a meager, unlaid ghost, to the wonder and alarm of the peaceable and well-disposed inhabitants of my uncle's house. (Godwin 1817: I, 136)

In Mandeville's mind, memory, false memories and history all coalesce into a fabric that is constitutive of both his conscious, and unconscious, mind. These jumbled, spectral visitations of written history, memory and fantasy repeatedly come upon Mandeville, who is represented as in a deep state of division, hatred and paralysis. Godwin's fictitious biography – ambitious, detailed, proliferating in the angles it takes and the lines of enquiry it pursues – is also an analytic form of national history; in short, a genealogy. It does not rest with the usual form of national history, but seeks to find a narrative language for the hidden preconditions of the present that only a third-order explanation can provide.

References

Alison, Archibald (1845), 'The Historical Romance', *Blackwoods Magazine*, 58: 341–56.
Barruel, Augustin (1798), *Memoirs, Illustrating the History of Jacobinism*, trans. Robert Clifford, London: Clifford.
Bradshaw, Charles C. (2003), 'The New England Illuminati: Conspiracy and Causality in Charles Brockden Brown's "Wieland"', *The New England Quarterly*, 76.3: 356–77.
Brown, Charles Brockden (1994) [1798, 1803–05], *Wieland and Memoirs of Carwin the Biloquist*, ed. Emory Elliott, Oxford: Oxford University Press.
Burke, Edmund (1791), *Reflections on the Revolution in France*, 2nd edn, London: J. Dodsley.
Christensen, Jerome (1994), 'The Romantic Movement at the End of History', *Critical Inquiry*, 20.3: 452–76.
Clemit, Pamela (1993), *The Godwinian Novel: The Rational Fictions of Godwin, Brockden Brown, Mary Shelley*, Oxford: Clarendon Press.
Foucault, Michel (1984), 'Nietzsche, Genealogy, History', in *The Foucault Reader*, ed. Paul Rabinow, New York: Pantheon, pp. 76–100.
Freud, Sigmund (1958) [1917], 'Mourning and Melancholia', in *The Standard Edition of the Complete Psychological Works: Volume XIV (1914–1916)*, trans. and ed. James Strachey, London: Hogarth Press, pp. 237–58
Gellner, Ernest (1983), *Nations and Nationalism*, Oxford: Blackwell.
Gilmore, Michael T. (1987), 'Constitution and the Canon', *The William and Mary Law Review*, 29: 35–40.
Godwin, William (1793), *An Inquiry Concerning Political Justice, and its Influence on General Virtue and Happiness*, 2 vols, Dublin: Luke White.
Godwin, William (1797), *Of History and Romance*, http://www.english.upenn.edu/~mgamer/Etexts/godwin.history.html (accessed 3 October 2018).
Godwin, William (1817), *Mandeville: a tale of the seventeenth century*, 3 vols, Edinburgh: Archibald Constable.
Godwin, William (2016), *The Plays of William Godwin*, ed. David O'Shaughnessy, New York: Routledge.
Hobsbawm, E. J. (1990), *Nations and Nationalism since 1780: Programme, Myth, Reality*, Cambridge: Cambridge University Press.

Hoeveler, Diane (2010), *Gothic Riffs: Secularizing the Uncanny in the European Imaginary, 1780–1820*, Columbus: Ohio State University Press.

Hofstadter, Richard (1996) [1952], *The Paranoid Style in American Politics*, Cambridge, MA: Harvard University Press.

Hume, David (1754), 'Of Superstition and Enthusiasm', in *Essays Moral, Political, and Literary*, http://www.english.upenn.edu/~mgamer/Etexts/hume.superstition.html (accessed 3 October 2018).

Leitch, Vincent B., et al. (eds) (2010), *The Norton Anthology of Theory & Criticism*, 2nd edn, New York: Norton.

Melville, Herman (2017) [1851], *Pierre; or, the Ambiguities*, ed. R. S. Levine and C. Weinstein, New York: Norton.

Murray, Hugh (1805), *Morality of Fiction*, Edinburgh: Mundell & Son.

Southam, Brian (ed.) (1968), *Jane Austen: The Critical Heritage*, vol. I, London: Routledge.

Stewart, Matthew (2014), *Nature's God: The Heretical Origins of the American Republic*, New York: Norton.

Warner, William B. (2013), *Protocols of Liberty: Communication Innovation and the American Revolution*, Chicago: University of Chicago Press.

Whateley, Richard (1968) [1821], unsigned review of *Northanger Abbey* and *Persuasion*, *Quarterly Review*, 24; repr. in Southam 1968: 85–7.

Wood, Gordon S. (1982), 'Conspiracy and the Paranoid Style: Causality and Deceit in the Eighteenth Century', *The William and Mary Quarterly: A Magazine of Early American History and Culture*, 3: 402–41.

Žižek, Slavoj (1999), 'Attempts to Escape the Logic of Capitalism', *London Review of Books*, 28 October, 3–6.

Zuern, John David (ed.) (1998), *Aristotle: Poetics*, CriticaLink edition, http://www.english.hawaii.edu/criticalink/aristotle/gloss/gloss9.html (accessed 3 October 2018).

Chapter 3

The Gothic in and as Race Theory
Maisha Wester

> I am a marked woman, but not everybody knows my name. 'Peaches' and 'Brown Sugar,' 'Sapphire' and 'Earth Mother,' 'Aunty,' 'Granny.' God's 'Holy Fool,' a 'Miss Ebony First,' or 'Black Woman at the Podium': I describe a locus of confounded identities, a meeting ground of investments and privations in the national treasury of rhetorical wealth. My country needs me, and if I were not here, I would have to be invented. (Spillers 1987: 65)

Race has long been a haunting discourse in Gothic literature. Often masked by a monstrous visage, racial minorities appear throughout traditional Gothic texts as figures around which authors spin debates about civilisation, enlightenment, freedom and human nature.

Minority bodies in such texts act as objects of discourse, rather than as social agents, allowing white subjects to meditate upon complex realities and behaviours without having to claim them. Hence, while Hortense Spillers's observation addresses the construction of black women in American society, my epigraph also defines the position of the racial other in traditional Gothic literature. Such constructions present a complex problem for minority authors who use the Gothic as a vehicle for enunciating the real terrors of racialised existence. Consequently, in navigating the Gothic's racial minefields, minority authors often reflect back upon how race has functioned in the Gothic generally and how this function contributes to wider discourses of oppression.

Black authors throughout the African Diaspora have particularly critiqued the reduction of blackness to monstrosity in the Gothic. Authors such as Edgar Mittelholzer, Helen Oyeyemi and Phyllis Alesia Perry have presented counter-narratives to the racial dynamics in traditional Gothic texts, explicitly critiquing the reciprocal dynamic between early Gothic texts and the institution of slavery, immigration reforms and the injustice of Jim Crow. From their perspectives, black theorists and realist writers such as W. E. B. Du Bois, Ralph Ellison and Ann Petry have turned to the Gothic to depict how the dynamics and ideologies of race produce horrific realities for black subjects. The Gothic and theory have thus come to be in a continual back-and-forth dialogue, exchanging articulations and critiques of race-based otherness in a conversation that ultimately challenges and destabilises constructions of whiteness – and of race in general.

The Gothic has proven profoundly useful to black theorists seeking to articulate the complex construction and use of blackness in white-dominated societies. For instance, Toni Morrison's *Playing in the Dark* (1992) discusses Gothic literary texts as contributors to the actual construction, function and location of racial difference within American democracy. She notes that the 'Not-Free, Not-Me' of the enslaved body has offered whiteness more than an abject body to make monstrous; it has helped to establish the parameters constituting proper citizenship. Her theoretical and literary forebear W. E. B. Du Bois also utilises Gothic tropes in elaborating his concept of 'double consciousness'. As James Smethurst explains, this idea originates in the Gothic and 'proposes a version of Spencer Brydon's split consciousness in Henry James's gothic influenced short story "The Jolly Corner" as a more or less permanent condition for African Americans' (Smethurst 2001: 30). Hence Du Bois's metaphor of the veil that hides the black subject from the white world and vice versa, obscuring the vision and perceptions of both, arises already redolent with Gothic suggestiveness. This metaphorical veil 'conceals the black subject as human, much like a concealed skeleton in a classic gothic novel' (Smethurst 2001: 30). The functions and impacts that Du Bois outlines for the veil in many ways, too, recall the reactions and behaviours witnessed in Nathaniel Hawthorne's story 'The Minister's Black Veil' (1832). In both cases, the veil is an indictment of the people who look upon the veiled figure – producing horror in the viewers that in truth stems from their own psyches and not the veiled body – even as the veiled figures themselves suffer beneath that cover, compelled to carry its burden to their deaths. Unsurprisingly, Ralph Ellison's *Invisible Man* (1952), which is a text that plays upon the Gothic in profound ways, frequently turns to the image of the veil in its depiction of chaotic racist society and the monstrous outbursts it can produce in the racial subject. Some of the novel's most grotesque and oft-referenced scenes – such as the blindfolding of the black boys in the Battle Royal (Ellison 1995: 21–3) and the bird-soiled statue of the Founder looming over a kneeling slave (1995: 27) – interrogate racial veiling in a Gothic fashion.

Exploration of the impact of systemic white domination upon black psychology has indeed produced theoretical statements and fictions loaded with Gothic tropes, but these also provide useful terms for specifying the shifting figurations of racial difference in the Gothic itself. Frantz Fanon's theory of the phobogenic object provides an especially useful intervention into the Gothic's racial discourse, particularly when aligned with Julia Kristeva's notion of 'abjection'. In *Black Skin, White Masks* (1952), Fanon argues that the phobogenic object – the black figure constructed as an object of fear – illustrates elements of a typical phobia in which neurosis is gathered around it as a symbol that arouses fear and revulsion. The object is overdetermined and

> does not come at random out of the world of nothingness; in some situations it has previously provoked an affect in the patient. His phobia is the latent presence of this affect at the root of his world; there is an organization that has been given a form. For the object, naturally, need not be there, it is enough that somewhere it exists: It is a possibility. This object is endowed with evil intentions and with the attributes of a malefic power. (Fanon 1967: 155)

The similarities of this scheme to Julia Kristeva's theory of abjection in *Powers of Horror* (1980) are worth noting (see also Chapter 6 below), considering the process of exile and purification that Kristeva's subjects undergo as they expel abjected othernesses from themselves. Fanon's theory proves useful in considering those texts in which the black subject/monster is not utterly exiled or, more significantly, the texts in which the monster 'wins'. Such plots suggest that society does not always require simple purification through abjection; instead it requires a phobogenic object against which to (racially) define itself and shudder in horror. Such dialogues between theory and Gothic tropes manifest themselves persistently – if differently – in traditional Gothic texts and black fictional texts, especially as each kind of writing both confirms and interrogates theory.

Competing Theories of Racial Difference: Traditional Gothic and the Black Writer

As theorists from H. L. Malchow to Judith Halberstam and Teresa Goddu have shown, eighteenth- and nineteenth-century Gothic texts often contain social discourses on racial politics concealed beneath a veil of monstrosity. Halberstam emphasises how particular kinds of bodies have been especially prone to being made monstrous because of European anti-Semitism and American racism. She notes *Dracula* (1897) and *Dr Jekyll and Mr Hyde* (1886) as examples of how the Gothic proves pleasurable mainly by 'fixing horror elsewhere, in an obviously and literally foreign body, and by then articulating the need to expel the foreign body. Both Dracula and Hyde are characters with markedly foreign physiognomies; they are dark and venal, foreign in both aspect and behavior' (Halberstam 1995: 13). Halberstam likewise reads Frankenstein's monster and his sexuality as a signifier of foreignness which threatens miscegenation; perhaps more usefully, she explains how the foreign and the sexual collide in the nineteenth-century Gothic in a composite production of otherness: 'where the foreign and the sexual merge within monstrosity in Gothic, a particular history of sexuality unfolds', given that sexuality 'is itself a beast created in nineteenth-century literature' (1995: 6–7). Moreover, while in the nineteenth-century Gothic, race 'was one of many clashing surfaces of monstrosity, in the context of twentieth-century Gothic, race becomes a master signifier of monstrosity and when invoked, it blocks out all other possibilities of monstrous identity' (Halberstam 1995: 5).

Malchow similarly interprets *Frankenstein* as the outgrowth of discourses stemming from the slave revolution in Haiti and the abolitionist struggle to end the slave trade in Britain (Malchow 1996: 11). Malchow's admission that Mary Shelley did not explicitly set out to construct a Negro monster in her novel helps us understand how the appearance and function of racial otherness in the traditional Gothic constitutes a kind of abjection. Malchow explains that Shelley 'dredged up a bogeyman that had been prepared by a cultural tradition of the threatening Other – whether troll or giant, gypsy or Negro – from the dark inner recesses of xenophobic fear and loathing' (1996: 18). Malchow's further analyses of works by other nineteenth-century writers such as Poe, Hawthorne and, later, Stoker illustrate that this xenophobia is often a reflection of anxiety about domestic white behaviour towards the racial other. The very notion of the Occidental tourist which often appears in critiques of *Dracula* acknowledges the abjection haunting such writers, as their texts repeatedly illustrate an anxiety about white behaviour towards racial others abroad returning home 'to roost'.

Morrison comments extensively on the appearance of racial abjection in Gothic literature in *Playing in the Dark*. She returns to the primal American scene of slavery as a source text, arguing that the slave master projected his own brutality on to the black slave body, where he could then whip it out of existence. Notably, she emphasises blackness as a metaphor in the white texts rooted in this cultural history; black bodies exist there only as trope and figuration, never as real and complex beings. Within figures in white (American) Gothic texts,

> the value of blackness resided in its metaphorical aptitude, whether literally understood as the fungibility of the commodity or understood as the imaginative surface upon which the master and the nation came to understand themselves [. . .] Blackness provided the occasion for self-reflection as well as exploration of terror, desire, fear, loathing, and longing. (Hartman 1997: 7)

Malchow similarly addresses the Gothic's abjection of racial others in his discussion of cannibalism in such texts, concluding that 'like assertions of racial inferiority, accusations of cannibalism establish the community of the virtuous by projecting onto others evils feared within' (Malchow 1996: 43). Thus, while texts (and society) shuddered for centuries in fear of brutal black rapists, the tales actually projected the institutionally sanctioned, violent consumption of black bodies – apparent in the regularised sexual assaults committed by white colonists and slave owners – on to the criminalised bodies of their victims.

By contrast, black writers throughout the Diaspora have been indicting such uses of black bodies in the service of whiteness since the nineteenth century. For instance, American ex-slave narrators heavily appropriated Gothic tropes to critique the sexualised abjection of blackness, locating in white men 'a patriarchal tyranny and a concomitant transgressive sexuality in which [. . .] female slaves [are forced] into unwanted sexual relations' (Smethurst 2001: 30). As I argue in *African American Gothic* (2012), ex-slave narrators used the Gothic to defy constructions of the slave as monstrous, emphasising the fictitious nature of such constructions while revealing the real, unimagined horrors of slavery and the actual monstrosity of slave owners. Ultimately, such narratives destabilise racial, geographical and intellectual boundaries through their Gothic appropriations. Building upon these early theorists, from Du Bois to Fanon and beyond, later generations of black Gothic writers explicitly critique the construction of whiteness and nation through and against black bodies. In *White is for Witching* (2009), Helen Oyeyemi explicitly illustrates the complex way in which Englishness, especially English womanhood, is constituted at the cost of black (women) migrants. Oyeyemi's text provides the racialised other with a face and a voice, a non-monstrous being, in order to reveal the very construct of Englishness as horrific and cannibalistic because it consumes and expels migrant bodies in its abject production of whiteness masked as 'Englishness'. Further, the notion of the nation as a domestic space, in which the performance and bodies of its women are essential to and constitutive of Englishness, is metaphorised by a sentient domestic space – the Dover House bed and breakfast – which exercises excessive control over the family's women in the pursuit of attaining and protecting racial and national purity.

When Miranda's mother Lilly goes to Haiti on an expedition in Oyeyemi's novel, the house wonders, 'Why do people go to these places, these places that are not for them? It must be that they believe in their night vision. They believe themselves able to draw images up out of the dark. But black wells only yield black water' (Oyeyemi 2009: 8). As much as the house disdains Lilly's expedition, her trip duplicates the connection between British colonial conquests and the making and maintenance of whiteness. Imperial and colonial conquest provided Britain with a sense of cultural and racial superiority, a way of defining Englishness on a global stage. As we have seen, the Haitian Revolution of the 1790s had ramifications for Gothic narratives because the location speaks to the end of Britain's colonial power and the intensified emphasis on Englishness as whiteness: 'the more potency they lost on the global stage after the eclipse of imperialism, the harder some Britons clung to the illusory status symbol that covered their bodies – their white skin – and the immutable cultural difference that it seemed to signify' (qtd in King 2013: 61). Consequently, Lilly's death in Haiti recalls the Revolution's threatened dissolution of whiteness and difference and the resulting Gothic nightmares it produced in colonial nations.

The Dover House's depiction of Haiti as one of the world's 'black wells' also concurs with white Western determinations to pathologise the country and 'the gross misperceptions people have held about Haiti throughout time. The house thus obsesses over blackness, for it deems itself and Britain not to be a "black well," and any contact it has with the Other becomes an instance of contamination' (King 2013: 62). While 'black wells' may be understood as a reference specific to the black Republic of Haiti, the house's disdain for 'these places' suggests that 'black wells' refers to an unknown quantity of locations; the whole of the remark importantly reasserts Paul Gilroy's contention that '"Race" is bounded on all sides by the sea. The effect of this ideological operation is visible in the way that the word "immigrant" became synonymous with the word "black" during the 1970s' (Gilroy 2002: 46). In Britain, skin colour is thus intimately conjoined with nation and citizenship, and people deemed 'white' in other locations are blackened in Britain because of their immigrant status. Importantly, Oyeyemi's novel speaks to and critiques this political reality and reveals the peculiar fiction behind designations such as black/white.

White is for Witching is, after all, set ironically in Dover, whose cliffs are famously chalk white. The setting emphasises the ways in which modern Englishness is overtly 'concerned with mechanisms of inclusion and exclusion' (Gilroy 2002: 45); the whiteness of the cliffs returns us to the conjoining of (imagined) racial difference, national legitimacy and citizenship. Dover's function as a gate through which immigrants are actually *denied* access to the nation is epitomised by the large immigrant detention centre – notably housed in a Gothic castle – on one of the cliffs's peaks. Significantly, the immigrant bodies suffer indefinite entrapment within the detention centre, thus making visible the irrational racialised nationalism that 'advances reasons for the segregation or banishment of those whose "origin, sentiment or citizenship" assigns them elsewhere' (Gilroy 2002: 45). Those immigrants who manage to make it out of the prison's walls find themselves employed as service support staff, and even then they are prey to numerous assaults. For instance, Sade – the maid to the Silver family – worries over the immigrants who go missing from the streets of Dover, even as she feels an unwelcoming evil in the house. Likewise, the house turns its animosity against black tourists who, by their very presence, sustain the home with their economic resources. Consequently, the detested minority body is marked as indispensable to the maintenance and support of the nation and its whiteness. And yet the house, in narrating its disdain for immigrants, repeats nineteenth-century 'imperialistic [and] colonial fantasies of other lands and peoples [. . .] concentrat[ing] its imaginative force upon the other peoples in "our" lands, the monster at home' (Halberstam 1995: 15). Oyeyemi's text suggests the nefarious ways in which this disdain continues into the twenty-first century, well beyond the rise of the European Union and the era of supposed globalisation. The house thus reveals the grotesque cannibalistic process of racial abjection, consuming – quite literally – the disdained racialised immigrant subject in order to sustain itself, 'metabolizing it, transforming it into shit, and eliminating it' (qtd in King 2013: 70).

Unsurprisingly, black theorists have long emphasised how such abjection is damning to black subjects. Fanon repeatedly articulates the horror of black existence throughout *Black Skin, White Masks*, acknowledging the ways in which Gothic tropes are deployed against black subjects in everyday exchanges. For instance, in recalling an encounter with a young white child and his mother, Fanon notes how black bodies are (irrationally) constructed as figures of terror:

> "Mama, see the Negro! I'm frightened" [. . .] My body was given back to me sprawled out, distorted, recolored, clad in mourning in that white winter day. The Negro is an animal. The Negro is bad, the Negro is mean, the Negro is ugly [. . .] the little boy is trembling because he is afraid of the nigger, the nigger is shivering with cold [. . .] the handsome little boy is trembling because he thinks the nigger is quivering with rage [. . .] Mama, the nigger's going to eat me up. (Fanon 1967: 112, 113–14)

Fanon's encounter illustrates the horrific 'experience of being taken over by a racial *imago* – of being intruded upon, displaced, and fixated by an imaginary double' (Marriott 1998: 418) manifestly informed by and constructed through the Gothic. The passage significantly juxtaposes the fantasised horror experienced by the white subject against that experienced by the black subject to reveal how entrapment within fictional Gothic narratives produces real horror for the person cast as monstrous. Notably, the sign of Fanon's suffering – he shivers with cold – is recast into a Gothic narrative that threatens his survival in its misreading of his body. Within such narratives, the 'Negro' can only be a mean, ugly animal, never a handsome, suffering human. Denied the prestige of his occupation or even ability to articulate his self, Fanon is ensnared within a prison of monstrosity: 'that child's words and look strip him of whatever imaginary coherence or identity he may have had, leaving him a crumpled, traumatized and amputated heap of fragmented parts [. . .] despite Fanon's (and others') high opinion of himself, he is reduced to the imago of a cannibal' (Marriott 1998: 420). Framed by the Gothic, which associates any and all black expression and movement with monstrosity, Fanon's shivering is denied the possibility of signifying anything other than violence.

Likewise, black novelists employing the Gothic suggest that horror stems from being condemned to spaces of aberration and monstrosity in racialised discourses. In *Native Son* (1940), Richard Wright deploys Gothic tropes – recreating the climactic scene of the *Frankenstein* film of 1931 with Bigger Thomas at its centre – in order to reveal how systemic racism and racist ideology produces black monstrosity. Evie Shockley observes a similar appearance of the Gothic in Ann Petry's

The Street (1946), which uses tropes of imprisonment, doubling and living burial in depicting 'Gothic Homelessness', a phrase she uses to describe the frightening uncertainty of the domestic boundaries that are supposed to safeguard those within its walls – or to evoke the horrifying exclusion (or potential for exclusion) from membership in one's would-be 'family' (Shockley 2006: 446). Through the trials and failures of its heroine, Lutie, Petry's novel exemplifies the ways in which Gothic Homelessness proves pervasive for black women, despite their subscription to the American Dream and thus the dominant social ideology. Lutie's race and gender imprison her within an externally defined identity explicitly at odds with the national ideal; she is consequently rendered prey to nightmarish violations.

Later generations of black writers continue this critique by depicting other ways in which minority bodies are exiled from the dominant national narrative, even as these very people subscribe to problematic white ideology. For instance, in *White is for Witching*, Ore – Miranda's British Nigerian girlfriend – attends Cambridge but acknowledges how the Gothic buildings and décor of the university mark her as a non-citizen. Upon arriving, she describes the college buildings as 'taut and strong as a flexed arm' (Oyeyemi 2009: 133); the image implies that the buildings offer assault to unwelcomed bodies and thus Ore thinks 'I can't live here' (2009: 133).

Likewise the dining hall is ornamented with pictures of former masters of the college, all of whom are white men; examining the portraits, in a scene which recalls the Gothic use of pictures as early as Walpole's *Castle of Otranto* (1764), Ore feels as if they are 'the same man, over and over again [. . .] readying himself to spit on [her] plate' (Oyeyemi 2009: 135). Ore's observations invariably correlate to her blackness, as these observations are woven into discussion of her racial heritage and status as a legal British citizen. That these observations circulate around Cambridge suggests that the novel is speaking more broadly about the place of racial minorities in the nation and its ideologies, given Cambridge's notoriety as an elite British university where heads of state send their children to be educated. Ore's encounter reveals the peculiar politics of 'the English/British case' where

> 'race' [. . .] is fired by conceptions of national belonging and homogeneity which not only blur the distinction between 'race' and nation, but rely on that very ambiguity for their effect. Phrases like 'the Island Race' and 'the Bulldog Breed' vividly convey the manner in which this nation is represented in terms which are simultaneously biological and cultural. (Gilroy 2002: 44)

Notably, Ore was adopted as an infant by white Britons; however, despite her birth in a Commonwealth nation and adoption into a British family, Ore is doomed to exile as a different 'breed' because of her race and immigrant origins.

As much as Ore understands herself as an outcast in this system, Oyeyemi's novel also depicts her as Gothically captured within it. Observing her dorm from the exterior, Ore concludes 'I could see we had made our beds in a tomb' (Oyeyemi 2009: 135). Later, visiting the Dover house, Ore suffers a frightening experience as she dries herself with a white towel:

> Where it had touched me it was stripped with Black liquid, as dense as paint
> [. . .]
> There were shreds of hard skin in it. [. . .]
> "The black's coming off," someone outside the bathroom door commented. Then They whistled "Rule Britannia!" and laughed.
> "*Bri-tons never-never-never, shall be slaves*" (2009: 198)

Importantly, as much as Ore reacts in horror to the stripping away of her skin colour, she expresses a desire to achieve a similar effect earlier on, explaining that she wished her adopted parents had indeed given her a more 'British' name such as 'Rose', thus illustrating her desire to linguistically erase her racial difference by wrapping herself in one of the nation's dominant images. Connected to Ore's wish for another name, the moment reveals the psychological stakes for the racial other and recalls the terrible ways in which black subjects are driven to neurotic states. Indeed, Oyeyemi recreates a troubling scene from Erik Erikson's psychological study 'A Memorandum on Identity and Negro Youth' (1950), in which a four-year-old girl compulsively tried to rid herself of her race, standing before a mirror each day attempting to scrub the 'stain' from her skin. While the little girl's behaviour reveals 'her obvious physical alienation before the mirror' (Marriott 1998: 421), Oyeyemi resists such complete alienation, which David Marriott reads as a sign of 'an unconscious that seems to be "white" [that] has displaced a conscious black identity' (Marriott 1998: 418). Ore, over-articulated before she can ever achieve any consciousness, is never allowed access to a consciousness besides otherness, as illustrated by her distress over her name. The scene rather reveals the extreme psychological violence inherent in the wish to become Rose instead of Ore, and defines this wish as externally imposed by a violating nation.

Equally important, the concluding line of the above passage marks Ore's exile from the dominant nation even as it marks her race as a point of abject identification. As a black body, Ore will 'never-never-never' be accepted as a 'Briton'. Yet the line also defines the idea of 'British' in terms of the exclusion of minority bodies in its invocation of slavery. To fit within the domestic, Ore has to somehow lose her blackness, which the text notably presents as a point of horror. Yet to be black in Britain is to be not-British but a 'slave'. Though 'slave' may be understood as historically specific in its reference, the text also implies that 'slave' has a meaning and ideological function in contemporary British society which is not all that different from the pre-Abolition experience. In both cases, the black subject is 'captured' and '(ab)used' by white British power.

Black Gothic's Redefinition of Race

In redressing ideologies of race through the Gothic, however, even as they acknowledge the ways in which racial production is a Gothic project and highlight the genre's contributions to the ways in which racial otherness has been imagined, black writers also access the destabilising power of the genre, a practice often visible in (but not exclusive to) postcolonial Gothic (see Chapter 4 below). Gina Wisker, after all, argues that the postcolonial Gothic denies the satisfactory conclusions pervasive in the traditional Gothic:

> Unlike conventional Gothic, which disturbs but frequently restores order, the postcolonial Gothic shifts what could be seen as order. So, at the end of the text, the reader cannot remain with a worldview free from the haunting of a newly exposed silence and hidden past, free from the hauntings of ghosted voices replacing hidden histories and versions and of a sense of living in a parallel universe where other people from other cultures perceive, interpret, value, and express quite differently from the orthodoxies influencing a reader unaware of postcolonial context. (Wisker 2007: 411)

Even as Wisker points to unknown histories that are expressively foreign to a (white) postcolonial readership, Black Diasporic Gothic outside of postcolonial nations and cultures also engages in this very practice. Indeed, black American and British authors similarly articulate unknown histories; the fact that these histories occur within the colonising and imperialist nations reveals that their absence is a consequence of being unacknowledged and, in some cases, actively disavowed. Consequently, while black American and British authors do concern themselves with the specific political concerns of their nations, they also acknowledge the ways in which these seeming differences inhabit the same discourses. Perhaps more importantly, modern black authors offer alternative constructions of racial difference, subjectivity and authority. Phyllis Perry's *Stigmata* (1998), for example, produces an alternative vision of history and of the black subject's relation to history, which allows for alternative understandings of the construction of whiteness. In the novel, whiteness is a haunting spectre positioned in stark contrast to the tangible black ancestral presence which accompanies the protagonist, Lizzie.

White figures appear only in the ancestors' memories of their actual experience, though these are narrated as if occurring in the present. Yet in the would-be present, whites are still defined as 'ghosts' leading their slaves into a 'land of walking ghosts' (Perry 1998: 97). The novel consequently suggests that whiteness, as a racial and cultural signifier, is an absence – like a ghost, a psychological manifestation lacking tangibility – which nonetheless troubles and impacts the black body. At another point, Ayo recalls a cannibalistic experience on the slave ship when, bleeding from wounds, she 'watched the blood run down onto the wood planks that soaked it up like the ship was thirsty. Drank it up. Drank it right up. A white man came [. . .] And he stepped in the blood. When he walked away he made a bloody footprint' (Perry 1998: 98). The broken bodies of the slaves provide sustenance for the slave ship, the primary method of material transport among the economies of several white nations during the eighteenth century. Together these scenes effectively define whiteness as Gothic exaggeration and excess: whiteness here exaggerates racial difference in order to conjure white authority out of nothing and thereby constructs itself, not through inherent self-definition, but through the excessive exercise of violence against non-whites. Such Gothic racial encounters in *Stigmata* consequently posit 'white' as non-material and, recalling Malchow's points, cannibalising.

White is for Witching also exemplifies the absence haunting the construction of whiteness and its consequent dependence on racial others. While the novel traces the haunting spectres of colonialism in contemporary society, it also illustrates how the threat of otherness is integral to stabilising the idea of Englishness as whiteness. Indeed, the novel is a response to and critique of the Conservative MP Enoch Powell's peculiar question and answer:

'what kind of people are we?' [. . .] 'We' were not muggers, 'we' were not illegal immigrants, 'we' were not criminals, Rastafarians, aliens or purveyors of arranged marriages. 'We' were the lonely old lady taunted by 'wide-grinning piccaninnies'. 'We' were the only white child in a class full of blacks. 'We' were the white man, frightened that in fifteen to twenty years, 'the black man would have the whip hand over us'. (Gilroy 2002: 48–9)

Although Gilroy concludes that Powell's comments construct black presence 'as a problem or threat against which a homogeneous, white, national "we" could be unified' (Gilroy 2002: 49), Oyeyemi's text reveals that the issue is more fundamental. There will always be a threat – there will always be an Ore/Sade/Tijana – because '[their] country needs [them], and if [they] were not here, [they] would have to be invented' (Spillers 1987: 67). Whiteness, as dominantly constructed, is ultimately a fiction that depends upon racial difference as a constructing referent, as Powell's list of what 'we are not' illustrates.

Whiteness as embodied and apparent in systemic structures therefore becomes a recurrent point of meditation, as modern black writers repeatedly critique the 'normativity' that whiteness claims. Further, they reveal the abjection inherent in whiteness and the horror of achieving such racist visions as a Union Jack absented of black(ness). Morrison, in one instance, discusses the myriad ways in which white American texts reduce themselves to a point of absolute whiteness, having rid themselves of all black characters. Richard Dyer's chapter 'White' in his collection *A Matter of Images* (1993) similarly acknowledges how, even in film, whiteness is beyond conceptualisation in isolation because 'when whiteness *qua* whiteness does come into focus, it is often revealed as emptiness, absence, denial or even a kind of death' (Dyer 1993: 126). Black fiction writers such as Richard Wright, Ann Petry and Ralph Ellison similarly reveal the triumph of whiteness as a point of horror, deploying the image of blizzards to allude to the freezing destructive force of whiteness and the massive system it spreads across the cultural landscape; each thus recalls Fanon's horrific moment of confrontation with the terrified child on a 'white winter day' (Fanon 1967: 113). Thus, for example, Bigger the black 'monster' runs through a hyper-white landscape on his way to the climax of Richard Wright's *Native Son*.

Petry's *The Street* even reveals the quiet death that occurs when whiteness dominates all arenas of social thought and life and exists as a form of undisputed power that seduces all and 'passes itself off as embodied in the normal' (Dyer 1993: 128). Throughout this novel, 'the invisibility of whiteness colonizes the definition of other norms' such as heterosexuality, gender, domesticity and even virtue (Dyer 1993: 128). The concluding scene problematises those associations, refusing their inherence within whiteness and revealing their dangerous snare:

> The snow fell softly on the street. It muffled sound. It sent people scurrying homeward, so that the street was soon deserted, empty, quiet. And it could have been any street in the city, for the snow laid a delicate film over the sidewalk, over the brick of the tired, old buildings; gently obscuring the grime and the garbage and the ugliness. (Petry 1998: 36)

While an initial reading may assume that this is a calming scene, the snow's covering of the street and its 'ugliness' alludes to the ways in which white ideals of normative gendered and familial life obscure the harsh economic and racial realities that force Lutie to kill a man and abandon her son. Consequently, the novel attacks the generally accepted associations of 'white with light and therefore safety, and black with dark and therefore danger' (Dyer 1993: 127). The hyperwhite world punctuating *The Street* is, in reality, one of cold silence, loss and looming destruction. This concluding scene links back to the novel's opening scene which, while not laden with snow, also alludes to the environmental forces that damn Lutie. Searching for an apartment, Lutie is accosted by a cold, violently assaulting wind, and the descriptions of the wind predict the racial and sexual assaults that Lutie will suffer throughout the novel. Thus the seeming calm of fallen snow is only a façade; its double is an explicitly assaulting environment. Together, the snow and wind allude Gothically to the eradicating and violent nature of whiteness understood as the established 'normative', which the novel highlights in depictions of all-white advertisements embodying the American Dream.

Ellison's *Invisible Man* similarly makes whiteness hyper-visible in its destructiveness; the novel even features a moment in which pervasive whiteness obliterates black peace. As the narrator enjoys a roasted yam on the snow-covered sidewalks of New York, he experiences a moment of revitalising cultural connection. Yet this reconnection is cut short once the narrator reaches the end of his delicious yam: 'the freedom to eat yams on the street was far less than I had expected upon coming to the city. An unpleasant taste bloomed in my mouth now as I bit the end of the yam and threw it onto the street; it had been frost bitten' (Ellison 1995: 267). The narrator's dismay at the limited freedom he experiences is thus underscored by the literal intrusion of whiteness, as figured by the snow, into important areas of his existence: it penetrates his mouth – quite important, given the novel's concern over black speech – and it contaminates his nourishment, thus threatening his internal state and functionality. In such novels, whiteness metaphorised through the environmental force of snow proves a 'system of supervision and control [with damning] effect on the black subject' (Smethurst 2001: 34). Equally important, as Richard Dyer has theorised, white power is hard to analyse because it is hard to see, positioned as it is as the normative; thus in making whiteness visible, such novels begin to dismantle its authority, revealing the horror beneath fantasies of all-white nations.

Such black texts also intimate that white subjects are both the villainous perpetrators and the oppressed victims of whiteness; in returning abjection to its source, black authors refuse the role of phobogenic object noted by Fanon and complicate the relationship between would-be fictionalised monster and colonising assailant. For instance, by invoking *Frankenstein* as a subtext for *Native Son*, Wright emphasises the moment when 'the line between the monster and the man who created him is blurred. Bigger, then, is a monster created by a [white] murderous society' (Smethurst 2001: 32). Indeed, we can and should read Bigger's behaviour as an understandable response to having a Gothicised racial imago imposed upon him. As Marriott notes, the displacement of self that occurs when a black subject is entrapped within a racial imago produces disorientation and trauma and gives birth to 'noticeable anger and confusion' and even a 'desire to hurt the imago of the body in a passionate bid to escape it' (Marriott 1998: 419). Understanding Bigger as a created monster – a projection of white vilification of black subjects – also clarifies his disturbing violence towards his family, friends and lover. They are all embodiments of the same imago-covered body that Bigger seeks to evade. Yet this violence and villainy originates within white desire, even as whites, like Victor Frankenstein and those he loves, are also the (accidental) victims of the Bigger-monster's rage.

The conclusion to Mittelholzer's *My Bones and My Flute* (1955) perfectly exemplifies this double-sided victim–villain aspect of abject whiteness, especially in its haunting character Myneer Voorman, an eighteenth-century Dutch slave owner killed in the 1763 Berbice slave uprising. The text emphasises whiteness's haunting of itself in Voorman's explanation of the demons' origins and their torment of him:

> Sometimes I see myself as I am, sometimes I see myself as they are, but it is all one [. . .] If a man shall defy his naturally beneficent urges and turn from his God to unnaturally malevolent practices [. . .] then shall he

emit emanations and influences – and these came out of that man himself [. . .] It is the evil from me that has taken unto itself shapes and odours of frightful nature. It is I myself who plague myself. (Mittelholzer 1955: 229–30)

Voorman, the tormented subject of demons he calls 'the Blacker Ones', reveals how his own desire and ambitions – notably supported by the racial economic system of the era – produce his destruction. Importantly, 'the unnaturally malevolent practices' he performs, though seeming to refer to demonic worship, in reality refer to the ideological violence stemming from white dominance and racial oppression; after all, this passage, like a good deal of Gothic, rejects the idea of demons as supernatural entities. Voorman, as a slave owner during an era that the text marks as pivotal in the devaluation of black bodies to less-than-human, participates in the shifting practices of slavery to produce a harsh, dehumanising system. This shift consequently signifies a moment when whiteness is rearticulated, its superiority and dominance gaining greater distinction as a consequence of the increased oppression of the racial object. In addition, his phrasing for the demons and the slave reveals how his death and damnation are also a result of his performance of white dominance; similar to the demons, he calls the rebelling slaves who ultimately kill him 'the black ones'. The repetition in the phrasing and his explanation of the demons' true nature thus reveal the violence of the slaves to be a product and manifestation of his own behaviour. Like Wright, Mittelholzer reveals how whiteness creates the monsters that torment it. Further, between the two, whiteness is ultimately the more monstrous as finally the source of 'the Blacker Ones'.

In such ways, black writers on both sides of the Atlantic reveal the ways in which whiteness is ultimately a magic trick hiding its monstrous dependence upon otherness. Oyeyemi's novel particularly exemplifies this conundrum in the house's praise of Miranda after it has worked its horror upon her: 'She looked so beautiful. Tiny. Immaculately carved; an ivory wand' (Oyeyemi 2009: 178). Miranda's body reflects the aesthetic ideals to which white womanhood subscribes and the function of these aesthetics as a tool of distraction. As an 'ivory wand', Miranda functions as a tool to hide the impurities and horrors of whiteness beneath the seeming perfection of its appearance. She is also meant to magically duplicate perfect whiteness from generation to generation without revealing its abject dependence upon racial minorities. In the end, the passage emphasises whiteness as artifice, a mere carving, though immaculate. There is nothing inherent or natural to it.

In this and other ways, then, black Gothic writers take up the tasks set forth by black theorists; both dismantle and dismiss racial constructions at play in dominant Western society and within the Gothic itself. Across the Diaspora, the writers repeatedly emphasise the terrors of whiteness. More importantly, they reveal the horrors of the process of racial construction, illustrating the costs for both the oppositional, overly determined black subject and the white subject, equally imprisoned by a society of systemic whiteness that demands allegiance to its definitions. White subjects are thus repositioned as the abject as defined by Kristeva, reconstituted as empty signifiers that primarily embody violence. Allegiance to racist ideologies and racial constructions, whether in statements of theory or in Gothic fictions, it turns out, only enables subjects to access and reproduce violence.

References

Dyer, Richard (1993), *The Matter of Images: Essays on Representation*, New York: Routledge.
Ellison, Ralph (1995) [1952], *Invisible Man*, New York: Vintage Books.
Fanon, Frantz (1967) [1952], *Black Skin, White Masks*, New York: Grove Press.
Gilroy, Paul (2002) [1987], *There Ain't No Black in the Union Jack*, New York: Taylor and Francis.
Halberstam, Judith (1995), *Skin Shows: Gothic Horror and the Technology of Monsters*, Durham, NC: Duke University Press.
Hartman, Saidya (1997), *Scenes of Subjection: Terror Slavery and Self-Making in Nineteenth Century America*, New York: Oxford University Press.
King, Amy K. (2013), 'The Spectral Queerness of White Supremacy: Helen Oyeyemi's *White is for Witching*', in Lisa Kröger and Melanie Anderson (eds), *Ghostly and the Ghosted in Literature and Film: Spectral Identities*, Newark: University of Delaware Press, pp. 59–73.
Kristeva, Julia (1982) [1980], *Powers of Horror: An Essay on Abjection*, trans. Leon S. Roudiez, New York: Columbia University Press.
Malchow, H. L. (1996), *Gothic Images of Race in Nineteenth-Century Britain*, Stanford: Stanford University Press.
Marriott, David (1998), 'Bonding Over Phobia', in Christopher Lane (ed.), *The Psychoanalysis of Race*, New York: Columbia University Press.
Mittelholzer, Edgar (1955), *My Bones and My Flute: A Ghost Story in the Old-Fashioned Manner*, Leeds: Peepal Tree.

Morrison, Toni (1992), *Playing in the Dark: Whiteness and the Literary Imagination*, Cambridge, MA: Harvard University Press.
Oyeyemi, Helen (2009), *White is for Witching*, New York: Nan A. Talese/Doubleday.
Perry, Phyllis Alesia (1998), *Stigmata*, New York: Hyperion.
Petry, Anne (1998) [1946], *The Street*, Boston: Mariner Books.
Shockley, Evie (2006), 'Buried Alive: Gothic Homelessness, Black Women's Sexuality, and (Living) Death in Ann Petry's *The Street*', *African American Review*, 40.3: 439–60.
Smethurst, James (2001), 'Invented by Horror: The Gothic and African American Literary Ideology in *Native Son*', *African American Review*, 35.1: 29–40.
Spillers, Hortense (1987), 'Mama's Baby, Papa's Maybe: An American Grammar Book', *Diacritics*, 17.2: 64–81.
Wester, Maisha (2012), *African American Gothic: Screams from Shadowed Places*, New York: Palgrave Macmillan.
Wisker, Gina (2007), 'Crossing Liminal Spaces: Teaching the Postcolonial Gothic', *Pedagogy: Critical Approaches to Teaching Literature, Language, Composition, and Culture*, 7.3: 401–27.
Wright, Richard (2005) [1940], *Native Son*, New York: Harpers.

Chapter 4

Postcolonial Gothic in and as Theory
Alison Rudd

As the Gothic has become established as a creditable field of enquiry in literary, film and cultural studies, among others, it has also expanded to emerging areas where it has proved to be a fertile mode of critique and theoretical analysis. Postcolonial Gothic is certainly one of these. Jerrold Hogle explains in this volume's introduction that Gothic stories are often critical interventions, aesthetically unstable and engaging actively in theory themselves. Postcolonial Gothic writers are no exception.

The postcolonial denotes the historical process of decolonisation and its aftermath, which during the mid-to-late twentieth century – following much resistance, struggle and anxiety – saw the major imperial powers relinquish their hold on their colonies and the people of those colonies take back substantial control for themselves, although for indigenous peoples, for example in Australia and New Zealand, control is partial, while anxiety, struggle and resistance persist. Postcolonial theory is therefore concerned with an analysis of the cultural history of colonialism and the effects of this history in the present. This intertwining of the colonial past with the present is at the heart of postcolonial discourse because of the impact that violent and disruptive history has had on most of the world and how much has determined present-day structures of power. As Robert Young explains, European colonialism and its relentless and comprehensive geographical, cultural and economic advance obliged societies with different historical, political and economic traditions to follow the same economic system developed and controlled by the West (Young 2001: 5). Just in the way Stuart Hall has argued, as the postcolonial restages the narrative of colonialism, it 'assumes the place and significance of a major, extended and ruptural world-historical event' (Hall 1996: 249). 'We always knew that the dismantling of the colonial paradigm would release strange demons from the deep and that these monsters might come trailing all sorts of subterranean material' (Hall 1996: 259).

In her ground-breaking work 'Postcolonial Gothic: Ruth Prawer Jhabvala and the Sobhraj Case' (1996), Judie Newman identifies postcolonial Gothic as a mode employed by writers from very different locations to address this very release. At the heart of postcolonial Gothic, she writes, lies 'the unresolved conflict between the imperial power and the former colony'. As a European and then American genre, the Gothic cannot entirely divorce itself from the West, but because it can 'retrace the unseen and unsaid of culture, the Gothic is very well adapted to expressing the untold and unspeakable stories of colonial experience' (Newman 1996: 171). Justin D. Edwards helpfully explains this aspect in the context of Canadian Gothic. He argues that Canada is caught in a liminal space between the colonial and the postcolonial and between a range of historical, cultural, political and economic influences from Great Britain as its former colonial master and the United States as its neighbour – and added to all this has been the impact of multiculturalism, which further destabilises a unified sense of national identity (Edwards 2005: xiv–xv). While this position allows Canada a unique perspective on colonialism, a 'cold eye' with which to gaze on the brutality of empire, is it also able to face its own demons, including its actions and attitudes towards its indigenous inhabitants, with the same level of detachment? It is this ambivalence and tension between the innocent victim and survivor and the guilty oppressor that enables the Gothic to be a productive mode of writing in a postcolonial context. The Gothic, in fact, is a mode of writing used by both settler and indigene to articulate the postcolonial experience, even while it also deals with the problems raised by more recent migrants. Gothic, after all, has always been obsessed with the past, while actually being really concerned with issues of the present. For David Punter, the relationship of the Gothic to the postcolonial lies in the way the Gothic views history as a troubling 'melodrama of rise and fall' where it is impossible to escape from a history that will 'reappear and exact a necessary price'. The postcolonial implies a time after, or an 'aftermath', opening itself up to 'the threat of return' (Punter 2003: 193).[1]

There are certain schemes in theory, consequently, that have proven especially suited for approaching the Gothic in general *and* Gothic of this kind: the uncanny and the abject. The uncanny, on the one hand, is defined by Freud as 'a class of the frightening that leads back to what is known of old and long familiar' (Freud 1997: 194–5) and translates as *unheimlich* or unhomely – to be un-homed. '*Heimlich* is a word the meaning of which develops in the direction of ambivalence, until it finally coincides with its opposite, *unheimlich*' (Freud 1997: 201). The uncanny effect is aroused by a recognition of the familiar in the unfamiliar, an old, familiar feeling, which through the process of repression has become alien (Freud 1997: 217). The notion of the unhomely is a particularly productive theory for the postcolonial, as Ken Gelder and Jane M. Jacobs discuss in their work on postcolonial Australia and as Homi Bhabha has argued about the postcolonial condition in general. This aptness does not mean that the postcolonial subject is literally homeless, but refers to a moment when the postcolonial subject is confronted by a disturbing vision of the past erupting into the present, effacing the boundaries between past and present, between public and private. What has been kept hidden as a personal trauma caused by historical events can, in the *un*homely moment, be brought to the surface to make visible the link between that personal tragedy and a wider political reality: 'The unhomely moment creeps up on you stealthily as your own shadow and suddenly you find yourself [. . .] taking the measure of your dwelling in a state of incredulous terror' (Bhabha 1994: 12).

An example of this very process can be found in Shani Mootoo's 2005 novel *He Drown She in the Sea*:

> Ahead loomed range beyond range of ice-capped mountains. Here and there were bursts of lavender, clumps of mustard golden-rod. Pride coursed through him; he had become an insider. By inviting him up, Kay was showing him something few people like him – he grinned at the thought – ever had the chance to glimpse. This was the Canada of postcards and tourism posters. In reality it was his backyard. He wanted to get out of the truck and look around but had the sensation, terror really, that at any time the land and road could simply slip away. (Mootoo 2005: 42)

Harry, the 'him' here, is a landscape gardener working in Vancouver, but originally from the Caribbean. What is described is clearly an unhomely moment in a sublime landscape where belonging and not-belonging coincide. Harry's fear that the land could 'simply slip away' is intimately tied to a precarious sense of identity that could also 'simply slip away' because it is a familiar tourist poster image of Canada, somehow inaccessible and therefore deeply *un*familiar to people like Harry, a recent migrant and person of colour.

Ken Gelder and Jane M. Jacobs have argued in a similar vein that the concept of the uncanny is productive for discussing Australian identity, particularly following the outcome of the *Mabo and Others v. Queensland* case in 1992, which ruled that indigenous custom and native title might exist over many land areas and was not dependent on government recognition. The case overturned the principle of *terra nullius*, which implied that Australia could be colonised without the need for treaties because there was no indigenous population prior to European settlement. The uncanny is valuable here in refusing a stable binary logic that would maintain Australia as a settler nation, focusing merely on settler guilt or innocence and a simplistic possibility of reconciliation. The way the uncanny oscillates between the familiar and the unfamiliar suggests that one can be both settled and unsettled at the same time, and can be both innocent and guilty too. Indeed, on the issue of reconciliation between Aborigine and non-Aborigine, Gelder and Jacobs argue that 'it is not simply that Australians will either be reconciled with each other or they will not; rather these two possibilities (reconciliation; the impossibility of reconciliation) coexist and flow through each other in what is often [. . .] a productively unstable dynamic' (Gelder and Jacobs 1998: 24). Jennifer Lawn, though, while acknowledging Gelder and Jacobs' postcolonial uncanny as persuasive and politically engaged, suggests that it risks normalising a condition of national melancholy. She posits the notion of the ghostly as a more productive descriptor for postcolonial Gothic. In her analysis, the postcolonial ghost possesses a certain monstrousness that arises in part from cross-cultural contamination and arrives when 'conditions are such that these ghosts can force their way into a sickly, static situation and open avenues to new modes of knowledge' (Lawn 2006: 147–9).

In *Powers of Horror* (1980), on the other hand, Julia Kristeva sets out a theory of abjection that has become equally useful in postcolonial analysis. She describes abjection as a pre-conscious process of 'throwing off' (the literal meaning of ab-ject) in which the 'abject' (the site that contains and conceals what has been thrown off as 'other' than a standard concept of identity) arouses a strong reaction that is at once both physical and symbolic, 'which is above all a revolt against an external menace from which one wants to distance oneself, but of which one has the impression that it may menace us from the inside' (Baruch 1996: 118). The abject is associated with expelled bodily fluids, the contaminated body, yet it is not caused by a lack of cleanliness or health, but rather by that which threatens identity and order, does not respect boundaries, 'the in-between, the ambiguous, the composite' (Kristeva 1982: 4; see also Chapter 6 below). Abjection has a number of aspects that can be applied to the analysis of postcolonial texts.

Abjection is rooted in the conflict bound up with the separation of the infant from the mother (half-'inside'/half-'outside') and the ambivalence of attraction and repulsion that the growing infant carries with it thereafter. It is therefore a useful analogy for white settler societies in separating from their imperial mother. Janet Wilson argues that the abject can be particularly productive for postcolonial writers who embrace it as an enabling condition, the abjection of the mother country, to facilitate the emergence of a postcolonial identity. With a focus on New Zealand writers, Wilson argues that they are drawn to the abject through an engagement with an unstable position of articulation, suggesting that 'the nation ... can be imaged as the emergent subject on the border of the thetic break, susceptible to being immersed by semiotic forces, under pressure from an affect-driven body' (Wilson 2002: 303).

However, in terms of the indigenous inhabitants of those societies, it has often been those very peoples who have been seen as abject, the 'outsiders' already within the colonised space and therefore a presence to be expelled. Deriving identity from a space that engrosses them as 'divisible, foldable and catastrophic', such peoples are excluded or made '*deject*' (Kristeva 1982: 8). In the postcolonial context, the abject can be seen to represent the underside of the imperial project, the fundamental hypocrisy at the very heart of the civilising mission's inability to account for both the indigenous peoples who were already there and the numerous cruel and inhuman practices employed in subjugating them and their land.

In *Postcolonial Imaginings* (2000), to be sure, David Punter makes the case for resisting too much of an overarching postcolonial Gothic theoretical framework. I have found in my own work that there is a compulsion to try to determine such a postcolonial framework to encompass all locations and historical contexts. But both postcolonial theory and the nature of Gothic itself resist an all-encompassing theory of everything postcolonial Gothic. Postcolonial theory demands that attention be paid to local contexts in defiance of the imposition of *any* imperial or metropolitan interpretation. It is also important to recognise where postcolonial Gothic is used as a critical frame to analyse texts – or alternatively where the author is engaging in an act of using the Gothic as a creative strategy. Postcolonial Gothic, after all, tends to fragment into countries, regions, ethnicities. Canadian Gothic, for example, breaks down into white settler, First Nations (for example Eden Robinson), English and French (for example *Kamouraska* by Quebec writer, Anne Hébert), Southern Ontario Gothic (Alice Munro), and even urban Gothic as an expression of lived experience by other migrants (*Brown Girl in the Ring* by the Canadian writer of Caribbean origin, Nalo Hopkinson).

A number of examples could be used to illustrate the way that postcolonial writers use the Gothic as a mode of writing, as well as forms of the uncanny or abjection, to question and highlight the postcolonial experience, usually in quite local ways. They work within a Gothic aesthetic, but many of them also within the critical environment of theory. I have chosen to focus on the Australian author Mudrooroo (the pen name of the writer born Colin Johnson), who uses the Gothic form in a deliberate way to interrogate and subvert representations of the Aborigine from the dominant white Australian perspective. The novels I want to discuss here are *Doctor Wooreddy's Prescription for Enduring the Ending of the World* and the *Master of the Ghost Dreaming* series, all written during the 1980s and 1990s, a crucial period, according to Eva Rask Knudsen, for the positioning of Aboriginal writing. Postcolonial theory was at that time attempting to 'centre the margins' and to locate indigenous space, while indigenous writers were keen to escape those particular confines in search of other positions more in tune with their creative sensibilities (Knudsen 2004: xiv). Mudrooroo was at the forefront of this movement-and-counter-movement with both his literary and academic works.

In *Doctor Wooreddy's Prescription* (1983), which is based on oral narratives, Mudrooroo reimagines the first contact between the first European settlers and the Aborigines of Tasmania (Bruny Island). The existence of the European settlers is incomprehensible to the Bruny Islanders unless they are seen as ghosts (*num*), demonic figures because of their different mentality, especially as the consequences of their actions result in disease, exploitation and death. The story is told from Doctor Wooreddy's point of view as he observes the advance of settlement with an increasing sense of dread, which is depicted through accompanying tropes of horror. The Kristevan notion of abjection can therefore be used to describe the world of *Doctor Wooreddy* as meaning collapses and he witnesses the annihilation of the Bruny Islanders. Unquestionably, this project of ever-advancing death is the 'utmost of abjection ... death infecting life' (Kristeva 1982: 4).

Mudrooroo's next project, the *Master of the Ghost Dreaming* series – *Master of the Ghost Dreaming* (1991), *The Undying* (1998), *Underground* (1999) and *The Promised Land* (2000) – provides another retelling of the first contact, subjugation and annihilation of the Tasmanian Aborigines. The first novel continues with the same sense of abjection as in *Doctor Wooreddy*. The opening of the *Master of the Ghost Dreaming* plunges the reader into a sense of unhomeliness felt by the Bruny Island Aborigines:

> *Now, we, the pitiful fragments of once strong families suffer on in exile, Pulled by Evening Star into the realm of ghosts, only some of us live on, ... All around us is an underlying silence of a land of death. ... Surrounded by ghosts, worse, in the arms of ghosts we die to ourselves. And even in that death, there is no surcease. Lost is the way to the skyland. Our souls wander forlornly in the land of ghosts.* (Mudrooroo 1991: 1, italics in original)

Here again, the corpse is the 'utmost of abjection' (Kristeva 1982: 4) as meaning collapses and the survivors become exiled from their own land, as '*dejects*', engrossed by a catastrophic space, a '*land of oblivion, that is constantly remembered*' (Kristeva 1982: 8).

The pity felt for the characters in *Doctor Wooreddy* as they strive to maintain dignity in the face of their inevitable annihilation is transformed in the *Master of the Ghost Dreaming* series as the characters attempt to shake off their victim status. The character of Robinson in this series was first introduced in *Doctor Wooreddy* and is based on a real historical character, George Augustus Robinson, who styled himself as the saviour of the Aborigines and was officially appointed as Conciliator and Protector of Aborigines. The Aboriginal characters are renamed and reimagined by Mudrooroo to reflect the change of tone in the new series. Jangamuttuk (the Doctor Wooreddy of Mudrooroo's previous work) enacts a series of rituals in order to gain possession of the dreams of the invading ghosts so as to subvert them and to put his people 'in contact with the ghost realm so that they could capture the essence of health and well-being' (Mudrooroo 1991: 2). In this way, his people should be able to reclaim the spiritual link with the land and their ancestors that had been so traumatically and brutally severed through colonisation. The ceremonies enacted by Jangamuttuk, the Master of the Ghost Dreaming, actually appropriate European reels and songs, in particular the convict ballad:

> *They made of me*
> *A ghost down under,*
> *Made for me*
> *A place to plunder,*
> *A place to plunder,*
> *Way down under.* (Mudrooroo 1991: 4–5, italics in original)

This song, the convict ballad 'Van Diemen's Land', demonstrates Jangamuttuk's sophisticated handling of chant, as Eva Rask Knudsen points out:

> He has gained access to the Ghost Dreaming by a deliberate deconstruction of the ghost world through a chink in its armour . . . the first European songlines in Australia, which were, or are, echoes of blind tracks completely out of harmony with place. (Knudsen 1997: 116)

Knudsen draws a link between Jangamuttuk gaining access to European mentality through the use of Aboriginal magic and his appropriation of the convict ballads. She then parallels that juxtaposition with Mudrooroo himself who gains access to the spiritual levels of Aboriginality through European print culture in his own academic works, especially *Writing from the Fringe*, which explores traditional oral narratives through the lens of European theory. Mudrooroo thereby demonstrates that he is as well versed in French theory as in Aboriginal narrative traditions, seeing as he makes use of every possible literary or strategic device at his disposal to excavate Aboriginality (Knudsen 2004: 231). This repertoire includes the Gothic.

Master of the Ghost Dreaming is a reimagining of *Doctor Wooreddy* into a *Moban* or shamanistic magic-realist narrative. That is partly because, since they were written more than half a decade after the first, the remaining books in the series, *The Undying*, *Underground* and *The Promised Land*, were influenced by Mudrooroo's reading of eighteenth-century Gothic novels during the years between. He notes that the invasion and settlement of Australia occurred during the eighteenth century, so for him this was a period of time that he describes as a

> *Gothic* monster which could not be ignored for long . . . [So] monsters entered with a rush in the last three books of the *Ghost Dreaming* series set during the so-called spread of settlement along the southern coast of Australia, a Gothic series of events indeed. (Mudrooroo 2011: 14)

It could also be argued that the controversy about Mudrooroo's racial identity and authenticity, which arose during this seven-year gap between the publication of *Master of the Ghost Dreaming* and *The Undying*, had a profound influence on his writing, But it is interesting to note that his response to the controversy around his identity was to introduce a vampire and one associated with cultural contamination.[2] As has already been stated, Mudrooroo was prepared to make use of a range of literary devices in pursuit of his project. He acknowledges that Aboriginal peoples are condemned to reconstruct their past through the coloniser's discourse, but the Gothic allows Mudrooroo to subvert the master's discourse through his engagement with a classic Gothic text, Bram Stoker's *Dracula* (1897).

In *The Undying*, the missionary, George Augustus Robinson, returns to England, leaving his son in charge of the mission. The Aborigines feel betrayed: 'Fada ate at our souls, and when he had finished eating, he abandoned us' (Mudrooroo 1998: 2). Jangamuttuk and his followers contrive to escape the prison that their island home has become. They eventually land on an unfamiliar stretch of coastline. George, the illegitimate son of George Augustus Robinson and adopted by Jangamuttuk, is the narrator of the series, but he loses control of the narrative at the point he is infected by a vampire, Amelia Fraser, who takes over as narrator. Gerry Turcotte argues that Amelia not only gains narrative control, but control over his dreaming, because her dreams replace his:

> For every possession, there is a dispossession. For a ghost to take over a soul, a soul must be lost. For land to be taken, someone must be dispossessed. For Aboriginal people, this moment of invasion is particularly uncanny. They are simultaneously possessed and dispossessed. (Turcotte 2003: 144)

While for Mudrooroo Australia is filled with spiritual forces, Turcotte shows that 'the ghostly – the *otherworldly* – is logically identified as a white, invading presence, literally from another world' (2003: 131, italics in original). The novel's Gothic mode is also identified as an alien, European, parasitic presence, infecting the magic realism of the Ghost Dreaming. As Wendy Pearson puts it, Mudrooroo depicts the Europeans and their culture as both vicious and incompetent and as 'both vampire and virus, a haunting and an infection' (Pearson 2003: 189–90). Importantly, and as also depicted in *Doctor Wooreddy*, cultural infection is linked to biological infection through descriptions of European diseases, for example the 'coughing demon', in order to emphasise the disastrous effect of both on the Aboriginal population.

Amelia's initial act of vampirism on an individual Aborigine metaphorically initiates and re-enacts the act of first contact and the process of colonisation in a parody of a first-contact narrative:

> I have need of this rude person. In this vast and cruel land I am entirely alone and must have someone to do my bidding [. . .] in his mind I explain to him his new position as I give him an advancement on his first wage.

> Now I am sucking on you and my tongue is in you. Now I am tasting your blood and I shall be your mistress. What is your language to me? I brush it aside and talk to you in pictures in your head. (Mudrooroo 1998: 93)

As with many first-contact encounters, the native other is renamed by the coloniser; in this case the name Renfiel is given by Amelia to her first Aboriginal victim. This is a direct allusion to Bram Stoker's *Dracula*, but the description above also alludes to twentieth-century American vampires that Nina Auerbach describes as 'psychic vampires'. As 'legatees' of Dracula that both pre-date him and gain new power from him, 'psychic vampires are a breed apart; instead of merely drinking blood, they sap energy [. . .] more absorbent than their rigid master, they drink energy, emotional generosity, self-control, creativity, talent, memories and importantly also identity' (Auerbach 1995: 101–2). Amelia could be described as a psychic vampire, but rather than being associated with female dependency, as representative of the British Empire she initiates and encourages colonial dependence. The Aborigines are transformed into vampires to become uncanny and abject at the same time. They are alienated from their land and their culture and, whereas in *Doctor Wooreddy* they are 'left to roam the land like phantoms' (Mudrooroo 1983: 96), in the *Master of the Ghost Dreaming* series, they are vampires who largely remain hidden in caves, sapped of their energy, creativity, memories and identity, their presence repressed by the dominant white culture, but *there* nonetheless.

The novels in this series offer a particularly appropriate misappropriation of Stoker's *Dracula*, seen for example in the doubling of the character Renfield (renamed Renfiel) and the behaviour of the character Mina in *The Promised Land* which replicates that of Lucy Westenra in Stoker's novel. In this way, through the deliberate reimagining of particular aspects of *Dracula*, Mudrooroo's novels are not just a transplanted (or transported) version, but an Aboriginal inversion of European Gothic where each is seen as abjecting the other. *Dracula* can be read as a narrative about the invasion of the metropolitan centre, reflecting the anxieties of late imperialism. Yet, as William Hughes points out, a postcolonial reading of the vampire as metaphor for reverse colonisation perhaps says more about twenty-first-century metropolitan guilt than late nineteenth-century anxieties:

> The vampire has to return home to the West, and has to colonise that central-imperial terrain, because the west, personified here as a

(twentieth-century) critical idiom, has anachronistically created him in order to preserve its own identity – or to express a perception of its own postcolonial guilt. (Hughes 2003: 92)

It would seem appropriate that this form of contamination should spread out to the empire in another wave in order to remind a postcolonial readership that the effects of colonialism are still felt, despite the end and the supposed burial of empire. For Turcotte the figure of the vampire as reanimated by Mudrooroo represents a colonial presence, which 'descends upon the Australian landscape to suck it dry, and to contaminate its spaces' (Turcotte 2003: 131). For Pearson, however, Mudrooroo's choice of vampire is reflected in the particular type of vampire narrative that he constructs 'consciously and ironically from the master-narrative of the European vampire' (Pearson 2003: 186).

While acknowledging a reading of reverse colonisation, Hughes offers an alternative reading of Count Dracula as a supreme individualist who, rather than representing the invasion of a race of vampires, represents the Great Man, or Imperial Hero, characters such as Cecil Rhodes who were not only important symbols of empire building, but used the wealth gained from their imperial adventures to fund and some might argue contaminate establishment institutions.[3] For Hughes, Dracula is such an individual, who, while he may symbolise perceived qualities of the nation he represents, acts on his own behalf and in his own individualistic and fiscal interests (Hughes 2003: 96). In this reading, *Dracula* becomes a portrait-in-disguise of the individuals who built the empire, and this link helps us to understand the *Master of the Ghost Dreaming* series. As Ross Gibson argues, the role of the individual is an important aspect of the building of the nation of Australia. White Australia's definition of itself, as distinct from Europe, claims a special association between the individual and the land he works; hence it is through individual and extraordinary heroism that the nation would be claimed:

> Implicitly, if it is taken as given that the society *en masse* cannot make a mark on the land, then the next most comforting myth would have to be a story of heroic individualism, adaptability, and ingenuity in the unwelcoming arena of national definition – the nation then becomes a motley gang of knock-about types, unified in the fact of their survival but not uniform or conformist according to rigid social schemes: a paradoxical nation, but a nation nonetheless. (Gibson 1992: 73)

This myth, however, has no room for the indigenous population, nor indeed for women, and therefore Mudrooroo's choice of a female vampire, Amelia Fraser, serves to further complicate the myth by suggesting what is both deeply repressed – and thus uncanny – and thrown off (abjected) in this myth.

Amelia Fraser appears in *The Undying, Underground* and *The Promised Land* and is presented as the fictional sister of Eliza Fraser, a real historical figure who has come to be one of the most controversial in Australian history. Eliza Fraser was the wife of Captain John Fraser, captain of the *Stirling Castle*, which in 1836 was shipwrecked off the Great Barrier Reef. Survivors were washed up on Thoorgine Island (now Sandy Island) and were captured by the indigenous islanders, the Badtjala people. There are a number of stories about Eliza's fate, but one of the most dominant is that the rescue party managed to secure her release only because their scout claimed she was the ghost of his dead Aboriginal wife (Brown 1998: 24). Ian McNiven and others point out that this first-contact story of a white woman victimised by 'savages' received a great deal of international media attention at the time, but it also had a significant impact upon the politics of empire at a crucial stage in Australia's colonial history (McNiven 1998: 1–2). As Turcotte suggests, Eliza thus became a signifier of Britannia pitted against the evil nature of the Aborigines, justifying punitive expeditions in support of white settlement (Turcotte 2003: 143).

According to Rod Macneil, the most widely read account of Eliza Fraser was *The Shipwreck of the Stirling Castle* (1838) by John Curtis, which represented her as Britannia's envoy upholding British ideals and rendered her story as a moral victory of the old world over the savagery of the new (Macneil 1998: 66). As Kay Schaffer comments in her article on twentieth-century responses to this legend, if Eliza Fraser had not existed, she would have had to be invented (Schaffer 1998: 79). Twentieth-century retellings of the myth have established a particularly masculine authority in the narrative that displaces the political and racial dimensions of the historical event and instead presents 'projections, repressions or fears about national identity held by aspects of the dominant white culture' (Schaffer 1998: 90). However, a re-gendered version of the myth, according to Jim Davidson, offers the possibility of a reconciliation myth for Australia, precisely because of the adaptability of the representations surrounding the story of Eliza as an individual. Where the individual male hero becomes the centre of his story, he is too individualised to become the progenitor of a myth. Eliza's relative lack of definition is ripe with subversive – and indeed uncanny and abject – possibilities (Davidson 1998: 123).[4]

Although Eliza Fraser might represent a figure for reconciliation for white Australians, this reconstruction is unacceptable to Aboriginal Australians. Mudrooroo's incorporation of the Eliza Fraser myth into his first-contact narrative, in which she is transformed into a vampire demonstrating the devastating effects of colonialism, illustrates the tension of reconciliation/non-reconciliation that such national myths might encompass. Mudrooroo's intervention into these myths can be seen as an attempt to re-indigenise them. As Turcotte says, the most terrifying aspect of the vampire, since it/he is uncanny, is the 'ability to colonize from within' (Turcotte 2003: 131). This ability is represented through a process of abjection. By reimagining the historical figure of Eliza Fraser as a vampire, into which is thrown many forms of infection and threats to the boundaries of order and identity, Mudrooroo also infects the white Australian contemporary myth from within. More importantly, he rejects the possibility of an Aboriginal acceptance of the Eliza Fraser story as a reconciliation myth.

Another Australian national myth that Mudrooroo engages with and subverts is the quite uncanny one of the lost child, which has been described as uniquely Australian by John Scheckter (1981), Peter Pierce (1999) and Felicity Collins and Therese Davis (2004). Pierce has made an extensive study of lost children stories, both real and imagined, which date back to the eighteenth century and have become lodged over time in the collective imagination, inspiring works of art, literature and film.[5] Scheckter argues that the stories of lost children in a hostile landscape become especially Australian because they are loaded with national symbolism and become archetypes of national determination (Scheckter 1981: 69). Pierce argues that the recurring trope is also a national anxiety, not only representing the real dangers of life in the outback, but deep anxieties about belonging:

> Symbolically, the lost child represents the anxieties of European settlers because of their ties with home which they have cut in coming to Australia [. . .] The child stands in for the apprehension of adults having to settle in a place where they might never be at peace. (Pierce 1999: xii)

Mudrooroo consequently engages with and infects the trope of the lost child. He himself was taken into the social welfare system and, despite the controversy over his racial origins, it is widely acknowledged that his background and early experience was that of an Aborigine. In *Underground*, much of the battle between the Aborigines and the vampire Amelia takes place in a series of caves, where Amelia infects an Afro-Caribbean slave and steals two Aboriginal children. This battle could be interpreted as a parody and critique of the Australian government policy that took mixed-race Aboriginal children away from their families to residential schools in order to assimilate them into the dominant white culture,[6] in which they become uncanny reminders of their repressed origins.

At the end of the vampire series, George, the main narrator of *Master of the Ghost Dreaming*, *The Undying* and *Underground*, remains one of the undead, uncanny and abject, and, as Pearson says, represents the failure of the Aborigines to repel the European invasion (Pearson 2003: 199). But this irony also demonstrates a failure on the part of the dominant white culture to erase the Aboriginal presence. At the end of *Doctor Wooreddy*, Wooreddy fades into dementia and death, and his corpse is buried on a beach in an unmarked grave, representing a site of abjection at the edge of empire. At the end of the *Master of the Ghost Dreaming* series, the undead vampires ('*dejects*') straying though a catastrophic space represent a repressed Aboriginal presence forced to the surface through the trope of abjection. While it may be impossible to recover precontact Aboriginal origins, for Mudrooroo it is important to attempt to recover an abjected Aboriginal presence for Australian history. The use of a vampire narrative seen through the lens of the Kristevan notion of abjection suggests a culturally contaminated presence that problematises a number of national myths.

I have drawn on Mudrooroo as one particular writer from Australia who has used the Gothic as literary trope, aesthetic, and critical framework with which to interrogate the history of Australia from the point of view of the Aborigines. The relationship between Gothic writing and Gothic theory, which Mudrooroo's total body of work manifests, turns out to be a complicated one. While theories about the Gothic can produce a productive framework for analysing a range of postcolonial texts from numerous different locations, it is important to pay close attention to the specific context of the writer. In his novels, Mudrooroo draws on and makes use of a range of literary and critical devices at his disposal in order to further his project of excavating and restoring an Aboriginal voice in Australia. Postcolonial Gothic as a distinct sub-genre thus has its own distinctive features, and each locale can produce its own sub-genre *of* that sub-genre. In some cases, theory is the framework or lens through which to analyse and discuss a text. In others – and I would argue that Mudrooroo is a good example – the text is itself the theoretical framework through which it is possible to witness an interrogation of history, society and culture.

Notes

1. For more on the wide range of reference in – and approaches to – the postcolonial Gothic, see Hughes and Smith (2003) and Khair (2009).
2. In 1996 Mudrooroo's sister claimed their father was African-American, rather than Aborigine, and he was denounced as 'inauthentic'. For discussions about this controversy, see Dixon et al. (1996), D'Cruz (2002), Hughes (1998), Goldie (2001), Oboe (2003), Pearson (2003), Nolan (2003), Shoemaker (2003, 2011) and Mudrooroo (2011).
3. One might note here the recent controversy over the 'Rhodes must Fall' campaign to remove the statue of Cecil Rhodes from outside Oriel College at Oxford University.
4. During the twentieth century, the legend has changed to include a romance between Eliza and a runaway convict, David Bracefell. This version alters the image of Eliza from victim of empire to seducer and betrayer, elements of a much larger narrative inscribed within Australian nationalism reflecting a sense of independence from Britain. In this narrative Bracefell plays the 'Aussie underdog' and Eliza represents a hostile and haughty Britannia (Schaffer 1998: 80).
5. Examples of writers include Henry Kingsley, Marcus Clarke, Henry Lawson, Joseph Furvey and Ethel Pedley. Frederick McCubbin is a notable example of an artist from the Heidelberg School who produced paintings of lost children. In terms of film, stories of lost children date back to the 1930s, for example, Charles Chauvel's *Uncivilized* (1936). The New Australian cinema of the 1970s saw examples such as *Lost in the Bush* (1970), *Walkabout* (1971) and *Picnic at Hanging Rock* (1975). The trope continues with, for example, *The Missing* (1998), *One Night the Moon* (2001) and *Rabbit-Proof Fence* (2002).
6. This policy has had a devastating effect on Aboriginal communities, as documented by the historian Peter Read (2000, 2003) and recounted by Doris Pilkington-Garimara in *Follow the Rabbit-Proof Fence* (1996) and the film *Rabbit-Proof Fence* directed by Phillip Noyce in 2002, which was a response to the controversial *Bringing them Home* inquiry into the Stolen Generations, published in 1997.

References

Auerbach, Nina (1995), *Our Vampires, Ourselves*, Chicago: University of Chicago Press.
Baruch, Elaine H. (1996) [1980], 'Feminism and Psychoanalysis', in Ross M. Guberman (ed. and trans.), *Julia Kristeva: Interviews*, New York: Columbia University Press, pp. 113–21.
Bhabha, Homi K. (1994), *The Location of Culture*, London: Routledge.

Brown, Elaine (1998), 'Eliza Fraser: An Historical Record', in Ian J. McNiven et al. (eds), *Constructions of Colonialism: Perspectives on Eliza Fraser's Shipwreck*, London: Leicester University Press, pp. 13–27.

Collins, Felicity, and Therese Davis (2004), *Australian Cinema after Mabo*, Cambridge: Cambridge University Press.

Davidson, Jim (1998), 'No Woman is an Island: The Eliza Fraser Variations', in Ian J. McNiven et al. (eds), *Constructions of Colonialism: Perspectives on Eliza Fraser's Shipwreck*, London: Leicester University Press, pp. 116–25.

D'Cruz, Carolyn (2002), '"What Matter Who's Speaking?" Authenticity and Identity in Discourses of Aboriginality in Australia', *Jouvert*, 5.3, http://english.social.chass.ncsu.edu/jouvert/v5i3/cdcr.htm (accessed 30 June 2017).

Dixon, Graeme, et al. (1996), 'The Mudrooroo Dilemma', *Westerly*, 41.3: 5–8.

Edwards, Justin D. (2005), *Gothic Canada: Reading the Spectre of a National Literature*, Edmonton: University of Alberta Press.

Freud, Sigmund (1997) [1919], 'The Uncanny', in *Writings on Art and Literature*, ed. James Strachey, Stanford: Stanford University Press, pp. 193–233.

Gelder, Ken, and Jane M. Jacobs (1998), *Uncanny Australia: Sacredness and Identity in a Postcolonial Nation*, Melbourne: Melbourne University Press.

Gibson, Ross (1992), *South of the West: Postcolonialism and the Narrative Construction of Australia*, Bloomington: Indiana University Press.

Goldie, Terry (2001), 'Who is Mudrooroo?', in Greg Ratcliffe and Gerry Turcotte (eds), *Compr(om)ising Postcolonialism(s): Challenging Narratives and Practices*, Sydney: Dangaroo Press.

Hall, Stuart (1996), 'When was the Postcolonial? Thinking at the Limit', in Iain Chambers and Lidia Curti (eds), *The Postcolonial Question: Common Skies, Divided Horizons*, London: Routledge, pp. 242–60.

Hughes, Mary Ann (1998), 'The Complexity of Aboriginal Identity: Mudrooroo and Sally Morgan', *Westerly*, 43.1: 21–7.

Hughes, William (2003), 'A Singular Invasion: Revisiting the Postcoloniality of Bram Stoker's *Dracula*', in Andrew Smith and William Hughes (eds), *Empire and the Gothic: The Politics of Genre*, Basingstoke: Palgrave Macmillan, pp. 88–102.

Hughes, William, and Andrew Smith (eds) (2003), *Postcolonial Gothic*, special issue of *Gothic Studies*, 5.2.

Khair, Tabish (2009), *The Gothic, Postcolonialism and Otherness: Ghosts From Elsewhere*, New York: Palgrave Macmillan.

Knudsen, Eva Rask (1997), 'Clocktime and Dreamtime: A Reading of Mudrooroo's *Master of the Ghost Dreaming*', in Dieter Riemenschneider and Geoffrey V. Davis (eds), *Aratjara: Aboriginal Culture and Literature in Australia*, Amsterdam: Rodopi, pp. 111–21.

Knudsen, Eva Rask (2004), *The Circle and the Spiral: A Study of Australian Aboriginal and New Zealand Maori Literature*, Amsterdam: Rodopi.

Kristeva, Julia (1982) [1980], *Powers of Horror: An Essay on Abjection*, trans. Leon S. Roudiez, New York: Columbia University Press.

Lawn, Jennifer (2006), 'From the Spectral to the Ghostly: Postcolonial Gothic and New Zealand Literature', *Australasian-Canadian Studies*, 24.2: 143–69.
Macneil, Rod (1998), '"Our Fair Narrator"' Down-under: Mrs Fraser's Body and the Preservation of the Empire', in Ian J. McNiven et al. (eds), *Constructions of Colonialism: Perspectives on Eliza Fraser's Shipwreck*, London: Leicester University Press, pp. 63–76.
McNiven, Ian J. et al. (1998), 'Introduction', in Ian J. McNiven et al. (eds), *Constructions of Colonialism: Perspectives on Eliza Fraser's Shipwreck*, London: Leicester University Press, pp. 1–10.
Mootoo, Shani (2005), *He Drown She in the Sea*, Toronto: McClelland and Stewart.
Mudrooroo (Colin Johnson) (1983), *Doctor Wooreddy's Prescription for Enduring the Ending of the World*, Melbourne: Hyland House.
Mudrooroo, Narogin (1990), *Writing from the Fringe: A Study of Modern Aboriginal Literature*, Melbourne: Hyland House.
Mudrooroo (1991), *Master of the Ghost Dreaming*, Sydney: Angus and Robertson.
Mudrooroo (1998), *The Undying*, Sydney: Angus and Robertson.
Mudrooroo (1999), *Underground*, Sydney: Angus and Robertson.
Mudrooroo (2000), *The Promised Land*, Sydney: Angus and Robertson.
Mudrooroo (2011), 'Portrait of the Artist as a Sick Old Villain "Me Yes I am He the Villain"': Reflections from a Bloke from Outside', *JASAL*, 11.2: 1–23.
Newman, Judie (1996), 'Postcolonial Gothic: Ruth Prawer Jhabvala and the Sobhraj Case', in Victor Sage and Allen Lloyd Smith (eds), *Modern Gothic: A Reader*, Manchester: Manchester University Press, pp. 171–87.
Nolan, Maggie (2003), 'Identity Crises and Orphaned Writings', in Annalisa Oboe (ed.), *Mongrel Signatures: Reflections on the Work of Mudrooroo*, Amsterdam: Rodopi, pp. 107–28.
Oboe, Annalisa (ed.) (2003), *Mongrel Signatures: Reflections on the Work of Mudrooroo*, Amsterdam: Rodopi.
Pearson, Wendy (2003), '"I the Undying": The Vampire of Subjectivity and the Aboriginal "I"', in Annalisa Oboe (ed.), *Mongrel Signatures: Reflections on the Work of Mudrooroo*, Amsterdam: Rodopi, pp. 185–202.
Pierce, Peter (1999), *The Country of Lost Children: An Australian Anxiety*, Cambridge: Cambridge University Press.
Pilkington-Garimara, Doris (1996), *Follow the Rabbit-Proof Fence*, Brisbane: University of Queensland Press.
Punter, David (2000), *Postcolonial Imaginings: Fictions of a New World Order*, Edinburgh: Edinburgh University Press.
Punter, David (2003), 'Arundhati Roy and the House of History', in Andrew Smith and William Hughes (eds), *Empire and the Gothic: The Politics of Genre*, New York: Palgrave Macmillan, pp. 192–207.
Read, Peter (2000), *Belonging: Australians, Place and Aboriginal Ownership*, Cambridge: Cambridge University Press.

Read, Peter (2003), *Haunted Earth*, Sydney: University of New South Wales Press.
Rudd, Alison (2010), *Postcolonial Gothic Fictions from the Caribbean, Canada, Australia and New Zealand*, Cardiff: University of Wales Press.
Schaffer, Kay (1998), '"We are like Eliza": Twentieth-century Australian Responses to the Eliza Fraser Saga', in Ian J. McNiven et al. (eds), *Constructions of Colonialism: Perspectives on Eliza Fraser's Shipwreck*, London: Leicester University Press, pp. 79–96.
Scheckter, John (1981), 'The Lost Child in Australian Fiction', *Modern Fiction Studies*, 27: 61–72.
Shoemaker, Adam (2003), 'Mudrooroo and the Curse of Authenticity', in Annalisa Oboe (ed.), *Mongrel Signatures: Reflections on the Work of Mudrooroo*, Amsterdam: Rodopi, pp. 1–23.
Shoemaker, Adam (2011), 'Mudrooroo: Waiting to be Surprised', *JASAL*, 11.2: 1–10.
Turcotte, Gerry (2003), 'Remastering the Ghosts: Mudrooroo and Gothic Reconfigurations', in Annalisa Oboe (ed.), *Mongrel Signatures: Reflections on the Work of Mudrooroo*, Amsterdam: Rodopi, pp. 129–51.
Wilson, Janet (2002), 'The Abject and Sublime: Enabling Conditions of New Zealand's Postcolonial Identity', in Andrew E. Benjamin et al. (eds), *Postcolonial Cultures and Literatures: Modernity and the (Un)Commonwealth*, New York: Peter Lang, pp. 300–19.
Young, Robert J. C. (2001), *Postcolonialism: An Historical Introduction*, Oxford: Blackwell.

Part II

The Gothic of Psychoanalysis and its Progeny

Chapter 5

The Gothic Body before and after Freud
Steven Bruhm

My title suggests one of those American-style 'extreme make-over' programmes, the kind of thing where we are given 'before and after' in a double exposure intended to show us the magnitude of the changes to what came before and the vast improvement of what came after. If you are like me, you often find that the 'after' is either not all that much different from the 'before' or that, sadly, the 'before' had a certain kind of allure that the 'after' has falsified or distorted. In fact, in some instances the 'after'-effect is something that our culture has taken to calling a 'Gothic body', as the internet offers us endless examples of excessive plastic surgery as a kind of 'monster-making' (Michael Jackson, anyone?). I find something about these ersatz-Gothic bodies – their before-and-after effect – to partake of the same kind of temporal continuity that we can see in Gothic bodies before and after the work of Sigmund Freud. The differences between the 'then' and the 'now' may be remarkable in some ways, but the bones, the structure and the self it encases are all too recognisable underneath. And perhaps that is because the very word 'Gothic', as it marks the aesthetic discussed in this entire collection of essays, is itself a temporal double exposure: since Horace Walpole's inaugural *The Castle of Otranto* of 1764, the Gothic has always looked back from the present, through the lens of the present, to attempt (and fail) to catch a 'back then' in anything legitimate, concrete and knowable.

How then to start thinking about this Gothic body before and after Freud? Indeed, which species of Gothic body are we talking about? The most revealing example, I would contend, is the body in demoniacal possession – not the only Gothic body, to be sure, but one whose historical longevity allows us to locate a past source for Freud's deliberations and to observe the interventions he makes (or does not make) into this narrative convention. For demonic possession, both in its originary texts and its contemporary popularity, throws into high relief the very purpose of Freud's late Enlightenment project: to demystify and debunk religious (dare I say superstitious?) explanations of behavioural pathologies or mental illness and to posit psychological causes for conditions for which metaphysical explanations once held sway. Yet – and here is the thrust of the argument that follows – the very language and theory that Freud brought to the seemingly possessed subject (his body *and* his mind) not only partook of the language of demonology that Freud inherited, but also renamed and codified for a new century a psychical demonology proceeding under the banner of science. As I want to show here, Freud may not have invented the Gothic, but he made possible and inescapable the Gothic as we now understand it.

For all that the phrase 'demoniacal possession' suggests an enclosed state, a personal diagnosis of an afflicted individual, the foundational narratives of possession in Western culture actually show us anything but. If we go as far back as the thrice-told tale of possession in the Christian Gospels (in Matthew 8:28–34, Mark 5:1–20 and Luke 8:26–39), we find a story of possession that is also a story of *movement* – a casting out, a sending elsewhere, what I shall refer to here as the demon's 'transferability'. Whether they appear in a herd of swine, hapless onlookers or a presiding exorcist, demons are always on the move; they have no fixed address or locus of influence. Later foundational narratives such as the possession of the Ursuline nuns at Loudun (in the early 1630s) and of Christoph Haizmann (1677–8) provided Freud with an archive of demons as figures for the interrelational, the communal, the 'legion' identities that can adhere to the body before and after scientific positivism, before and after psychoanalysis, before and after the Enlightenment. The shuttlings between the one and the many, the old and the new, the sacred and the secular, also define a trope of the contemporary Gothic: I am thinking, of course, of those psychoanalytically trained priests of exorcism narratives, analysts doubly schooled in the motility of demons: Father Gregory Sargent in Ray Russell's 1962 novel *The Case Against Satan*; Father Damien Karras in *The Exorcist* (both William Peter Blatty's 1971 novel and William Friedkin's 1974 film); Father Delaney (Rod Steiger) in *The Amityville Horror* film of 1979; and the Protestant minister Reverend Eckhardt (Richard Waugh) in the 2000 TV movie *Possessed* – all of whom probably owe a debt to Abraham Van Helsing in the *Dracula* of Freud's own time. These men stand sentinel over a trans-historic Gothic body, staging for us the very conflict of the spiritual and the medical that Freud had thought to explain and to explain away.

Curiously, Freud appears never to have written on the group possession of Ursuline nuns in France – a hotbed of other demonological theorising (as well as Ken Russell's film, *The Devils* [1971], and at least one modern opera) – but he devoted an entire case study to the travails of the possessed Bavarian painter, Christoph Haizmann. 'A Seventeenth-Century Demonological Neurosis' (1923) relates how Haizmann, following the death of one of his parents, began to experience repeated convulsive attacks in 1677. Upon the recommendation of the priest of a church in Pottenbrunn, where he lived, Haizmann was admitted to the Styrian Shrine at Mariazell, where he was declared to be possessed by the Devil. The chief evidence for this diagnosis was his own story of visitation by a demon who originally appeared to him in the form of a respectable burgher, but who, on repeated visits, became increasingly grotesque and demonic. Haizmann claimed to have entered into a pact (written in blood) with this demon nine years before, and, as the end date of the pact was drawing nigh, the persecutions (and his terror of them) began. He was first exorcised in September of that year, during which he witnessed the appearance of the Devil, from whom he snatched back the pact he had signed. This exorcism seemed to do the trick, in that Haizmann lived some weeks in relative quiet, taking up residence with his sister and her husband in Vienna. On 11 October 1677, however, the demoniacal assaults renewed themselves, and in May of the next year Haizmann returned to Mariazell to undergo a second exorcism. Here it was revealed that he had signed another, earlier pact (this one in ink) with the Devil, which was returned to him during the second exorcism, which duly quieted him. During his ordeal, Haizmann recorded his physical tribulations and demonic visitations in his diary as well as in a series of eight paintings and a votive triptych, which are included in the manuscript that Freud read (see Macalpine and Hunter 1956). Haizmann's history concludes with him joining the Order of the Brotherhood Hospitallers and living quietly until his death in 1700. During his time with the order he was visited by demonic tempters (especially when in his cups) but was able to withstand their wiles. His papers have been kept in the National Library in Vienna, where they were discovered by the director Rudoph Payer-Thurn and handed over to Freud, in the hope of a collaborative essay that never came to be.

Freud's key statement on the 'causes' of Christoph Haizmann's demoniacal visitations (1923) demonstrates as much Enlightenment demystification as do the common-sense explanations of the supernatural in an Ann Radcliffe novel. But whereas Radcliffe's world usually deals with very positivist physical machinations, Freud's Gothic scenario is fundamentally psychological, invoking a *meta*physical reality that Radcliffe would abjure. Freud writes,

> demons are bad and reprehensible wishes, derivatives of instinctual impulses that have been repudiated and repressed. We merely eliminate the projection of these mental entities into the external world which the middle ages carried out; instead, we regard them as having arisen from the patient's internal life, where they have their abode. (Freud 2001: 72)

For Freud, any consideration of Gothic madness and demonological mayhem must begin *not* in the theological world-view of angels and devils but in the subject's own desires: 'Why', asks Freud, 'does anyone sign a bond with the Devil?' (2001: 79). What is being gained in this sacrifice? Freud's answers locate a libidinal economy where theology would posit a salvational one: 'Here was a person [. . .] who signed a bond with the Devil in order to be free from a state of depression' (2001: 81), a depression begun by the death of Haizmann's father and ignited into pathology by the ambivalence of love and hate that the painter had felt towards his parent. What is crucial for Freud are the transferential energies that he sees as projections out into a demon but which are really quite circular in nature: conflicting libidinal investments arise in the psyche to be doubled back upon it in grotesque distortion. The projections in question are manifold: Haizmann imagines his father both as a tyrannical persecutor who castrates his child and as a castrated, effeminised figure himself, appearing in some of the later paintings with multiple breasts. This effeminising, Freud argues, is evidence of yet another projection – that of Haizmann's affection for his *mother*, who is being invoked to save the young man from his persecuting father and from depression over his loss of a father for whom he felt such ambivalence. If demoniacal possession suggests the emptying out of a subject by the invading demonic spirit, as it may have for the medievals, such an emptying-out connotes for Freud the active *need* of the patient rather than the passive usurpation by another, and it manifests itself in bodies defined by projection and incorporation. Freud's demoniacal possession is thus a long way from a personal battle with a personal demon: it stages a psychic conflict across a number of bodies, relying upon the transferability of those libidinal investments.

Towards a Gothic Demonology

One of the things that strikes the modern reader of Freud's case history of Haizmann is that the early modern painter does not appear to be *possessed* in the way contemporary Gothic figures such as Regan MacNeil or Ray Russell's Susan Garth are possessed – that is, Haizmann is not completely taken over by an invasive demon; rather, his problem is more recognisably Faustian, since he is visited upon, pestered, seduced and attacked. Yet the diagnosis of possession that Freud makes twice in his introduction to 'Demonological Neurosis' is not mere sloppiness (although Macalpine and Hunter do criticise Freud for cherry-picking Haizmann's symptoms); instead, it reflects a slipperiness of terminology bequeathed to modernity by the Middle Ages. As we learn from Craig E. Stephenson (and the *OED*), medieval demonology prior to the thirteenth century used the word 'possession' as all but synonymous with 'obsession': both words named states in which a person is being attacked by a malignant demon who compels the subject to act strangely and against his own will. (Indeed, one *OED* definition of 'possession' is 'Domination or a person by an idea, thought, feeling, etc. Also ... the thought or feeling itself, a preoccupation, an obsession' [3b]. Hence, we still speak of 'a man possessed' in the sense of his being *ob*sessed with an idea.) Towards the end of the Middle Ages, the terms began to diverge in meaning. '[An] *obsessive* spirit was thought to assail, haunt, harass a person from outside, while a *possessing* spirit was considered to have taken up residence *inside the body*', to 'occupy', to tyrannically 'take over the seat of the self' (Stephenson 2014: 132, my emphasis). By these lights, Christoph Haizmann was not *pos*sessed but *ob*sessed, harassed by a tempter who always remained outside his skin, never really taking him over from inside. Such external harassment is surely the seed of the Faust story so popular in the classic Gothic, which appears directly in Goethe's *Faust*, Byron's *Manfred*, and fictions ranging from Matthew Lewis's *The Monk* (1796) to Charlotte Dacre's *Zofloya* (1806) and Charles Maturin's *Melmoth the Wanderer* (1820).

Yet Haizmann's type of devil *is* a possessor as far as early medieval and more recent demonologies are concerned. According to T. K. Oesterreich (whose *Possession, Demoniacal and Otherwise* [1930] remains the touchstone on the history of demoniacal possession), 'possession' has come in the twentieth century to denote two things: 1) 'demoniacal somnambulism', in which '[a demon] makes [the subject] lose consciousness and then seems to play in his body the part of the soul: he uses, at least to all appearance, his eyes to see with, his ears to listen, his mouth to speak with, whether it be to those present or to his companions' (Poulain quoted in Oesterreich 2017: 77); and 2) 'the state of inner division in which the individual imagines he feels the demon as a second self within him' (Oesterreich 2017: 77). This second sense of possession seems to have absorbed something of medieval 'obsession', in that the afflicted person remains conscious of a demon which exists at enough cognitive distance from the afflicted to be recognised as other, yet which the possessed person cannot escape. To make sense of this amalgam, Oesterreich posits a third condition – 'lucid possession' – in which one is certainly invaded by a malignant spirit but remains completely aware of the assaults on one's body; those assaults remain available to memory after they cease. While Haizmann's manuscript records incidents of his body and will being completely taken over by the demon, there are no clear instances when he is not conscious of this usurpation or where his experiences are lost to memory. In this sense, Haizmann is the subject of 'lucid possession', not just a troubling obsession. Moreover, Oesterreich notes that 'obsession', 'demoniacal somnambulism' and 'lucid possession' fluctuate as diagnostic terms, given the degree of severity evidenced in the patient's symptoms: 'it must be said', he observes, 'that this terminology has not always been strictly observed. The more nearly the state of obsession approximates, at least apparently, to possession, the more readily is this designation applied' (2017: 77).

A number of things are fascinating here for students of the Gothic. First, the idea of somnambulism versus lucidity allows us to think about the ideological implications of who gets to remember what about their demoniacal experiences. It is surely important that a modern figure such as *The Exorcist*'s Regan MacNeil, enveloped as she is by twentieth-century ideologies of childhood, purportedly leaves the story unable to remember anything of it: thanks to the repressive agencies of somnambulism, no lucidity threatens her delicate adolescent purity. Second, and on a grander scale, the body in the history of possession is not just the vessel for demoniacal habitation, but actually seems to *determine* how such spiritual hijacking is to be codified. Stephenson explains that, in the early Middle Ages, the Devil was understood only to be able to affect a person's *imagination*, to attack his *will* in ways that would result in unwanted behaviour. Temptation proceeded by the Devil's deployment of seductive images – *fantasmata* – such as might appear in an erotic dream (and Christoph Haizmann, we note, had such dreams). However, in the thirteenth century, theologians revised their thinking to engage the subject's body more directly. 'A pontifical constitution rendered nocturnal dream voyages into quasi-religious meetings marked by physical, not imaginary, acts of incest, sodomy, and infanticide', which is to say that, if one dreams of illicit sex, one is actually guilty of *having had that sex*. 'Witches and sorcerers were henceforth described as have [sic] abjured their Christian faith by inviting devils into their bodies' (Stephenson 2014: 132). We need only think here of Lewis's monk, Ambrosio, who lustfully dreams of (his future sex partner) Matilda alongside his 'quasi-religious' erotic interest, the Madonna: 'while sleeping . . . his unsatisfied desires placed before him the most lustful and provoking images, and he rioted in joys till then unknown to him' (Lewis 2004: 86). It is a scene we see again, with a different affective valence, in Rosemary Woodhouse in Ira Levin's *Rosemary's Baby* (1968). Here Rosemary 'dreams' she is having sexual congress with the Devil, only to learn later that she actually *did* have sexual congress with the Devil. To paraphrase Keats, the demoniacal imagination in these stories is, sexually speaking, like Adam's dream: the dreamer awakes to find it truth and suffers its consequences.

For Michel Foucault, the kind of *fantasmata* or image by which the Devil might lead the soul to ruin becomes, in the medical demonology of the fifteenth and sixteenth centuries, the way not just for the Devil to assault the individual's will or soul (over which Satan is thought to have some sway), but also the means by which the Devil might attach himself corporally to the body, the *physical* world that Satan had erstwhile been understood not to be able to affect. Attending closely to Henricus Institoris and Jacob Sprenger's *Malleus maleficarum* of 1486 and Johann Wier's *Cinq livres de l'imposture et tromperie des diables* of 1564, Foucault traces the ways by which late medieval demonology made the organs that receive images – 'the senses, nerves, humours' – into 'the domain of the Devil' (Foucault 1999: 53). Foucault is talking specifically about witchcraft, but his words are relevant to all Gothic bodies in commerce with a demon. In a way that prefigures the Associationists of the mid-eighteenth century (John Locke, David Hartley et al.), the authors of the *Malleus* and the *Cinq livres* see not just the mind or soul of the sinner as the point of demoniacal ingress, but his very *body*. Foucault summarises them thus:

> Satan knows how to mobilize all the solids of the body: when he shakes the nerves next to the brain, he needs at the same time to excite the organs of the senses, so that the fantasy can be taken for reality itself and that the body can be taken in by this great trickery, which makes the Devil appear to the enfeebled spirit of witches. (Foucault 1999: 53)

Foucault's gloss on this demonology, not surprisingly, is that the institution of religion, which thought it was liberating the possessed body from its demon, was actually subjecting it to the demoniacal all the more:

> if it is no doubt true that, under the impetus of a whole religious evolution, the thinkers of the sixteenth century increasingly spiritualized the power of the Devil, they only gave him more complete powers over the body's interior machinery [. . .] The demonic has not been dismissed; quite the opposite, it is brought closer, and infinitely so: embedded in the joining of spirit and body *where the imagination is born*. Paradoxically doctors of the sixteenth century freed up from the demonic only those things which were inanimate; they place the demonic in the immediate environs of the soul, at the contact surface of the body. (Foucault 1999: 52, 55, my emphasis)

In a way that anticipates Freud's theories of incarnate libidinal conflict, early modern diagnosticians, such as those of Haizmann's time, concretised the animate body's connection to the soul, thus underwriting the mental relationship that the body would have to an imagined devil inside it.

This is not to say that early modernity understood all maladies of the mind to be demonic possessions. As Richard Noll points out, many psychological disorders prior to the age of scientific enlightenment were understood to be caused by biology or to have a 'behavioral basis' (as opposed to a spiritual one) (Noll 1992: 142), a thesis first advanced by Hippocrates, and what Freud would later call 'actual neuroses' because they had organic rather than metaphysical causes. Hence the need for elaborate protocols (as in *The Exorcist*) to determine whether a person's erratic, sacrilegious behaviour was organic, demonic or even faked (what Freud would call 'malingering'). But while the Middle Ages may have furthered the work of Hippocrates in distinguishing between organic maladies and demonic possessions, it was the very instability of the binary that, for Joel Faflak, becomes key to the rise of the Gothic in Enlightenment rationalism and the body that it would figure forth. As Faflak argues, the eighteenth-century body inherited from John Locke contained an epistemological problem that would fuel the explosion of interest in the irrational mind (Faflak 2003: 94). Lockean empiricism helped to posit a subject in whom the organs of sense perception made a larger and different kind of 'sense' for the human subject in the world; 'thought' began by assembling the myriad stimulations the sense organs received and then shaped them into ideas. (One such idea, I have sought to show through Foucault, is the idea of demoniacal possession, whose mechanics pre-date Locke.) However, argues Faflak, this rationalist sense-making sensorium also began to betray a reservoir of illogic, dark vision or untrammelled passion. Using the very materialist discourse of mesmerism in James Hogg's 1824 novel, *The Private Memoirs and Confessions of a Justified Sinner*, as his primary example, Faflak argues that the 'eighteenth-century empiricist body also had a mind of its own that the modes of sentiment and sensibility attempted to speak ... a psychosomatic *corpus* of perception and cognition' that proceeded from sensory stimulation but that could not be controlled by the mind responsible for it (Faflak 2003: 94). Hence Foucault's notion of the Devil residing for the late medievals in the place 'where the imagination is born'. Cast in etymological terms, the *daemon* that we inherited from the Greeks as our (morally neutral) sense of genius, inspiration or guiding spirit, the *daemon* that animates the 'rapt imagination' in Percy Bysshe Shelley's *The Daemon of the World* (1816: l. 206): this *daemon* became fractured into the *demon* that we come to know in the medieval narratives of possession, one not so invested in the salubrious feats of Romantic creativity as Shelley might wish. It is the 'daemon' that both guides and destroys Victor Frankenstein; it is both Victor *and* his creature, his 'guiding spirit', that leads him to his monster and is clearly possessed by it (Shelley 2003: 212).

At one level, Hogg's *Justified Sinner* recycles the Faustian demoniacal obsession narratives that I have listed above: his is the Scottish Protestant retelling of stories already told in Lewis, Byron and Maturin. However, the novel goes one better in its treatment of the demoniacal by melding the earlier Faustian traditions and their 'lucid possessions' with those of the somnambulistic and elusive: the persecuted self in *Justified Sinner* is also the self often lost to the demoniacal other, as the transference of the Devil into the human is, at times, complete. The second part of the novel is told by the titular Sinner, Robert Wringhim, who has been persuaded by his (demonic) interlocutor, Gil-Martin, that he (Wringhim) is both above the law of the land and responsible to God for ridding that land of sinners: to wit, Robert's brother, George, his mother and anyone else who stands in the way of his divine calling. As their relationship intensifies, Wringhim begins to fragment, developing a feeling that he is more than one person: 'seized with a strange distemper', Wringhim notes that 'I generally conceived myself to be two people. When I lay in bed, I deemed there were two of us in it; when I sat up, I always beheld another person, and always in the same position from where I sat or stood' (Hogg 1999: 153–4). This splitting becomes more alarming when he confronts charges for wrongdoings that he has no memory of committing, doings clearly carried out by Gil-Martin: 'Either I had a second self, who transacted business in my likeness', he reasons, 'or else my body was at times possessed by a spirit over which it had no control, and of whose actions my soul was entirely unconscious' (1999: 182). Such unconsciousness – such somnambulistic possession – illustrates Faflak's dictum that the Enlightenment body came to have a mind of its own, but for Wringhim, it has another *body* of its own as well: he complains of Gil-Martin that 'to shake him off was impossible – we were *incorporated* together – identified with one another, as it were, and the power was not in me to separate myself from him' (1999: 183, emphasis added); 'I was doomed to remain in misery, subjugated, *soul and body*, to one whose presence was become more intolerable to me than ought on earth can compensate' (1999: 189, emphasis added). If demoniacal possession has always been defined by *movement* – be it Christ's exorcisms in the Gospels or Freud's libidinal motilities in 'A Seventeenth-Century Demonological Neurosis' – the Gothic cements the illegibility of that movement by its deployment of the doppelgänger, a literary motif that its chief psychoanalytic theorist, Otto Rank, locates in the heyday of Romantic narratives (Rank 1971: 9). On the one hand, the demon can move in and out of the human body at will, and on the other, the human can never know for sure if his condition is one of possession, obsession, or an amalgam of the two.

To the degree that *Justified Sinner* builds its doppelgänger narrative upon demoniacal possession, and to the degree that such possession moves from Faustian 'lucidity' to somnambulistic incorporation, the novel inaugurates a proto-psychoanalytic version of the unconscious. For Faflak, this unconscious has all the makings of Jacques Lacan's 'mirror': 'one is made aware [in this novel] that the possession is never one's own: one only has the possession of being possessed by the other' (Faflak 2003: 106). I agree. As the *pas de deux* between Freud's *The Uncanny* and his *On Narcissism* makes clear, the *heimlich* as the familiar and comforting always carries with it seeds of the unfamiliar, the undoing or *unheimlich* sense of what has been repressed, buried, disavowed or distorted. The ego itself, a structure both built and unbuilt by needing the other to recognise itself, renders us uncanny to ourselves. However, I would go one step further to insist that in the Gothic, as psychoanalysis has framed it, the possession is *also always* one's own as well. We are subject to the demonic transfers of others, to be sure, but like Robert Wringhim, we are powerless to determine when that other is demoniacally other and when it is daemon-iacally our 'selves'. In other words, demoniacal possession – as it is represented in Hogg and later theorised in psychoanalysis – forecloses our awareness of the source or origin of the demon we are forced to confront. Wanting to be sure that we are free from the oppressive control of others (parents, Church, society), we remain *self*-possessed, always demonised by our own demons, always a proto-Gothic subject. We are thereby doomed to encounter the other in ourselves that, doppelgänger-like, is always already projected outward, always and ever our own *obsession*, always and *never* our own *possession*. Possession, then, is not only what we subjects *do*; it is what we as subjects *are*. As post-Enlightenment subjects, we have never not been medieval.

The Gothic Body after Freud

It is both the inheritance and the curse of Freudian psychoanalysis, then, that the psyche can best be understood only when it seems to be split, narcissistically embattled, at war with itself. I find enormously useful Faflak's observation that Hogg's *Justified Sinner* presents 'a radically stymied psychoanalysis perversely elaborated as a process of introspection working against itself, a sense-making that stops making sense' (Faflak 2003: 100). At the same time, though, the daemoniacally possessed psyche insists to itself that it make sense, that it pose implacably as a unified whole, a 'subject', and it is this dialectic of possession that marks the post-Freudian Gothic body (to be understood now not merely as the physical body of the Christian sinner but as the over-stacked warehouse of psychic investments). Richard Noll's discussion of 'polypsychism' – the theory in the early twentieth century that the mind is composed of many minds or spirits (as in Virginia Woolf or baby Quincey at the end of *Dracula*) – places such self- and other-possession on a trajectory towards the late twentieth century, when psychologists have actually come to advocate the practice of exorcism for patients with multiple personality disorder who *believe* that a devil resides within them (see Schendel and Kourany 1992: 198). It is not a big leap from Haizmann's devil as a libidinal projection, a polyvalent *condensation* of his father, his mother, his God and himself, to the legion of identities Regan MacNeil claims to have incorporated into her own body: the Devil, Damien Karras's late mother, the homeless 'old altar boy' who addresses Karras in the subway, her mother's dead friend Burke Dennings. All of these beings are 'in here with us', Regan says, because 'in here' is always plural and multiple, a daemon-ology constructed in the Middle Ages and absorbed – incorporated, as Nicholas Abraham and Maria Torok would say (1994) – by the Enlightenment Gothic and psychoanalysis.

Hence the 'curse' of which I just spoke. If demonology in all its guises presents the body as both an absorbent sponge and a leaky vessel in relation to the spirits that define it, how can we ever know which of the legion we are encountering – or whether there is a demon at all? Possession narratives from the medieval to the contemporary always stage a careful protocol of tests to determine if there really is a demon, but such protocols quickly betray the degree to which demon-hunting can be an exercise in finding what you are looking for. Exorcisms are forms of the talking cure, in that they are composed of highly leading questions in search of meaningful speech-acts, but the problem with the talking cure is that it is, like a confession, a dialogue, so that the 'disinterested' other person also gets his say. In that case, the Devil may be neither a metaphysical transference nor a homegrown daemonic presence, but rather a clerical (or clinical) *im*plantation, the invention of the exorcist/analyst. We read the following in the letter from Johann Leopold Braun, the priest of Pottenbrunn who wrote the letter of introduction to admit Haizmann to Mariazell, regarding the initial inquiry into Haizmann's condition:

> As [another] attack recurred soon afterwards and lasted with increasing severity until the following day, the Prefect of the Seigniory of Pottenbrunn of his own accord quietly questioned [Haizmann] as to what kind of thoughts occupied him; and whether perhaps he practiced the forbidden arts or was entangled in a pact with the Devil. (Macalpine and Hunter 1956: 58)

Such presumptions of diabolical influence permeate this case history, despite the protocols intended to prevent a premature conclusion. The Prefect seems to have fed Haizmann his diagnosis in the very act of seeking it, just as Freud seems to have determined that it was *paternal* grief and ambivalence that led Haizmann to depression, even though there is nothing in the original manuscript to indicate that it was the *father* who died (Macalpine and Hunter 1956: 104). And in the much later *Exorcist* of Blatty, Father Merrin assumes upon arrival at the MacNeil home that the Devil is about and is the 'only one' in Regan's bedroom, despite Karras's more sensible adherence to the preliminary questions one is to ask. Demoniacal possession here is not just the ineluctable human condition of modernity but also what Foucault would call a perverse implantation, the transferential embedding of a power-rich concept into the subject so that it can later be torn from its hiding place inside the body (Foucault 1980: 41–2).

While any configuration of a traumatic experience runs the risk, since Freud, of being considered an implantation, which drives both sides of the polemic regarding 'recovered memory', it is the fact of the unconscious and its relation to trans-historical demonology that haunts the Gothic body since Freud. Regardless of where we might want to locate the 'origin' of a demon within us, it is the unconscious – that which continually eludes, contradicts or distorts the self that the ego shows to the world – that psychoanalysis and the Gothic always has us confront. And in the Gothic, as in psychoanalysis, that unconscious acts the part of the medieval Satan, in that it makes of the psyche the Father of Lies. Freud has taught us to mistrust both what the psyche confirms and what it denies, making negativity as generative in the Freudian hermeneutic as the positive presence of a symptom. *The Case Against Satan*, for example, turns on the very Freudian question of how Susan Garth's demoniacal possession connects with Father Sargent's belief that Susan's father Robert raped her (or tried to rape her, or wanted to try). Sargent's key piece of evidence is a negative: '*Susan has told me there is a blank day in her life, a day she can never remember*', leading the analyst-priest to conclude '*that Susan, horrified and repelled, suppressed the entire loathsome incident*' (Russell 1962: 131, italics original). This novel remains undecided on the question of the father's guilt, but not on the importance of absence in diagnosing trauma. *The Exorcist*, conversely, is less certain about the legibility of symptoms and the functions of absence. Consider the scene in which Damien Karras 'tests' Regan's body to see if it truly lodges a demon or if her behaviour is an acting out of some deep psychic mechanism. He sprinkles her with what he tells her is holy water, and her writhing, enraged response indicates to him that there may really not be a devil, since the water came from the tap and was not blessed. This is as far as the film takes the matter, leaving us perpetually wondering (with Ellis Hanson [2004]) whether we can ever get to the heart of Regan's matter, just as we cannot get to the heart of Susan's. But the novel presents a more complicated problem. The next time Karras returns to Regan's bedside, she taunts him for his hubris:

> 'So you're back', it croaked. 'I'm surprised. I would think that the embarrassment over the holy water might have discouraged you from *ever* returning. But then I forget that a priest has no shame.' (Blatty 1972: 315)

In actual fact, Karras had no embarrassment because he didn't recognise that the demon was lying to him when she writhed under the procedure, that, in pretending to be burned, she was really just playing his game; clearly, the demon's reaction to the holy water was as fake as the water itself. Karras had forgotten what medieval theologians (and usually Freud) always remembered: that the Devil, like the tortured psyche, lies. Symptoms may be telling, but what they may tell are inconvenient truths – including that sometimes they mean nothing at all.

If the analyst, be he priest or physician, is presumed to know a condition that may continually dupe him, that is not only because the Freudian symptom migrates, translates or transmogrifies, but because the analyst can never safely be quarantined from the *daemon* he is analysing. As we saw in the Prefect of Pottenbrunn above, the priest/analyst always stands ready as the (too) helpful parent, what Jacques Lacan would call 'the subject presumed to know' in reference to Freud (Lacan 1998; see especially chapter 18), thus setting himself up to be the good parent who might rescue the patient/sinner from the torment(or). The analyst/priest whom the afflicted invests with salvational knowledge and who responds in turn with the narcissistic pleasure of being the saviour: this is the dynamic of transference and counter-transference that Freud came to understand as the crucial problem for psychoanalysis, that our ubiquitous demons, yours *and* mine, are always on the move. And such transference is not just clinically dangerous, it is Gothically horrifying. To the degree that modern exorcism narratives are about uncovering dark and dirty secrets (especially from children, especially from little girls), their subject is most often the kind of incorporated knowledge that the exorcist himself needs to repress. Regan's string of blasphemies includes showing Karras his own guilt with regard to his mother's death, his failures of pastoral care, and in more general ways the fear of homosexual desire infiltrating the priesthood. So too Susan Garth in *The Case Against Satan*, who meets the priests' questions with: 'your interest is not legitimate; it is not priestly – it is lascivious! Details, you say you want. Oh, and how you will lick your lips over those details, won't you?' (Russell 1962: 98). Given the threat of priestly paedophilia that is repeatedly invoked in the novel, and given Father Sargent's research on how, 'at the highest peak, sexual, artistic and religious ecstasy are surprisingly similar' (Russell 1962: 26), Susan Garth is probably not wrong. What these possessed girls really know is what the priests already know, or refuse to know, writ large. Gone are the Christ-like assurances that the truth will set them free, because it is precisely the truth of their own lusts that imprisons them in the first place, and it is the Freudian dynamic of transference that will act as judge and executioner. This irony, perhaps, is one of Freud's greatest gifts to the Gothic. To my knowledge, no cases of demoniacal possession either in medieval Europe or in the religious revivals of Early America ever turned upon the possessed's or the alleged witch's telling the priest/pastor *his own dirty secrets*; a witch's testimony may have bespoken truths about a culture's misogyny (see Traister 2016), but these early stories never cast the exorcist in the role of repressing subject or counter-transferring analysand. Rather, Freud made possible this trope and, along with it, the disabusing enlightenment of the already-Enlightened subject, as networks of disavowals become staged upon the other. Analysts ever so quickly transfer into analysands, confessors into the confessing.

If Freud has left us with the interminable (daemonic) transfer of selves and others, if he has birthed a Gothic that is, as Faflak contends, a haunted corpse of empirical bodily knowledge, then we can turn to this failed dialectic one more time to read the crisis moments of our possession stories. Let us go back to the Enlightenment's 'common sense' and read how Father Gregory Sargent's housekeeper, Mrs Farley, would deal with Susan's purported possession: 'A booby hatch is where she belonged, the wild creature. A paddle across her little round bottom . . . knock a little sense into her, a little of the wildness and looniness out of her' (Russell 1962: 61). Farley's prescription for dealing with the shenanigans of wayward youngsters is soon put to the test as Sargent, enraged by Susan's refusal to 'tell', slaps her hard across the face. This act produces nothing other than the momentary realisation that Talk – both the Catholic rite of exorcism and the talking cure of psychoanalysis – has failed. A similar scene in *The Exorcist*, though, does take us further. When Karras enters Regan's bedroom to find the exorcist Father Merrin dead on the floor, he too retires his words (religious and psychoanalytic) in favour of his hands, holding them out as 'great, fleshy hooks' in the novel and using them as fists to punch Regan's face in the film, all the while desperately goading, 'Take me! Come into me!' (Blatty 1972: 389). Karras seems to have heeded Mrs Farley's advice about trading in intellectual niceness for a good crack on the head, but what makes this scene so remarkable is how the *failure* of the talking cure(s) heralds their *success*: the brute violence against Regan results in the demon transferring from her and into Karras. The narrative has found its way past the transference/counter-transference dilemma of interminable analysis, showing us a body that the Gothic has always delighted in showing us: as I have shown elsewhere (Bruhm 1994), the Gothic body is a conservative limit-point of any democratising attempt to enter into or alleviate another's physical tribulations. Formalised language may not be effective, but brute bodily contact sure is.

As Father Merrin lies dead on the floor and Father Karras lies dying in the street, we wonder how successful these exorcism narratives may be at the project of redressing the 'doubt' (Russell 1962: 51) and 'despair' (Blatty 1972: 369) of our late age. Stories of demoniacal possession throughout Western culture figure the body as a conduit for transferability, yet demoniacal possessions since Freud also figure the body as a closed circuit of libidinal transfer. We exorcise demons by calling them out of the body (pre-Freud), only to find that they either must go into another body (our own), or that they were in our own bodies to begin with, as projections and incorporations (post-Freud), or as the perverse implications (post-Foucault) of a Western subjectivity always unable to exorcise itself. Thus does the Freudian body become the Gothic body *par excellence*: its very porosity offers the possibility for a transfer of spirits between subjects – what our priestly analysts would doubtless call 'love' – but it betrays its own intransigence in disallowing this transfer. It remains *self*-possessed, refusing to expel its own demons for congress with another. Analysis interminable, indeed.

References

Abraham, Nicholas, and Maria Torok (1994), *The Shell and the Kernel: Renewals of Psychoanalysis, Vol. I*, trans. Nicholas T. Rand, Chicago: University of Chicago Press.
Blatty, William Peter (1972) [1971], *The Exorcist*, New York: Bantam.
Bruhm, Steven (1994), *Gothic Bodies: The Politics of Pain in Romantic Fiction*, Philadelphia: University of Pennsylvania Press.
Faflak, Joel (2003), '"The clearest light of reason': Making Sense of Hogg's Body of Evidence', *Gothic Studies*, 5.1: 94–110.
Foucault, Michel (1980) [1976], *The History of Sexuality, Volume I: An Introduction*, trans. Robert Hurley, New York: Vintage.
Foucault, Michel (1999) [1962], 'Religious Deviations and Medical Knowledge', in Jeremy R. Carrette (ed.), *Religion and Culture: Michel Foucault*, New York: Routledge, pp. 50–6.
Freud, Sigmund (2001) [1923], 'A Seventeenth-Century Demonological Neurosis', in *The Complete Psychological Works of Sigmund Freud*, ed. and trans. James Strachey, London: Vintage, XIX, pp. 69–105.
Friedkin, William (dir.) (1973), *The Exorcist*, Warner Brothers.

Hanson, Ellis (2004), 'Knowing Children: Desire and Interpretation in *The Exorcist*', in Steven Bruhm and Natasha Hurley (eds), *Curiouser: On the Queerness of Children*, Minneapolis: University of Minnesota Press.
Hogg, James (1999) [1824], *The Private Memoirs and Confessions of a Justified Sinner*, ed. John Carey, Oxford: Oxford University Press.
Lacan, Jacques (1998) [1973], *The Four Fundamental Concepts of Psychoanalysis*, trans. Alan Sheridan, New York: Norton.
Levin, Ira (1968) [1967], *Rosemary's Baby*, New York: Dell.
Lewis, Matthew Gregory (2004) [1796], *The Monk*, ed. D. L. Macdonald and Kathleen Scherf, Peterborough, ON: Broadview Press.
Macalpine, Ida, and Richard A. Hunter (1956), *Schizophrenia 1677: A Psychiatric Study of an Illustrated Autobiographical Record of Demonic Possession*, London: William Dawson and Sons.
Noll, Richard (ed.) (1992), *Vampires, Werewolves, and Demons: Twentieth Century Reports in the Psychiatric Literature*, New York: Brunner/Mazel.
Oesterreich, T. K. (2017) [1930], *Possession, Demoniacal and Other among Primitive Races, in Antiquity, the Middle Ages, and Modern Times*, trans. D. Ibberson, London: Kegan Paul, Trench, Trubner; repr. Middletown, DE: Old South Books.
Rank, Otto (1971) [1914], *The Double: A Psychoanalytic Study*, trans. Harry Tucker, Jr, Chapel Hill: University of North Carolina Press.
Russell, Ray (1962), *The Case Against Satan*, New York: Penguin.
Schendel, Eric, and Ronald-Frederic C. Kourany (1992), 'Cacodemonomania and Exorcism in Children', in Richard Noll (ed.), *Vampires, Werewolves, and Demons: Twentieth Century Reports in the Psychiatric Literature*, New York: Brunner/Mazel, pp. 198–209.
Shelley, Mary (2003) [1818], *Frankenstein*, ed. Maurice Hindle, New York: Penguin.
Shelley, Percy Bysshe (2013) [1816], *The Daemon of the World*, http://www.gutenberg.org/files/4654/4654-h/4654-h.htm (accessed 14 October 2017).
Stephenson, Craig E. (2014), 'The Possessions at Loudun', *The Psychologist*, 27.2: 132–5.
Traister, Bryce (2006), *Female Piety and the Invention of American Puritanism*, Columbus: Ohio State University Press.

Chapter 6

Abjection as Gothic and the Gothic as Abjection
Jerrold E. Hogle

When Julia Kristeva articulated her now famous theory of 'abjection' in her *Powers of Horror* (1980; English trans. 1982), she produced a revolutionary and still influential advance in the analysis of Gothic fiction. Abjection for her, since she takes its roots (*ject* plus *ab*) seriously, is the pre-conscious *throwing-over* or *casting-out-and-down* of what 'disturbs identity, system, order' at the most primordial levels of our existence (Kristeva 1982: 4). This chaotic manifold deep in our unconscious is projected outwards into an 'abject', a site of the repulsively 'other', as though a fundamental otherness-from-ourselves within ourselves can appear entirely outside us and look abhorrently alien. A perfect example, we have since come to see, is the fabricated 'creature' in Mary Shelley's *Frankenstein* of 1818, whom his maker finally realises is 'my own vampire, my own spirit let loose from the grave' (Shelley 2012: 51). Part of what we abject, Kristeva writes, is any form of 'death infecting life' (1982: 4), the undercurrent in us that we are moving towards death from the moment of our birth, even as we also emerge from and partly retain elements from the dying bodies of our parents. Victor Frankenstein's creature is thus an 'abject' because he is a living composition born from fragments of the dead – hence, like a 'vampire', a reanimated corpse, the 'utmost of abjection' in Kristeva's theory (1982: 4). The inseparability of death from birth, which Frankenstein wants to throw off from himself in a galvanising of stitched-together cadavers, suddenly confronts him in a being of 'strange nature' visibly intermingling what should be the ultimate opposites: life and death (Shelley 2012: 51).

As an 'abject' Gothic image that crosses between and blurs these distinctions, thus making him/it a 'monster' (always a combination of discordant ingredients), the creature both obscures and manifests a heterogeneity fundamental to Frankenstein's, and every human's, being that threatens his quest, and all of our longings, for a homogeneous identity supposedly distinct from such anomalies as the creature's death-in-life. Such an appearance of the strangely *unfamiliar* that actually recalls what is all-too-familiar at a repressed unconscious level, of course, is like what Sigmund Freud calls 'the Uncanny' in his 1919 essay of that name, which has long been associated with Frankenstein's creature in theory-based criticism (Sherwin 1981). There Freud sees such returns of the repressed as stemming from a compulsion to repeat, much as the creature repeats unconscious inclinations in Frankenstein himself. Such a process intimates the death-drive, the impulse to return to an undifferentiated state like that in the womb, lurking deep within us from the moment we come to life (Freud 1949: 391–7). But Kristeva's theory connects this return of the repressed to a level even deeper than such drives, to a chaos of un-differentiation (where death is inseparable from birth) that actually underlies them. She thus makes the abject a self-obscuring but still frightening signifier of what we very dimly recall as a primordial disorder at the foundations of our being, and remember, if we do at all, with the profoundest horror, towards which we can nevertheless be recalled, as *Frankenstein* shows us, by a Gothic figuration.

That disorder for Kristeva, moreover, is not just death-in-life at birth, and Mary Shelley's novel, it turns out, is quite prescient about what she adds to it. As *Powers of Horror* further claims, 'abjection preserves what existed in the archaism of pre-objectal relationship, in the immemorial violence with which a body becomes separated from another body in order to be' (Kristeva 1982: 10). It

> confronts us ... within our personal archeology, with our earliest attempts to release the hold of *maternal* entity even before ex-isting outside of her ... a violent, clumsy breaking away, with the constant risk of falling back under the sway of a power as securing as it is stifling. (1982: 13)

What has to be abjected by us for any distinct identity to be attempted is the traumatic moment of birth at which we are half-outside/half-inside the mother, half-ourselves/half-another, half-alive/half-not-fully (hence the death-state haunting birth), and consequently anomalous, heterogeneous, multiple, yet undifferentiated, an interfusion of what will later be articulated as opposites that, at our most 'archaic' point, are inseparable. Even the impulse to abject, at both early and later stages of it, is a tug-of-war between linked contradictions, a seeking for differentiation from the maternal alongside a desire to be reabsorbed back into it/her (the end point of the death-drive in Freud 1949: 397).

Shelley's Victor Frankenstein, when half-conscious/half-pre-conscious, could not agree more. As he recalls swooning from exhaustion after beholding the grotesquely anomalous visage of his finished creature for the first time, he also remembers having this now-much-discussed dream:

> I thought I saw Elizabeth [his fiancée], in the bloom of health, walking in the streets of Ingoldstat [where he has made his creature]. Delighted and surprised, I embraced her; but as I imprinted the first kiss on her lips, they became pale with the hue of death; her features appeared to change; and I thought I held the corpse of my dead mother in my arms; a shroud enveloped her form, and I saw the grave-worms crawling in the folds of the flannel. I started from my sleep with horror . . . when, by the dim and yellow light of the moon, as it forced its way through the window-shutters, I beheld the wretch – the miserable monster whom I had created. (Shelley 2012: 36)

In making his creature without involving a woman, this dream reveals, Victor has ironically produced a heterogeneous construct that recalls what most deeply motivates him and so what he has tried his utmost to throw off, his desire to be half-distinguishable from and half-rejoined to his own deceased mother. She is the ultimate object that he unconsciously seeks, while anxiously avoiding it too, in creating a 'child' without a mother. She is the end-point of desire that beckons to him behind both his creature and his ostensible love-object. His mother had explicitly designated Elizabeth as her replacement, we must remember, when she lay dying from a disease she had caught from Elizabeth herself (Shelley 2012: 25). This contagion is reversed in the dream as the death-state spreads from the mother's body to Elizabeth's, a transfer that is prophetic, we ultimately find, of the creature strangling Victor's bride on her wedding night, a regressive pulling back to the desire and the contagion of death in the dream (2012: 140–1).

This dream is horrifying, not just because of its 'death infecting life', but because, when a distortion of Frankenstein's and everyone's primal birth-state breaks into a dream-consciousness like a light 'through window-shutters', that very displacement intimates both the longing for such a reunion and the fear (again in Kristeva's words) of 'falling back under the sway of a power as securing as it is stifling', as much the site of ultimate death as it is of the dawning of life. Hence the re-embracing of the birth of the self here can *only* be the embracing of its dissolution, and all of these anomalies are conflated – and thus turn out to be abjected – into the face of the creature, the 'abject' that now looms over Victor's bed as he awakens. Such supremely Gothic moments, combining symbolic depth with a powerful *frisson* effect, precede Freud by many decades and help make possible some of the terms and imagery of psychoanalysis, which Kristeva has radically extended. Consequently, they are, as Anne Williams has said, irrefutable evidence of how many male constructs, such as Frankenstein's, attempt to suppress woman as the source of life by abjecting her primacy for men (and everyone) into something apparently non-feminine, especially in Gothic texts. Such efforts involve 'the "sublimation" of the culturally female', along with what Kristeva terms 'our personal archeology', and are thereby 'a smuggling' of 'the repressed maternal' into what Jacques Lacan has called the 'Symbolic' Order that is male-dominated public language (Williams 1995: 79). That primal link of manhood to the feminine is thus a principal cause of the frequent Gothic 'tension between the Symbolic and the inexpressible other', a tension obscured yet incarnated by the abject, that the Symbolic strives to contain within and keep distant from itself at the same time (Williams 1995: 66).

But what allows Williams in the 1990s to add 'culturally' to 'female' as she so suggestively does? Kristeva provides part of the answer. In her later book *Strangers to Ourselves* (1988; English trans. 1991), she finds an 'uncanny strangeness' like abjection in the 'fascinated rejection that any *foreigner*', a figure who can assume many different forms, 'arouses in us' precisely because anyone identified as foreign 'takes up again our infantile desires' and their links to 'fear of the other', including the mother who threatens to reabsorb us (Kristeva 1991: 191, my emphasis). The otherness in the 'foreign' figure can prompt repulsion in the observing subject (us) because it recalls by displacing our deep otherness-from-ourselves within ourselves, because of which each subject 'projects out of itself what it experiences as dangerous or unpleasant in itself, making of it an alien *double,* uncanny and demoniacal' – hence foreign (1991: 183–4). The process of abjection now reaches for Kristeva beyond 'personal archeology' to become collective, cultural, interpersonal (hence Williams's use of 'culturally') as a means by which threats of anomalies that are widely shared – such as the anomalous birth-state we all seek to throw off, but also our springing from heterogeneous mixtures of classes and races, as well as sexes – are turned into diametric differentiations that intensify a pervasive social antagonism simmering at all times, whether we or not we consciously act on it. It is just this underlying 'traumatic social division' that Slavoj Žižek, at about the same time as Kristeva's *Strangers* in *The Sublime Object of Ideology* (1989), sees as the 'insupportable, real, impossible kernel' covered over and kept distant, hence abjected, by the 'fantasy-construction' that is cultural ideology, the hegemonic 'illusion' that provides us the 'social reality' that we believe to be the actual truth so as to 'escape from [that] traumatic, real kernel', which he also calls a primordial 'maternal Thing' (Žižek 1989: 45).

Here Žižek, after all, like Kristeva, is developing Lacan's notion of the unrepresentable 'Real', the chaotic material alterity, which includes the heterogeneous birth-state, deeply feared and yet unreachable by all representation and conscious knowledge. There manmade distinctions dissolve, entities both contend with and flow into each other, and 'traumatic social divisions' seethe with potentials for chaos and violence (Žižek 1991). On occasion, for both Žižek and Kristeva, hyperbolic, densely eclectic and self-contradictory articulations, as in Gothic fictions such as Frankenstein's creature, can arise in the Symbolic order of the everyday as 'symptoms' suggesting, while disguising, the 'terrifying, impossible' Real (Žižek 1989: 69–71), thereby arousing an affect of fear that really does shake us to our foundations. While they cannot represent it directly, they can hint at its antagonisms and blurrings of boundaries by discordantly manifesting both intertwined opposites and the intermingled yet clashing ideologies that stem from the desires of different groups competing for cultural power. They can even do so, Žižek adds, by enacting 'the paradox of the Sublime', the production of an apparently meaningful representation that raises to great aesthetic expansiveness 'the very impossibility' that is the 'permanent failure' to represent the lurking but inaccessible Real (1989: 203), as when Shelley's creature appears to his maker during a thunder-and-lightning storm in the towering Alps (Shelley 2012: 50).

Given these expansions of abjection by Žižek, Williams and Kristeva herself, we have therefore come to realise in Shelley's *Frankenstein* (as I have, for example, in Hogle 1998) that the process of abjection throws over into the creature more than just the contradictions in the death-in-life birth-state. It also sequesters there the deep social antagonisms in the Western culture of Shelley's time and ours – hence the ongoing adaptations of *Frankenstein* – that appear in how the discordances in the 'monster' half-conceal/half-expose the unresolved conflicts among competing ideologies in several different spheres. As various interpreters of the Shelley novel have described them, usually without connecting them to Kristevan theory, these ideological conflicts (symptoms of the Real) abjected on to the creature include the simultaneous hopes *and* fears in the 1810s about the industrial revolution turning human creation into mechanical reproduction (O'Flinn 1983); the hesitation then and since between older, divinely sanctioned, even alchemical science and the post-Enlightenment science that sees life as an electrical transmission into and within material bodies (Butler 2012); middle-class aspirations for self-advancement as they confront – while trying to avoid – their role in the creation of the enormous and exploited working class manifestly suggested by the creature (Vlasopolos 1983); strivings towards the perfectibility of the human race haunted by anxious racist fears about humanity's ethnic diversity, as in the several *colours* on the creature's face (Malchow 1993; Mellor 2001); the possibilities of greater education for women conflicting with a diminution of their role in giving birth with the rise of new technologies (Homans 1986: 100–19); and the increasing difficulty of separating the human being from the beast, seeing as fragments of both humans and animals come together in the creature, and conscious from unconscious drives in people, considering Victor's dream of re-embracing his dead mother right after he beholds the first breath of a creature whom he has brought to birth without a mother at all (Shelley 2012: 31–6). Just as anomalous as the desires to both rejoin and escape the mother and death, these complexes, all caught betwixt and between, are aspects of a cultural unconscious haunting collective and individual thinking with hints of a cacophonous Real. It is all this that the modern Western and male psyche, albeit rooted in every one of these contradictions, must 'other' away from itself and see as a horrific alterity, as Frankenstein does, if it is to claim a coherent, and clearly male, identity for itself. Gothic texts such as this one may have crafted precursor-images that the more recent theories of Kristeva and Žižek provide concepts to explain, but there can be no doubt that abjection theory has transformed Gothic studies retroactively and permanently from the 1980s onwards, especially as its 'personal archeology' has expanded to be seen as a cultural one too.

I want to argue here, however, that abjection is not just prefigured by prominent monster-Gothic texts, though much of what has been said above about the 1818 *Frankenstein* can also be found in Edgar Allan Poe's 'The Fall of the House of Usher' (1839), Robert Louis Stevenson's *Strange Case of Dr Jekyll and Mr Hyde* (1886), Bram Stoker's original *Dracula* (1897) and Gaston Leroux's French *Phantom of the Opera* (1910), among many other Gothic fictions (see Hoeveler 1992; Hogle 2012). As much as *Powers of Horror* draws its examples from very modern Continental writers, what really enables Kristeva to even conceive of abjection as being symbolised in Gothically based literature – and indeed what enables Freud to hunt for subconscious 'memory-traces' haunting conscious awareness in Shakespeare or the dreams of his patients – is also what lies behind those 'monster' tales: the special nature of Gothic symbol-making as it develops in and out of Horace Walpole's *The Castle of Otranto* (1764), the first narrative to be labelled a 'Gothic Story' by its author. I now want to show, therefore, that the theory of abjection as a symbol-making process and more recent expansions on it, as well as the Gothic novels that prefigure both, develop out of the underlying assumptions within Walpole's very particular scheme, which he both fictionalised and theorised in the mid-1760s. There could hardly be a clearer instance of a recent theory applicable to the Gothic that is so fully anticipated by the Gothic itself and by the earliest manifestations and theorisings of it.

Walpole's genre-designation of 'Gothic' – at his time, we must remember, a floating signifier that could mean 'imaginative in a medieval manner' or 'barbarous and pre-civilized' by more modern standards (see Tucker 1967: 149–55) – was added by him to the 1765 second edition of *Otranto*, and he justified it with a second Preface, while reprinting the first one too, in order to define what this new aesthetic combination should mean henceforth. In the new Preface, a 'Gothic Story' is an antithetical 'blend' of 'two kinds of romance, the ancient and the modern' (Walpole 1996: 8), a combination as blatantly two-faced as that old Roman god Janus, who looks backwards and forwards simultaneously. The most backward-looking of these 'kinds', 'ancient romance', is rooted in still attractive but antiquated (indeed, medieval Catholic) beliefs in interventions by the supernatural, in the blood and body of Christ really inhabiting symbols of him (such as the Holy Grail), and in hierarchies and destinies fixed by the order of God's cosmos, the crux of the ideologies that support aristocratic supremacy, albeit in a receding, because increasingly 'ancient', past. The second, more forward-looking, of these, the 'modern romance', as in the emerging middle-class novel of the eighteenth century, increasingly assumes knowable truth to be based on earth-bound, Protestant-supported, empirical perceptions and the associated ideas that stem from reflecting on them. These are the associations that John Locke in his *Essay Concerning Human Understanding* (1690) sees as the combining into mental constructs of what are already spectral perceptions, like

Freudian memory-traces, that have become the ghosts of initial sensory impressions and even the 'Tombs' of their original imprints if the latter are 'effaced by time' and not *'refreshed'* by similar or analogous impressions, themselves in the process of becoming spectral memories (Locke 1979: 151–2). This ideological scheme allows individual development to be less predetermined, more psychologically motivated, and more open to future possibilities that eventuate, not because of external destiny, but out of internal, empirically based understandings developed from the mind reflecting on and combining memory-traces over time, a scheme valued in middle-class systems of belief as underwriting self-advancement with no predetermined nature or outcome. Indeed, in the Preface to his first *Otranto* edition, the anti-Catholic Walpole asks his readers to accept his medieval images of the 'preternatural' as by now 'exploded' (1996: 6), as not to be believed in by his enlightened readers even if they *are* credited by his quasi-medieval characters. Those readers are thus faced with the pull of archaic visions towards the apparent security of older, divinely grounded schemes in a fading way of thinking. But they face just as much the metaphysical emptiness of those spectres, now, like Lockean perceptions, just ghosts of old images, spectres of the already spectral. These symbols are no longer embodiments (no longer 'refreshed') but fragments and dead letters uprooted from what once seemed grounded, whole and alive. That empiricist hollowing-out, while husks of the past still linger, enables the prospect of a supposedly freer, less predestined individual, whose 'powers of fancy' in Walpole's second Preface are thus 'at liberty to expatiate' by giving new meanings to old forms now emptied of their original grounds (1996: 9), and for whom knowledge and behaviours emerge from experiences based on interpreted, if ghostly, impressions, even though these keep calling the mind back towards receding or absent foundations.

The most influential Gothic images in *The Castle of Otranto*'s main text, moreover, like the label 'Gothic' itself at Walpole's time, exemplify this ancient-and-modern scheme while also adding some dimensions to it. There is a Janus-faced quality in all of the ghosts, for example, that loom before this novella's central characters: the monstrously enlarged and armoured fragments of the Ghost of Alfonso, Otranto's original founder, which refer back mainly to the black marble effigy on Alfonso's tomb in the castle's crypts (Walpole 1996: 21); the portrait of Ricardo, the grandfather of the current Prince Manfred and the poisoner of Alfonso decades ago, which walks out of its frame and makes Manfred react almost exactly like Hamlet faced with the ghost of his father in Shakespeare's play (1996: 26); and the 'phantom' of the Hermit of Joppa, who appears suddenly before Frederic, a Marquis who also aspires to the ownership of Otranto, precisely in the manner of the skeletal figures in medieval *danse macabre* paintings who confront usually 'noble' beings with the sinfulness in them that could mean eternal death (1996: 106). While these figures do look backwards to old assumptions about aristocratic inheritance and icons of cautionary spirits, they are also, like Locke's interpreted perceptions, spectres of the merely spectral, figurations of what are only figurations already (statues, paintings, texts of 'ancient' romance) without the apparent solidity of a body behind them that makes Hamlet refer to this first sighting of his sire's ghost as 'King, father, royal Dane!', embodied exactly as he was 'in complete steel' when he killed old Fortinbras of Norway (*Hamlet* I.iv.45–52). In fact, since Walpole's first *Otranto* preface has declared the beliefs behind such 'ancient romance' elements to be 'exploded', these monster/spectres are indeed the ghosts of outdated representations only. They leave readers caught between disbelieving such apparitions, except as they exist in the minds of this tale's medieval characters who accept the antiquated ideologies, and being drawn towards believing in what such Gothic images betoken anyway, at least while the story lasts, because the characters do – but, then again, that is not entirely true of Walpole's characters either. Prince Manfred especially, when faced with such figures and others' reactions to them, is repeatedly torn between conflicting attitudes, more internally than characters in old romances, to the point where he 'even doubted whether [a late] discovery was not a contrivance' instead of an actual truth outside of him matching his initial perceptions (Walpole 1996: 57). On one level, such a character verges on becoming an Enlightenment, Lockean perceiver, free to decide, although fearful about, what to think, given the spectral nature of perceptions that may or may not be grounded in what Catholicism and aristocratic ideologies have claimed for centuries. On another level, he faces the prospect of what medieval Catholic imagery was for Walpole: *fake*, a purveyor of now false beliefs that arouse doubtful responses, that consequently can refer to new as well as old contents of thought, even as both his readers and characters – Janus-faced like his concept of the Gothic (already a conflicted term) – may be called backwards to old ways of thinking that still have compelling features, productive of real fear-affects in the reader as well as the characters, and so continue to haunt, while still being questioned by, more progressive systems of belief.

This conundrum in the inaugural 'Gothic Story' is one reason I have elsewhere referred to every such emptied-out-yet-terrifying image in Walpole and his successors as 'the ghost of the counterfeit' (Hogle 2012: 496–503). It is a phrase that I would also apply to Frankenstein's creature and Dr Jekyll's Mr Hyde (both spectres of 'contrivance' and closer to their projectors than they first appear) as much as to the ghost-figures in *The Castle of Otranto* or to the internal imaginings that appear as external apparitions in the 1790s Gothic 'romances' of Ann Radcliffe (Castle 1987) and even *The Monk* by Matthew Lewis (1796; see Hogle 1997). Another reason for using this term, however, appears in the debt that *Otranto* admits it owes to Shakespeare's *Hamlet* in Walpole's second Preface (Walpole 1996: 10–14). Although the ghost of old Hamlet first appears fully embodied, its/his entrance into the Queen's bedroom later in the play follows Prince Hamlet confronting his mother with portraits of both his father and his uncle, the usurper King Claudius. The Prince demands that she compare the 'counterfeit presentiment of two brothers' (*Hamlet* III.iv.53), one of which for young Hamlet is authentically noble and the other a false, corrupted substitute 'like a mildewed ear' (III.iv.64), all of which has the ghost making his entrance as though walking out of one of these pictures, as Ricardo does in Walpole's *Castle*, right as Hamlet says the line 'A king of shreds and patches', albeit in reference to Claudius (III.iv.102). That line can drift, if only momentarily, from Claudius to old Hamlet for the audience because the Prince has used the word 'counterfeit' to describe both pictures, even though the implication of 'fake' in that word applies only to the portrait of Claudius in Hamlet's eyes.

As Jean Baudrillard has shown in a study of how assumptions about signs develop and change across Western history, 'counterfeit', the governing view of signs in Baudrillard's view at the time of *Hamlet* (first staged 1600–1), could mean both a representation of supposedly true accuracy *and* a fake representation or false front. At this time, the rising mercantile classes, from which Shakespeare came himself, were forcefully affecting beliefs about self-representation in a British culture also inclined towards the aristocratic thinking that connected modes of dress and expression with natural birth into fixed classes. Hence representations of individuals began oscillating between 'nostalgia for the natural reference of the sign' within a set class scheme, favoured by aristocrats, where 'assignation is absolute' (the portrait/counterfeit as 'true to nature', if only nostalgically) and an increased 'transit of values or signs of prestige from one class to another' (the counterfeit uprooted from past reference points no longer pre-ordained and thus transferable to class-climbers, fakes by older standards) – a heterogeneity that reared its head when the middle-class Shakespeare purchased and displayed a family coat of arms (Baudrillard 1993: 50–1). This state of the sign, after all, reflected an early stage of the shift towards 'modernity' in Western culture, which Charles Taylor has defined as the movement from belief in an ontic *logos*, where fixed hierarchies manifest the dictates of a 'transcendent' God, to a wide acceptance of free-floating contests between that retrogressive scheme and other, more emergent systems of belief, 'multiple modernities' (Taylor 2007: 21). Within these, individual class-climbing is now thought of as possible, and symbols of a higher class can be expropriated to become visible definers of entrepreneurs who come from a lower one. The 'counterfeit' in Shakespeare's day, then, to which Walpole's 'Gothic' ghosts clearly look back, is itself a Janus-faced notion caught between the lingering attraction of waning and the increasing appeal of waxing ideologies. Even when Hamlet sees his father's ghost for the first time, the latter is already a counterfeit in this anomalous sense. His shocked son, in starting to interpret what this apparition might be and mean, hesitates whether to call it 'a spirit of health' or a 'goblin damn'd' (*Hamlet* I.iv.40). He reveals himself and his audience to be torn between the long-standing Catholic and aristocratic belief that ghosts are harbingers of ultimate revelation (*true* counterfeits) and the Protestant and more middle-class view that ghosts are agents from Hell who may deceive the unwary with appearances that falsify ultimate reality (*fake* counterfeits; see Frye 1984: 11–29).

Consequently, Walpole's Gothic spectres referring back to such counterfeits are Janus-faced on two levels in ways that make possible *both* the capacity in later Gothic figures to be sites of abjection for ideological conflicts *and* the more recent advent of abjection theory to explain what those figures suggest. In their pointing only to what are already representations, ones even emptied of believable content by his first Preface while they still have haunting power over characters and readers, these show the ancient-and-modern-romance combination that defines the 'Gothic Story' to be suggesting profound disagreements between ideologies (old aristocratic vs. rising middle-class ones in the main), an undercurrent of contestation seething unresolved in British and much of Western culture at the time *Otranto* was written. E. J. Clery therefore reads Walpole's Gothic insightfully when she sees it as intimating a 'contradiction between the traditional claims of landed property', now 'estranged, defamiliarized' by the 1760s in a more mercantile economy, and the surging bourgeois 'claims of the private family' still partly longing for the apparent sureties of an ageing class-system that they want both to empty out *and* to climb up (Clery 1995: 77). Moreover, in referring back to older counterfeits that are themselves sites of ideological contestation, even though there is stronger 'nostalgia for the natural referent of the sign' in the Shakespearean counterfeit (Baudrillard 1993: 51), Walpolean Gothic figures reveal the 'grounding' of their symbols for the ideological conflicts of their own time to be similar, and equally unresolved, contestations – older Janus-like tugs-of war – inherent in the medieval-to-Renaissance counterfeit sign as it appears in *Hamlet*. Gothic figurations that are the heirs of Walpole's monster-ghosts, such as Frankenstein's creature, which Mary Shelley admitted to be based on the walking spectre of a portrait 'clothed like the ghost in Hamlet' in her Introduction to the revised *Frankenstein* of 1831 (Shelley 2012: 166), are therefore, by the very nature of their Gothic construction, sites into which ideological debates of their time *as they also recall signs of such contests from an earlier age* can be abjected, thrown over and made alien, by authors and readers who seek both to manifest and to obscure a pervasive and deeply feared aporia regarding conflicting beliefs in the cultural unconscious.

Indeed, in such Gothic figures, which are always signs of other signs harkening back to still other ghost-like memory-traces, there is no solid grounding point to be accessed behind or beneath them. That is because, in their figuring of unresolved ideological conflict that refers mainly to figures for earlier (if partly different) conflicts, they point to, while they also strive to keep distant from full awareness, the 'traumatic social division' that Žižek sees as an ongoing, pervasive social Real, the terrifying, underlying turbulence of a potential chaos in all cultures, even as its ingredients and inequalities change across history. By keeping this Real at a far remove in its half-hyperbolic ('ancient romance') and half-realistic ('modern romance') style, the Gothic sets up and enables Žižek's theory by hinting at the threatening alterity of traumatic underlying conflict even more than so-called 'straight realism' can do, since the latter merely depicts the ideological illusion of 'reality' that actually masks the Real. Given its *Otranto* foundations in tensions between different modes of fiction, then, Gothic can suggest the wars of ideas looking back to other such wars that both underlie each text's Gothic surface and dimly indicate the deep social antagonism that ideologies rise from, yet work to bury beneath, their conflicts. After all, the Walpolean Gothic reveals such contests to be ultimately fictive, Žižek's hyper-Marxist sense of the hegemonic 'reality' produced by every ideology, precisely by overemphasising ideological schisms and the Gothic's own fictionality in representing them via monsters and spectres.

At the same time, though, figures based in Walpole's Gothic can also suggest, while distancing, other dimensions of the Real, the ones that become most vital to Kristeva, beyond just the social traumas masked by irresolutions among belief-systems. However much each of his ghosts recalls another representation that itself refers to another past figure rather than a body, they all suggest the anomaly of death-in-life that Kristeva will make the 'utmost of abjection'. It is not simply that they are mobile representations of dead people; they are also Lockean impressions already turned into 'Tombs' or dead letters that point to fading points of reference and encourage the receding and dying of those referents to carry over into the newer representation, especially after Walpole's first Preface refuses to reinforce the belief-system in which most of his medieval icons used to be grounded. By extension, then, the Gothic reveals any attachments of newer meanings to older figures to be ominously subject to the same entombment themselves as time and belief-systems move on. Hence the longing of Gothic characters, from Manfred to Frankenstein to Dracula, for the apparent security of older counterfeits in the past (as in the promises of medieval effigies or alchemy or Transylvanian warlord culture) that seem more grounded than the newer ones may ever be, even though any revival of those old counterfeits will always produce no more than an anomalous figure of the living dead that Kristeva will call 'abject'.

On top of this aspect of his Gothic figures, and as noticed in 1773 by John and Anna Laetitia Aiken (later Mrs Barbauld; see Clery and Miles 2000: 129), Walpole carries forward into his *Otranto* and its spectres the theory of the sublime as rooted in terror presented in his fellow Whig Edmund Burke's *Philosophical Enquiry into the Origin of our Ideas of the Sublime and Beautiful* (1757). Whether they depict broken-down old ruins, 'vast extent', profound 'obscurity' or a '*spirit*' from '*visions of the night*', figurations of any of these in art, especially verbal art, arouse for Burke associations in observers or readers not just of fear, but of possible 'death' while they live, the death-in-life that Kristeva says we abject while we also feel a very deep *frisson*, 'the strongest emotion [of] which the mind is capable', when we behold a suggestion of it (Burke in Clery and Miles 2000: 113–15). At the same time, Burke adds, such representations, by being art, can achieve 'certain distances' that make their figures 'not [actually] conversant about the present destruction of the person' observing or reading and can thereby arouse 'delightful terror', rather than 'noxious' horror, as a sublime aesthetic response (Clery and Miles 2000: 113, 121). Death in Burke is always suggested by sublime representations, which always imply some dissolution going on within or behind them. Yet the sublime representation can veer away from a direct confrontation with the wrenching disorder of a body's actual death by obscuring that traumatic welter behind a distancing construct about it, much as Kristeva believes we throw it off, and much as Žižek sees ideology as 'sublime' in covering over much of the destructive/constructive Real that it claims to organise and explain. It would seem that such a distance from death, and hence the sublime, is indeed achieved by Walpole's ghosts of counterfeits being images of older images rather than material corpses.

At the same time, however, Burke's theory connects the power of sublimity with its capacity to make the observer feel the immanence of death in the 'affecting idea' of it that sublime constructions arouse (Clery and Miles 2000: 113). What is distanced by aesthetics is restored in the affect, the mental response of a spectator or reader, which does not escape apprehending death in sublime works. The perceptions arousing the mind's fearful associations, as I have noted above, are themselves inclined, if not refreshed, to become 'Tombs' that kill themselves and what they have perceived for a Lockean Associationist, as Burke clearly was in the 1750s. Hence the terrifyingly sublime opening scene in Walpole's *Otranto*, where Manfred, trying to stage the wedding of his son to ensure his family's continued possession of Otranto, suddenly 'beheld his child dashed to pieces, and almost buried under an enormous helmet, an hundred times more large than any casque ever made for human being' (Walpole 1996: 19). This passage moves quickly away from a brief reference to the son's dead body and pans upward, like a film camera, to behold a vast enormity far beyond human size, thus arousing the sublime affect of superhuman, if frightening, associations that almost 'bury' the body from sight, as indeed the giant helmet does in Walpole's words. Lest we be allowed to escape the real death involved, however, some spectators soon note that the helmet is an enlargement of the one 'missing from Alfonso's statue' in the castle crypt (1996: 21). We are drawn, as a result, towards thinking of the 'casque' as part of a grave harbouring what begins to seem the remains of a suspect death. In addition, some terrified spectators from Walpole's opening scene extend that reconnection by supposing that whoever has apparently 'stolen the helmet' has 'dashed out the brains of our young prince' (1996: 21), recovering his shattered body – and thus physical death – for the reader's attention from its earlier burial. True, we later find the 'enormous' helmet to be one portion of the gigantic Spirit of Alfonso, with its fragments reunited, when it finally rises from within the now-ruined castle to ensure the restoration of his own family line to the principality of Otranto; what thus appears is another sublime figure. Yet even this one still carries death with it, while attempting to rise above it, because it helps enunciate on the same page the long-hidden secret of Alfonso's murder (1996: 112–13), of which his ghost is incontrovertible evidence. Meanwhile, we have also been told by Walpole's first Preface that such supernatural prodigies are based on 'exploded' beliefs, a precondition of our reading that renders this one a dead letter to more Enlightenment understandings even as it prompts a sublime affect by Burkean standards, albeit in its hollowed-out display of what is still death-in-life.

Undergirded by such paradoxes in Gothic symbol-making, Kristeva therefore connects the sublime with abjection in a quite similar way. For her it seems that 'the sublime has no object', or rather that anything that might be its 'object dissolves in the raptures of a bottomless memory' (Kristeva 1982: 12), much as Walpole's reunited ghost arouses multiple associations in the minds of its onlookers with apparently no attention to the dead body left behind in the crypt or the fragmentation of its effigy (Walpole 1996: 113–15). But its objects, such as death-in-life, can be distanced, the way they are in Burke and Walpole, only because the sublime's 'spree of perceptions and words that expands memory boundlessly' (Kristeva 1982: 12) includes disembodied recollections that, precisely in their multiplicity, both refer to and have deliberately sublimated the 'heterogeneous flux', the Real, of individual and cultural being (1982: 10) that has been cast off by abjection into frightening 'others', such as the looming dark fragments of the black effigy in *Otranto* viewed as dealing death, as crushing bodies and brains. The sublime in Kristeva is the counterpart of the abjection that ultimately enables it and that it therefore recalls in sublimated form, just as the sublime in Burke and the Gothic sublime in Walpole strive to rise above the death they suggest only to intimate it again, and preserve its threat, in ideational (and ideological) forms.

Not surprisingly, then, the abjection of the birth-state in *Powers of Horror*, the 'breaking away' that is also 'at constant risk of falling back' into the '*maternal* entity' (Kristeva 1982: 11), is just as thoroughly prefigured by Walpolean Gothic symbol-making. The spectres of spectres looking back to still other ones in *The Castle of Otranto*, apparently without a solid bottom to be reached, nevertheless pull readers and characters towards uncovering the long-buried secret of Alfonso's past that reveals the true Otranto lineage that exposes Manfred as a usurper like his grandfather. That probing establishes the supposed peasant Theodore, like the young King Arthur, as the true Alfonso heir, and the priest in the tale, Father Jerome, as his father and Alfonso's grandson – but only because they and Alfonso can be linked back to the most hidden part of the whole mystery and the last one revealed: the woman, 'Victoria', whom Alfonso once met and secretly married in Sicily and then abruptly left to continue on to the Crusades, though he did leave her pregnant with the eventual mother of Jerome, of whom Victoria 'was delivered' right about the time 'she heard the fatal rumor of her lord's death' (Walpole 1996: 114). This revelation, conveyed by Jerome, is sketchy at best about Victoria herself and says nothing at all about her daughter, despite the latter being Jerome's own mother. Instead Jerome refers, for final evidence, to 'an authentic writing' he carries (perhaps from Victoria, perhaps not) and to further augmentation by 'Theodore's narrative' (1996: 114–15), leaving the story of the *and his* primal mother mostly buried and entirely in male hands. He thereby repeats the pattern throughout *Otranto* of memorials being texts mostly of older texts, of which the exact origins, already dead – in this case *the* maternal origins in the story – are apparently impossible to determine, even regarded as entombed like the grounds of belief in 'ancient' romance. No wonder Anne Williams has seen Walpole as thereby inaugurating a procession of Gothic fictions in which both men, such as Victor Frankenstein, and their self-representations, such as his creature, deliberately avoid, while still desiring, the primal mother, all by putting forth representations related but not clearly connected to her. In that way, Williams writes, they sublimely intimate yet distance the 'horror', the affect that Kristeva rightly associates 'with the pre-Oedipal separation from the mother [or primal] material [the Real] that both predates and impels the construction of the speaking subject' (Williams 1995: 72–3). In this very crucial realm of the cast-off self-in-the-mother, the most primal heterogeneity that must be abjected for Kristeva, as well as in all the other dimensions discussed above, her theory of abjection, as an articulated scheme, proves to have deep roots in the Gothic ghost of the counterfeit. It is precisely because of that foundation that abjection theory has provided and continues to provide an unusually apt way of interpreting works in the Gothic mode that Horace Walpole both inaugurated and theorised in the eighteenth century.

References

Baudrillard, Jean (1993), *Symbolic Exchange and Death*, trans. Iain Hamilton Grant, London: Sage.

Butler, Marilyn (2012), '*Frankenstein* and Radical Science', *Times Literary Supplement*, 9 April 1993, pp. 12–14; repr. in Mary Shelley, *Frankenstein: The 1818 Text*, 2nd edn, ed. J. Paul Hunter, New York: Norton, pp. 404–16.

Castle, Terry (1987), 'The Spectralization of the Other in *The Mysteries of Udolpho*', in Felicity Nussbaum and Laura Brown (eds), *The New Eighteenth Century: Theory, Politics, English Literature*, London: Methuen, pp. 231–53.

Clery, E. J. (1995), *The Rise of Supernatural Fiction, 1762–1800*, Cambridge: Cambridge University Press.

Clery, E. J., and Robert Miles (eds) (2000), *Gothic Documents: A Sourcebook, 1700–1820*, Manchester: Manchester University Press.

Freud, Sigmund (1949) [1919], 'The Uncanny', in *Collected Papers*, ed. and trans. Joan Riviere, London: Hogarth Press, IV, pp. 368–407.

Frye, Roland Mushat (1984), *The Renaissance Hamlet: Issues and Responses in 1600*, Princeton: Princeton University Press.

Hoeveler, Diane Long (1992), 'The Hidden God and the Abjected Woman in "The Fall of the House of Usher"', *Studies in Short Fiction*, 29: 385–95.

Hogle, Jerrold E. (1997), 'The Ghost of the Counterfeit – and the Closet – in *The Monk*', *Romanticism on the Net*, 8 (November), http://id.erudit.org/iderudit/005770ar (accessed 6 November 2018).

Hogle, Jerrold E. (1998), '*Frankenstein* as Neo-Gothic: From the Ghost of the Counterfeit to the Monster of Abjection', in Tilottama Rajan and Julia Wright (eds), *Romanticism, History, and the Possibilities of Genre*, Cambridge: Cambridge University Press, pp. 176–210.

Hogle, Jerrold E. (2012), 'The Gothic Ghost of the Counterfeit and the Progress of Abjection', in David Punter (ed.), *A New Companion to the Gothic*, Oxford: Wiley-Blackwell, pp. 496–509.

Homans, Margaret (1986), *Bearing the Word: Language and Female Experience in Nineteenth-Century Women's Writing*, Chicago: University of Chicago Press.

Kristeva, Julia (1982) [1980], *Powers of Horror: An Essay on Abjection*, trans. Leon S. Roudiez, New York: Columbia University Press.

Kristeva, Julia (1991) [1988], *Strangers to Ourselves*, trans. Leon S. Roudiez, New York: Columbia University Press.

Locke, John (1979) [1690], *An Essay Concerning Human Understanding*, ed. Peter H. Nidditch, Oxford: Clarendon Press.

Malchow, H. L. (1993), 'Frankenstein's Monster and Images of Race in Nineteenth-Century Britain', *Past and Present*, 139: 90–130.

Mellor, Anne K. (2001), '*Frankenstein*, Racial Science, and the Yellow Peril', *Nineteenth-Century Contexts*, 23: 2–28.

O'Flinn, Paul (1983), 'Production and Reproduction: The Case of *Frankenstein*', *Literature and History*, 9: 194–213.
Shakespeare, William (1974), *The Riverside Shakespeare*, ed. G. Blakemore Evens et al., Boston: Houghton Mifflin.
Shelley, Mary (2012) [1818], *Frankenstein: The 1818 Text*, 2nd edn, ed. J. Paul Hunter, New York: Norton.
Sherwin, Paul (1981), '*Frankenstein:* Creation as Catastrophe', *PMLA*, 96.5: 883–903.
Taylor, Charles (2007), *A Secular Age*, Cambridge, MA: Harvard University Press.
Tucker, Susie I. (1967), *Protean Shape: A Study in Eighteenth-Century Vocabulary*, London: Athlone Press.
Vlasopolos, Anca (1983), '*Frankenstein*'s Hidden Skeleton: The Psycho-Politics of Oppression', *Science Fiction Studies*, 10: 125–36.
Walpole, Horace (1996) [1764], *The Castle of Otranto: A Gothic Story*, ed. W. S. Lewis and E. J. Clery, Oxford: Oxford University Press.
Williams, Anne (1995), *Art of Darkness: A Poetics of Gothic*, Chicago: University of Chicago Press.
Žižek, Slavoj (1989), *The Sublime Object of Ideology*, London: Verso.
Žižek, Slavoj (1991), 'Grimaces of the Real, or When the Phallus Appears', *October*, 58: 44–58.

Part III

Feminism, Gender Theory, Sexuality and the Gothic

Chapter 7

Unsettling Feminism: The Savagery of Gothic
Catherine Spooner

Feminism and the Problem of Gothic

Gothic has always provided both problems and opportunities for feminism. On the one hand, it is a form that, from the later eighteenth century onwards, has been associated predominantly with women writers and readers. As a result, the first generation of feminist critics of the Gothic novel in the 1970s and 1980s found it uniquely suited to expressing women's fears and desires. Nevertheless, there is also much within Gothic fiction that is troubling to feminists, in particular a sado-masochistic dynamic that appears to enjoy the spectacle of violence against women and the reaffirmation of cultural stereotypes projecting women as either victims, monsters or *femmes fatales.*

It is not my business in this chapter to offer a feminist reading of Gothic texts. That has been done exhaustively elsewhere, to the degree that it has arguably become a dominant paradigm of Gothic criticism. Rather, I seek to demonstrate how feminism itself is troubled by the Gothic, a problem it cannot easily resolve, which replays feminism's own grand narrative in uncanny form. Mary Russo argues that, since the 1990s, in an attempt to reassure and avoid alienating the mainstream, feminism 'has stood increasingly for and with the normal' in its 'prescription of correct, conventional, or moralizing behaviour or identity' (Russo 1994: vii). She deploys what she calls the 'female grotesque' to challenge the 'cultural and political disarticulation of feminism from the strange, the risky, the minoritarian, the excessive, the outlawed, and the alien' (Russo 1994: vii). While Gothic and the grotesque are not reducible to one another, they occupy a similar cultural space. Gothic acts as an unsettling force within contemporary feminism, revealing its aporias and rubbing against the grain of political correctness. In doing so, it opens up new spaces for debate and critique and, potentially, for a different kind of feminism. The seeds of this unsettling feminism were sown in Ellen Moers's foundational *Literary Women* (1976): her formulation of the 'female Gothic' offers the potential of what I call 'savage' or 'barbaric' feminisms, feminisms that may unsettle the rational, orderly and proper body of feminism itself.

In Chapter 6 here and elsewhere, Jerrold E. Hogle provides a more detailed account of this process of unsettling in his identification of the way that Gothic enacts what Julia Kristeva in *Powers of Horror* calls 'abjection': the 'throwing off' or 'throwing under' of properties or substances that threaten the integrity of the self. For Hogle, Gothic conventionally identifies the clean and proper self as bourgeois, rational and progressive and allows that self to cast off its horrifying and fascinating others in monstrous form (Kristeva 1982; Hogle 2012). Mainstream feminism is likewise bourgeois, rational and progressive, and Gothic likewise provides a means for the movement to abject its horrifying and fascinating others, thus shoring up its boundaries and its legitimacy as a liberal politics. More than this, however, Gothic is itself one of the others that feminism periodically abjects. Feminism is riven by its attempts to separate itself from the Gothic even as it finds its grand narratives and most productive metaphors within Gothic texts.

Modern feminism is intrinsically bound up with the Enlightenment project: it emerged as one of a range of political voices in the eighteenth century calling for liberty and equality, and its rationale rests on the notion that women should have the same rights extended to them as any other human subject. Feminism, therefore, is inherently humanist and tied to ideologies of reason and progress. If other forms of feminism have emerged, they have done so in response to and in negotiation with these central tenets. As Patricia Waugh points out, 'even if [feminism] draws upon postmodern aesthetic forms of disruption, it cannot repudiate entirely the framework of Enlightened modernity without perhaps fatally undermining itself as an emancipatory politics' (Waugh 1992: 195). Feminism thus finds itself in a double bind: it wants to contest the hierarchies and power structures entailed in the dominant ideologies of the West, but it is at the same time dependent on them for its existence and purpose.

Gothic, too, emerged during the eighteenth century and is similarly attached to the Enlightenment project. As Fred Botting writes, 'the definition of Enlightenment and reason ... requires carefully constructed antitheses, the obscurity of figures of feudal darkness and barbarism providing the negative against which it can assume positive value' (Botting 2014: 3). Crucially, Botting's account suggests that Gothic is *productive*, that only with a dark ground can the light of reason be fully visible. In feminist terms, the Gothic denunciation of the injustices of the past allows the emancipatory principle of feminist discourse to be apprehended and realised. The progress of feminism is premised on a Gothic repudiation of past oppression.

The beginnings of Gothic, then, were entwined with the beginnings of feminism, and feminist criticism has tended to find in Gothic texts a model of its own grand narrative. This grand narrative, in which the female subject flees the house of patriarchy, is inscribed into the foundational texts of Western feminism. Mary Wollstonecraft, author of the ground-breaking *A Vindication of the Rights of Woman* (1792), strikes the key note in her novel *Maria, or The Wrongs of Woman* (1798), when she expands the Gothic prison there to envelop all women, asking 'Was not the world a vast prison, and women born slaves?' (Wollstonecraft 1992: 64). *Maria* describes a middle-class, educated female protagonist who is committed to a lunatic asylum by her husband in an attempt to force her to give up her fortune, whence she contrives to escape with the assistance of her working-class warder, Jemima. The novel relocates the characteristic pattern of imprisonment and escape found in the Gothic novel from a reassuringly distant past to the eighteenth-century present and thus reveals its continuing resonance. Nevertheless, in *Maria*, the fantasy resolution of the female Gothic novel, in which the general threat of patriarchy is particularised into a villain whose tyranny may be thwarted, is unsettled. Wollstonecraft died before she was able to complete the book, and two endings exist, one in which Maria is reunited with her lost daughter and one that is summarised as 'Divorced by her husband – Her lover unfaithful – Pregnancy – Miscarriage – Suicide' (Wollstonecraft 1992: 147).

The Gothic model of incarceration and flight continues to inform feminist writing long after the first phase of the Gothic novel has passed. The language of imprisonment pervades Simone de Beauvoir's *The Second Sex* (1949, trans. 1953), a foundational text of second-wave feminism. Informed by her Existentialist standpoint, de Beauvoir argues that women, like men, must embrace individual liberty and avoid being turned into a thing. She describes her project as asking 'in what kind of universe [woman] is confined, what modes of escape are vouchsafed her'? (de Beauvoir 1997: 31); women's biology, in patriarchal thought, 'imprison[s] her in her subjectivity, circumscribe[s] her within the limits of her own nature' (1997: 15); the term female 'imprisons [woman] in her sex' (1997: 35); most Gothically, women are 'the heirs of a burdensome past, who are striving to build a new future' (1997: 31). The language of imprisonment thus informs de Beauvoir's articulation of women's relationship with their bodies and with political, economic and social systems. Meanwhile, she suggests, women face the ultimate threat of becoming a being-as-object, anticipating another Gothicised grand narrative that emerges in second-wave feminism: the threat of becoming a doll.

These themes are taken up repeatedly in Anglo-American feminism throughout the second half of the twentieth century. If Gothic imagery remains implicit in many of these theoretical works, the emergence of feminist literary criticism in the 1970s brought the underlying connections to visible notice. Sandra Gilbert and Susan Gubar's iconic book *The Madwoman in the Attic* (1979) frames the themes of imprisonment and objectification in explicitly Gothic terms. Indeed, they argue that 'dramatizations of imprisonment and escape are so pervasive in nineteenth-century literature by women that we believe they represent a uniquely female tradition in this period', implying that the entire tradition of women's writing following the emergence of Gothic in the late eighteenth century is intrinsically bound up with the Gothic mode (Gilbert and Gubar 1984: 35). Although theirs is a work of literary criticism, it does not only produce readings of literary texts; it also reads the position of women in patriarchal culture through a series of Gothic metaphors: women's literary tradition is a Gothic tradition because patriarchy enacts a Gothic narrative. Their monumental study addresses a very wide range of texts and authors, but in Charlotte Brontë's *Jane Eyre* (1847) they find an archetypal model:

> Her story, providing a pattern for countless others, is . . . a story of enclosure and escape, a distinctively female *Bildungsroman* in which the problems encountered by the protagonist as she struggles from the imprisonment of her childhood toward an almost unthinkable goal of mature freedom are symptomatic of difficulties Everywoman in a patriarchal society must meet and overcome. (Gilbert and Gubar 1984: 339)

Famously, they read Jane's employer's mad wife, Bertha Rochester, as a dark double to the heroine, a projection of her violent rage. They present this doubling as a metaphor for the plight of the woman writer in patriarchal culture, whose repressed rage can only be expressed in the margins of the narrative.

A Gothic model of feminism in which rebellion is staged through flight is a potentially problematic one, however, in that it stages what has come to be known as 'victim feminism'. At its most basic, it is a version of the 'good girl' story identified by Angela Carter in the Marquis de Sade's *Justine* (1791). Justine, whom Carter designates 'woman as ... escape artist', adheres dogmatically to the position of passive virtue inculcated by late eighteenth-century Western culture; she does not, however, achieve a happy ending: her virtue is rewarded by repeated rape and abuse (Carter 1979: 56). As Carter states, 'The piety, the gentleness, the honesty, the sensitivity, all the qualities she has learned to admire in herself, are invitations to violence; all her life, she has been groomed for the slaughterhouse' (1979: 55). Carter contrasts Justine with her sister, Juliette, who takes on the role of victimiser and revels in her potential for sexual pleasure and cruelty. She does not present Juliette as a model for women, but argues that, in her de-sacralisation of the female body and repudiation of its reproductive function, she helps tear down the patriarchal constructs that have enabled women's oppression.

Similarly, in *Gothic Feminism* (1998), Diane Long Hoeveler identifies what she calls Gothic feminism as 'a version of "victim feminism," an ideology of female power through pretended and staged weakness' (Hoeveler 1998: 7). She traces how the characteristic heroine of eighteenth- and nineteenth-century Gothic novels positions herself 'as the deserving and innocent victim of oppression, malice, and fraud', thus enabling her to use her suffering as a kind of currency for which she can barter financial support and emotional security (Hoeveler 1998: 18). Like Gilbert and Gubar, Hoeveler sees this model functioning not only as a strategy within the texts, but also as a strategy for their female authors, through which they could negotiate their status within a male-dominated literary marketplace. By inventing 'her own peculiar form of feminism ... mixing one part hyperbolic melodrama with one part Christian sentimentalism', the Gothic feminist propagated the fantasy that women's 'socially and economically weak positions could actually be the basis of their strength' (Hoeveler 1998: 19).

Hoeveler identifies a feminism that is to a certain degree unsettling in that, to a modern reader, it is too complacent in its acceptance of patriarchy as the status quo and in the way it revalues the conventionally feminine rather than challenging gender binaries. For Hoeveler, eighteenth- and nineteenth-century Gothic writing by women protests by way of a passive aggression that is a long way from the 'hunger, rebellion, and rage' that Gilbert and Gubar identify in *Jane Eyre* (Gilbert and Gubar 1984: 338). Moreover, this is a distinctively white, middle-class and disembodied kind of feminism, ideologically motivated by the 'dream of riding above the corrupt body, the dream of becoming masculinized – all mind, all reason' (Hoeveler 1998: 245).

In Gothic feminism as Hoeveler presents it, therefore, there are a number of cultural others that are uncomfortably elided. We are thus reminded of Wollstonecraft's comparison of women to slaves, a statement that resonates problematically through second-wave feminism. Eighteenth-century discussions of slavery ranged from ancient times to white slavery in Russia and elsewhere and were not confined to the slavery of black Africans. However, its appropriation as a metaphor by white feminists is a source of anger for many black women. bell hooks points out that

> Theoretically, the white woman's legal status under the patriarchy may have been that of 'property', but she was in no way subjected to the dehumanization and brutal oppression that was the lot of the slave. When white reformers made synonymous the impact of sexism on their lives, they were not revealing an awareness or sensitivity to the slave's lot; they were simply appropriating the horror of the slave experience to enhance their own cause. (hooks 1981: 126)

In 1790, as the first phase of the Gothic novel approached its peak, there were an estimated 480,000 black slaves in the British colonies and 700,000 in the United States. Toni Morrison, citing Orlando Patterson, argues that slavery was an essential precondition to the emergence of the Enlightenment: 'The concept of freedom did not emerge in a vacuum. Nothing highlighted freedom – if it did not in fact create it – like slavery' (Morrison 1992: 38). The white heroine is knowingly or unknowingly complicit in this system: behind her flight lies the erasure of a black body. Again, *Jane Eyre* provides the critical paradigm: for Gayatri Spivak, it is the history of colonialism and not Jane's anger that forms the suppressed material of the text. For Spivak, Jane's narrative of personal development is a form of Western imperialist individualism that allows Jane to achieve a sense of self only at the expense of the colonial subject Bertha's oppression. Jane's narrative of self-discovery is therefore co-extensive with the narrative of imperial domination. As Spivak puts it, Bertha must 'set fire to the house and kill herself, so that Jane Eyre can become the feminist individualist heroine of British fiction' (Spivak 1985: 251).

The Gothic heroine remains a potent figure in contemporary feminist discourse, but, as her contradictions have become more apparent, feminists have increasingly looked elsewhere for a model of opposition to patriarchal hegemony. In particular, they have sought a model that addresses the condition of embodiment without returning women to patriarchal definitions of femininity as associated only with the body. Gothic fiction has obliged with another grand narrative, in the form of Mary Shelley's *Frankenstein* (1818) and the figure of the monster.

Revisionary Monsters

The term 'female Gothic' has become predominantly associated with the narrative of the imperilled heroine fleeing a male persecutor through an imprisoning space that takes the place, in more or less symbolic fashion, of the domestic environment. However, the book that first introduced the term, Ellen Moers's *Literary Women* (1976), presents a rather more diverse range of narratives under the title of 'female Gothic' and repays revisiting. The most celebrated passage is that in which Moers describes Mary Shelley's *Frankenstein* (1818) as 'a horror story of maternity' (Moers 1986: 95). As the twentieth and twenty-first centuries have worn on, Shelley's 'hideous progeny' has become as significant as the heroine in flight as a model for the Gothic (Shelley 1968: 264). While the theme of monstrous maternity on Frankenstein's part is never far from these tales, it is the creature itself that increasingly becomes the central focus.

Moers argues that '"Freaks" is a better word than monsters for the creations of the modern female Gothic' (Moers 1986: 108). She perversely appropriates the phrase that T. S. Eliot hoped would *not* be applied to Djuna Barnes's *Nightwood* (1936), 'a horrid sideshow of freaks', and reclaims it as a positive expression of the ways in which female writers and artists including Barnes, Isak Dinesen, Carson McCullers, Diane Arbus and Sylvia Plath have given '*visual* form to the fear of self' (Moers 1986: 107–8). The psychoanalytic reading of the freak as an image of the suppressed self – popularised by Leslie Fiedler's *Freaks: Myths and Images of the Secret Self* (1978) – has now largely been discarded in light of the emergence of disability studies in the 1990s and its emphasis on the social construction of disability. Nevertheless, a preoccupation with monstrous embodiment and the 'freak' body outside of societal norms continues to inform contemporary Gothic writing and, in particular, Gothic feminism. In the 1990s and beyond, a new generation of feminists appropriated and extended Gothic metaphors in a form of feminism that is most often labelled 'posthumanist', but which has its roots in the challenge to the unitary human subject mounted by the Gothic.

In an essay first published in 1993 and reprinted in *Nomadic Subjects*, Rosi Braidotti argues that women and the monstrous have always been allied in Western culture. The tradition of Enlightenment science is troubled by hybrids and mixtures, which disrupt logical taxonomy and do not fit the order of things. 'Monsters', Braidotti claims, 'represent the in between, the mixed, the ambivalent as implied in the ancient Greek root of the word *monsters*, *teras*, which means both horrible and wonderful, object of aberration and adoration' (Braidotti 2011: 216). Likewise, the 'morphologically dubious' female body 'is troublesome in the eyes of the logocentric economy' (Braidotti 2011: 226). Women's bodies change shape in pregnancy and childbirth and, as such, have been constructed as different and threatening by the patriarchal order, which is reified through scientific and medical enquiry. For Braidotti, monsters and women are aligned in that their difference is perceived negatively, although, as she points out, this perception is not inevitable; the response to difference could be wonder rather than horror.

The Gothic archetype of posthumanism is Frankenstein's creature, a marvellous body who in his monstrous birth, hybrid form, superhuman capabilities and studied socialisation shows the limits of the human. The creature, and sometimes his abortive bride, has become a potent metaphor for feminist posthumanism. Spivak identifies the potency of the novel as lying in its refusal to 'speak the language of feminist individualism which we have come to hail as the language of high feminism within English literature' (Spivak 1985: 254). This potential is realised in Donna Haraway's 1985 essay 'The Cyborg Manifesto', which deploys the concept of the artificially created being in order to construct a new feminist myth, one that in its inherent piecemeal nature refuses the totalising discourses of phallocentrism. Haraway's cyborg, 'a hybrid of machine and organism, a creature of social reality as well as a creature of fiction', straddles numerous binary oppositions, embracing 'contradictions that do not resolve into larger wholes' (Haraway 1991: 149). Its hybridity gives it both its monstrous qualities and its critical purchase on existing systems of power. Reflecting more widely on the cultural construction of monstrosity, Jeffrey Jerome Cohen writes,

> The monster always escapes because it refuses easy categorization . . . This refusal to participate in the classificatory 'order of things' is true of monsters generally: they are disturbing hybrids whose externally incoherent bodies resist attempts to include them in any systematic structuration. And so the monster is dangerous, a form suspended between forms that threatens to smash distinctions. (Cohen 1996: 6)

Where Cohen invests the monstrous with inherently deconstructive properties, Haraway distinguishes between real-life cyborgs, the product of the military-industrial complex, and the cyborg as 'ironic political myth' (Haraway 1991: 149). For Haraway, the cyborg is a 'rhetorical strategy and . . . political method' and thus a form of disruptive praxis rather than ontology (1991: 149).

True to her principle of feminist 'blasphemy' (1991: 149), Haraway both invokes and dismisses *Frankenstein* (and its most significant intertext, *Paradise Lost*) in her text, stating,

> Unlike the hopes of Frankenstein's monster, the cyborg does not expect its father to save it through a restoration of the garden; i.e., through the fabrication of a heterosexual mate, through its completion in a finished whole, a city and cosmos. The cyborg does not dream of community on the model of the organic family, this time without the Oedipal project. The cyborg would not recognize the Garden of Eden. (1991: 151)

For Haraway, the potential of the artificial being lies in the fact that it was made, not born, and therefore possesses the ability to evade the Oedipal maturation narrative and heterosexual family structures that pervade Western culture. She considers, however, that Shelley's myth-making does not go far enough; it is too invested in patriarchal and Christian structures to be truly liberating. This is a problem for her cyborg too, which is 'the illegitimate offspring of militarism and patriarchal capitalism' (1991: 151). However, as Chris Baldick points out in *In Frankenstein's Shadow*, 'long before the monster of Frankenstein, monstrosity already implied rebellion, or an unexpected turning against one's parent or benefactor' (Baldick 1987: 13). Haraway echoes this pattern when she suggests that the cyborg, like other 'illegitimate offspring', is 'often exceedingly unfaithful to [its] origins' (Haraway 1991: 151). What the creature provides as a model for the cyborg is not only its hybridity but also its irreverence to existing systems of power. It is no accident that in late twentieth- and early twenty-first-century Gothic, from Alisdair Gray's celebrated novel *Poor Things* (1992) to Shelley Jackson's hypertext fiction *Patchwork Girl* (1995) and the television series *Penny Dreadful* (2014–16), it is the female creature who becomes invested with the politics of resistance and disruption of heteronormative patriarchy. The female creature, whose capacity for resistance so frightens Frankenstein in Shelley's novel that he cannot bring himself to complete her, can be imagined but is not realised by the novel; she remains outside normative discourse. Frankenstein describes the 'unparalleled barbarity' of such a creature and his fear that 'she might become ten thousand times more malignant than her mate' and 'might refuse to comply with a compact made before her creation' (Shelley 1968: 435). The female creature's existence outside of and beyond a social compact drawn up between men is what terrifies Frankenstein but has inspired subsequent feminists.

The revisionary freaks and monsters of late twentieth-century feminism are suggestive, but they run the risk of idealising or fetishising the disabled body they seek to reclaim. Work within twenty-first-century disability studies emphasises the particularity of the disabled body, its embodiment and its social construction. The conflation of the female body with the monster runs similar risks to the conflation of women and slaves; it collapses specific kinds of otherness and ignores the intersectionality of distinctive kinds of oppression. In both these cases, the imbrication of feminism with the Enlightenment project creates an aporia, whereby the desire for subjective autonomy, on the one hand, and corporeal integrity, on the other, come into contradiction with the exclusions these concepts entail. The monster, no less than the heroine, is an uncomfortable figure for many feminists, who regard it as irretrievably shaped by misogyny and ablism. While Haraway's 'illegitimate' cyborg goes some way towards challenging these ideologies and developing a new feminist language, or what Haraway calls a 'powerful infidel heteroglossia', its utopian dreams have foundered in the gendered realities of the twenty-first-century tech industry (Haraway 1991: 181). There is one more narrative that Gothic offers feminism, however, and that is the story of the wild girl, or what I am calling, with a nod to Haraway's invocation of the infidel, 'barbaric feminism'.

Towards a Barbaric Feminism

In a less frequently discussed passage in *Literary Women*, Moers draws attention to Catherine Earnshaw's exclamation in Emily Brontë's *Wuthering Heights* (1847) that 'I wish I were a girl again, half savage and hardy, and free . . . and laughing at injuries, not maddening under them' (Brontë 2002: 118). For Moers, Catherine's longing for her brutal and tempestuous childhood, and her ghostly reappearance in childhood form, articulates 'the savagery of girlhood' (Moers 1986: 107), another cornerstone of the female Gothic as she conceives it. If female Gothic has, to date, been associated primarily with either the heroine fleeing the dark house or metaphors of monstrosity, Moers's formulation here offers a further possibility.

Moers's evocation of savagery is a suggestive one. To be savage is to be 'fierce, ferocious, cruel, harsh', according to the *Oxford English Dictionary*, but also a 'primitive or uncivilized person'. Inevitably in the nineteenth century the primitive or uncivilised was associated with non-white races, a link given additional resonance in this case by the fact that Catherine's childhood playmate and lover Heathcliff is repeatedly described by Brontë as dark-skinned and even as a 'gypsy' or 'little Lascar' (Brontë 2002: 61). Savagery has a dual resonance; while the term was used negatively to identify otherness, it also carries positive connotations of the 'noble savage', a phrase first adapted from the French notion of *le bon sauvage* or 'the good savage' by John Dryden in *The Conquest of Granada* (1672). In this play, savagery is associated with freedom, "Ere the base Laws of Servitude began,/ When wild in woods the noble Savage ran' (Dryden 1978: I.i.208–9). For eighteenth-century British writers, the noble savage was closely associated with the Germanic tribes described by Tacitus in the first century AD and conflated by them with the Goths. The Goths' notoriety as the tribes that had sacked Rome was revised in the eighteenth century, and they then became associated with what James Beattie identified as a particularly British 'invincible spirit of liberty' that continued to inform national identity and politics (Beattie 2000: 89). For many late eighteenth-century writers, including Coleridge, barbarism became invested with a sublimity and passion that was absent from the harmonious and rational works of ancient Greece and Rome. The position of women in barbarian society, moreover, was held up for particular remark: drawing on Tacitus, Beattie favourably compared the freedom of 'Gothick' women and the mutual respect in which they lived with their partners with conditions 'little better than slavery' in modern Asia, and in ancient Greek and Rome (2000: 89). Although there is an orientalising gaze at work here, and Beattie's commendation of women's role 'as friends and faithful counsellors, and frequently as sacred persons' is not unproblematic to a modern feminist, the association of Gothic with a notional sense of women's liberty is potent nevertheless (2000: 89).

Despite the revaluation of the Goths by Beattie and others, which was instrumental in supporting the Gothic Revival, both the Goths themselves and the Gothic aesthetic named after them retained more conventional connotations of barbarism for most eighteenth- and nineteenth-century readers. To be barbaric is to be 'Uncivilized, uncultured; savage; savagely cruel' (*OED*). As Chris Baldick and Robert Mighall demonstrate, the Gothic novel in the eighteenth and nineteenth centuries was a characteristically Whiggish genre in which a barbaric past is evoked and vicariously enjoyed, only to be suppressed in favour of a more enlightened modernity or its avatars (Baldick and Mighall 2012: 278). The Goths' destruction of Rome provides a conceptual model for a tension between a barbarism that arises to disrupt civilisation, enlightenment and modernity and the need to contain or suppress this threat.

If barbarism was crucial to the meaning of the Gothic as it developed in the eighteenth century, then, that meaning was not always clear-cut. On the one hand, the term Gothic (or Gothick) was often used in a negative sense, meaning that which was rude and undeveloped, opposed to the finer achievements of literature and culture. On the other, Gothic represented a national temperament founded in individual liberty and a society in which women were treated with relative equality. Both of these meanings are compacted in Catherine's 'half savage' girlhood, which represents both freedom and oneness with nature prior to assuming the burdens of adult femininity, and wild, unconstrained, violent passions opposed to and outside the constraints of reason, modernity and enlightenment. The savage femininities offered by the Gothic thus remain open to a feminist reading while also in some senses troubling the feminist project.

The word 'savage' plays a significant part in *Jane Eyre*: it appears eleven times in the novel. Its register is profoundly ambivalent. It first appears when Jane is explaining her childhood belief that the elves 'were all gone out of England to some savage country where the woods were wilder and thicker, and the population more scant' (Brontë 1966: 53). Savagery is here associated with a displaced and inaccessible childhood realm that stands in contrast to Jane's oppressive childhood existence at the Reeds'. In a key passage, Helen Burns tells Jane that only 'Heathens and savage tribes' resist unjust punishment, an ambivalent moment when Christian acquiescence is put into tension with Jane's impassioned rebellion (1966: 90). St John Rivers is also headed to colonial territories as a missionary for 'savage tribes' (1966: 433). The overt message of the text is that savagery must be tamed and the heathen converted, whether through the imperialist project or as part of the disciplining of the self. The savage without or within provides the ground for what Spivak refers to as Christian 'soul making' (Spivak 1985: 247). Nevertheless, savagery is also a vehicle for impassioned protest, and not only from Bertha: Jane is described by the term three times in contrast to two each for Bertha and Rochester. Jane's savagery creates lines of connection between her and Bertha that cannot be neatly contained by the conclusion, indicating their shared oppression and prompting the question: why can these two victims of patriarchy not see each other?

As this discussion of *Jane Eyre* shows, concepts of savagery and barbarism cannot be entirely dissociated from their colonial history, and in that sense they must remain problematic. There is another problem, too, in that both barbarism and girlhood can only be appraised retrospectively, from a position of civilisation/adulthood. Barbarism appears in the Gothic novel as anachronism: as a survival or relic from an outmoded past. The same might be said of girlhood. Karin Lesnik-Oberstein explains: '"Childhood" ... functions as an exponent of the "non-adult" and "non-reason". Childhood can only speak through the memories, observations, or selections and interpretations of adults' (Lesnik-Oberstein 1994: 26). In *Wuthering Heights*, Catherine's girlhood is recalled from an adult present, whether by Catherine herself or by the housekeeper Nelly. Nevertheless, through the recollected savagery of girlhood, *Wuthering Heights* indicates a resistance to the linear narrative of maturation and self-discovery validated in conventional feminist criticism: Catherine longs to be a girl again, and takes that form as a ghost, despite having died as an adult woman in childbirth. Savage girlhood returns to disrupt adult decorum. As such, it exists in precarious tension with the civilised, rational voice of adult feminism. It is not necessarily bound by limitations of age (or indeed biological gender), but it is a subject position that can be temporarily and perhaps ironically inhabited in order to allow the expression of fierce passions, ferocious anger, harsh truths. Barbarism, meanwhile, stands outside and contests Enlightenment values but it is not necessarily antithetical to them; it offers a different route to liberty.

Just as the heroine and the monster provide grand narratives for earlier phases of feminism, the savage girl or barbaric feminist is becoming recognisable in what is sometimes called fourth-wave feminist discourse. The savage girl's modern incarnation has its roots in Riot Grrrl, a subcultural movement of the early 1990s that combined the self-conscious and politicised imagery of girlhood with DIY activism. At the same time, female musicians such as Kat Bjelland of Babes in Toyland and Courtney Love of Hole drew on similar imagery in a Gothicised register. Twenty-first-century feminist social media activism is less invested in girlhood imagery, but its prioritisation of anger over social decorum suggestively enacts the barbaric overthrow of 'civilised' values. In a piece responding to Katie Roiphe's call for a more measured response to sexual harassment claims in the wake of the Harvey Weinstein scandal and the #MeToo movement of the 2010s, journalist Jane Gilmore argues,

> Roiphe wants us to take the anger out of women's rejection of sexual harassment, she wants us to be calm and reasoned ... Powerlessness and rage, suppressed for too long, is not reasoned when it finally surfaces. Nor should it be ... The power of anger, collectively harnessed anger, is required to force change. (Gilmore 2018)

Social media feminists as Gilmore describes them are the new Goths, rising up to overthrow Rome.

A passionate outpouring of rage also informs a new wave of female-written and/or directed horror films including *Ginger Snaps* (2000), *Jennifer's Body* (2009), *The Moth Diaries* (2011) and *American Mary* (2012), some of which also exploit more familiar metaphors of monstrosity. In *American Mary*, for example, the heroine is a medical student who turns to illicit surgery to support herself and enacts her revenge on a rapist professor by mutilating and torturing him; in *Jennifer's Body* a cheerleader turns into a succubus who consumes her male victims. It is hard to read either of these as conventional feminist fables, as neither torture nor eating your date can be endorsed within the liberal humanist framework of contemporary feminism. Moreover, the excessive rage expressed by the protagonists of these films cannot be sustained and is ultimately contained by the narrative, usually through their deaths. Nevertheless, these films challenge the tyranny of the normal; their barbaric feminism enables risky, complex, provocative meditations on the double standards women face in contemporary culture.

While the savagery of girlhood plays out in these popular cultural narratives in fairly loose and imprecise ways, it is given more complex expression in contemporary fiction. Helen Oyeyemi's novel *White is for Witching* (2009) provides a particularly rich example. As Alison Rudd points out in Chapter 4 of this volume, Oyeyemi is a Black British writer born in Nigeria and brought up in the United Kingdom. *White is for Witching*, her third novel, is a perplexing, poetic, highly intertextual narrative. It is set in 29 Barton Road, a guesthouse in Dover, where the famous white cliffs provide an omnipresent symbol of Britain's borders. The central character is Miranda Silver, a white teenage girl suffering from 'pica', an eating disorder that prompts her to eat inedible substances such as chalk and plastic. The novel's preoccupation with what is and is not food, alongside a topical concern with national borders and immigration, inevitably invites a reading of the novel drawing on Kristeva's theory of abjection (see Chapter 6 here). However, the novel consistently invokes abjection only to refuse or turn away from it, and does so through what I am calling a barbaric register.

In many ways, Oyeyemi's novel is a meditation on *Jane Eyre* and its 1966 rewriting by Jean Rhys, *Wide Sargasso Sea*. Miranda may or may not have been taken over by a soucouyant, a vampire-like creature from Caribbean folklore. This occupied state links her directly with Brontë's Bertha, described by Jane as a vampire, and Rhys's Antoinette, compared to a 'soucriant' (Rhys 1999: 70). Miranda, however, is not the marginalised colonial subject but the privileged, middle-class white girl; her eventual disappearance leaves a vacuum at the centre of the text that cannot be filled by Spivak's 'feminist individualist heroine of British fiction', for she is that heroine (Spivak 1985: 251). Instead, the book reveals the savagery at the heart of the white female subject.

Oyeyemi's novel eschews temporal linearity both in plot and structure: the novel begins with its own end, and is replete with hauntings, doublings and repetitions of different kinds. As Helen Cousins shows, Oyeyemi incorporates elements of folklore from her Yoruba heritage into her Gothic schema; Miranda's female ancestors inhabit her house and intervene in her daily life (Cousins 2012). Among these, Miranda's great-grandmother, Anna Good, appears as Britannia on a television show as a child and represents the force of British imperialism in the text: her racism is an attempt to shore up whiteness and by extension the borders of Britain. However, the house at 29 Barton Road tells Anna, 'there was another woman, long before you, but related' (Oyeyemi 2010: 24). This woman is a savage, barbarous ancestor who self-cannibalises her body and is 'thought an animal'; her anachronistic incursion into the narrative provides a precedent and a mythology for Miranda's present-day eating disorder (2010: 24). In contrast to Anna, the woman refuses abjection, for rather than expelling bodily substances to shore up the boundaries of her body, she consumes bodily substances to erode the boundaries of her body. In her frenzy, she insists on her own embodiment even as she attempts to destroy it. In a similar move, Miranda eats chalk, associated in the novel with the white cliffs of Dover, consuming her own whiteness even as she symbolically erodes the borders of Britishness that her great-grandmother fought so hard to shore up. Like the savage woman, her self-immolation at the end of the novel is a paradoxical form of agency: 'She chose this', her girlfriend Ore insists, 'as the only way to fight the soucouyant' (2010: 1). Nevertheless, the recursive structure of the novel implies that snow-white Miranda, buried (like the fairy-tale Snow White) with a slice of apple in her throat, may awaken and return and the story begin again. A conclusion in which progress and reason are triumphant is denied.

White is for Witching's barbaric feminism is troubled and troubling: it disrupts innumerable racist and misogynist paradigms, including that of the clean and proper, white, bourgeois, female subject, but provides no clear feminist message. Trouble, therefore, may be an end in itself, as Donna Haraway writes in her 2016 book, *Staying With the Trouble*:

> In urgent times, many of us are tempted to address trouble in terms of making an imagined future safe, of stopping something from happening that looms in the future, of clearing away the present and the past in order to make futures for coming generations. Staying with the trouble does not require such a relationship to times called the future. (Haraway 2016: 1)

Barbaric feminism, as I am proposing it, can be said to stay with the trouble; it disrupts the dream of progress towards an imagined safe future with its temporal discontinuities and returns. It does not clarify, rationalise or sanitise; it is risky, difficult and it does not aim to please. Rather, it offers an arrested space, in which the savagery of girlhood plays out, an unsettled and unsettling – and distinctly Gothic – feminism.

References

Baldick, Chris (1987), *In Frankenstein's Shadow: Myth, Monstrosity and Nineteenth-Century Writing*, Oxford: Oxford University Press.
Baldick, Chris, and Robert Mighall (2012), 'Gothic Criticism', in David Punter (ed.), *A New Companion to the Gothic*, Oxford: Wiley-Blackwell, pp. 267–87.
Beattie, James (2000) [1783], 'On Fable and Romance', in E. J. Clery and Robert Miles (eds), *Gothic Documents: A Sourcebook 1700–1820*, Manchester: Manchester University Press, pp. 88–92.
Botting, Fred (2014), *Gothic*, 2nd edn, London: Routledge.
Braidotti, Rosi (2011), *Nomadic Subjects: Embodiment and Sexual Difference in Contemporary Feminist Theory*, 2nd edn, New York: Columbia University Press.
Brontë, Charlotte (1966) [1847], *Jane Eyre*, ed. Q. D. Leavis, Harmondsworth: Penguin.
Brontë, Emily (2002) [1847], *Wuthering Heights*, ed. Diane Long Hoeveler, Boston: Houghton Mifflin.
Carter, Angela (1979), *The Sadeian Woman: An Exercise in Cultural History*, London: Virago.
Cohen, Jeffrey Jerome (1996), 'Monster Culture (Seven Theses)', in Jeffrey Jerome Cohen (ed.), *Monster Theory: Reading Culture*, Minneapolis: University of Minnesota Press, pp. 3–25.

Cousins, Helen (2012), 'Helen Oyeyemi and the Yoruba Gothic: *White is for Witching*', *The Journal of Commonwealth Literature*, 47.1: 47–58.
de Beauvoir, Simone (1997) [1949, trans. 1953], *The Second Sex*, trans. H. M. Parshley, London: Vintage.
Dryden, John (1978), *The Works of John Dryden, Vol. XI, Plays: The Conquest of Granada, Marriage a-la-Mode, The Assignation*, ed. John Loftis and David Stuart Rhodes, Berkeley: University of California Press.
Fiedler, Leslie A. (1978), *Freaks: Myths and Images of the Secret Self*, New York: Doubleday.
Gilbert, Sandra, and Susan Gubar (1984) [1979], *The Madwoman in the Attic: The Woman Writer and the Nineteenth-Century Imagination*, New Haven, CT: Yale University Press.
Gilmore, Jane (2018), 'Has Social Media Ruined Feminism?', *Sydney Morning Herald*, 7 February, https://www.smh.com.au/lifestyle/has-social-media-ruined-feminism-20180207-h0v6zl.html (accessed 27 February 2018).
Haraway, Donna (1991), *Simians, Cyborgs and Women: The Reinvention of Nature*, London: Free Association Books.
Haraway, Donna (2016), *Staying With the Trouble: Making Kin in the Chthulucene*, Durham, NC: Duke University Press.
Hoeveler, Diane Long (1998), *Gothic Feminism: The Professionalization of Gender from Charlotte Smith to the Brontës*, University Park: Pennsylvania State University Press.
Hogle, Jerrold E. (2012), 'The Ghost of the Counterfeit and the Progress of Abjection', in David Punter (ed.), *A New Companion to the Gothic*, Oxford: Wiley-Blackwell, pp. 496–509.
hooks, bell (1981), *Ain't I a Woman: Black Women and Feminism*, Boston, MA: South End.
Kristeva, Julia (1982) [1980], *Powers of Horror: An Essay on Abjection*, trans. Leon S. Roudiez, New York: Columbia University Press.
Lesnik-Oberstein, Karin (1994), *Children's Literature: Criticism and the Fictional Child*, Oxford: Oxford University Press.
Moers, Ellen (1986) [1976], *Literary Women*, London: The Women's Press.
Morrison, Toni (1992), *Playing in the Dark: Whiteness and the Literary Imagination*, London: Picador.
Oyeyemi, Helen (2010) [2009], *White is for Witching*, London: Picador.
Rhys, Jean (1999) [1966], *Wide Sargasso Sea*, ed. Judith L. Raiskin, New York: Norton.
Russo, Mary (1994), *The Female Grotesque: Risk, Excess and Modernity*, London: Routledge.
Shelley, Mary (1968) [1818/1832], *Frankenstein*, in Peter Fairclough (ed.), *Three Gothic Novels*, Harmondsworth: Penguin, pp. 257–497.
Spivak, Gayatri Chakravorty (1985), 'Three Women's Texts and a Critique of Imperialism', *Critical Inquiry*, 12.1: 243–61.

Waugh, Patricia (1992), 'Modernism, Postmodernism, Feminism: Gender and Autonomy Theory', in Patricia Waugh (ed.), *Postmodernism: A Reader*, London: Edward Arnold, pp. 189–204.

Wollstonecraft, Mary (1992) [1798], *Maria*, in Mary Wollstonecraft and Mary Shelley, *Mary/Maria/Matilda*, ed. Janet Todd, Harmondsworth: Penguin, pp. 55–148.

Chapter 8

Gothic Fiction and Queer Theory
George E. Haggerty

After Horace Walpole published *The Castle of Otranto* (1764), he wrote to his antiquarian friend the Reverend William Cole in order to explain how his imagination gave rise to such an eccentric work:

> Your partiality to me and Strawberry have I hope inclined you to excuse the wildness of the story ... Shall I even confess to you what was the origin of this romance? I waked one morning in the beginning of last June from a dream, of which all I could recover was, that I had thought myself in an ancient castle (a very natural dream for a head filled like mine with Gothic story) and that on the uppermost banister of a great staircase I saw a gigantic hand in armour. In the evening I sat down and began to write without knowing in the least what I intended to say or relate. The work grew on my hands, and I grew fond of it – add that I was very glad to think of anything rather than politics – In short I was so engrossed with my tale, which I completed in less than two months, that one evening I wrote from the time I had drunk my tea, about six o'clock, till half an hour after one in the morning, when my hand and fingers were so weary, that I could not hold the pen to finish the sentence, but left Matilda and Isabella talking, in the middle of a paragraph. You will laugh at my earnestness, but if I have amused you by retracing with any fidelity the manners of ancient days, I am content, and give you leave to think me as idle as you please. (Walpole 1937–81: I, 88, 9 March 1765)

The 'Strawberry' that Walpole mentions in the first paragraph is Strawberry Hill, his home in Twickenham, which he had reconstructed as a mini-Gothic castle. This letter has been discussed in a variety of ways in order to help explain the origin of the Gothic novel. For the purposes of this chapter, though, it is also the origin of queer theory about the text. Horace Walpole, a lifelong bachelor, takes us directly into his dreams in order to explain the 'wildness of his story'. But what does this specific dream explain?

Walpole was an inveterate collector, especially of material left over from the Middle Ages, which he used to decorate his Gothic villa and to turn it into something of a mini-masterpiece of its kind. He could not collect this material without imagining a past world in which to place it, and that is what he means when he tells Cole that his head was 'filled with Gothic story'. His head is so filled with Gothic story, he says, that he readily 'thought myself in an ancient castle' when he dreamt. Walpole had such a staircase at Strawberry Hill, or a least a miniature version of one, and it is fair to imagine that the ancient castle he dreamt about was his own. 'A gigantic hand in armour', though, is harder to place. Gothic statues and suits of armour were large but not usually gigantic, and it is this size that first alerts us to the strangeness of this dream. Queer theory, with a nod to psychoanalytic theory, can offer the notion of the fetish to help us explain this image: we might say that this gigantic hand is detached from some supernatural, gigantic body as a protection against the implicit fear of castration, the cutting-off of an appendage, that this dream implies. This is how a fetish works: it serves as a protection against a larger threat. The fear of powerlessness before the unknown is lessened because of the presence of this giant hand. Yet it is almost as if this image 'hands' Walpole the power to write the 'romance': it invites him to engage with all the private hopes and desires that consumed him as he collected and constructed his Gothic abode.

Early critics of the Gothic were not hesitant to turn such implications into lurid anathemas. Although Thomas Babington Macaulay may have been talking about Walpole himself and his letters, rather than his novel, he nevertheless includes it all in this phobic response:

> The faults of Horace Walpole's head and heart are indeed sufficiently glaring. His writings, it is true, rank as high among the delicacies of intellectual epicures as the Strasburgh pies among the dishes described in the *Almanack des Gourmands*. But, as the *pâté-de-fois-gras* owes its excellence to the diseases of the wretched animal which furnishes it, and would be good for nothing if it were not made of livers preternaturally swollen, so none but an unhealthy and disorganized mind could have produced such literary luxuries as the works of Walpole. (Macaulay 1987: 312)

Macaulay uses his image of *fois-gras* to suggest an unhealthy and disorganised mind. What Macaulay calls 'literary luxuries' is a code for what would later be called decadence: a diseased form of expression that suggests sexual as well as social transgression.

Walpole's dream thus allows us to probe the 'queer' inner reaches of his psyche for the source of Gothic fiction. An avid collector is threatened by his own collection and is in a state of anxiety concerning his place in the world. Queer theory does not need much more to go on, especially not when Walpole's own sexuality is always a question mark (see Haggerty 1999: 152–74). This dream invites us to think more about how and why Gothic impulses are connected to the secrecies of private desire that are well outside public norms, which makes them very like queer theory itself, which is concerned, not only with so-called homosexuality, but with the wide range of *all* non-normative sexualities. Therefore, you might say that Walpole is the first Queer Gothic theorist and that he offers us the very terms by which to interpret his work.

Another Gothic writer who offers a dream to explain the origins of a Gothic romance is, of course, Mary Shelley. In the preface to the 1831 edition of her *Frankenstein*, she tells the now-familiar story of a rainy 1816 summer which she and her husband-to-be, Percy Shelley, spent with Lord Byron and others. Byron proposed that they all come up with a ghost story in order to amuse each other. Mary thought and thought and had many conversations with her friends, especially about experimental inquiries into the origins of life and the hope that electricity might give life to inanimate objects. Then:

> When I placed my head on my pillow, I did not sleep, nor could I be said to think. My imagination, unbidden, possessed and guided me, gifting the successive images that arose in my mind with a vividness far beyond the usual bounds of reverie. I saw – with shut eyes, but accurate mental vision, – I saw the pale student of unhallowed arts kneeling beside the thing he had put together. I saw the hideous phantasm of a man stretched out, and then, on the working of some powerful engine, show signs of life, and stir with an uneasy, half vital motion. Frightful must it be; for supremely frightful would be the effect of any human endeavor to mock the stupendous mechanism of the Creator of the world. His success would terrify the artist; he would rush away from his odious handiwork, horror-stricken. He would hope that, left to itself, the slight spark of life which he had communicated would fade; that this thing, which had received such imperfect animation, would subside into dead matter, and he might sleep in the belief that the silence of the grave would quench for ever the transient existence of the hideous corpse which he had looked upon as the cradle of life. He sleeps, but he is awakened; he opens his eyes; behold the horrid thing stands at his bedside, opening his curtains, looking on him with yellow, watery, but speculative eyes.
>
> I opened mine in terror. The ideas so possessed my mind, that a thrill of fear ran through me, and I wished to exchange the ghastly image of my fancy for the realities around. (Shelley 1980: 9)

This dream, like Horace Walpole's, offers us a story of origins while at the same time suggesting the very terms for understanding it. In this case, discussions about scientific discoveries and electricity have encouraged these night-time images. But Mary Shelley takes us into her bedroom, even into her very bed, which becomes Victor Frankenstein's in the novel (1980: 57–8): for, as she builds to the climax of the description, the hideous creation, driven by 'some powerful *engine*', is looking 'with yellow, watery but speculative eyes' into her own. Feminist and psychoanalytic critics have made much of this, and the essays about 'Mary Shelley's Hideous Progeny' – placing her at the very centre of this horror – are legion. Queer theory would go just one step further to say that this secret personal horror is a cultural horror as well. This isolated figure tormented by the monster he has created, this identification with a transgressive act (the genesis of a child without conventional sexual intercourse), the impossibility of hiding or hiding from such a monstrosity – and ultimately in the bedroom: this whole configuration could be called queer. When this queerness is so vividly associated with death and the drive towards death in the making of a creature from corpses, it might call to mind the situation that Lee Edelman describes in *No Future*. Edelman's 'queer' embraces the death drive because he needs to resist the overwhelming cultural force of reproductive futurism, seeing as he is engaged in some form of sexually non-reproductive activity in the present; being true to ourselves, that is, means accepting the symptom that reveals the basic flaw of this future-obsessed cultural moment. Rather than ignoring death, Edelman's queer confronts death and what it tells us about our lives. This moment of confrontation in Shelley's dream suggests that the stakes are exactly this high. Shelley is confronting life with death, and she does so by means of the trope of the 'pale student of unhallowed arts', alone in his study, turning his ideas into a monstrous creation. Grant F. Scott makes much of the visual impact of the bedroom scene, then others, in Shelley's novel to show how they all suggest queerness, in his 2007 essay 'Victor's Secret'.

These two Gothic dreams take us a long way into the complicity between Gothic fiction and queer theory from the former's very beginnings. These evocative dream-worlds make it only too easy to delve into the boundary-blurring inner workings of subjectivity. However, Gothic fiction generates queer theory in other ways as well. If we return to *The Castle of Otranto*, we discover another familiar and extraordinarily generative trope. One of the heroines, Isabella, is fleeing the villain Manfred, who, in order to press his suit on her – he wants to marry her to sire an heir because her fiancé, his son Conrad, has died – follows her into the labyrinthine caverns underneath the castle. The passage that results has rightly been called the first Gothic moment of erotic fear:

> The lower part of the castle was hollowed into several intricate cloisters; and it was not easy for one under so much anxiety to find the door that opened into the cavern. An awful silence reigned throughout those subterraneous regions, except now and then some blasts of wind that shook the doors she had passed, and which grating on the rusty hinges were re-echoed through that long labyrinth of darkness. (Walpole 1982: 25)

Walpole establishes this image of the victimised female – very much the object of sexual victimisation – as a central Gothic trope. In a single image, he combines the sexual anxiety of a victimised female, the incestuous desire of a libidinous male (since Manfred demands sex from his own son's betrothed), the use of the actual physical features of the castle to represent political and sexual entrapment, and an atmosphere deftly rendered to produce terror and gloom (Walpole 1982: 22).

Walpole's subterranean regions are easily internalised: they could represent the internal workings of desire and fear before the Walt Disney Company made the images of that world so cosy and familiar in its animated *Inside Out* (2015). Through these externalised, psychological tropes, Walpole does not so much invite as he initiates a queerly theoretical investigation of his material. The innocent woman is pursued for incestuous purposes, for no other reason than her availability and her assumed capacity for producing an heir. She is always already sexualised, always already pursued as a tool for continuing patriarchal dominance, simply by her incipient presence in the family. This image of ready-made victimisation is available in the culture from which it springs – and not just eighteenth-century masculinist culture but Western culture itself is implicated in Manfred's pursuit. If queer theory pushes against the regulated sexual agendas labelled as 'normativity' by exposing this oppressive system as it traps and 'undergrounds' anyone inclined to evade it, then Horace Walpole is the Gothic novelist who first shows that push-back in operation.

If Walpole could set out a trope that would serve Gothic novelists well – the erotic victimisation of a powerless but resourceful female and anyone else who resists 'normative' sexual pressures – then Ann Radcliffe manages to transform that trope into a sophisticated device that accomplishes all that Walpole's image achieves and more. Offering her own commentary on female victimisation in such novels as *The Mysteries of Udolpho* (1794) and *The Italian* (1797), Radcliffe offers a cultural critique that queer theorists can embrace. In a typical Radcliffe novel, the hero, though devoted to the heroine, proves utterly worthless and debilitated, not in moral but in narrative terms. Her heroes are never where the heroine needs them to be, and when they do appear they lead the heroines into deeper danger. They are, moreover, usually wounded or detained in ways that are beyond their control. This marginalisation leaves Radcliffe's heroines to struggle against their Gothic villains on their own in a stance that places them both inside *and outside* the 'normal' positioning of sexualised women.

In *The Mysteries of Udolpho* specifically, Emily St Aubert becomes the victim of the aloof and threatening Montoni, who has locked Emily and her aunt away in his castle in the Apennines. Emily is fearful for herself and for her aunt, and when she suspects that her aunt has died, whether by natural or unnatural causes she is not sure, Emily is left on her own. This is where Radcliffe wants Emily, because through her the novelist can experiment with her theories of the sublime. The sublime as based fundamentally on terror was, of course, the aesthetic theory promulgated by Edmund Burke in *A Philosophical Enquiry into the Origin of Our Ideas of the Sublime and the Beautiful* (1757). Burke argued that there was aesthetic pleasure to be taken from observing terrifying images or experiences, and he calls that aesthetic pleasure 'the sublime'. For Burke, awe-inspiring landscapes and harrowing situations produce a similar emotional and psychological response. Death and the fear of death are included in Burke's panoply, not as just another effect, but as the most important effect of all. Radcliffe was among the Gothic novelists who took Burke's theory to heart, and as Emily trembles in the corridors of the Gothic castle, deeply in fear for her life and that of her aunt, she experiences a very refined version of the sublime. Emily is attempting to find her aunt in this remarkable passage:

> At length she obtained something like a direction to the east turret, and quitted the door, from whence, after many intricacies and perplexities, she reached the steep and winding stairs of the turret, at the foot of which she stopped to rest, and to reanimate her courage with a sense of her duty . . . As she surveyed the dismal place, she perceived a door on the opposite side of the stair-case, and, anxious to know whether it would lead her to Madame Montoni, she tried to undraw the bolts, which fastened it . . . As she gazed, now willing to defer the moment of certainty, from which she expected only the confirmation of evil, a distant footstep

reminded her, that she might be observed by the men on the watch . . . Trembling came upon her, as she ascended through the gloom. To her melancholy fancy, this seemed to be a place of death, and the chilling silence, that reigned, confirmed its character . . . The image of her aunt murdered – murdered perhaps by the hand of Montoni, rose to her mind. She trembled, gasped for breath – repented that she had dared to venture hither . . . At length a track of blood, upon a stair, caught her eye; and instantly she perceived, that the wall and several other steps were stained. She paused, again struggled to support herself, and the lamp almost fell from her trembling hand. (Radcliffe 2008: 322–3)

This passage has the quality of a set-piece in the experience of the sublime. Darkness, the intricacy of the passages, blood and death all work together to make Emily tremble and doubt herself. Radcliffe insists on every little detail of this scene in order to lead her heroine to the brink of collapse. In doing so, she not only invokes the sublime for the reader but also demonstrates how deeply *abjection* is embedded within this psychological theory. As Chapter 6 above has reminded us, we are familiar with abjection from the work of Julia Kristeva, who articulates it as a form of violence against the self. In *Powers of Horror: An Essay on Abjection*, Kristeva reveals that abjection occurs 'when narrated identity is unbearable, when the boundary between subject and object is shaken, and when even the claim between inside and outside becomes uncertain' (Kristeva 1982: 141). Emily is nothing if not abject in that sense, since she fears her own and her aunt's dissolution in an imprisoning labyrinth that is both internal and external to her, and it is out of that abjection that she must find a way to survive. Kristeva would classify this abjection as 'sublime' (Kristeva 1982: 9) and, in doing so, she implicitly connects it with its Gothic contours as they are displayed in this novel. Queer theory latches on to this abjection and makes it a key feature of queer subjectivity, but it also looks for ways to transform this abjection into something less isolating and more positive. Emily does not collapse here, but she pushes into a darkened chamber and finds the bloody remains of a soldier's uniform, imagines her aunt murdered, and then confronts Montoni himself. The experience has not destroyed her; in fact almost the reverse is true: being led to this very extreme of terror and isolation, she finds the strength to proceed. Queer theory in fact teaches us that being placed in a position of abjection can be a source of strength. As one of the best-known queer theorists, Judith Halberstam, argues in *The Queer Art of Failure*, 'Under certain circumstances failing, losing, forgetting, unmaking, undoing, unbecoming, and not knowing may in fact offer more creative, more cooperative, more surprising ways of being in the world' (Halberstam 2011: 2). What Halberstam claims here, and throughout her book, is that abjection itself can offer modes of creativity. That is exactly what Radcliffe teaches us.

This transformation is even clearer in a similar moment in Radcliffe's later novel, *The Italian*. Ellena, the heroine, has been locked away in the prison-like convent/monastery of San Stephano. There she is desperate to escape the confines of her cell, and a kindly nun, Olivia, appears to take pity and offers her access to a turret that opens from near her room. When she ascends, she looks out on a sublime scene of cliffs and precipices:

> These precipices were broken into cliffs, which, in some places, impended far above their base, and, in others, rose, in nearly perpendicular lines, to the walls of the monastery, which they supported. Ellena, with a dreadful pleasure, looked down them, shagged as they were with larch, and frequently darkened by lines of gigantic pines bending along the rocky ledges, till her eyes rested on the thick chestnut woods that extended over their winding base, and, which softening the plains, seemed to form a gradation between the variegated cultivation there, and the awful wildness of the rocks above. (Radcliffe 1998: 90)

The 'dreadful pleasure' that Ellena feels is Burkean sublimity for sure, as is the 'awful wildness of the rocks', so Ellena seems to take strength from these views of the landscape. She somehow finds hope in them because in looking at them she finds hope in her self: in her own powers of observation, to be sure, but also in her imagination and her ability to think clearly in a moment of crisis. Through abjection she finds this strength. In addition, almost to underline that hope and make it a function in the novel, the nun who helps her by this point becomes a friend, her only friend, in the convent. Without this friend and without this access to the turret, the sublime experience would not be available to Ellena. She finds it in a sense through this other woman, who attracts her and also challenges her to be her best self.

This kind nun turns out to be Ellena's long-lost mother, for whom she feels a very deep attraction long before she knows of any pre-erotic connection, and as she embraces this woman and thanks her for all her kindness, it becomes clear on what her hope is founded. This kindly, encouraging and helpful nun becomes Ellena's closest friend, and the affection these two characters share becomes an emotional alternative to the horrors of the convent. This woman-to-woman love, intense and utterly unexpected, only later to become a mother–daughter relationship, takes Ellena out of the confines of abjection and offers an almost erotic intimacy on which to build her bond with the hero, Vivaldi. This relation with her mother becomes one based on loss, but it is also one of deep originary, as well as erotic, attachment that in a certain way defines her.

Judith Butler, a philosopher and gender theorist whose work has been basic to the concept of queer theory itself, argues something similar in *The Psychic Life of Power*. Butler explains how and why all desire finds its sources in the erotics of loss. Butler quotes from Sigmund Freud's discussion of his earlier essay 'Mourning and Melancholia' in *The Ego and the Id* (1923), where he remarks that 'when it happens that a person has to give up a sexual object, there quite often ensues an alteration of his ego which can only be described as a setting up of the object inside the ego, as it occurs in melancholia' (Freud 1974: 29). Butler's helpful gloss on Freud's remarks suggests that

> melancholic identification permits the loss of the object in the external world precisely because it provides a way to *preserve* the object as part of the ego and, hence, to avert the loss as a complete loss ... Giving up the object becomes possible only on the condition of a melancholic internalisation or, what might for our purposes turn out to be even more important, a melancholic *incorporation*. (Butler 1997: 133–4)

For Butler, this *incorporation* is the way in which identification becomes a 'magical, a psychic form of preserving the object' (Butler 1997: 134). This is a form of psychic experience that could also be labelled 'uncanny': psychic life preserves this loss in a form that means that, if it ever is found, it will be found with a specifically Gothic mode of recognition, fearfully strange and yet deeply familiar (like Ellena's attraction to Olivia). Radcliffe works out this dynamic in *The Italian*. Rather than making it utterly melancholic, however, she gives Ellena hope: hope that she can maintain a relationship with Olivia at the same time that she turns to Vivaldi.

José Estabon Muñoz, a queer theorist who also looks beyond loss and self-destruction, makes an important point about such a politics of hope in *Cruising Utopia: The Then and There of Queer Futurity*: 'Queerness is a longing that propels us onward, beyond romances of the negative and toiling in the present. Queerness is the thing that lets us feel that the world is not enough, that indeed something is missing' (Munoz 2009: 1). Radcliffe works with hopes such as these: hopes that there is still a way forward from the hideous complications into which she throws her heroines, all of which are based on traditional constructions of patriarchal power that seek to sequester or imprison the many forms of sexuality and sexual expression, such as the one between Ellena and Olivia, that do not fulfil their imperatives. The hope she offers these lost and isolated females is connected to this hope of queer theory at its most challenging.

A bleaker account of queer experience, to be sure, is dramatised in Matthew Lewis's *The Monk* (1796). What seems early in the novel to be a potentially innocent homoerotic encounter between the young novice, Rosario, and a proud but (at first) kindly monk, Ambrosio, turns oddly lurid and starts to expand into multiple forms of 'queer' sexuality when Rosario confesses to being a woman in disguise. This woman, Matilda, indulges Ambrosio in criminal sexual passion, and when he becomes tired of her and lusts after an innocent girl who he meets from the town, Matilda leads him into a demonic encounter in which he barters with an angelic-looking, yet seductively male demon for access to the girl he now desires. Later Matilda confesses to being a succubus – an emissary from the Devil – and the objects of Ambrosio's lustful desire turn out to be his long-lost sister and his mother, Elvira, whom he kills in his effort to penetrate his new object of desire. All these scenes are violent and sexually charged; when Ambrosio is overcoming the girl's mother, he does so in a scene that comes close to rape. Elvira's murder is one of the most brutal scenes of Gothic fiction:

> Turning round suddenly, with one hand He grasped Elvira's throat so as to prevent her continuing her clamour, and with the other, dashing her violently to the ground, He dragged her towards the Bed . . . The Monk, snatching the pillow from beneath her daughter's head, covering with it Elvira's face, and pressing his knee upon her stomach with all his strength, endeavoured to put an end to her existence. He succeeded but too well . . . The Monk continued to kneel upon her breast, witnessed without mercy the convulsive trembling of her limbs beneath him, and sustained with inhuman firmness the spectacle of her agonies, when soul and body were on the point of separating. [At last he completed his task and gazed on her] . . . a Corse, cold, senseless, and disgusting. (Lewis 2008: 303–4)

Lewis takes time over this description, as if he knows that he is composing what will come to seem like a case study of Ambrosio. That this abandoned child, now grown into a violent, repressed and victimising adult, should murder his mother in this sexually suggestive encounter would almost be too much for Sigmund Freud himself. Lewis, only a teenager when he composed this novel, is surely tapping into some profound personal knowledge, for what he writes is deeply unsettling for the reader in its intensity. Incest when driven to these extremes – perhaps the definition of non-normativity – can be called queer because the queer emerges in the struggle against the force of the normative (which is Elvira, the unknown mother, in this scene). When oppressed as much as it is in this case, the horrifying outcomes are almost understandable. Lewis creates this horrific image in order to shock his readers, to be sure. He wants to shock them out of their complacency and confront the intricacies and potentialities of violent incest. This almost primal image has a queer potential because it rewrites the past within a haunting, horrifying present in 1796.

In 'Queer Spectrality: Haunting the Past', Carla Freccero, a queer theorist and scholar of early modern literature, writes about the potential homoerotics of the colonial encounter: 'the impossible task of retracing and listening, of locating desire in the (not quite total) silences of texts, articulates a complex interplay of desire and identification' (Freccero 2007: 198). That interplay of desire and identification is also at work in *The Monk*. Ambrosio is a Gothic villain to be sure, but he also harbours the queer potential of isolation and sensational sexual transgression. We may not be like Ambrosio, but we can recognise his pain. Lewis makes him the quintessential Gothic villain, in part because he can identify with the transgressive quality of his innermost desires.

Charlotte Dacre's *Zofloya, or The Moor* (1806) pushes these concerns even deeper into the human psyche. This novel's heroine, Victoria, also harbours illicit desires, in this case for her husband's younger brother, Henriquez. When the dashing Henriquez appears initially, he is accompanied by the elegant Moor, Zofloya. When Victoria first dreams of her attraction to Henriquez, she is also tormented by the presence of the innocent Lilla, Henriquez's fiancée, who enrages Victoria by her very presence. The Moor appears in the dream in order to aid Victoria, and when she encounters him again, outside the dream, he seems ready to do the same. Anne Mellor rightly calls the result a 'lurid tale of Victoria's sexuality' (Mellor 2002: 172). Eventually Zofloya assists her in poisoning her husband and removing the young girl. He gives Victoria access to Henriquez by first changing her image into that of Lilla. Henriquez has a wild night of sex with her, and then, in the morning, when he realises what has happened, he kills himself. Victoria is distraught, and she murders Lilla in another violent scene. In an ending reminiscent of that of *The Monk* but even more scandalous in its use of *cross-racial* queerness, Zofloya presents himself as the Devil, and he passes judgement on the heroine in these terms:

> 'Dost thou mark me, vain fool!' he cried in a terrific voice, which drowned the thundering echo of the waters – 'Behold me as I am! – no longer that which I appeared to be, but the sworn enemy of all created nature, by men called – SATAN! – 'Tis I that lay in wait for frail humanity . . . Few venture as far as thou hast ventured in the alarming paths of sin – thy loose and evil thoughts first pointed thee out to my keen, my searching view, and attracted me towards thee in the eager hope for prey . . . I found thee, oh! most exquisite willingness, and yielding readily to all my temptations.' (Dacre 1997: 254)

To use demonic possession in this way as a means of talking about transgressive desire, here as in *The Monk*, is already to theorise about its meaning and force. If we look into Victoria's soul and find these 'loose and evil thoughts', what would we discover if we looked into the souls of most adolescents? If everyone is loaded with loose thoughts, even ones that are never acted on, then Dacre is diagnosing what it is to become an adult. Freud could learn a lot from her. If I once again turn to Butler, I do so because she also understands the deepest realms of subjectivity to be always already a mode of transgression. As she says in *The Psychic Life of Power*,

> If there is no formation of the subject without a passionate attachment to those by whom she or he is subordinated, then subordination proves central to the becoming of a subject. As the condition of becoming a subject, subordination implies being in a mandatory submission. Moreover, the desire to survive, 'to be', is pervasively exploitable by desire. (Butler 1997: 7)

So much so that transgression of what seems the 'master text' turns out to be part of that subordination. Dacre seems to be outlining how such a procedure would work. As Zofloya damns Victoria, he also points out to her that her own desires have been her undoing.

Mary Shelley's *Frankenstein* addresses these very same issues, and it does so in ways that all of us recognise. After viewing the human activity in an isolated cottage and attempting to approach the family, only to be spurned, Frankenstein's creature observes the failed leavings of domesticity: the hut where he hoped to find succour is left abandoned at the horror of encountering him. Now that home is closed to him because the family unit itself is always already paranoid and defensive about what it represents. The DeLacey family does not so much represent an ideal as it does the failure of an ideal. As if to underline this fact, the creature dances around the cottage and sets it on fire:

> I lighted the dry branch of a tree, and danced with fury around the devoted cottage, my eyes still fixed on the western horizon, the edge of which the moon nearly touched. A part of its orb was at length hid, and I waved my brand; it sunk, and, with a loud scream, I fired the straw, and heath, and bushes, which I had collected. The wind fanned the fire, and the cottage was quickly enveloped by the flames, which clung to it, and licked it with their forked and destroying tongues. (Shelley 1980: 138–9)

This nocturnal scene of almost ritualistic destruction has the quality of a purging or purification. It is as though the creature must destroy the vestiges of the family life to which he has become devoted. His disillusionment with the family is measured in this violent scene (Haggerty 2017: 118).

If we recall Freccero's 'Queer Spectrality', we might think we recognise this lost figure howling in the night-time, suddenly realising that he is utterly friendless. Even more, this creature is given life by the mad scientist who then disowns him right after the creature has approached him in his bed: this pattern calls to mind the struggles of a young gay man, monstrous to himself in so many ways and confused about how he has come into being. *Frankenstein*, in other words, goes to the heart of queer relations in explaining the contempt one man can feel for another who has been closest to him and has in fact been his 'creator'. Mary Shelley may or may not have had such a configuration in mind, but given the boundary-stretching relations among her closest friends, it is not at all clear that she was not caught up in the intrigues of contemptuous intimacies. *Frankenstein* exerts this queer spectrality because it haunts us with its familiarity (Haggerty 2017: 118–19).

I am not saying that we all create monsters, but we do create ourselves, and in doing that we sometimes destroy those we love, whether we want to or not. Mary Shelley makes clear in her 1831 Introduction that she herself identifies with the mad scientist, and she places herself in the bed in which her hero confronts the creature for the first time: 'He sleeps; but he is awakened; he opens his eyes; behold the horrid thing stands at his bedside, opening his curtains, looking at him with yellow, watery, but speculative eyes. I opened mine in terror' (Shelley 1980: 9). Shelley confronts the horror of a creation – 'How I, then a young girl, came to think of and dilate upon so very hideous an idea?' – by explaining that the very same creature haunted her dreams. Every queer reader knows that her or his or their own dreams are deeply threatening, first to themselves and then to everyone around them. This is queer spectrality at its most trenchant: those dreams of non-normative desire enacted are damning and unnerving in unexpected ways, and the fondest hopes become excuses for acts of treachery if they even begin to see the light of day.

If I seem to end on this note of despair, I would also like to claim, not overly glibly, as several queer theorists have said, that perhaps 'it gets better'. I started this discussion of Queer Gothic fiction theory with hope, and I would like to end in hope as well, taking us back to José Estabon Muñoz. '*Cruising Utopia*'s first move is to describe a modality of queer utopianism', he argues, 'within a historically specific nexus of cultural production before, around, and slightly after the Stonewall Rebellion of 1969' (Muñoz 2009: 1). It is no accident that Muñoz turns to this historical moment of liberation to counteract the centuries of self-hatred I have hinted at. Gothic fiction, film and television of recent years has embraced this spirit of liberation and changed Gothic interiority for good. From *True Blood* to *Buffy the Vampire Slayer* – both of which cross normative sexual boundaries repeatedly – we are discovering ways in which the dictates of reproductive futurity can be challenged and undermined, in ways that Muñoz and all the queer theorists noted would certainly applaud.

References

Burke, Edmund (2015) [1757], *A Philosophical Enquiry into the Origin of Our Ideas of the Sublime and Beautiful*, ed. Paul Gurey, Oxford: Oxford University Press.

Butler, Judith (1997), *The Psychic Life of Power: Theories of Subjection*, Stanford: Stanford University Press.

Dacre, Charlotte (1997) [1806], *Zofloya, or the Moor*, ed. Adriana Craciun, Peterborough, ON: Broadview Press.

Edelman, Lee (2004), *No Future: Queer Theory and the Death Drive*, Durham, NC: Duke University Press.

Freccero, Carla (2007), 'Queer Spectrality: Haunting the Past', in George E. Haggerty and Molly McGarry (eds), *The Blackwell Companion to Lesbian, Gay, Bisexual, Transgender and Queer Studies*, New York: Blackwell, pp. 194–213.

Freud, Sigmund (1974) [1923], *The Ego and the Id*, in *The Standard Edition of the Complete Psychological Works of Sigmund Freud*, ed. and trans. James Strachey, London: Hogarth Press, XIX, pp. 19–27.

Haggerty, George E. (1999), *Men in Love: Masculinity and Sexuality in the Eighteenth Century*, New York: Columbia University Press.

Haggerty, George E. (2006), *Queer Gothic*, Champaign-Urbana: University of Illinois Press.

Haggerty, George E. (2017), 'What is Queer about *Frankenstein*?', in Andrew Smith (ed.), *The Cambridge Companion to Frankenstein*, Cambridge: Cambridge University Press, pp. 116–27.

Halberstam, Judith (2011), *The Queer Art of Failure*, Durham, NC: Duke University Press.

Kristeva, Julia (1982) [1980], *Powers of Horror: An Essay on Abjection*, trans. Leon S. Roudiez, New York: Columbia University Press.

Lewis, Matthew (2008) [1796], *The Monk. A Romance*, ed. Howard Anderson, Oxford: Oxford University Press.

Macaulay, Thomas Babington (1987), unsigned review of *Letters of Horace Walpole, Earl of Orford, to Sir Horace Mann*, *Edinburgh Review*, 57 (October 1833); repr. in Peter Sabor (ed.), *Horace Walpole: The Critical Heritage*, London: Routledge, pp. 311–26.

Mellor, Anne (2002), 'Interracial Sexual Desire in Charlotte Dacre's *Zofloya*', *European Romantic Review*, 13.2: 169–73.

Muñoz, José Estaban (2009), *Cruising Utopia: The Then and There of Queer Futurity*, New York: New York University Press.

Radcliffe, Ann (1998) [1797], *The Italian, or The Confessional of the Black Penitents*, ed. Frederick Garber and E. J. Clery, Oxford: Oxford University Press.

Radcliffe, Ann (2008) [1794], *The Mysteries of Udolpho*, ed. Bonamy Dobrée and Terry Castle, Oxford: Oxford University Press.

Scott, Grant F. (2016) [2012], 'Victor's Secret: Queer Gothic in Lynd Ward's Illustrations to *Frankenstein*', in Mary Shelley, *Frankenstein*, ed. Johanna M. Smith, Boston: Bedford/St Martins, pp. 400–45.

Shelley, Mary (1980) [1818, 1831], *Frankenstein*, ed. M. K. Joseph, Oxford: Oxford University Press.

Walpole, Horace (1937–81), *The Yale Edition of Horace Walpole's Correspondence*, ed. W. S. Lewis et al., 48 vols, New Haven, CT: Yale University Press.

Walpole, Horace (1982) [1764], *The Castle of Otranto, A Gothic Story*, ed. W. S. Lewis and Joseph Reed, Oxford: Oxford University Press.

Part IV

Theorising the Gothic in Modern Media

Chapter 9

The Gothic at the Heart of Film and Film Theory
Elisabeth Bronfen

While Don Draper, the ad-agency 'creative director' in the American television series *Mad Men* (2007–15), is best known for a self-reliance that often helps him to recover from personal and professional setbacks, he is also a haunted man. Since the identity theft on the Korean War front that led to the burial of his CO under a false name, Dick Whitman (Don's original name) has been living a double life. Even after he has succeeded in becoming a celebrity in the Madison Avenue world of advertising, this secret past continues to have a hold on him. Thus, while series creator Matthew Weiner has garnered praise for his accurate reimagination of American culture in the 1960s, Gothic moments that render visible Don's haunting by his former self trouble what is otherwise an artful revisitation of Hollywood's office-film genre of the 1950s–1970s. Visually performing the disturbance of the ordinary so prototypical of a Gothic sensibility, these moments not only speak to the psychological consequences of Don's duplicitous existence, they also draw attention to my subject here: what is Gothic about *any* filmic representation, namely that its doubling of the world on screen – developing the Gothic penchant for doubles in an especially visual manner – is always predicated on a spectral play between absence and Gothic presence.

In contrast to the way Don recalls his war experiences, an ominous mood permeates those *Mad Men* flashbacks that reveal the destitution and moral depravity of his childhood and adolescence. These include the death of his mother and the stillborn child of Abigail Whitman, whose place he assumes in the family of his biological father, and the fatal injuring of his father by his horse while he was attempting to mount it in a drunken state. While the dark colours in which these memory scenes are cast underscore the contrast with Don's apparent good fortune, his imaginary resuscitation of these phantoms of the past seeps into the places he currently inhabits, rendering his ordinary world uncanny. As the editing moves between these two temporal moments, the past sense of foreboding does more than displace all sense of security. This visual splice renders Don's present a ghostly space as well, the backdrop for the far more powerful recollections that cannot be contained. In that Don assumes a spectral presence in these reimagined scenes, neither fully in the past nor in the present but rather hovering between the two, self-reflexivity comes into play. In relation to the camera as the device producing these hallucinations, his remembering eye/I is the point of interconnection between actual experience and spectral recollection.

Even more markedly Gothic are those sequences in which the dead make an appearance as ghosts, bearing an encrypted message regarding the precarious state of Don's double existence. After his real brother, Adam, has committed suicide because Don refuses to let him be part of his new life, his apparition returns more than once – an embodiment of a murky sense of guilt but also a figure of warning. More felicitous, yet equally Gothic, is the moment when Anna Draper, the wife of the man whose identity Don has assumed, appears in the office where he has fallen asleep on a sofa while he waits for a call from California to say she has died. A translucent figure, Anna enters with a suitcase in her hand, and, as if looking for him, scans the room. Her steps wake him up, and, once their eyes meet, she smiles at him before turning away to leave him again. In a similar spirit, his former lover, Rachel Menkin, appears to him in a scene that recalls the casting session with which the episode 'Severance' (Season 7) begins. Wearing only a fur coat, she first poses in front of a mirror, similar to the other models, but then turns towards Don, explaining that 'I am supposed to tell you, you missed your flight.' Only later will Don discover that she, too, has died. The scene begins with Ted opening the door to let Rachel in, but closes with Pete telling Don that it is time to get back to work. Her apparition is weird in a manner reminiscent of the Gothic films and television series of David Lynch; rather than being staged as a hallucination, it is presented as an alternate reality into which Don enters in his sleep.

The narrative climax of these spectral visions has, however, already occurred in 'A Tale of Two Cities' (Season 6), when Don, intoxicated during a party in California, has his own near-death experience. The comment made by a spectral one-armed soldier he espies among the guests – 'dying doesn't make you whole, you should see what you'd look like' – prompts a vision of himself, standing at the edge of a pool, looking down at his own corpse. Seconds later, we see him resuscitated by Roger, who has pulled him out of the pool. The doubling of his body, one alive and the other dead, again reflects on the precarious duplicity of his current existence by having recourse to a Gothic sensibility. As messengers from the past, all these apparitions serve as a form of self-knowledge. They call upon Don to acknowledge that, because he is always in flight, running as much from the constraints of the ordinary as from a past life he does not want to relinquish, he is himself living a ghostly existence.

By rendering visible the threat that looms beneath the surface of the stylish world that Draper is passing through, the filmy dead who have returned to the world of the living point, in extradiegetic terms, to the fault lines in the optimism so pervasive in post-war American culture. Yet these Gothic interpolations have a message for us in a further sense, embodying the spectral force on which any historical reimagination is grounded. By virtue of having recourse to montage as a cinematic device that splices together different moments in time, introducing the past back into the present, these markedly Gothic moments allow *Mad Men* to think about its own aesthetics. Don, lying on the edge of the pool, once more gasping for breath, can be read as a trope for the entire show's project, predicated as it is on drawing attention to the way the past is never gone. Instead, the haunting past overshadows and even encroaches on the world of the early twenty-first century, cinematically as well as narratively (see Bronfen 2016 for more on *Mad Men*).

To explore the Gothic at the heart of film theory thus entails focusing on the correspondences between a thematic concern with the presence of death in life and the cinematic work used to perform and transmit such disruptions of our ordinary experience of the world. The claim of this essay, building mainly on some insights from Stanley Cavell (who argues that cinema satisfies our magical wish to view a world on screen from which we are absent, unseen), is that film is most markedly self-reflexive when it involves stories of haunting because these speak to the fact that there is something inherently ghostly about cinema itself (see Cavell 1979). The Gothic as a mode in fiction, after all, arose under the influence of, and also influenced, the phantasmagoric magic-lantern shows of the eighteenth century that vividly projected spectral figures from the past, often to arouse fear, on to screens or walls or even darkness itself (Castle 1995: 140–67), very like the old portrait that walks out of its frame into the air in Horace Walpole's *The Castle of Otranto* (1764), the first narrative to call itself 'a Gothic Story'. Playing with and to our fascination with bringing what has disappeared back to life by rendering the past present again, albeit as embodied visions, the technical devices of modern cinema quite self-consciously bank on the affective effect of haunting just as their magic-lantern ancestors did. Even if the actors in a given film story are not dead, they are of course not actually present to us. Given the importance that lighting and the cadrage (the director's viewfinder) have for their existence as film images, they are also never the same on screen as in reality. We are, thus, always seeing after-images of people, things and spaces, manipulated to tell a particular film narrative.

Furthermore, what is rendered present *again* are not living people, but rather moving images that double and stand in for them. Affected by these apparitions, we see and experience film characters and the world they inhabit as animate even as we know them to be nothing other than a spectral illusion. As such, cinema renders fluid the boundary between actual/corporeal and imaginary/psychic experience. The magic of cinema consists in eliciting an uncanny ambivalence of response. The bodies that appear to us are spectres, yet they have a somatic impact on us. We are drawn in and affected by a conjured image world not *although* but *because* we know it to be a technical manipulation of our sight. Cinema's power of resuscitation affects objects as well in an ambivalent manner. Like Gothic spectres, filmed objects take on a life of their own. In the process of being animated, they not only reflect on cinema as the art of endowing still images with life. They also draw attention to the way that lighting, framing and *mise-en-scène* can have the opposite effect, namely that of transforming living bodies into inanimate signs. The logic of classic shot/reverse shot editing is such that, detached from the body by virtue of montage editing, an eye and the object on which its gaze focuses not only appear on the same diegetic level of the film but are both inanimate images on film, albeit in motion.

The affective ambivalence at issue is such that, by assuming the position of the camera in the act of viewing a film, we can use our imaginary capacities, like a Victor Frankenstein, to animate what is absent or lifeless. By the same token, too, we are partaking in a process that renders the world inanimate, freezing it into moving images of fragmented and spliced bodies. The spectral play between presence and absence, on which the illusory power of cinema is predicated, is thus doubled by an equally uncanny exchange between animation and de-animation. If, in turn, the film image doubles the movie star playing a fictional character, this duplication implicates us as well. Insofar as sharing in the phantasmagoria involves projecting myself on to and empathising with, not just a stranger, but one who is the effect of cinematic devices, this whole process, like magic-lantern shows, entails a moment of self-destabilisation. The power of my imaginary capacities consists in allowing me to experience something as phenomenologically real to which, in fact, I am absent. This means, however, that, at least for the period of my engrossment in a given film, I am absent to myself, absorbed instead in the emotion – be it fear, suspense or excessive enjoyment – enacted on screen.

Regarding the correspondence between Gothic concerns and cinematic devices, it is useful to recall Sigmund Freud's discussion of the uncanny, related as it is to a return from repression that arouses dread and horror. He significantly bases his analysis of the types of situations that arouse in us the feeling of uncanniness on the claim that '*heimlich* is a word the meaning of which develops in the direction of ambivalence, until it finally coincides with its opposite, *unheimlich*' (Freud 1955: 226). Such a blurring of distinctions is key for the viewing effect on which the ghostly quality of cinema is predicated because it creates an ambivalence regarding whether what emerges on screen is present and/or absent, bodily and/or psychic, real and/or imagined, alive and/or dead. Consequently, it is precisely this intellectual uncertainty that speaks to why the Gothic is at the heart of cinema's self-reflection. Particularly the phenomenon of the double, singled out by Freud, involves epistemological hesitation when rethought in terms of cinematic effect. Imaginary reduplication may, as Freud demonstrates, include sharing knowledge, feelings and experiences with someone who is considered identical to oneself, such as when we empathise with a film character to the extent that she or he is perceived as an extension of ourselves. Or it may involve the self-doubt that arises from this identification, namely when, in extreme situations, we are cajoled into completely substituting the film character for ourselves. In either case, the doubling, dividing and interchanging at issue involve a blurring between me and the other, here and there, being and not being.

However, the double also touches on cinema's concern with reanimation in another sense. As Freud points out, while guardian spirits and a belief in the afterlife of the soul allow for the double to be conceived as 'an assurance of immortality', its reverse aspect transforms this figure into 'the uncanny harbinger of death' (Freud 1955: 235). For Freud, the ambivalence between sustainability and disappearance of the self that is negotiated with the use of a double speaks to the human capability for self-observation and self-criticism. Detached from the rest of the ego, the mental part of ourselves, by offering reactive comments, affords insights into ourselves that are not possible through direct experience. Reconceiving all this in terms of cinematic language, one can say that, along with a blurring of the boundary between absence and presence, in-animation and re-animation, movies make use of the technical ability to double characters such that they can be in two places at once – acting and observing themselves act. At the same time, by virtue of our absorption in the cinematic spectacle, we also find ourselves split between an imaginative empathy with the world being viewed and an intellectual distance from it. We also become a double of ourselves in that, at one and the same time, we emotionally indulge in and intellectually observe what is facing us on the screen.

If Freud, in turn, privileges the fear of damaging or being robbed of one's eyes for his discussion of the uncanny, an alteration of vision pertains to the spectral logic of cinema as well. While all moving images perform ocular manipulation, it is precisely when the camera and the editing translates a Gothic concern with excessive emotions into an extreme visual distortion that one can speak of an 'assault on our eyes'. Such reanimism is as ambivalently marked as other Gothic motifs, not least because it serves as the source for an omnipotence of thoughts crucial to any emotional transference between a spectator and characters on screen. In terms of cinematic language, the magical thinking that purports to have a psychic influence over others transforms into the conviction that I am privy to the thoughts of those who appear in the film-image. The close-up is, perhaps, the most salient cinematic device to support this fantasy, especially when, in connection with reverse shots, we are called upon to share one and then another character's subjective gaze.

Freud's special emphasis on animism is, therefore, seminal for my own discussion because it is what is common to all uncanny viewing effects. Be it a belief in the return of the dead, in the division and interchangeability of the double, or in the power of one's psychic life, it is also at the heart of cinema's affective effect. As Freud concludes, 'an uncanny effect is often and easily produced when the distinction between imagination and reality is effaced, as when something that we have hitherto regarded as imaginary appears before us in reality' (Freud 1955: 244). This is as true for film characters who indulge in their fantasies by enacting them with their own body as it is for us sharing in such magical thinking. Such a doubling between Gothic themes and cinematic techniques ultimately revolves around the fact that both – the film's story and the effects that its *mise-en-scène* and editing have – are predicated on seeing something out of the ordinary, even if it remains uncertain whether this apparition is real or not. Along with the visceral engagement of the hero and heroine, that of the audience hinges on taking such blurring of the boundaries between imagination and reality to a fundamentally Gothic excess.

Alfred Hitchcock, the master of the thriller genre, is a paradigmatic example for the Gothic at the heart of film and film theory precisely because he is working in direct line with the pre-cinematic and Gothic phantasmagoria. Being preoccupied with uncanny disturbances of the ordinary – haunting, doubles, madness and murder – he not only uses the psycho-thriller to develop his singular vision as a film-maker, he also self-consciously reflects and reflects upon the Gothic inheritance of the cinematic medium per se. The manner in which his films produce suspense makes use of narrative uncertainty in more than one sense. The outbreak of something strange not only unsettles the familiar everyday in his pictures. Hitchcock also deploys a disruption of the seamless construction of coherent space which continuity editing is meant to afford, producing a disturbance of ordinary vision. The outbreak of excessive emotion and violence around which his narratives circle may be doubled by top-down or bottom-up shots that distort the appearance of the characters, or by a pronounced use of shadows, reminiscent of the also Gothic *film noir* of the 1930s–1940s, that enmesh them in an imaginary web. Such disruption is usually, however, also accompanied by camera work and editing that draws attention to itself. We are not only meant to notice that something has gone awry with the hero's or heroine's perception of the world, we are also meant to realise that what we see on screen is the result of technical artifice, not a mimetic representation of the world. We are thus left in an *aporia*, suspended between sharing emotionally in the intense excitement of the characters *and* taking notice intellectually of the visual devices that produce this suspense. We are caught up equally in the obsessions of the characters *and* in Hitchcock's obsession with the cinematic techniques that produce intense affects effectively.

Indeed, Gothic excess in Hitchcock's oeuvre has, above all, to do with the way the camera is deployed to produce a visual enchantment that is tantamount to robbing us (along with the characters) of any ordinary vision of the world. The opening credit sequence of *Vertigo* (1958), a film that revolves around a woman allegedly haunted by her suicidal ancestor, draws our attention from the start to the way the spectral vision the film narrative is about to present is concerned with a manipulation of our eyes. While a close-up shot initially focuses on a woman's mouth, across which the name of the main actor, James Stewart, appears, it soon glides upwards along the nose to capture a pair of eyes, moving cautiously from the right to the left. Once they have come to rest, staring straight at us, the name of the female star, Kim Novak, appears just beneath them. Then, as the camera zooms in on the left eye, the words 'in Alfred Hitchcock's' pop up in the same lettering to indicate his authorship, while also bringing with it an even closer move towards the woman's eye.

Now, filmed through a red filter, this eye is wide open, as in fear, but also so as to allow the film's title to emerge from the pupil. The word 'Vertigo' is soon followed by a purple spiral, which is initially superimposed over the shape of the pupil and iris it replicates, until, having filled the screen, it blocks out the woman's eye completely. In its stead, a series of revolving circular shapes in different colours, now accompanied by Bernard Herrmann's billowing score, emerge from a black backdrop and keep moving forward from the centre of the screen where the woman's eye used to be. Even as their vertiginous movement sets the tone for the hero's obsessed gaze at the heroine, it produces for us a double vision. In our mind, we retain an after-image of the woman's eye, which has been displaced by the circular shapes that recall it, until they are, once more, reabsorbed by it. In other words, as part of Hitchcock's self-reflection, the image of the eye and the geometric shapes replace each other, even while blurring the boundary between realistic and abstract cinematic representation. The woman's eye engenders shapes while she is also subsumed by them. The final shot of the credit sequence returns to an extreme close-up of the woman's eye, once more captured through a red filter. Gazing at us, although now no longer wide open in fear, it serves as the source for the words 'directed by Alfred Hitchcock' that emerge from it. Epistemological uncertainty remains, as it often does in Gothic tales where we cannot tell the actual status of spectres (are they supernatural or mental projections?). Is the woman's eye the object of the director's gaze, or is her vision equated with his? Does he control her gaze (the shapes emerging from and reabsorbed by her vision), or is he the product of her eye? And what are we meant to anticipate, given that the hero, aligned in words with the woman's mouth, is not part of this visual game?

The film narrative itself discloses the lethal core at the heart of all this ghost-seeing. Scottie Fergusson, a retired SFPD detective, takes on the job of watching over the beautiful Madeleine Elster, because her husband has convinced him that, haunted by her ancestor, mad Carlotta, she has become suicidal. After she subsequently succeeds (it appears) in jumping from the tower of a Spanish mission close to San Francisco, Scottie falls into a deep depression. Then, upon meeting Judy, who uncannily resembles the dead woman, his obsession for her takes a new turn. Compelling her to become Madeleine for him, to put on her clothes and change both her hairstyle and her make-up, he hopes to resuscitate the dead woman at the expense of the separateness of the one still living. The suspense of the story, in turn, hinges on the fact that Hitchcock lets us in on the ruse that has been played on his clueless hero. Judy is actually an actress, who is playing Madeleine at the behest of Gavin Elster, so that he can kill his wife. Knowing that Scottie has been suffering from vertigo, Gavin and Judy are sure he will never make it to the top of the church tower to discover that the woman he loved as Madeleine was not a suicidal ghost-seer but rather the scheming double of Elster's real wife. When, upon discovering the deception, Scottie forces Judy/Madeleine to return to the scene of the crime, his repetition-compulsion takes on yet a further Gothic turn. Because Judy sees a darkly clad figure emerging from the stairway, she does fall from the tower, thus fulfilling her impersonation of the luckless wife, even while, as in several horror stories by Poe, she turns into a ghost that will now forever haunt the man who has hunted her down.

At various moments in *Vertigo*, meanwhile, Hitchcock uses the Gothic motif of the revenant to speak to the lethal power of his camera. The premise of Elster's murder plot, after all, consists in Judy not only posing as his wife, but remodelling her appearance along the lines of the portrait of mad Carlotta hanging in a museum – a device, again, reminiscent of those portraits that come to life in Gothic fiction. Madeleine is thus the double not of an actual woman but of an imaginary one, modelled Gothically on a painting. Hitchcock's camera, in turn, repeatedly catches Madeleine in poses that present her performance of a haunted woman as a *tableau vivant* performed – in a flower shop, at Carlotta's grave, in front of her portrait in the museum, at the window of a hotel – exclusively for Scottie's eye. In the first part of the film, the performed illusion is twofold. While Scottie is oblivious to the fact that Madeleine knows he is following her and is posing only for him, we also are cajoled into perceiving her as a woman suspended uncannily between a portrait and its embodiment.

The epistemological uncertainty posed by the faux ghost story at the start of the film also speaks to the spectral power of cinematic representation itself. Hitchcock uses the other woman in Scottie's life, his maternal friend Midge, to debunk his hero's obsession, even while disclosing the artifice of his own medium. One evening, after Scottie has driven her home, Midge, mocking his belief in ghosts, leaves him sitting in his car and threatening to take another look at the portrait. Suddenly uncertain himself, Scottie picks up the museum catalogue he has tucked away beneath the dashboard and opens it to the relevant page. The editing segues into a cinematic performance of Scottie's ghost-seeing. In a lap dissolve, the profile of Madeleine comes to be juxtaposed over the black-and-white reproduction of Carlotta's portrait in the catalogue, only to once again fade. The double vision sustains the uncertainty about whether Madeleine embodies an uncanny resuscitation of the dead woman on which Scottie's necrophilial desire thrives.

At the same time, we are called upon to remember that this profile is, in fact, the same shot as the one at the climax of the scene when Scottie saw Madeleine for the first time at Ernie's restaurant. So as to underscore that his hero privileges an imagined picture – and not a direct view – of the woman he is to follow, Hitchcock has Scottie turn away from Madeleine as she approaches the bar where he is sitting. When she finally comes to stand in profile directly in front of the camera, her pose is one performed not for him but for us. The image that Scottie's enchanted eye juxtaposes over the reproduction in the catalogue, in his effort to cast aside the doubt Midge has raised, is consequently not one he remembers. What appears to be his subjective gaze is, in fact, Hitchcock's signal that he is playing with our vision.

This break in the diegesis that foregrounds its artifice corresponds to the fact that the woman who shows herself in profile at Ernie's restaurant is not Madeleine posing for Scottie, since she has noticed that he has turned his back to her and cannot see her. Rather, this is an extradiegetic shot, in which the star, Kim Novak, presents herself to us as the director's new leading lady. Then, too, the lap dissolve melds together the reproduction of a painted portrait with the reappearance of a previous shot. Scottie's hesitation over whether the woman he has fallen in love with is real or a ghost is thus doubled by our own hesitation over whether this face belongs to a fictional character or is an image detached from the diegesis to highlight the film's enactment of stardom. Scottie treats this composite image as proof of Madeleine's haunting. By using not the hero's memory image but rather a recycled shot, moreover, Hitchcock robs us of our ocular certainty. What is the status of this double portrait? Is there any reference adhering to it or is it a free-floating, cinematic image? The Gothic excess that Hitchcock self-reflexively taps into makes us see the fabrication, yet we are nevertheless taken in by its charm.

In Hitchcock's film of Daphne du Maurier's *Rebecca* (1940), the return of a dead woman does not so much involve an enchantment of the heroine's eye as reveal her willingness to be engulfed by the imagined body of this predecessor. Since the housekeeper at Manderley, Mrs Danvers, not only staunchly keeps alive the memory of Maxim de Winter's first wife but also imposes this spectral presence on to his second wife, the distinction between psychic and material reality blurs in this film more and more. Yet, as befits the Gothic mode of the original novel, uncertainty pervades this spectral haunting. Is the heroine, who throughout the film has no given name, the victim of a dead woman's malice, or is this ghost an expression of her own death wish? Is Rebecca really haunting Manderley or is her presence merely a fantasy that Danvers and then the second wife entertain? Is the fantasy that Rebecca is trying to evict her from her uncanny home in fact the heroine's recasting of her troubled marriage in Gothic terms, sometimes in a dream-state?

In *Rebecca*, the engulfment by a spectral force, which aligns the spectator's emotional position with the heroine's dream-work, becomes particularly noticeable in the self-reflexive use to which Hitchcock puts lap dissolves. During the heroine's whirlwind romance with Maxim de Winter, many of the transitions from one scene to the next are signalled by a juxtaposition between the ending of the former and the beginning of the latter. As the heroine comes closer to Manderley, however, what up to that point was nothing more than an editing convention takes on real significance for the plot. To mark the period of time that passes between her perfunctory marriage ceremony in the south of France and her arrival at her new home, Hitchcock offers a poignant visual juxtaposition. The bunch of flowers that Maxim buys just before they drive off is so enormous that it covers not only her upper body but also half of her face. In the lap dissolve that follows, this half-hidden face is, in turn, superimposed on the iron gate that the heroine had dreamt about passing through like a spirit in the narrative frame that begins the whole film. Now her face fades into the bars just before the servant, noticing the approaching car, opens the two gates to let their car pass through. By merging these two distinct images – the bride's head and the gated entrance to the estate – the lap dissolve produces a non-mimetic representation that anticipates the heroine's uncanny absorption by and into the mansion at the end of the drive. The ambivalent manner in which she both fades into this edifice even as it emerges from her head suggests that what is about to happen is as much the product of her imagination – and of lap dissolve and editing – as it is a threat to her existence.

Even more eerie is the transition between the moment when Danvers draws her mistress's attention to the portrait of Lady Caroline hanging in one of the dark hallways in Manderley and the costume ball where the second Mrs de Winter will wear this ancestor's dress, not knowing that Rebecca had chosen the same outfit the year before. While the heroine, dwarfed by the enormous painting, walks out of the frame, the camera pans towards the painted woman. Then, as her painted body fades out, an image of the nocturnal mansion, shot from the same angle as in the film's opening frame, fades into view. The uncanny impression effected by the visual juxtaposition is that Rebecca is hovering over the house. As such, this lap dissolve anticipates that Rebecca will not be displaced by any impersonator, even an unwitting one. After Maxim demands that his wife take off the tell-tale costume, the festivities are, indeed, interrupted because the boat containing Rebecca's corpse has suddenly re-emerged from the sea. The evidence of foul play to which this material return from death speaks further underscores the power that the dead woman continues to hold over the de Winter mansion.

The fact that an invisible force seems to draw the camera to Lady Caroline's portrait, however, also speaks to the way Hitchcock makes use of the space that is offscreen throughout *Rebecca* to produce some of his most pointed Gothic effects. Early on in the film, Danvers shows the heroine the door leading to Rebecca's room, invoking its magnificence. Then, while both women, as if suddenly in a trance, walk out of the frame, the camera proceeds towards the door. For a brief moment, the dog guarding it raises its head but, as if to signal that the figure approaching is not a stranger, it does not stir. The lap dissolve, juxtaposing this portentous door with the napkin bearing Rebecca's initials, supports the effect that the person whose gaze the camera is transmitting at this point is that of the dead woman herself. Rebecca's offscreen presence is, furthermore, repeatedly invoked by Danvers as she tries to convince the unwelcome second Mrs de Winter that her predecessor has come back to watch the living – and in so doing compelling us to imagine her being there as well, just as we are doing with the insubstantial figures on the screen.

Maxim does the same in the scene at the boathouse, during which he confesses to his wife the violent argument that he had with Rebecca on the night of her death. As Hitchcock's camera pans around the room, re-enacting the dead woman's movements, she is resuscitated as the spectral object of our gaze. Once he has reached the point in his confession when he recalls that at the height of her taunting remarks she had come to stand face to face with him, the camera itself has come full circle and is now also facing Maxim. For a brief moment, as Maxim finishes his story by describing how he struck her, Rebecca's ghost is no longer the invisible object but rather the gaze behind the camera. The reverse shot focuses on the spot where she stumbled and fatally fell, followed by a shot that now brings the transfixed gaze of the *heroine* into play. If she is fully absorbed not only by her husband's tale but also by the magical evocation of Rebecca's ghost, she is also the one to put an end to the spectacle by realigning our gaze with hers. It is this moment at which we recognise that we have been captivated by a cinematic ploy that not only allowed us to imagine Rebecca's spectral presence, but more importantly to gaze with her at all those still living, turning us into ghosts as well. The Gothic motif of a woman who returns from the dead to haunt those who have survived her thus allows Hitchcock to exploit the phantasmagoric possibilities of the cinematic medium that have always been basic to the Gothic too, even while drawing us into the force-field of this illusion.

The psycho-thriller *Suspicion*, in turn, which came out one year later, also starring Joan Fontaine, can be read as a counter-piece to *Rebecca*. While the Gothic mode here, too, supports the heroine's path to self-knowledge, at issue is less the psychic torment resulting from a young bride's imaginary rivalry with her dead predecessor and more a young bride's uncertainty about whether she may have married a murderer. Rather than indulging in the fantasy of being haunted by the past, Lena's excessive fantasy pertains to a danger that is possibly still to come. Her hallucinations allow her to experience crimes that have not yet been committed as spectral events taking place before her inner eye. The minute she begins to doubt the integrity of her spendthrift husband, Johnnie Aysgarth, by linking his irresponsible attitude towards money (including an act of embezzlement) to a perhaps unlawful killing, the suspense of the narrative falls back on her. We are less concerned with when he might kill her. Our uncertainty revolves instead around whether she is right in assuming that he is the danger she imagines him to be.

The mood of uncertainty is fostered in part because her new home is rendered as a Gothic site even if it is not as architecturally 'Gothic' as Manderley. From the moment the newlyweds move in, interwoven shadows cover the walls of the entrance hall, as though the characters are caught in a web. As the heroine's paranoia becomes more intense, so too the shadows grow more pronounced, taking over the entire house. Employed as an architectural double of her psychic doubt, the grid on the walls that Lena keeps passing by intensifies the contrast between the imagined darkness inside the house and the brightly lit reality outside. The psychic hesitation they effect is that, as in *Rebecca*, it not only remains uncertain whether the threat they render visible is first and foremost her projection. Equally ambivalent is whether this imaginary prison is one that she has become caught in or one that she is producing and projecting on to her husband. This, again, is Hitchcock's self-reflexive comment on the way his camera work imprisons us in his heroine's excessive imagination even while showing his sleight of hand.

As in *Rebecca*, Lena's excessive absorption in her fantasy work corresponds with an excessive disturbance of continuity editing; it is only in *Suspicion*, though, that uncanniness becomes self-reflexive, particularly regarding the very power of reanimation so central both to the Gothic and to the cinematic medium. At one point in the mounting tension between this young couple, Johnnie sharply forbids Lena to intervene in a business venture he intends to carry through with his friend, Beaky. She has already begun to harbour the fantasy that her husband is merely using their plans to develop a piece of coastal land as a way to get at his clueless friend's money. A Scrabble game the following evening is introduced with a lap dissolve, in which the truncated word 'doub' is juxtaposed over Lena's puzzled face. Then, as the two men discuss going to the site early the next morning, she begins to put together the word 'murder' from the pieces lying face up on the table. Hitchcock's montage produces a phantasmagoria on screen, again recalling magic-lantern Gothic, in which the inanimate letters, in conjunction with a photograph of the coastal road, become animated. As a close-up of Lena's excited face is superimposed over the photograph, the still image transforms into a live backdrop in a brief sequence showing Johnnie pushing Beaky off the cliff. Drawn completely into his fall and the turbulent waves about to swallow him up, both juxtaposed over the close-up of her face, we share her lethal thoughts, as if gifted with the magic of telepathy. Overwhelmed by her own enjoyment of this imagined death, which she (and we) experience by proxy, she faints. The falling of her body puts an end to both her excessive fantasy and the excessive montage.

The climax of this uncanny animation of objects in *Suspicion* is, of course, the famous scene in which Johnnie carries a glass of milk up the stairs, while Lena, waiting for him in her bedroom, is convinced that he has found a poison that cannot be detected after death. Functioning as the reverse shot to her gaze, we see the portentous glass first as a shadow on the completely darkened floor of the entrance hall, cast by the light from the kitchen, which, upon entering, Johnnie immediately extinguishes. Even if the scene is an enactment of what Lena imagines is happening outside her door, the danger is staged only for us. Thus, as Johnnie walks up the stairs in the darkened hall, the milk glass now alone shines luminously; it becomes alive with its secret force only for the audience, while his face is indistinguishable in the darkness. Given that, by virtue of an implicit animism, we share Lena's thoughts throughout the film narrative, it remains uncertain whether this scene actually takes place or is happening only in her mind. We are drawn into her fantasy, even when she is not explicitly present. If this is Hitchcock's joke on us, it is also a reflection on the inherently Gothic rhetoric of cinema.

The most uncanny of all houses in Hitchcock's oeuvre still has to be the home of Norman Bates in *Psycho* (1960). Reminiscent of many a haunted house in black-and-white cinema, while it also recalls Edward Hopper's painting *House by the Railroad* (1925), it is another Gothic reanimation of what was already a spectral picture. As in *Rebecca*, moreover, this house is the scene where a dead woman has returned so as to haunt the living, although, in this case, the house contains the spirit, as well as the skeleton, of the murdered mother, kept alive thanks to her son's impersonation of her. If the point of his double act is that it allows him to kill in the guise of the mother he himself killed, then the distinction between the murdered woman and the murdering man collapses into a hybrid body. The inanimate maternal fetish that Norman has preserved, hiding it in the cellar when visitors threaten to come, is not attached to the scolding woman's voice which the hapless heroine, Marion Crane, hears emanating from the house. The ventriloquism pertains to the house itself, which seems to be alive, the windows appearing like eyes looking down at her. As in *Suspicion*, this home's uncanny effect draws attention to the fact that for us it exists mainly as the effect of the psychic reality of the deranged hero.

But if, with Norman's voyeurism, which culminates in his gaze through a hole in the wall at the naked Marion about to step into the shower, we return once more to the issue of enchanted eyes at the centre of *Vertigo*, what also looms in *Psycho* is Hitchcock's idiosyncratic mix of Gothic terror and self-reflexive comic wit (itself like that oxymoronic condition of the Gothic as early as Walpole's *Otranto*). In the final scene, Norman sits alone in a locked room in the County Court House. Once again the camera, like a spirit, has passed through a barred door and is alone, facing not Manderley, as in the opening sequence in *Rebecca*, but the face of a lonely young man. Once more a female voice-over offers a narrative commentary as the camera slowly pans towards the object of her discourse. Only now, in contrast to the narrating heroine in *Rebecca*, this voice is attached to the body about which she speaks. What Hitchcock, once again, appeals to is our Gothic belief in animism, allowing us to share in the thoughts running through this hybrid figure's mind, fusing son and mother. Then, once more relying on an excessive disturbance of continuity editing to suggest a disturbance of normality, the body that is host to this spectral voice transforms into a composite image that is pure cinematic virtuality. As the camera moves into a close-up, capturing Norman's face, his intense, inward gaze transforms into the grin of a madman. At that point, the illusory reanimation of the maternal fetish, as in the climactic cellar scene where Norman is finally caught, is now superimposed over this grimace. Just as in *Vertigo*, the lap dissolve not only juxtaposes two separate images, but, by recycling an earlier sequence, two temporal moments.

Cinematically what is staged in the final lap dissolve of *Psycho* is a double birth. Norman's face fades out, replaced for a few seconds first by the face of the maternal fetish and then by a car (Marion's) being pulled out of the swamp behind the motel. If the son has died off completely, he has given birth not to the actual mother, but to the fetish body he had created along with Marion's corpse, now contained in the car, with its two front lights becoming a face of sorts. This montage recalls *Rebecca*'s dead body, emerging once more from the sea, indicating not only that the dead will return over and again on screen, but that as such we are dealing with a form of spectral recycling. The final title in *Psycho*, 'The End', puts closure, not to the haunting, but to the visual excess, detached from all mimetic reference. As the screen turns black before the car has been fully retrieved, Hitchcock signals a theoretical position basic to the Gothic and to cinema alike. The kernel of excessive enjoyment can never be fully disclosed. It moves from body to body, from film image to film image, gaining ever more layers of articulation along the way. *Psycho* is Hitchcock's cinematic Frankenstein-ian monster, an amalgamation of visual fragments and story partly taken from previous films and images. In this overdetermination of spectral images superimposed, the Gothic at the heart of film and film theory finds its perfect articulation.

References

Bronfen, Elisabeth (2016), *Mad Men, Death and the American Dream*, Chicago: University of Chicago Press.
Castle, Terry (1995), *The Female Thermometer: Eighteenth-Century Culture and the Invention of the Uncanny*, New York: Oxford University Press.

Cavell, Stanley (1979), *The World Viewed: Reflections on the Ontology of Film*, Cambridge, MA: Harvard University Press.
Freud, Sigmund (1955) [1919], 'The Uncanny', in *The Standard Edition of the Complete Psychological Works*, ed. and trans. James Strachey, London: Hogarth Press, XVII, pp. 217–56.
Hitchcock, Alfred (dir.) (1940), *Rebecca*, Selznick International Pictures/United Artists.
Hitchcock, Alfred (dir.) (1941), *Suspicion*, RKO Pictures.
Hitchcock, Alfred (dir.) (1958), *Vertigo*, Paramount Pictures.
Hitchcock, Alfred (dir.) (1960), *Psycho*, Paramount/Universal Pictures.
Weiner, Matthew (creator) (2007–15), *Mad Men*, Weiner Brothers/Silvercup Studios/Lionsgate Television.

Chapter 10

Techno-Terrors and the Emergence of Cyber-Gothic

Anya Heise-von der Lippe

'You're the realest'

One of the most prominent areas of liminality explored by various forms of the Gothic is the question of the human and its Others: the monster, the stranger, the alien and, most recently, the posthuman in its various figurations. The Gothic's explorations of the intersections of embodiment and technology harken back to Mary Shelley's *Frankenstein* (1818), of course, which envisions the creation of life with the help of science in the wake of post-Enlightenment trepidations about scientific hubris. The growing possibilities of late twentieth- and early twenty-first-century techno-science have done nothing to assuage these fears. On the contrary, they seem to indicate drastic changes in our understanding of what it means to be human. In the light of further human–technology integrations, it is no longer a question of coming to terms with a clearly delineated posthuman Other; we now face our own 'posthuman becomings' (Botting 2012: 19) and the long-building realisation that 'the human' is just as much a theoretical construct as the posthuman. As Rosi Braidotti points out, drawing on Cary Wolfe,

> [n]ot all of us can say, with any degree of certainty, that we have always been human, or that we are only that. Some of us are not even considered fully human now, let alone at previous moments of Western social, political and scientific history. Not if by 'human' we mean that creature familiar to us from the Enlightenment and its legacy: 'The Cartesian subject of the cogito, the Kantian "community of reasonable beings", or, in more sociological terms, the subject as citizen, rights-holder, property-owner, and so on.' (Braidotti 2013: 1)

For Braidotti 'human' is a term that has undergone – and is continuously undergoing – historical and cultural fluctuations, and the challenge to humanity's sense of wholeness and conceptual stability is, consequently, not an entirely new one. The contemporary ubiquity of technology and the myriad ways in which we rely on it in almost every aspect of our lives, however, serves as a constant reminder of the precariousness of the human as an ontological construct. Wolfe himself argues:

> posthumanism names a historical moment in which the decentering of the human by its imbrication in technical, medical, informatic, and economic networks is increasingly impossible to ignore, a historical development that points toward the necessity of new theoretical paradigms (but also thrusts them on us), a new mode of thought that comes after the cultural repressions and fantasies, the philosophical protocols and evasions, of humanism as a historically specific phenomenon. (Wolfe 2010: xv–xvi)

While Wolfe's argument suggests no less than a complete renegotiation of the philosophical conceptualisation of the human and a call for what is now frequently being termed the 'critical posthumanities' to address these questions, the impact of this paradigm shift, which has its roots in post-Enlightenment and modernist thought (Nietzsche's work, in particular), is also tangible in contemporary popular culture. The dependence on and the simultaneous fear of technologies that dominate our everyday lives resonate throughout contemporary Western cultures, and popular media therefore abound with narratives of human–technology interactions gone awry. Moreover, they often do so by drawing on the meta-narrative mechanisms of the Gothic.

The speculative TV series *Black Mirror* (2011–), for instance, explores the proliferating forms of media technology, which permeate almost every aspect of contemporary culture, as these forms build on long-standing Gothic paradigms to challenge such basic categories as life and death, real and virtual, factual and fictional. Season 2's episode 'Be Right Back' explores the possibility of recreating a dead person from their online presence. 'You're just a performance of stuff that he performed without thinking and it's not enough!', the female protagonist admonishes her replicated boyfriend, suggesting that, taken in sum, our online personalities would occupy a slightly less-than-human position at the lower end of the 'uncanny valley' (see Mori 1970; Winfield 2012: 72–3). Season 3's 'Men Against Fire' and 'Hated in the Nation' take a similar approach by showing how virtual narratives change people's perceptions of reality and influence their moral standards and actions.

Black Mirror's depiction of the near future suggests that it is precisely our deep involvement with various technologies that turns this brave new media world into a nightmare of fourth-order simulacra (signs that refer only to signs of other signs of other signs), an aesthetic of infinite surfaces, doubles and mirrors prefigured in the Gothic since Horace Walpole. As Jean Baudrillard argues about our postmodern world pervaded by *Simulacra and Simulations*, '[t]here is a plethora of myths of origin and of signs of reality – a plethora of truth, of secondary objectivity, and authenticity' which leads to '[p]anic-stricken production of the real and of the referential, parallel to and greater than the panic of material production' (Baudrillard 1994: 6–7). In a post-factual, technologically mediated world, any narrative can carry the same weight as any other, while we seem to be trapped in an endless regress of looking for an obsolete concept called 'the real thing'. Cyber-Gothic texts draw attention to this discrepancy by highlighting narrative constructions of reality, particularly those based on human–technology interactions. 'You're the realest', the technician tells the operator of an artificially grown body in James Tiptree's tale 'The Girl Who Was Plugged In' (1973), because she is as real as anything else in this novella's world of the 'gigabuck mainstream [. . .] that's pumping the sight and sound and flesh and blood and sobs and laughs and dreams of reality into the world's happy head' (Tiptree 2014: 59–61). In a system of medially enhanced consumerism anything seems possible: 'Whatever turns you on, there's a god in the future for you, custom made' (2014: 43), but these gods are empty idols, controlled for the profit of 'consumer industries' because it is 'economic to have a few controllable gods' (2014: 56).

This warning of highly mediatised techno-capitalist consumerism may seem superficial, referring to an identity crisis that we as overconnected citizens of what is increasingly termed the 'Global North' have largely brought upon ourselves. In the light of globally operating corporate greed, however, our actions have far-reaching consequences, as Braidotti further argues, drawing on Achille Mbembe's concept of 'necropolitics' (Mbembe 2003: 11): 'the bodies of the empirical subjects who signify difference (woman/native/earth or natural others) have become the disposable bodies of the global economy' (Braidotti 2013: 111). The consequences of our media-technology addiction are especially dire in countries of the Global South, where lives are at stake in the production (and decay processes) of an obsolescent stream of consumer electronics (see Mantz 2013). Moreover, with austerity measures in place throughout the Western world, the boundaries that separate the human from the dehumanised Other have become substantially more permeable, as citizens of highly industrialised countries also face the possibility of economic marginalisation.

Rather than a clearly delineated subject position of us (humans) versus them (non-humans/machines), our 'imbrication in technical, medical, informatic, and economic networks' (Wolfe 2010: xv) therefore poses an epistemological challenge to our understanding of what it means to be human. As Michael Sean Bolton argues, the 'threat in the posthuman Gothic [. . .] is not that of consumption by the machine but of subsumption into the machine' (Bolton 2014: 4). Whether this occurs at the level of production or consumption seems to be a question of degree, rather than ontological difference. Technological speculation is, of course, a central aspect of the science fiction genre; but it is within a framework of Gothic textuality that these fears can be explored in a more self- and theory-conscious manner. There is, after all, a close affinity between Gothic textuality and technology. As Fred Botting argues, 'Gothic fiction begins in an age of mechanism and deploys an array of machines' (Botting 2005: 1). In the Gothic, these are inextricably 'tied to the mechanisms of narrative' (Botting 2005: 6) and replicable modes of textual production. In the cyber-Gothic they undermine common conceptions of reality by showing that everything is virtual/constructed and there is no reality beyond an intricate system of narratives. Starting at this intersection of science fiction and the Gothic, I propose a meta-critical reading of Tiptree's 'The Girl Who Was Plugged In' in the light of one of the central questions of cybernetics – that of control. Drawing on Donna Haraway's 'Cyborg Manifesto' and *Frankenstein*'s concerns with gender, aesthetic creation and narrative authority, all of which are closely entangled with the cyber-Gothic, I propose to discuss Tiptree's novella as a key text, an epitome, of the self- and theory-conscious cyber-Gothic mode that has emerged quite powerfully in the late twentieth and early twenty-first centuries. In the process, I also plan to show how posthumanist concerns bridge the divide between critical theory, narrative and lived reality, as well as questions of mediation and gendered embodiment, by creating a challenging dialogue within the posthuman cyber-Gothic itself.

The Biomediated Body: 'her nervous system hanging out'

In their preface to the 2009 issue of *Gothic Studies* on 'Theorising the Gothic', Jerrold E. Hogle and Andrew Smith trace the Gothic's involvement with theory back to the beginnings of the genre in late eighteenth-century political and aesthetic debate, arguing that 'the Gothic actively instigates discourses appropriate to it rather than just passively providing evidence for theory's retrospections about literature, art, drama, and film' (Hogle and Smith 2009: 2). Theoretical interest in the Gothic, however, seems to diminish when the Gothic becomes an established mode of literary production, focusing on imitation rather than innovation. As Botting points out, '[f]amiliar monsters [. . .] continue throughout popular fiction, culture and media, repetitively recycled in novels, films, magazines, games, cartoons, comics, clothes and commodities' (Botting 2014: 199). It would be tempting to read this development, in Jacques Derrida's terminology, as a kind of 'domesticat[ion]' of the monster (Derrida 1995: 386), but such a reading discounts the Gothic's potential to renew itself in the light of new cultural and technological developments. It is, as Christopher Keep argues,

> a recurring moment within the history of modernity, that point in which the material substrate of signification, whether it takes the shape of the book or a computer-mediated network, is momentarily visible, when it has not yet become so much a natural fact of our reading practices as to disappear from view. (Keep 2006: 12)

This definition highlights the Gothic's potential to address and expand on technological innovations on various textual levels, including metanarrative explorations of its own production processes. Indeed, one of the main functions of the Gothic's 'negative aesthetics' lies in its unique ability to textually embody our deep-seated fears that 'disturb the borders of knowing' (Botting 2014: 1–2). The horror film *The Ring* (2002), as an example of the monstrous crossing diegetic boundaries, establishes a constant cycle of its own textual reproduction by suggesting that those who watch the film must also keep themselves and the monster alive by copying the video of it. A printed example of this type of Gothic textuality, Mark Z. Danielewski's hypertext novel *House of Leaves* (2000), creates an unnamed and unknown monstrous threat, which traverses diegetic levels, suggesting that the text itself possesses monstrous qualities.

The creation of this kind of textual monster depends on the use of frames – a diegetic device both typical of the Gothic and easily translatable to new production technologies – as well as an understanding of corporeality as subject to discursive changes that are enacted on the level of narrative form, as in 'The Girl Who Was Plugged In'. Patricia Clough refers to this combination as the 'biomediated body'

(Clough 2010: 208). Heralding changes not only to the genetic composition of our bodies but also to the narratives we use to constitute them, the 'biomediated body' posits a 'challenge to autopoiesis of the body-as-organism' (Clough 2010: 208), as well as to the basic understanding of the human as a fixed category. In the context of the Gothic, this shift in perception emerges as a set of fears. As Bolton argues, 'the posthuman Gothic finds instances of terror and horror arising from the interfaces and integrations of humans and technologies' (Bolton 2014: 2). Drawing on earlier Gothic fears of technology, the source of these anxieties, however, 'lies not in the fear of our demise but in the uncertainty of what we will become and what will be left of us after the change' (Bolton 2014: 3).

Contemporary anxieties about the impact of technology are historically rooted in an understanding of the body as a fragmented narrative, which emerged from eighteenth-century anatomical perceptions of the organic body as automaton, a collection of exchangeable machine parts. As Stefani Engelstein argues,

> Once the body is formulated as an amalgam of organ systems, each of which plays a specific role in the body, then the body itself can no longer be seen as the smallest meaningful organic unit. At this point, the body ceases to *belong* to an individual whose rational control it serves and becomes an assemblage with a multitude of purposes or drives of its own that threaten to usurp the identity of the human. (Engelstein 2008: 2)

Frankenstein plays out these very concerns and channels them into a modern myth of biomediated bodies. Mary Shelley's novel is 'deeply concerned with the nature and function of "information" and especially with media(tion)' (Burkett 2012: 581), so 'the novel's diegesis inspires, or perhaps instigates, a type of thinking that the novel's structure itself comes to embody' (Burkett 2012: 583). While critics have described the various diegetic levels of *Frankenstein* as a Chinese box system (Botting 1991: 42) or a 'Matryoshka chain' (Heiss 2008: 156), the 1818 Preface and 1831 Introduction, although (meta-)narratives in themselves, are not usually considered part of this system. The multiple frames in *Frankenstein* draw attention to the constructedness of the text, raising questions of authority and narrative authenticity that can also be traced throughout the paratexts. Shelley's reticence to claim authority and responsibility over her work reflects views on female authorship at her own time and points to a post-Enlightenment understanding of writing as a technology, rather than the infusion with a divine spark of authoritative genius. It also, however, seems to posit the text as a work of art without an artist. As Ann Marie Adams has argued, 'Mary Shelley's authorial experience demonstrated how a literary artist could be rendered almost superfluous to the artwork that she created' (Adams 2009: 403).

A lack of authority and control over one's own writing is, as Joanna Russ argues (2005: 20), one of the reasons why female authors throughout literary history have chosen to write under a male pseudonym. For Alice Sheldon, 'James Tiptree, Jr.' was certainly more than a convenient pen name. *Being* Tiptree was inextricably linked with her creativity and sense of authority as a writer. When her identity was revealed in 1977, she felt she could no longer write as Tiptree: 'I had through him all the power and prestige of masculinity; I was – though an aging intellectual – *of* those who own the world' (quoted in Phillips 2007: 422–3). As Julie Phillips argues in her biography of Tiptree/Sheldon:

> Tiptree never pretended to be a man in person. Yet Alli's appropriation of the male mind is even more exciting. It's a much deeper challenge to the established narrative order, and promises greater freedom. It questions all our assumptions about writing and gender. (2007: 6–7)

Tiptree's masquerade, then, while almost watertight and upheld for several decades, only existed in writing, which raises a number of questions about how gender is perceived when it is (technologically) mediated, independently of corporeality – for instance in online communication or through the medium of printed text. As Phillips points out, Tiptree's writing was influenced by the 'questioning of perspective. Who's looking? How does who they are influence what they see?' (2007: 225) Her stories, such as 'The Women Men Don't See' (1973) as well as 'The Girl Who Was Plugged In', reflect questions of gender and cultural representation through the lens of a male voice (see Phillips 2007: 302). While women are thus perceived and presented from the outside, these narrative constructions offer striking insights into gender inequality and social power structures, control and textual production.

Writing Cyborgs/Cyborg Writing: 'she hasn't spoken through her own mouth'

In 1974 'The Girl Who Was Plugged In' won the Hugo award (the most prestigious literary honour in science fiction) for best novella. Amid wide-ranging speculations about Tiptree's identity, 'frustrated detectives [at the World Science Fiction Convention in Washington] began to claim that he could alter his molecular structure at will and had been assuming the form of Coke machines and ashtrays in order to mingle undetected with the crowd' (Phillips 2007: 376). There is a serious core to this humorous speculation: in the absence of actual 'knobby flesh to be scanned in vain for what makes the words come out' (Tiptree quoted in Phillips 2007: 375), anything seems possible: the writer's mind might just as well reside in a machine.

In 1950 Alan Turing addressed this issue in a hypothetical experiment to determine the question 'Can machines think?' Today, this experiment is known as the Turing Test for artificial intelligence. To avoid definition problems, Turing suggested the following analogy:

> The new form of the problem can be described in terms of a game which we call the 'imitation game.' It is played with three people, a man (A), a woman (B), and an interrogator (C) who may be of either sex. The interrogator stays in a room apart from the other two. The object of the game for the interrogator is to determine which of the other two is the man and which is the woman. (Turing 1950: 433)

Only in a second step would one of these subjects be replaced with a computer, using the same basic setup to avoid visual identification. The most striking factor of this 'imitation game' is its focus on the mediation of communication between the interrogator and the subjects. As Turing stresses, '[t]he ideal arrangement is to have a teleprinter communicating between the two rooms' (1950: 433). This setup completely eliminates physical attributes (such as voice or handwriting), reducing the determination of gender to the answers given by the subjects alone. What Turing saw as a means of clarifying the basic setup of his test has been interpreted by fellow mathematician Andrew Hodges (1997) as 'confus[ing] the point', a 'bad analogy' and 'asking for trouble by bringing sex into it'. From a cultural studies point of view, however, the analogy raises a number of interesting questions about gender and mediation, as noted by N. Katherine Hayles:

> If your failure to distinguish correctly between human and machine proves that machines can think, what does it prove if you fail to distinguish woman from man? Why does gender appear in this primal scene of humans meeting their evolutionary successors, intelligent machines? (Hayles 1999: xii)

Hayles argues that the inclusion of gender in this mediated form (via a computer terminal) implies 'the possibility of a disjunction between the enacted and the represented bodies' of the test subjects (1999:

xiii). The basic disconnect between the physical representation and virtual enactment of the body in technologically mediated scenarios is tied to the Greek root of the term *cyber-** (from κυβερνάω, to guide, to steer), which suggests an emphasis on control, a distinction between the person of the controller and the apparatus or machine being controlled, as well as a form of mediation between the two. The simple presence of mediation (whether through a computer or other medium, such as printed text) consequently adds a dimension of authority and control to communication scenarios – specifically in those contexts where women and minorities would traditionally be perceived as inferior or otherwise divergent from the norm – simply by taking the (marked) human body out of the equation.

As Donna Haraway argues in 'A Cyborg Manifesto', after all, technologically mediated bodies have a political dimension. The cyborg, 'a hybrid of machine and organism' (Haraway 2000: 291), is 'a creature in a post-gender world', which will end the 'border war' between 'organism and machine' over 'territories of production, reproduction and imagination' (2000: 292). Haraway's 'ironic dream' (2000: 291) explores the cyborg as a feminist myth, suggesting that the *'translation of the world into a problem of coding'* (2000: 302) resting on a 'theory of language and control' (2000: 303) is a necessary step, since '[c]ommunications technologies and biotechnologies are the crucial tools recrafting our bodies' (2000: 302).

Haraway's vision is based – in part – on Tiptree's fiction (see Genova 1994: 7), clear evidence of how the Gothic often advances beyond and even instigates theory, rather than simply reflecting and exemplifying it. Indeed, 'A Cyborg Manifesto' acknowledges a debt 'to writers like Joanna Russ [. . .] James Tiptree, Jr., Octavia Butler [. . .] These are our story-tellers exploring what it means to be embodied in high-tech worlds. They are theorists for cyborgs' (Haraway 2000: 310). Haraway's interchangeable use of both 'theory' and 'story' (for her own writing, as well as Tiptree's, Russ's and Butler's) is indicative of her viewing the task of theorising cyborg embodiment as a form of narrative myth-making to undermine authoritative systems of thought associated with traditional patriarchal structures. Writing is, as Haraway argues, 'pre-eminently the technology of cyborgs' (2000: 312), a mediation through text that allows women to 'subvert [. . .] the force imagined to generate language and gender, and [. . .] the structure and modes of reproduction of "Western" identity, of nature and culture, of mirror and eye, slave and master, body and mind' (2000: 312).

To be sure, interpretations of 'The Girl Who Was Plugged In' have tended to read it as 'a condemnation of appropriated female bodies and agency' (Stevenson 2007: 87), a negative version of Haraway's cyborg myth. But the narrative structure of Tiptree's novella creates a meta-level that allows a different reading: while the novella's cyborg does not speak 'through her own mouth' (Tiptree 2014: 61), the interplay of narrative voice and representations of different narratives is specifically constructed to draw attention to questions of perception and control (as in Shelley's *Frankenstein*). The shiny surface of perfect, artificial bodies advertising the products of global corporations is undermined, not only by the pronounced ugliness of the operator controlling the artificial body, but also by the fact that the reader is made aware of the corporation's machinations and control mechanisms: 'They've got the whole world programmed! Total control of communication', the rebellious Paul Isham rages, but it is really the narrator's offhand commentary about 'inputs [guarded] like a sacred trust' (Tiptree 2014: 68) that drives home the argument. Rather than any rebellious act on the operator's part, it is this juxtaposition of different narratives – and the revelation that they are, in fact, all narratives – that suggests alternative ways of reading and writing.

Controlled Cyborg Embodiment: 'the greatest cybersystem [. . .] ever known'

Haraway's ironic myth is an attempt to read human involvement with technologies as the advent of the cyborg and as a chance for 'women in the integrated circuit' (Haraway 2000: 291) to shake the boundaries imposed on them by gender and the globalised capitalist economy. Yet it is ironic only insofar as its alternative would suggest an acceptance of the status quo. 'The Girl Who Was Plugged In', concerned with similar questions, reflects the fear of losing one's identity and perceived physical integrity, as the human becomes obliterated by machine embodiment. This fear is underlined by the double-layered structure of the novella: it is the narrator's distanced commentary, describing the story's protagonist as the Other, as a human–technology hybrid 'spouting wires and blood' (Tiptree 2014: 78), which creates a sense of the abject. Julia Kristeva describes the process of 'abjection' as an integral part of identity construction, in which those anomalies that cannot be reconciled with the self are 'thrown' over into a radical Other (Kristeva 1982: 2–4). It is in this sense that 'The Girl Who Was Plugged In' uses the Gothic's negative aesthetic to create a brave new world of physically flawless bodies, which are, in fact, empty shells, or 'waldos' (Tiptree 2014: 54), remote-controlled by humans, trying to uphold a performance of normative human embodiment with a 'forty-thousand mile parenthesis in [their] nervous system' (2014: 54). In a society that has officially banned advertisements, the 'remotes' offer the possibility of controlled product endorsements in the media, a service that the corporations controlling the media describe as 'a genuine social contribution' to help 'the good people who make' the products (2014: 52). That this is just a narrative among others is made clear by the narrator's casual references to 'the other speech' (2014: 53), which the corporate representative saves for reluctant subjects.

Steeped in the social hierarchies of media 'gods' and 'mortals' (2014: 43), the protagonist, P. Burke, sees her waldo, 'Delphi', as an opportunity to escape her own 'rotten' body and circumstances. Her 'self-alienation' only heightens her 'terrific aptitude' (2014: 58) as an operator, so that, with the waldo's growing popularity, the operator becomes almost obliterated:

> Of course it's really P. Burke down under Carbondale who's doing it, but who remembers that carcass? Certainly not P. Burke, she hasn't spoken through her own mouth for months. Delphi doesn't even recall dreaming of her when she wakes up. (2014: 61)

Cyborg-embodiment, it seems, has a contrary effect on the protagonist compared to what is envisioned by Haraway: instead of empowering P. Burke, it silences her and further suppresses her sense of self. Moreover, as the narrator's sarcastic comment suggests, escape into the more desirable body can only ever be temporary and the original body must be kept alive for the mind to still function. Thus, while P. Burke hopes to '*die and be reborn again in Delphi*' (2014: 72), the text makes it clear that this is '[g]arbage, electronically speaking' (2014: 72).

By reiterating the connection between the mind and its original body as both tenuous and inseparable, the novella draws the reader's attention to the theoretical implications of this technologically induced mind–body divide. One of these implications, as Hayles argues, is that 'human being is first of all embodied being, and the complexities of this embodiment mean that human awareness unfolds in ways very different from those of intelligence embodied in cybernetic machines' (Hayles 1999: 283–4). Hayles's argument draws on her own discussion of Hans Moravec's concept of 'mind uploading' (see Moravec 1988), the idea that human consciousness could be disconnected from the human body and transferred to a computer in a stab at immortality. In all likelihood, a transfer of the 'self' into some kind of virtual environment is not an option, as neuro-ethicists Michael Madary and Thomas Metzinger argue: 'it is not that some mysterious "self" leaves the physical body and "enters" the avatar'; instead, 'users experience an illusion of ownership of the virtual body (the avatar is my body), as well as an illusion of agency (I am in control of the avatar)' based on a 'functional configuration in which two body representations dynamically interact with each other' (Madary and Metzinger 2016). Cyberpunk nevertheless explores 'uploading' as a possibility based on transhumanist suggestions: William Gibson's *Neuromancer* (1984) envisions the character of the 'Dixie Flatline' (1984: 49), a hacker turned 'firmware construct' after his death, whose predominant wish for non-existence suggests that being a disembodied consciousness inside a computer or network – technological feasibility aside – might not actually be a viable subject position for a human being.

In her discussion of Moravec's transhumanist dream of uploading (and his perception of human identity as informational, rather than embodied), Hayles posits that our idea of what it means to be 'human' is inseparable from our understanding of what it means to inhabit a human body: 'Interpreted through metaphors resonant with cultural meanings, the body itself is a congealed metaphor, a physical structure whose constraints and possibilities have been formed by an evolutionary history that intelligent machines do not share' (Hayles 1999: 284). Hayles suggests that what we understand as 'human' is a discursive construct based on how we perceive our bodies in the world. These perceptions will be influenced by our gender, ethnicity, age, body shape, (dis-)ability, for instance, and not least by how others frame us in terms of these categories. To separate our sense of self from these defining categories is almost impossible, even if we do not fit into them easily. Humanity's relationship and integration with advanced technology is, thus, a double-edged sword discursively speaking: while the combination of advanced medicine and technology (and, within a capitalist framework, the availability of funds) promises an unprecedented sense of 'wholeness', the substitution of biological components and functions with technological prostheses also challenges traditional human identity constructions based on physical integrity and control.

These metaphorical constructions of the human are undermined by the 'Cyborgothic', which 'imaginatively create[s]' sentient, articulate, non-human beings (Yi 2010: 41). Focusing on aesthetic rather than scientific aspects, Dongshin Yi reads *Frankenstein* as a key text in its genealogy. Such 'aesthetic machines' (Yi 2010: 41) as the creature and its descendants, he argues, inhabit a subject position of difference, which aligns itself with that of women in Haraway's claim that 'the cyborg is our ontology' (Haraway 2000: 292). 'The Girl Who Was Plugged In' revolves around the 'abject' that is this kind of 'aesthetic machine' in the light of techno-capitalist narratives and its systematic framings of the Other. Delphi/P. Burke's stretched out nervous system, which is presented as numb on the part of the remote body and over-sensitive and stretched out towards the machinery of control on the part of its operator, visualises the protagonist's lack of aesthetic control over the different components of her biomediated embodiment.

Abject Narrative: 'One rotten girl in the city of the future (That's what I said)'

As a cyber-Gothic narrative, too, 'The Girl Who Was Plugged In' reflects this sense of losing control on the level of narrative perspective as well as content. The homodiegetic narrator is instrumental to the main character's predicament while positioning himself at a safe local and temporal distance from the events he narrates. 'Listen, Zombie. Believe me' (Tiptree 2014: 43), the novella begins, addressing its readers directly: 'you with your silly hands leaking sweat on your growth stock portfolio' (2014: 43). This direct address serves the combined purpose of drawing the reader into the story and introducing its general context (capitalist greed), as well as the narrator's condescending manner. The narrator's use of the present tense underlines the novella's complex temporality. While the narrator is, ostensibly, addressing a reader in the present (the Nixon era referred to in the penultimate paragraph), he also suggests that he can 'show' the reader 'the city of the future' (2014: 43). This destabilisation of the narrator's temporal position challenges his reliability and creates narrative distance, underlined by the narrator's constant commentary on reader expectations, which are going to be thwarted – '(You thought this was Cinderella transistorized?)' (2014: 47) – as well as foreshadowing questions: 'Do you need a map?' (2014: 85). These comments are often delivered in parentheses, setting them apart from the rest of the narrative and drawing attention to certain aspects by the contrary means of suggesting that they '([. . .] need not concern us.)' (2014: 63). The narrator's frequent comments, as a result, also draw attention to his own bias and involvement in the events.

As Phillips argues, 'Tiptree's [early] stories often contain a sympathetic male narrator [who] turns out to be just another part of the problem' (Phillips 2007: 143). In 'The Girl Who Was Plugged In', the narrator is not exactly sympathetic, even if his role in the protagonist's downfall is only revealed through a shift in perspective at the end. While the narrator frequently refers to 'weasel boy' (Tiptree 2014: 71) or 'ferret-face' (2014: 73) who calls P. Burke 'that pig' and a 'damn freak' (2014: 74), the connection to the 'sharp-faced lad' whose meddling has 'bugged quite a few people' (2014: 78) is only made in the last paragraph. The story comes full circle to the narrator's comments about 'the future' in the first paragraphs, when the sharp-faced lad 'stands where somebody points him during a test run' of a 'temporal anomalizer' and 'wakes up lying on a newspaper headlined NIXON UNVEILS PHASE TWO' (2014: 78).

The narrator, it turns out, is explicitly not cast in the role of a villain, but rather appears as a petty 'seventh-level' bureaucrat (2014: 60) trying to better his position in the corporation by discouraging the doomed relationship between the well-connected Paul Isham and Delphi, the remote-controlled walking ad. His attempts, which include physical torture, are consequently hidden between the lines of intricate descriptions of future technology, thereby suggesting a criticism of technocratic capitalism's exploitative tendencies. The fact that a 'delicately unbalanced' feedback of the remote connection between P. Burke and Delphi can have 'striking results' on the operator (2014: 70) is only revealed, paragraphs later, as causing 'agony' (2014: 71) for P. Burke. The episode has a contrary effect on Paul, who resolves to save Delphi from what he perceives to be the controlling grasp of 'headquarters' and his father (2014: 70), but is actually P. Burke's remote control of the Delphi body.

This misunderstanding has tragic results, but the problem, the story suggests, is a systematic one. After all, the only person who misses P. Burke is Joe, the technician, 'the only one who had truly loved her' (2014: 78), if only on the basis of her abilities as a remote operator: 'P. Burke, now a dead pile on a table, was the greatest cybersystem he has ever known' (2014: 78). But even for Joe, she is, to some extent, replaceable. The waldo called 'Delphi lives again', albeit operated by 'a different chick' (2014: 78). The new operator's lack of a name underlines the necropolitical exchangeability of the human in this constellation, but the story's main argument against a technocapitalist framing of the human body is Paul's eventual ascent to 'the GTX boardroom' (2014: 78), which suggests that the economic and political system remains unaffected by the events. The company will continue to use remotely operated waldos to circumvent society's consummate ban on open advertising. In the narrator's view, the Global Communications Corporation's boardroom is not cast as villainous:

'If you're looking for the Big Blue Meanies of the world, forget it' (2014: 45). What the company represents, instead, is an 'orderly' (2014: 45) system combining economic interests with technological progress – to the detriment of human individuals – especially those who don't conform to its concept of normality. P. Burke becomes an operator because her ugliness (2014: 44), her lack of family (2014: 46) and her suicide attempt make her an outsider, an abject Gothic Other, someone who is vulnerable to the system. The complex narrative setup manages to draw the reader's sympathies towards this monstrously 'ugly duckling' with the 'horrible body' (2014: 47) by showing the system as both ruthless and highly effective. As Tiptree wrote in a letter to Joanna Russ: 'I was early impressed with the idea that "orderly" societies can wreak considerable ravage on the deviant individual' (quoted in Phillips 2007: 41). Like Braidotti and Haraway, Tiptree locates the problem not in technological progress itself, but in the broader context of capitalist greed and what it is capable of doing if coupled with unchecked technological progress.

As the story suggests, P. Burke is certainly a 'disposable bod[y] of the global economy' (Braidotti 2013: 111), but, at the same time, she is a cyborg undermining gender stereotypes (in the worst possible way): 'P. Burke is about as far as you can get from the concept *girl*' (Tiptree 2014: 55). The narrative further reinforces this impression by dwelling on the 'meldings of flesh and metal', which make her look '[i]f possible, worse than before' (2014: 47), the operation which turned her into an operator. P. Burke's love for Paul makes her seem even more grotesque, as the discourse of abject Gothic monstrosity employed to describe their final, tragic meeting suggests:

> The doors open and a monster rises up.
> 'Paul, darling!' croaks the voice of love, and the arms of love reach for him.
> And he responds.
> Wouldn't you if a gaunt she-golem flab-naked and spouting wires and blood came at you with metal-studded claws?
> 'Get away!' He knocks wires.
> It doesn't matter which wires. P. Burke has, so to speak, her nervous system hanging out. (2014: 76)

There are various levels of discrepant awareness at work in this narrative construction. The reader is shown P. Burke's narrative of 'love' and her vulnerability alongside the narrator's rhetorical question addressed to the reader and demanding sympathy for Paul's distorted version of the situation. This juxtaposition of interpretations not only creates an ambiguous subject position (who is the reader supposed to side with?) but draws attention to the constructedness of the different narratives at work.

Paul's misunderstanding of Delphi's biomediated embodiment, of course, is consistent with the cultural background within the narrative, which keeps the waldos a secret, and also echoes predominant Western beauty myths. As Philips argues, '[i]n the classic fairy tale, the lover discovers the true beauty beneath the ugly surface [. . .] Tiptree says the reverse: the world loves the beauty on the surface and can't abide the monster in the mind' (Phillips 2007: 301). In this sense, 'The Girl Who Was Plugged In' is 'a horror story about performing the feminine: the beautiful, numb outer self, the female impersonator, houses the unacceptable true self' (Phillips 2007: 301). The introduction of biomediated embodiment into this classic scenario of beauty and beast further complicates the narrative, since the presence of mediation suggests a liminality that undermines the binary structure of inside and outside.

'Listen, Zombie'

By foregrounding the constructedness of narratives of biomediated embodiment, Tiptree's novella draws attention to problematic practices of looking and perceptions of gender in normative cultural discourses, addressing in its own way the lack of feminist, posthuman cultural myths that Haraway points to in her 1985 'Cyborg Manifesto'. The juxtaposition of conflicting narratives of technological mediation in the story suggests a reading in the context of Baudrillard's concept of the disappearance of 'the Real', which posits that '[i]n our virtual world, the question of the Real, of the referent, of the subject and its object, can no longer be posed' (Baudrillard 2000: 62). 'By shifting to a virtual world', he argues, the Other – and any possible myths based on radical otherness – 'will be eradicated, because it will be immediately realized, operationalized' (2000: 66). Situated at the intersection of early cyberpunk and feminist science fiction, 'The Girl Who Was Plugged In' addresses the human fear – not of being (as suggested by the concept of 'the singularity') one day outsmarted by intelligent machines, but of being subsumed into and consumed by the necropolitical machinery of global capitalism, which creates its own narratives of humanity. By employing the 'negative aesthetics' (Botting 2014: 1) and narrative plurality of the cyber-Gothic, 'The Girl Who Was Plugged In', in line with other Gothic texts before and after it, draws attention to the constructedness and resulting contestability of these biomediated narratives of the human and its Others.

References

Adams, Ann Marie (2009), 'What's in a Frame? The Authorizing Presence in James Whale's *Bride of Frankenstein*', *The Journal of Popular Culture*, 42.3: 403–18.
Baudrillard, Jean (1994), *Simulacra and Simulation*, trans. Sheila Faria Glaser, Ann Arbor: University of Michigan Press.
Baudrillard, Jean (2000), *The Vital Illusion*, ed. Julia Witwer, New York: Columbia University Press.
Bolton, Michael Sean (2014), 'Monstrous Machinery: Defining Posthuman Gothic', *Aeternum*, 1.1: 1–15.
Botting, Fred (1991), *Making Monstrous*, Manchester: Manchester University Press.
Botting, Fred (2005), 'Reading Machines', in Robert Miles (ed.), *Gothic Technologies: Visuality in the Romantic Era*, University of Maryland, http://www.rc.umd.edu/ (accessed 21 November 2016).
Botting, Fred (2012), 'Love Your Zombie – Horror, Ethics, Excess', in Justin D. Edwards and Agnieszka Soltysik Monnet (eds), *The Gothic in Contemporary Literature and Culture*, New York: Routledge, pp. 19–36.
Botting, Fred (2014), *Gothic*, London: Routledge.
Braidotti, Rosi (2013), *The Posthuman*, Cambridge: Polity.
Brooker, Charlie (creator) (2013), 'Be Right Back', *Black Mirror*, London: Zeppotron/House of Tomorrow.
Brooker, Charlie (creator) (2016), *Black Mirror*, Season 3. London: Zeppotron/House of Tomorrow.
Burkett, Andrew (2012), 'Mediating Monstrosity: Media, Information and Mary Shelley's *Frankenstein*', *Studies in Romanticism*, 51.4: 579–605.
Clough, Patricia (2010), 'The Affective Turn', in Melissa Gregg and Gregory J. Seigworth (eds), *The Affect Theory Reader*, Durham, NC: Duke University Press, pp. 206–25.
Delaney, Kate (2004), 'Cyber Dreams and Nightmares', in Jaap Verheul (ed.), *Dreams of Paradise, Visions of Apocalypse*, Amsterdam: VU University Press, pp. 172–82.
Derrida, Jacques (1995), 'Passages – from Traumatism to Promise', in *Points . . . : Interviews 1974–1994*, ed. Elisabeth Weber, trans. Peggy Kamuf et al., Stanford: Stanford University Press, pp. 372–95.

Engelstein, Stefani (2008), *Anxious Anatomy*, Albany: State University of New York Press.
Genova, Judith (1994), 'Tiptree and Haraway: The Reinvention of Nature', *Cultural Critique*, 27: 5–27.
Gibson, William (1984), *Neuromancer*, New York: Ace.
Haraway, Donna (2000) [1985], 'A Cyborg Manifesto', in David Bell and Barbara M. Kennedy (eds), *The Cybercultures Reader*, London: Routledge, pp. 291–324.
Hayles, N. Katherine (1999), *How We Became Posthuman*, Chicago: University of Chicago Press.
Heiss, Lokke (2008), 'Frankenstein and the Matryoshka Chain', *The South Carolina Review*, 41.1: 156–61.
Hodges, Andrew (1997), 'Some Pink Herrings', in Andrew Hodges (ed.), *The Alan Turing Internet Scrapbook*, http://www.turing.org.uk/scrapbook/test.html (accessed 21 November 2016).
Hoeveler, Diane Long (2004), 'The Secularization of Suffering: Toward a Theory of Gothic Subjectivity', *The Wordsworth Circle*, 35.3: 113–17.
Hogle, Jerrold E., and Andrew Smith (2009), 'Revisiting the Gothic and Theory – An Introduction', *Gothic Studies*, 11.1: 1–8.
Keep, Christopher (2006); 'Growing Intimate With Monsters', *Érudit*, 41–2, http://id.erudit.org/iderudit/013156ar (accessed 21 November 2016).
Kristeva, Julia (1982) [1980], *Powers of Horror: An Essay on Abjection*, trans. Leon S. Roudiez, New York: Columbia University Press.
Madary, Michael, and Thomas K. Metzinger (2016), 'Real Virtuality: A Code of Ethical Conduct', *Front. Robot. AI*, 3.3, doi: 10.3389/frobt.2016.00003 (accessed 21 November 2016).
Mantz, Jeffrey W. (2013), 'On the Frontlines of the Zombie War in the Congo: Digital Technology, the Trade in Conflict Minerals, and Zombification', in Maria Levina and Diem-My T. Bui (eds), *Monster Culture in the 21st Century*, London: Bloomsbury, pp. 177–92.
Mbembe, Achille (2003), 'Necropolitics', *Public Culture*, 15.1: 11–40.
Moravec, Hans (1988), *Mind Children*, Cambridge, MA: Harvard University Press.
Mori, Masahiro (1970), 'The Uncanny Valley', *Energy*, 7.4: 33–45.
Phillips, Julie (2007), *James Tiptree, Jr.: The Double Life of Alice B. Sheldon*, New York: Picador.
Russ, Joanna (2005), *How to Suppress Women's Writing*, Austin: University of Texas Press.
Shelley, Mary (2012) [1818], *Frankenstein*, ed. J. Paul Hunter, 2nd edn, New York: Norton.
Stevenson, Melissa Colleen (2007), 'Trying to Plug In', *Science Fiction Studies*, 34.1: 87–105.
Tiptree, Jr, James (2014), *Her Smoke Rose Up For Ever*, London: Orion.
Turing, A. M. (1950), 'Computing Machinery and Intelligence', *Mind*, 59: 433–60, http://loebner.net/Prizef/TuringArticle.html (accessed 21 November 2016).

Walpole, Horace (1991) [1764], *The Castle of Otranto*, ed. W. S. Lewis, Oxford: Oxford University Press.
Winfield, Alan (2012), *Robotics*, Oxford: Oxford University Press.
Wolfe, Cary (2010), *What is Posthumanism?*, Minneapolis: University of Minnesota Press.
Yi, Dongshin (2010), *A Genealogy of Cyborgothic*, Farnham: Ashgate.

Part V

The Gothic before and after Post-structuralism

Chapter 11

The Gothic as a Theory of Symbolic Exchange
David Collings

Several chapters into the final volume of *The Mysteries of Udolpho* (1794), Ann Radcliffe inserts 'The Provençal Tale', interpolating it on the verge of the novel's final resolution (Radcliffe 1980: 552–7). In this tale, a baron, alone at night in his chamber, is visited by a knight unknown to him, who leads him into a recess in the nearby forest, where the stranger reveals the body of a man, recently murdered, 'stretched at its length, and weltering in blood', with a 'ghastly wound' on its forehead (1980: 556). Noticing that the features of this corpse match those of his visitor, the baron turns to the knight in surprise, only to see the latter melt away as a voice declares that the stranger knight, on his way back to England from the Holy City, was murdered. The voice goes on: 'Respect the honour of knighthood and the law of humanity; inter the body in Christian ground, and cause his murderers to be punished. As ye observe, or neglect this, shall peace and happiness, or war and misery, light upon you and your house for ever!' The baron accordingly gives the body of Sir Bevys due burial, 'with the honours of knighthood', and presumably fulfils all the demands given to him (1980: 556, 557).

This tale is unusual for Radcliffe's fiction, for it features an instance of supernatural visitation that it does not eventually explain away. Yet, since it is an interpolated tale, it does not violate the premises to which she otherwise adheres over the course of her romance. Indeed, one might take it to articulate a set of premises that she refuses to endorse. Even so, this tale provides a remarkably useful template for the novel's narrative, for before Emily St Aubert can fully enter into adulthood, she must discover the crime that haunts her family, Signora di Laurentini's murder of her father's sister, the Marchioness de Villeroi; understand the motives for that crime in sexual passion taken to excess; come to terms with aspects of her family history that her father kept secret from her; and absorb the consequences of what she has learned into her own life. In short, before she can enter her adult estate, she must carry out the psychic equivalent of confronting her ghosts, burying her dead, and according honours to those who came before her. While the novel translates the supernatural terms of the tale into a psychological idiom, it nevertheless foregrounds this tale at a suitably strategic moment as if to make clear that it finds in the tale a precise counterpart of its own form. Indeed, insofar as this insertion reprises Horace Walpole's *The Castle of Otranto* (1764), which similarly features the murder of a knight who has returned from a holy place, it transforms that initial Walpolean scheme into a template for Gothic romance.

The tale's presence in a Radcliffe novel is more striking because it also exemplifies the narrative pattern that informs Matthew Lewis's *The Monk* (1796), ostensibly written as a defiant rebuke to *The Mysteries of Udolpho* (Collings 2009: 131–60). In one of its more notorious scenarios, *The Monk* features an unexplained instance of the supernatural, the ghost of the Bleeding Nun, who haunts the living in part because she, too, indulges in sexual passion to excess leading to murder, disturbs the world of the living in the form of a bloodied corpse, and can be laid to rest only when her descendant Raymond causes her to be buried with all due respect and ceremony. In a more naturalistic vein, the novel also narrates how Agnes, after taking her vows as a nun, indulges her passion for her lover; punished for her fault through the equivalent of live burial in the dungeons of the convent, she is rescued, brought into the light of day, repents of her sin and is eventually permitted to legitimise her passion by marrying her lover.

The narrative pattern exemplified by 'The Provençal Tale' and the tale of the Bleeding Nun is clear: a corpse that has not received a proper burial is anomalous, out of place, an affront to the peace of the world. Such a body endures a condition no longer alive yet not quite dead, hovering in the space between recognised categories, and thus cries out for a ritual that can confer upon it the status of the dead. According to the premises of these tales, death is not a biological category, a condition one enters automatically on ceasing to live, but rather a status that one can attain only through the symbolic actions of the living. The ghost represents the profoundly unsettling condition of the literal body that has not yet been symbolised *as* dead; it is not a specious entity, the product of mere superstition, but the figure of a demand that it be given a clear and honourable status. While the dead can no longer participate directly in the world of the living, it turns out that a demand to respect them nevertheless has a certain imperative force, one that will haunt the living as long as they ignore its appeal.

It follows on these premises that the living body must impose a similar demand to be given more than a merely biological condition, to enjoy a status that can only be given and received in acts of formal bestowal. Both stories in *The Monk*, for example, suggest that the sexualised feminine body, exemplified by the Bleeding Nun and Agnes, is similarly unsettling, for it instances a form of embodiment that has not yet attained an authorised status through the ritual of marriage. The burial of the Bleeding Nun and the marriage of Agnes are parallel events, homologous (if contrasting) symbolisations. *The Monk* is not alone in exploring this homology; the Bleeding Nun's tale, after all, echoes that of Laurentini, who similarly murders for love. Moreover, much as Raymond must first learn of the tribulations of his ancestor and bury her with due honours before he can marry Agnes, Emily must confront the legacy of Laurentini's actions before she can marry Valancourt. In these tales, it seems, one must bury the dead before one can symbolise one's embodied passion in matrimony. One must confront an aspect of the literal body, the corporeality of both mortality and passion, before assuming its cultural significance in one's own right.

That logic, in turn, points to the implication that, insofar as sexual passion can lead to murder and thus an unburied corpse, the sexual body and the corpse share a common condition, as is evident in both of the tales in *The Monk*. In effect, the body riven by its passions mutilates itself; it is a murderous and murdered figure. The demand of the ghost has its counterpart in the demand of the passionate body, an imperious call to attain a human status through a suitable symbolic act. Without due symbolisation, the passionate body, like the corpse, disturbs the peace of the world. In effect, these tales suggest a counterpart to the symbolic relations between the dead and the living, this time in the symbolic exchange between sexual partners. According to this logic, far from being a biological fact, sexual passion is an uncanny presence whose disturbing effects can only be defused through symbolisation. The opposite of an authorised status, it turns out, is not any merely literal condition but transgression, not biology but a destabilising excess, the sole exit from which is symbolic exchange.

Although Radcliffe and Lewis explore these questions through apparently opposed scenarios, the explained and unexplained supernatural, this divergence may be less significant than what they share, the narrative theorisation of symbolic exchange. The fact that tales otherwise so distinct have this theorisation in common invites one to consider it as fundamental to Gothic narrative; indeed, as if to confirm this intuition, later Gothic tales frequently complicate this theorisation even further, creating a problematic remarkable in its range and sophistication. Twentieth-century critical reflection begins to theorise symbolic exchange with Marcel Mauss and anthropologists working in his wake; it is also a central concern for Jean Baudrillard, who deploys it in the course of his critique of the hegemonic forms of value under capitalism. As we have seen, however, these Gothic tales proleptically complicate such accounts, proposing that symbolic exchange operates not only between the living but also through those familiar gestures, embedded in virtually every society, whereby the living confer a recognised status on the newly deceased. In the Gothic account, social agents participate in a mode of exchange that takes place over a span of time much longer than the individual lifespan; one's place within the collective is received, just as one gives it to others, in a mode of reciprocity that applies not to objects but to subjects. According to this logic, human beings are to be understood as moments in a sequence of symbolic acts, each of which implies and calls for the rest; one does not own oneself, as in the ideology of liberal modernity, but rather owes oneself to others, occupying a position within a series of relations far wider than the self.

One might object that such a theory tends to subordinate the individual to the tradition in Burkean terms, for it seems to absorb the subject into what Burke calls the 'great mysterious incorporation of the human race' that includes 'those who are living, those who are dead, and those who are to be born' (Burke 2004: 120, 194–5). Yet Burke invokes this notion of an enduring, perpetually renewed body out of hostility to the French Revolution, taking his repudiation of the latter so far that he refused to be buried in a marked grave on his estate at Beaconsfield (Kramnick 1977: 189). Ironically, Burke's paranoid repudiation of what may come denies the alterity of the future, an element intrinsic to the very continuity he pretends to value (see Collings 2009: 59–94). This gesture thus reveals what might otherwise remain unmarked: symbolic exchange is not a practice that simply maintains the tradition, for its practices encode a certain antagonism between the living and the dead. That antagonism, in turn, foregrounds the fact that a tacit antagonism operates even within gift exchange in the irreducibility of any gift to any other, of any symbolic gesture to a standard of measure or a medium of equivalence. In giving a gift, one can never be certain that it will call forth a return; it is thus at least in part an instance of expenditure, a gesture without a final calculation. As a result, symbolic exchange refuses any explicit recognition that one trades an act directly for another, introducing a temporal interval between them to defuse the potential violence implicit in such an overt comparison (Collings 2009: 49–54). This deferral – evident as well, for example, in the interval between receiving a symbolic status at birth and giving such a status to the dead – tacitly recognises the incommensurability of each subject, bringing each not into a synchronic symbolic order, as Jacques Lacan might propose, but rather into a collective enacted through a sequence of acts across time. As a result, symbolic exchange produces no smooth continuity but a discontinuous continuity, an antagonistic reciprocity, which transmits a symbolic status between generations that retain an irreducible alterity to each other.

If all this is the case, then the relation of gift and counter-gift across generations is far more subtle and capacious than any Burkean stance. But Burke is not alone during the Romantic period for failing to understand the complexity of generational exchange. Indeed, his suppressed burial affiliates him with an apparently opposed figure, the Marquis de Sade, who out of an extravagance of defiance asked to be buried in an unmarked grave on which trees would be planted so that his remains would be effaced forever (Lever 1993: 563). Such a defiance of traditional norms rehearses in another form Burke's repudiation of alterity. In this period, further ironic instances of troubled burial abound. One might think, for example, of Burke's most famous respondent, Thomas Paine, who famously insisted, 'It is the living, and not the dead, that are to be accommodated', and who, denied burial in sacred ground in the United States because of his supposed infidelity, was eventually disinterred by his admirer, the radical journalist William Cobbett, who wished to give him honourable burial in a mausoleum in England but failed to do so, leaving Paine's bones unburied (Paine 1984: 42; Collins 2006). These and other instances indicate that in the ferment of this period, thinkers of various sorts at times imagined that they could overleap alterity and forcefully assert their agency against all the odds, only to reveal instead that the relations of symbolic exchange are not amenable to any such imposition.

What I have discussed so far suggests that, while the demand to bury the corpse may seem to be obvious, an instance of common sense, in fact its codification in narrative constructs a theory of social relations more nuanced than one might suspect: a theory homologous with notions of the gentry–plebeian reciprocity crucial throughout this period. Insofar as the Gothic builds on such a theory, elaborating it at times with great care across its various narratives, it explores an understanding of culture considerably more sophisticated than most of the familiar political, economic or social theories on offer in the period – including traditionalism and revolution, or utilitarianism and liberalism, to be sure, but also any stance that conceives of social agents in primarily biological terms, such as the biopower of Thomas Malthus (see Collings 2009: 161–92). Indeed, its strategy in this regard suggests that the practices upon which it draws, far from expressing simplistic or credulous beliefs superseded in the modern era, continue to obtain even under these new conditions and, what is more, urgently require renewed attention under the threat of conceptual systems that are intending to eradicate them. Even where practitioners of the Gothic appear to differ widely in their priorities, as in the cases of Radcliffe and Lewis, the Gothic tale insists that familiar conceptions of past and future, as well as modes of social and economic agency, rest on more fundamental practices of antagonistic reciprocity than they care to theorise. According to the Gothic, no such thing as wholesale traditionalism or full-throated revolutionary insurrection, for example, can succeed, for each generation necessarily demands to confer a human status on the next and to receive a human status in turn; continuity makes its demand felt, even when, or especially when, something has drastically interrupted that sequence.

Adopting this reading of the Gothic might seem to underline a broadly historicist account of its emergence. Indeed, there can be little doubt that the Gothic addresses itself to the question of symbolic exchange precisely because revolutionary challenges to the tradition in the later eighteenth century made it unusually difficult for the living to inherit the institutions of the past. The generation of the 1790s thus faced what they took to be the vexed question of how to confront the secret crimes of that past, the forms of violence and abuse intrinsic to its forms of power, and the flawed gender roles and sexual relations inscribed into those forms, as well as the problem of the violence implicit in condemning that past and in enduring the loss of continuity between generations. Hence they found it necessary to invent a discursive mode through which they could rethink that past and repair the breach. No doubt the tales of Radcliffe and Lewis, oriented as they are to the question of the supernatural, set themselves apart from the vast array of romances of their moment; as James Watt argues, most of the romances of this period focused on the drama of usurpation and the restoration of rightful ownership, placing such concerns within an overtly patriotic and didactic framework (Watt 1999: 7, 42–69). But in that case, what appears to be generic variation actually reinforces the central burden of what we would now call 'Gothic' tales, for they, alongside other romances, rather than being simply the product of a particular history, attempt to respond to and reinterpret that history, to think through what is at stake in the reception of the past and the articulation of its legacy.

It might thus be tempting to argue that the Gothic participates in formulating the terms of a historicism that becomes dominant in the initial decades of the nineteenth century – and one that underlies the historicist imperatives even of our moment (Chandler 1998). But the Gothic pursues another strategy. Rather than taking cultural discontinuity to be a historical question, an event within the complex interweaving of various causes and effects, it reads that interruption as the sign of a fundamental threat to culture: because the symbolic relations between the living and the dead have been altered, the human status of both is in danger (see Castle 1987: 241–4). In its view, the task is not to explain the breach in a discourse of knowledge but to heal it through a form of narrative reparation that revives and reconceives archaic practices in doing so. Rather than constituting a historicist response to the dilemmas of history, then, it provides in a fictional medium a quasi-anthropological response to what it considers a crisis in the basic practices of culture.

Undoubtedly, differing Gothic tales interpret this crisis in idiosyncratic ways. Sharing the post-Revolutionary anxiety of her moment, Radcliffe expands it to encompass a broader question: how to reconceive of the cultural traditions that precede the literature of sensibility in the new contexts imposed by the 1790s. Her tales typically centre on protagonists of sensibility encountering a world shaped by lack of sympathy, obsession with property, manipulation of law, the imposition of personal will and the indulgence in reckless expenditure or passionate murder. In effect, she places protagonists of feeling in a rather Hobbesian world, as if to expose the subjectivity of late eighteenth-century British literature to the realities of an alternative regime not shaped by its disciplines (Poovey 1979). Her work attempts to reinterpret those realities within the terms of an aesthetically capacious and psychologically coherent ethical life. It strives to incorporate a now alien past, as well as the breach between that past and the present, into a narratively rendered sensibility that can do justice to them while rewriting them in new terms. But since *The Mysteries of Udolpho* treats Emily's consciousness as perpetually 'preoccupied' with familiar cultural tropes, including commonplace emotions and their received representations (Pinch 1996: 111–36), it is no simple matter to bring her incrementally towards less derivative insights. The novel thus presents the reworking of that past and its continued impress as the labour of years in a process conducted under perpetual duress.

Within this overarching emphasis on the revision of a prior cultural mode, the novel can reach its completion only through a surprisingly subtle engagement with the violence against which it is written. Never having learned of the legacy of family violence from her father, who keeps the murder of his sister a secret and thus in some sense unburied and unaddressed (Miles 1993: 130–1), Emily in *Udolpho* at last understands the history of her family thanks to her direct encounter with Laurentini, as if to suggest that she can defuse the threat of passionate violence only through a face-to-face exchange with its perpetrator (Radcliffe 1980: 641–9, 654–64). Moreover, having apparently signed over her property to Montoni, Emily receives a testament from Laurentini, retaining her privileged status in part because of a gesture of reparation from the person who committed violence against her family. The novel thus converts the sign of interruption into that of restoration, providing Emily a solution, not through her development alone, but also through a gift from the agent of violence. Here the detective tale held in solution throughout the novel's plot is resolved not simply in Emily's gaining access to a particular knowledge – a requirement voiced as well in the interpolated tale, in which the deceased stranger makes a murder known in order to demand that the perpetrator be brought to justice – but also in the novel's placing such knowledge within the dynamics of exchange, confession, acceptance and reparation. Both knowledge and property thus operate under the imperative to bury the dead and heal the breach. A similar reworking of disruption is in play when Valancourt, having indulged himself at the gaming tables of Paris, stakes all on one last play and bestows his winnings on a friend, restoring him to his family, enabling him to marry, and thus in the novel's terms to enter responsible adulthood (Radcliffe 1980: 652–3). In these narratives, the novel converts the site of transgression into bestowal, incorporating sensibility and transgression alike into its sense of the demands of antagonistic reciprocity.

Where Radcliffe often places her focus on such a negotiation with a troubled past, Lewis in contrast emphasises the implications of the breach itself, organising his tale around the excessive enjoyments of sexual transgression and its close analogue, destructive insurrection (Paulson 1983: 219–25). These two approaches to the disturbance in continuity ultimately shape two contrasting, yet mutually implicated, traditions of the Gothic tale: Radcliffe's 'terror' and Lewis's 'horror' Gothic. As we have seen, in Lewis's novel, Raymond lays his ancestor the Bleeding Nun to rest and later receives his beloved Agnes back from a living death, completing the complex interplay between homologous tales. But this novel innovates on the Radcliffean tradition by providing a further tale in which no such resolution takes place, one that depicts what transpires when a protagonist chooses absolute transgression. In doing so, it complicates the Gothic's core concerns, suggesting that such a choice ironically takes shape through a demonic version of symbolic exchange, the act whereby Ambrosio signs his soul over to Lucifer. The novel thus proposes that the repudiation of symbolic exchange cannot help but participate in a darker version of the same. Absolute transgression does not merely abrogate reciprocity, creating the conditions for disaster, for in the view of the Gothic even this apparent instance of fierce self-assertion must ultimately constitute another version of symbolic exchange, a horrific gift to a nihilistic alterity. For the Gothic, even the repudiation of reciprocity must be read as reciprocity, albeit a demonic one. Yet the Gothic tale also suggests that such a version of exchange must ironically cancel itself. As the final twist in Ambrosio's tale suggests, the monk's fidelity to disaster meets with its own undoing in a Satanic contempt that annihilates whatever he hoped for in signing the contract in the first place. Fidelity to disaster is a disaster for fidelity itself. By the same token, such a fidelity also leads to a world where even the most fundamental relations of symbolic exchange collapse: on the novel's final page, as he dies over seven days, Ambrosio endures the scene of a cosmic anti-creation, an undoing of the divine gift of the world.

Because the novel provides no answer for this development, leaving Ambrosio's corpse unburied in its final lines, it refuses to incorporate this plot into the scenario of ceremonial burial visible elsewhere; in its overall form *The Monk* thus provides us with both a narrative of symbolic exchange and an account of its radical collapse, giving neither version final authority. It thus initiates a key counter-tradition in the Gothic mode, bringing into play, along with a theory of culture, one of anti-culture, showing that the rituals of culture can form no permanent defence against anti-creation. It suggests, in short, that the acts constituting the apparent foundation of the world in fact do not found it but only attempt to ward off the perpetual threat of its dissolution, remaining caught within a contest that is ultimately unresolvable.

By initiating this exploration, *The Monk* also conceives of the form that a relation to sheer transgressive enjoyment might take. Through the figure of Matilda, Lewis provides a figure who perpetually incites Ambrosio to further transgressions, promises gratifications still to be pursued, and encourages his final, lethal contract with Satan. Embodying the quintessence of seductive agency, a form of enjoyment that few desiring subjects could resist, Matilda cuts against any participation in symbolic exchange, voicing a demand to defy it instead. While the incitement to enjoyment might seem to emanate from the protagonist's own desire, in this novel it takes the form of an external – or what Lacanian theory would describe as an 'extimate' (Miller 2008) – agent, bearing out once again the Gothic insight that one's apparently autonomous, anti-relational acts transpire in another mode of relation. Moreover, that relation, as in any instance of symbolic exchange, remains unstable, partly antagonistic; although Matilda seems to play a subservient role in fulfilling each of Ambrosio's wishes, by perpetually enabling their satisfaction she eventually begins to dominate those wishes, commanding what she would fulfil. Much as Lacanian theory juxtaposes the moral imperatives of the superego with the superego's command to enjoy, proposing that under the harsh demands of the moral law lurks a hidden injunction to obscene pleasure (Žižek 1991: 9–11, 237–41; cf. Townshend 2007: 329–31), this novel interweaves the strictures of conscience with their repudiation, suggesting that the norms of the law inevitably bear within them a similarly imperious, but demonic, command. The figure of Matilda, of course, is an instance of the disastrous alterity discussed above; her perpetual incitement to transgression thus constitutes an ongoing invitation to choose anti-creation, to opt for a fidelity that would erase symbolic relations *tout court*. Such a figure becomes pivotal for further Gothic explorations of the underside of symbolic exchange. The extimate agent, too evil to be human and too intimate not to be, reappears variously in Charlotte Dacre's *Zofloya* (1806) as a racially marked, Satanic tempter; as the theologically seductive Gil-Martin in James Hogg's *The Private Memoirs and Confessions of a Justified Sinner* (1824); and much later (1897) as Stoker's Dracula, a figure that even Mina Murray, exemplar of married virtue, personal stability and savvy resourcefulness, cannot resist.

Insofar as *The Monk* creates mutually implicated scenarios of restoration and transgression, it ultimately points to that aspect of the subject – and of the collective – which occupies a precarious position between symbolic exchange and its demonic counterpart.

This position, which some might describe as a place of radical freedom, was especially palpable in the years during and immediately after the French Revolution, when the collective hovered between the prospects of further insurrection or restoration. Insofar as the Gothic reduces this instability to a dimension of the fictional subject, it creates scenarios in which the subject's volatility remains distinct from either narrative option. Perhaps the most notorious result of this development takes shape in Lord Byron's Oriental tales, where the visage of the so-called Byronic hero hints at a subjectivity whose previous acts and enduring commitments remain inscrutable.

These renderings, however, may only articulate in another idiom what is present in a seemingly benevolent figure such as La Luc in Radcliffe's *Romance of the Forest* (1791), who after the death of his wife withdraws from sexual interest in others and daily meditates on the one he hopes to join in the afterlife (Radcliffe 1986: 273–5). Insofar as he insists on sustaining his relation to her even after her death, he transforms her into a version of the undead, even if a beloved one. His condition thus nearly shades into that of Raymond in *The Monk*, who inadvertently finds himself pledged body and soul to the Bleeding Nun through his notorious mistake at the gates of the Castle of Lindenberg. In these tales, Radcliffe and Lewis explore a further complication to symbolic exchange, the prospect of marriage not to a mortal but an immortal, and thus potentially undead, partner. A marriage of this kind, while apparently within the terms of symbolic exchange, actually transforms it into something like fidelity to what such exchange normally excludes, the claims of a partner even after death, creating a paradoxical construction not far removed from the contract into which Ambrosio enters with Lucifer.

These various renditions of marriage to the undead hint that something uncanny takes place in marriage that it cannot fully defuse. La Luc's undying attachment to his wife and Raymond's inability to relieve himself of his involuntary receptivity to the visits of the Nun suggest that an aspect of the undead inheres in the living subject; marriage may thus be an exchange between immortals despite the marriage ceremony's reference to a fidelity until death. That prospect, in turn, suggests that an uncanny, undead element remains in each partner, a queer aspect of the subject that cannot fully defer itself in symbolic action. Yet as we have seen, the Gothic proposes that this aspect of the subject does not exemplify autonomy or self-ownership but rather is itself to be conceived as owed to another. Thus the Gothic tale proposes that symbolic exchange, rather than defusing the demands of the ghost, creates the conditions for mutual haunting, producing a reciprocity of undead subjects, both of whom will forever be vulnerable to the welcome or unwelcome visits of the other. In effect, the Gothic takes the fictions of romantic love so far that it transforms them into their uncanny counterpart, into tales of horrific – or horrifically blissful – undead romance.

These aspects of the Gothic tale directly anticipate the themes that Freud explores a century later, for they suggest that the *unheimlich* – 'uncanny' or un-home-like – is intrinsically interwoven with the *heimlich*, the home-like itself. The uncanny is the unacknowledged element of the homely, the demonic persistence within those rituals of mutual bestowal that create the conditions for home and comfort in the first place. To bestow the human condition, it seems, is also to take the risk of accepting an inhuman condition at the same time. Uncanny alterity is never mastered, never deferred for good. The Gothic captures this motif in part by suggesting that the resolution to its plots can take place only by means of a fault: Raymond sets in motion the narrative that culminates in his marriage to Agnes only through a plot to help her escape, much as Laurentini, the one who violates the St Aubert family, becomes the only one capable of giving Emily the knowledge she seeks. Such a fault bears the trace of antagonism intrinsic to the rituals of symbolic exchange: without a hint of transgression, there would never be occasion for those rituals of reciprocation across the generations or between sexual partners to take place at all.

The prospect that a hint of the inhuman persists even in the rituals of symbolic exchange almost inevitably produces a religious or metaphysical horror, the unbearable fear that even the sacred bears the traces of evil. Taken far enough, such a horror touches on the prospect that Christianity is stained with that which repudiates its conception of the ultimate act of symbolic exchange between humanity and divinity: the crucifixion. Within the folkloric traditions on which the Gothic relies, no figure exemplifies this repudiation better than the Wandering Jew, who in the traditional telling refuses to come to the aid of Christ on his way to the cross. This figure, redolent of old Europe's anti-Semitism, serves throughout the Gothic tradition as the supreme outsider; the tormentor of Christ himself, he is excluded from the sacrificial community and from death, forced to endure existence as a living version of the undead. In *The Monk*, this wanderer appears in the guise of the Grand Mogul, whose outsider status at once accurses him and gives him a privileged knowledge by which he can release others from their undead status. Here Christianity's implication in its own inhuman other leads to the further complication that this other can help restore the sacrificial community itself, as if he is necessary for the relations of symbolic exchange themselves to function. In effect Lewis explores the logic of the Greek *pharmakos*, the sacrificial victim who attains a certain redemptive agency, suggesting that the one who violates symbolic exchange becomes, through that very event, a sacred outsider capable of restoring it (cf. Girard 1977: 94–6, 296–7).

But perhaps the most complex formulation of a Gothic religious horror appears in Bram Stoker's *Dracula* (1897), especially in the scene in which Mina, by now Mina Harker, is seen sucking blood from the breast of the undead Dracula (Stoker 1996: 281–2). This sublimely transgressive scene evokes the prospect that vampiric transmission constitutes a demonic parody of the Eucharist, producing a community of outcasts who share the exact contrary of a redemptive, sacrificially authorised, gender-normative and ethnically and sexually legitimate blood (Herbert 2002: 115–19; O'Malley 2006: 158–60). Even worse, the novel suggests that its virtuous characters are vulnerable to being converted to this unholy community merely because the vampire can gain access to their bodies, hinting that virtually anyone who enjoys the condition of embodiment hosts an involuntarily vampiric disposition. The sacrificial community, it seems, is at least potentially the host to its hellish counterpart. Still worse, the chief agent of this horrific Eucharist is almost impossible to destroy; to bury him is only to provide him a base for endless wandering, giving him his properly improper position as the perpetual contrary of the sacrificial community, a late version of the Wandering Jew. Thus Stoker must invent Van Helsing, a character who mediates between Britain and its Eastern European other and who, through his strange knowledge, can help construct symbolic exchange on a new level, enabling what one might call the emplotment of a second death, a further kind of burial, for Dracula and his acolytes – a death that can usher them into a state of eternal rest. In providing this new construction, however, the novel innovates yet again on the themes central to the Gothic, for its rendition of the passage from undeath to a truly final, peaceful death proposes an ultimate level of symbolic action: in its view symbolic exchange can definitively respond to the call of transgressive enjoyment only by producing a second version of burial that surmounts undead pleasure in the even more imperative bliss of peace. In that case, as it works through the themes of Radcliffe's interpolated tale on a second level, *Dracula* proposes that the final form of the symbolic relation of the dead to the living is to exchange the peace of the grave for the peace of the earth.

One could argue that in this tale the complex role of the Grand Mogul, who is at once outcast and redemptive, is split into the more consistently transgressive Dracula and the consistently restorative Van Helsing, considerably simplifying the ambiguities of *The Monk*. But a similarly complex role reappears elsewhere in *Dracula*, as Mina, partially infected through her contact with Dracula, uses her unconscious knowledge to aid the mission of her peers in tracking him down and laying him to rest. Here an unconscious vulnerability to undeath becomes an asset, a means of restoring the Eucharistic community, suggesting that Mina has some of the attributes of the *pharmakos* herself. That suggestion, in turn, hints that any subject infested by the persistence of undeath can through a second-order symbolic act lay that intimate vampiric agency to rest. In this account, the subject's vulnerability to the death drive goes only so far; even this dimension, cryptically inscribed within the relations of symbolic exchange itself, can be overcome through the bestowal of a state that exceeds any haunting, that goes beyond the mere immortality of the subject to an anonymous eternity, an alterity beyond all desire.

The appearance of a figure such as Van Helsing within the Gothic tale – an expert in the revenants of old Europe who, through his shadowy knowledge, can become a resource in laying them to rest – brings that tale within the vicinity of psychoanalysis, whose initial Freudian formulations appeared during the same decade as *Dracula*. The role that Stoker gives to Van Helsing is soon to be taken over by the analyst, who similarly aspires to a knowledge of the soul's uncanny dimensions. Where Van Helsing relies on hypnosis to capture Mina's cryptic knowledge, Freud moves from using hypnosis to inviting a certain mode of speech, bringing him closer to aspects of the literary evocation of the unspoken and thus to central terms in the Gothic tradition. In these and other ways, the analyst becomes the heir of the Gothic project, attempting to tease out the inhuman attributes of the haunted social subject and to bring those attributes into the light of day, allowing them expression through the interchange of speech. In this way, the analyst enables the subject to assume a more fully conceived relation to desire and to place it more consciously in relation to others.

Within the trajectory I have traced in this essay, then, psychoanalysis extends Radcliffe's reinscription of the interpolated tale, following through on the attempt to find the unburied corpse, to recognise its alterity through appropriate symbolic action and to lay the unquiet dimensions of the soul to rest. Like the Gothic, psychoanalysis contemplates the various challenges of modernity from within premises it inherits from a distant past, sustaining imperatives that modernity has striven to forget and that as a result haunt it with redoubled force. Moreover, as we have seen, like the Gothic it conceives of the subject's desire not as its innermost essence, an instance of its autonomy, but rather as a further instance of alterity; as a result, in its mapping of the subject and its relations, psychoanalysis refuses the terms of fictional realism and its attendant psychologically 'deep' or round subject, as well as the fictions of liberal social agency inscribed in such literature. It thus carries forward the broadly Gothic project of conceiving even of modernity in non-modern terms (cf. Collings 2009: 31–4), making explicit what the entire ensemble of apparently secular modernity otherwise would miss, the insistence of symbolic exchange.

A full rendition of the consequences of the Gothic for our own moment would thus need to interpret how the Gothic tale, psychoanalysis and their heirs, taken together, place symbolic exchange under the care of one who, knowing its ways, can tend to its practices within the nearly lethal context of liberal modernity. Heirs of all its sub-modes – Radcliffe's explained supernatural, Lewis's unexplained supernatural, and a wide range of further renditions of seduction, insurrection, usurpation and restoration – this ensemble of Gothic and psychoanalysis shows that its proper form inheres, not in any one of them, but in the dialectic between them and thus in the gradual elaboration of a core set of questions into ever more explicit and capacious terms. The Gothic, in short, is not a specific narrative form or mode but a theorisation of symbolic exchange that can range beyond narrative boundaries to incite and enliven a range of further discourses and practices enduring into our own moment. It is the site where a supposed modernity conceives of itself otherwise, accepting the demand to recognise and symbolise its vexed relation with a repudiated past.

References

Baudrillard, Jean (1981), *For a Critique of the Political Economy of the Sign*, trans. Charles Levin, St. Louis: Telos.
Beckford, William (1995), *Vathek and Other Stories*, ed. Malcolm Jack, Harmondsworth: Penguin.
Burke, Edmund (2004) [1790], *Reflections on the Revolution in France*, ed. Conor Cruise O'Brien, Harmondsworth: Penguin.
Castle, Terry (1987), 'The Spectralization of the Other in *The Mysteries of Udolpho*', in Felicity Nussbaum and Laura Brown (eds), *The New Eighteenth Century: Theory, Politics, English Literature*, New York: Methuen, pp. 231–53.

Chandler, James (1998), *England in 1819: The Politics of Literary Culture and the Case of Romantic Historicism*, Chicago: University of Chicago Press.

Collings, David (2009), *Monstrous Society: Reciprocity, Discipline, and the Political Uncanny, c. 1780–1848*, Lewisburg, PA: Bucknell University Press.

Collins, Tom (2006), *The Trouble with Tom: The Strange Afterlife and Times of Thomas Paine*, London: Bloomsbury.

Dacre, Charlotte (1997) [1806], *Zofloya, or The Moor*, ed. Kim Ian Michasiw, New York: Oxford University Press.

Freud, Sigmund (1959) [1919], 'The Uncanny', in *Collected Papers*, trans. Joan Riviere, New York: Basic Books, IV, pp. 368–407.

Girard, René (1977), *Violence and the Sacred*, trans. Patrick Gregory, Baltimore: Johns Hopkins University Press.

Herbert, Christopher (2002), 'Vampire Religion', *Representations*, 79: 100–21.

Hogg, James (1981) [1824], *The Private Memoirs and Confessions of a Justified Sinner*, ed. Ian Duncan, New York: Oxford University Press.

Kramnick, Isaac (1977), *The Rage of Edmund Burke: Portrait of an Ambivalent Conservative*, New York: Basic Books.

Lever, Maurice (1993), *Sade: A Biography*, trans. Arthur Goldhammer, San Diego: Harcourt Brace.

Lewis, Matthew (1998) [1796], *The Monk*, ed. Howard Anderson, New York: Oxford University Press.

Maturin, Charles Robert (1989) [1820], *Melmoth the Wanderer*, ed. Douglas Grant, New York: Oxford University Press.

Mauss, Marcel (1967), *The Gift: Forms and Functions of Exchange in Archaic Societies*, trans. Ian Cunnison, New York: Norton.

Miles, Robert (1993), *Gothic Writing 1750–1820: A Genealogy*, New York: Routledge.

Miller, Jacques-Alain (2008), 'Extimity', *The Symptom*, 9, www.lacan.com/symptom/extimity.html (accessed 4 October 2018).

O'Malley, Patrick R. (2006), *Catholicism, Sexual Deviance, and Victorian Culture*, New York: Cambridge University Press.

Paine, Thomas (1984) [1791, 1792], *Rights of Man*, ed. Henry Collins, Harmondsworth: Penguin.

Paulson, Ronald (1983), *Representations of Revolution (1789–1820)*, New Haven, CT: Yale University Press.

Pinch, Adela (1996), *Strange Fits of Passion: Epistemologies of Emotion, Hume to Austen*, Stanford: Stanford University Press.

Poovey, Mary (1979), 'Ideology and "The Mysteries of Udolpho"', *Criticism*, 21: 307–30.

Radcliffe, Ann (1980) [1794], *The Mysteries of Udolpho*, ed. Bonamy Dobrée, New York: Oxford University Press.

Radcliffe, Ann (1986) [1791], *The Romance of the Forest*, ed. Chloe Chard, New York: Oxford University Press.

Stoker, Bram (1996) [1897], *Dracula*, ed. Roger Luckhurst, New York: Oxford University Press.
Townshend, Dale (2007), *The Orders of Gothic: Foucault, Lacan, and the Subject of Gothic Writing, 1764–1820*, New York: AMS.
Watt, James (1999), *Contesting the Gothic: Fiction, Genre and Cultural Conflict, 1764–1832*, Cambridge: Cambridge University Press.
Žižek, Slavoj (1991), *For They Know Not What They Do: Enjoyment as a Political Factor*, New York: Verso.

Chapter 12

Incorporations: The Gothic and Deconstruction
Tilottama Rajan

When deconstruction is linked to the Gothic, commentators often evoke Jacques Derrida's *Specters of Marx* (1993; e.g. Wang 2011). Yet Derrida's emphasis on the spectre as harbinger of the future and the obligation to redeem the 'debt' (Castricano 2001: 9) implies a utopianism at odds with a Gothic heart of darkness that has already made itself felt in deconstruction's precursors: in Maurice Blanchot's focus on language, death, solitude and night in *The Space of Literature* (1955) or Emmanuel Levinas's 'horror' of (non-)being in *Existence and Existents* (1947; see Rajan 2002: 62–75, 82–4). Derrida's defanging of the spectre is evident when he converts his own potentially horrific *image* of the philosopher Jean-Paul Sartre – as the revenant who keeps running after his decapitation to convey a message about the Greek victory at Marathon – into the tamer *concept* of a legacy not fully grasped (2002: 267–8). Likewise, *Specters of Marx* links the revenant to inheritance, the *à venir* (or still-to-come), and a 'messianism without content'. The spectre becomes the 'nostalgic waiting for a redemption' or 'a spirit' (Derrida 1994: 28, 136) in the idealist sense of 'spirit' that Derrida criticises in Heidegger, a sublimation from which Derrida's own late work is not immune. At the same time, however, the muting of the spectre's deathly threat remains haunted by what Paul de Man has called the 'rudderless signification' behind language (de Man 1996: 61) that for deconstruction always marks the slipping away of every referent from every signifier. Accordingly, this chapter examines a broader constellation of texts than those by Derrida in order to probe the unresolved differences in deconstruction that the Gothic can help unpack. It suggests that Gothic moments in deconstructive thinkers disclose something unprocessed, rather than a settled methodology reducible to formulae such as language as a site of non-identity or an 'opening to the other'. The Gothic, as the unprocessed *par excellence*, as an incoherent materiality outside concepts, provides a unique environment for bringing the unfinished project of deconstruction back from attempts to systemise or make it whole, whether its own or those of commentators.

The softening of deconstruction began, as Tom Cohen argues, when the 1980s controversy over de Man's wartime writings made it desirable to model a 'good' rather than 'bad' deconstruction that could not be charged with nihilism: Derrida in the 1990s rather than de Man or Derrida himself in the 1970s and early 1980s (Cohen 1998: 35; 2012a). In the wake of revelations that the young de Man had written literary columns for a Belgian collaborationist journal, deconstruction had to be expediently identified with Derrida alone, who became separated from literature and re-domiciled in philosophy, in a move that forgets his close focus on language as 'the process of death at work in signs', or what he calls writing, *écriture* (Derrida 1973: 40). Derrida had to be reconstructed, and indeed refashioned himself, as a humanist concerned with cosmopolitanism, friendship and democracy. To craft these 'apps', as Cohen bitingly puts it, Derrida himself entered 'contracts of dependency' with various 'groups' (Cohen 2012a): political or social thinkers and, to satisfy the philosophical side, (post-)Heideggerians such as Levinas and Jean-Luc Nancy through whom deconstruction was made less threatening by being identified with an ontology of radical passivity (see Rajan 2012: 298–9). The result was a certain 'occasionalism' in his work;[1] as Cohen notes, Derrida almost always wrote *on* someone, 'graft[ing] his writing into what was there' (Cohen 2012a). Derrida took up occasions for dialogue in fields that went well beyond his earlier triad of philosophy, literature and linguistics: politics, medical humanities or theology, among others. We can see this as 'response-ability' (Silverman 2007: 304–5). But the effect can be to fragment his later work, and arguably this attempt to renew deconstruction and make it speak to a wider audience has been accomplished with less compromise by others who rigorously engage with a single new field: Friedrich Kittler in technology, Cohen himself in film/cultural theory, and Lee Edelman in queer theory.

By contrast, de Man, according to Cohen, did not try to please. He adhered uncompromisingly to the trauma, disclosed in 'Shelley Disfigured' (1979), of language as a 'positional power' whose very randomness obliterates its meaning (de Man 1984: 116–19) and exposes the subject to machinic 'pre-inscriptive sites of memory formation' that Cohen now links to biosemiosis and the neural turn (Cohen 2012a; 2012b: 110). Whether or not de Man escaped becoming a 'franchise'

(Cohen 2012a) any more than Derrida (Guillory 1993: 176–268), it is true that his work is traversed by tropes of disfiguration and defacement that materialise an 'inhuman' quality of language that the late Derrida skirts. But de Man's barely avoided Gothicism – his terms are often wilfully dead metaphors – also raises the question of whether his deconstruction confronts its heart of darkness. Or is the Gothic a scar, a limit to the intellectualising and abstracting impulses of theory that also sometimes characterise deconstruction itself?

Of course it would be crude to describe either de Man's work or deconstruction as 'Gothic'. The major theorists of deconstruction, if they write on literature, do not choose Gothic texts. The Gothic is not an allegory of deconstruction, nor is deconstruction a key to the Gothic. Hence, in putting the two into an asymmetrical dialogue, I avoid translating Gothic tropes in deconstruction into concepts that make the latter's use of the 'crypt', for instance, too simply the place of an 'unresolvable contradiction' whereby a word works in more than one way (Castricano 2001: 7). These *topoi* are often catachreses (or figures for what has no name), which is to say they enter deconstruction as what Slavoj Žižek calls an anamorphic distortion that affectively registers how theoretical translation can include contortions of its logic that are symptomatically revealing (Žižek 1997: 97). But more than just a symptom, the Gothic is also an environment for reading: a way of approaching deconstruction outside the hagiography of defences of de Man after the revelations about his journalism or commentaries on the late Derrida that adopt his own theories of legacy and survival (e.g. Silverman 2007). The Gothic is, in Žižekian terms, a kind of Real, a primal chaos of conflicted differences, such as life and death, that blur into each other (the 'traumatic social division' underlying all civilisation, for one thing), in which the Real is not barred from symbolisation, as it is for Lacan, but erupts or implodes within the symbolic order (Žižek 1989: 45, 147–8).

In arguing all this, I am still using 'Gothic' to evoke a set of conventions or 'gestures' (Sedgwick 1986) including castles, spectres, vaults, secret passages, crypts and live burial – *topoi* associated with secrecy, the hollowed-out, abjection, terror, horror and, at some level, death and the void. As such, signs in the Gothic function as what Derrida, taking apart Husserl's logocentric theory of language, calls 'indications' that point to something *other* rather than 'expressions' that convey it (Derrida 1973: 17, 27–9), intimating an absence that cannot be articulated in concepts. Gothic *moments* or *traces* in deconstruction thus register an excess or gap or hole in the conceptual edifice; *tropes* of the crypt or the secret agent, such as we will find in Abraham and Torok or Cohen, are more self-conscious about the Gothic as an affective source for theory. Much has also been written about the conventional nature of these signifiers that seem like the *bric à brac* of a B-movie. But as Jerrold Hogle argues, the Gothic combines a 'sham' quality with the suggestion of 'deep foundations . . . in unconscious desires' (Hogle 1994: 23). So, as we consider these indications, signs and symptoms that withhold something as an apparatus or space for reading deconstruction, Hogle's description of the Gothic as a receptacle into which unsorted material is 'abjected', 'thrown off' or 'thrown down and under' is also useful (Hogle 1998: 178).

However, unlike Julia Kristeva, from whom Hogle draws the term abjection, the figure of a receptacle can also imply material that is sheltered in a kind of archive for the future. Hogle uses Walpole's own mini-castle, Strawberry Hill, as a synecdoche for the way the Gothic houses sediment or peripheralise traces, part meanings that have been stored up and emptied out because they no longer work or have not yet been worked through (Hogle 1994: 23). A literary example is Sophia Lee's novel about the secret daughters of Mary Queen of Scots, whose title, *The Recess* (1783–5), refers to a subterranean labyrinth of rooms that sheltered Catholic priests after Henry VIII's destruction of the monasteries, with each priest adding a new room, all connected by 'secret passage[s]' (Lee 2000: 8, 22). This architecture creates the space for reading Lee's multi-generational, partly epistolary novel, which moves from the reign of Elizabeth to that of James I, and from chivalric to ordinary life, but in a circular rather than progressive structure that allows for the eternal return of unassimilated material that is not yet done with (see Rajan 2017). But as my account suggests, rather than seeing the Gothic as a 'complex' that is a transitional moment in a residual > dominant > emergent timeline, I prefer to see it as a permanent 'matrix' of possibilities that are alternately blocked, productive and disjunctive (Rajan 2015: para. 13–14). As a matrix, the Gothic, as I argue elsewhere, can be approached through what Hegel, in the period of its inception, called 'symbolic' art, which is also monstrous, fantastic or mechanically put together, and thus, like Mary Shelley's *Frankenstein* (1818) or her husband's earlier Gothic novel *St Irvyne* (1810), a turbulent amalgam of undead possibilities. Although, of course, Hegel does not use these examples, the point is his distinction of symbolic from a more aesthetic 'classical' art. Where the classical is the 'adequate embodiment of the idea', symbolic art is premature, its 'idea' still 'indeterminate'. Its 'restless fermentation' indicates a consciousness 'labour[ing]' to make itself 'clear to itself' rather than resting in 'settled' ideas (Hegel 1970: 76–7, 438–9; Rajan

2015: para. 5–6, 10–13). In all these respects, the Gothic 'matrix' goes far deeper than the superficial motifs that are its 'indications', as its distortions point to a kernel of error at the heart of all conceptualisation (Rajan 2015: para. 9, 13).

The story of deconstruction's ferment, which makes it a conceptual edifice haunted by unresolved issues rather than a single method, zigzags through de Man, the early Michel Foucault, and others in the next generation through whom de Man, himself abjected and thrown down and under, returns in different forms. During that process, key moments or 'knots' arise in which the Gothic kernel surfaces, albeit indistinctly and fleetingly. Derrida's first decade-and-a-half of work provides some examples, since what opens up in language for him then is the 'relation of an "existent" to his death' (Derrida 1973: 10). Crucial to this 'Gothic' Derrida is 'Fors', his introduction to Nicholas Abraham and Maria Torok's *The Wolf-Man's Magic Word* (1976), which deals more broadly with their psychoanalytic work, including their essays from 1956–86 collected in *The Shell and the Kernel* (1987). Abraham and Torok repeatedly circle round the figures of phantom, crypt, tomb, burial, secret. Given Freud's failure to grasp the structures of what is 'buried alive' in the Wolf-Man's psyche, these Gothic conventions provide the apparatus for Abraham and Torok's 'cryptonymy', which replaces Freud's procedures with an 'anasemic' reading that works through the homonyms and anagrams that populate the Wolf-Man's private 'verbarium' to get at the unspoken word under or beside its spoken counterpart (Abraham and Torok 1986: 107–13). One could claim, with their translator Nicholas Rand, that Derrida's essay makes *Magic Word* and their larger corpus an 'allegory of deconstruction', distilling the figures of cryptonymy into a logic of concepts, though admittedly 'antiphilosophical' concepts such as 'remainder, *différance*, dissemination' etc. However, 'Fors' is not an exegesis of Abraham and Torok but, as Rand concedes, 'an encounter with [Derrida's] own modes of research' (Rand 1986: lxvi–lxix). As such it does not epitomise Derrida's mastery of his own method, unlike his essays on Husserl and Hegel, but is rather an encounter with deconstruction across the screen of what Foucault, writing on Blanchot, calls 'a thought from outside': an alien, yet interior, thought that opens thought to its own crypts. For Torok's suggestion that Freud's relation to the Wolf-Man's trauma incorporates his own trauma (Abraham and Torok 1986: 85–6) – in what psychoanalysis calls the counter-transference – invites us to subject both psychoanalysis and theory to the tools they use to read their object.

Anasemic reading clearly resonated with Derrida by 1976 because it was itself a product of Jean Starobinski's rediscovery (1971) of Ferdinand de Saussure's work on anagrams, which inaugurated a key moment of 'theory' in the twentieth century by disclosing a dark matter in language. Like the linguistic turn in Lacan, Abraham and Torok's anasemic reading and cryptonymy shift the focus from the content to the structures and language of the unconscious: from transparency to opacity. The homonyms and anagrams, which exist only at a level of formalisation that refuses 'referential reading' (de Man 1986: 36), are 'words buried alive' inside a crypt and kept safe behind a 'door silently sealed off like a condemned passageway'. This crypt is a 'pocket of resistance' inside the self, an interior 'partitioned off from the interior', so that the more the 'self keeps the foreign element as a foreigner inside itself, the more it excludes it' (Derrida 1986: xv–xix, xxxv). That paradox recalls Freud, for whom consciousness is not at the core of being but at the 'surface of the brain' in the cerebral cortex. In trauma, some radical event bypasses this outermost layer and lodges inside, a 'fragment of living substance' protected from 'stimuli' by an outer 'shield' that has become 'inorganic' (Freud 1955: 25–9). Such a topology, of course, describes the structure of the Gothic in which hidden depths of fragmentation and dissolution – or 'disarticulation' in de Man's term (1996: 79) – are indicated yet shielded by an outer layer of castle walls, locked rooms and vaults that is almost too predictable.

Taking up this architecture of the unconscious, 'Fors' emphasises the notion of a *double* crypt: a crypt that shields a further crypt. Derrida writes of a 'cryptic enclave', 'walls, leaning the power of intolerable pain against an ineffable, forbidden pleasure', of an 'inner safe' or 'artificial unconscious' that constitutes the crypt itself 'as an outer safe' that is 'caulked or padded along its inner partition'. But in this 'fortress' there are also 'partitions, cavities, corridors, niches', which generate crossings and 'disguises' (Derrida 1986: xiv–xv, xix–xx). The double crypt is the site of what Abraham and Torok call 'incorporation', which they distinguish from the 'introjection' (or internalisation) of the lost object that allows it to be sublimated in normal mourning. The de-synonymising of these two terms, which are not clearly distinguished by Freud and Karl Abraham, is considered Abraham and Torok's major contribution to psychoanalysis. Briefly, incorporation is to introjection or internalisation as melancholia in Freud is to mourning. In introjection, the lost thing is recovered and distanced in words or concepts. But incorporation, which Abraham and Torok develop in a Gothic direction, has a traumatically physical aspect: in order not to 'have to "swallow" a loss', we literally swallow or 'ingest' it, burying it alive inside us as the undead (Abraham and Torok 1994: 126–7), as in Poe's 'The Cask of Amontillado' or 'The Premature Burial'.[2] But what the crypt, 'as the incorporated object's "tomb"', encloses is 'not the object itself but its exclusion' from 'the introjection process', to which psychoanalysis gives the name 'the Thing', which is in effect a nothing (Derrida 1986: xvii).

Starobinski's reconstruction of an *other* Saussure whose work was contemporaneous with Freud's (Lotringer 1973: 6–9), an insane double who had to be locked away by a suppression that embargoed his work on anagrams and published only the *Course in General Linguistics* (1916), has been hugely influential on theorists including Derrida, de Man, Baudrillard and Deleuze. Still, despite their metapsychological innovations, Abraham and Torok's decrypting of the Wolf-Man's words misses this double crypt that Derrida emphasises and so does not fully break with Freudian dream interpretation and its eventual recovery of a signified. Moreover, despite going well beyond Freud in distinguishing 'incorporation' and 'introjection', and despite centring *The Wolf-Man's Magic Word* on the Gothic concept of incorporation as swallowing something and being swallowed alive, Abraham and Torok as therapists remain Freudian rationalists in wanting to cure the Wolf-Man's refusal to mourn, arguing that 'the magical "cure" by incorporation exempts the subject from the painful process of reorganization' (Abraham and Torok 1994: 127). Curiously, too, they did not actually analyse the Wolf-Man, they only read his case; hence their cure, therapeutically untested, is more a theory of reading. As such, it stops short of realising its potential, instituting its own 'magic cure' by terminating the analysis in *decryption*. In this move they resemble Ann Radcliffe, who wants to explain the supernatural and thus return to normality. By contrast, Derrida dwells on the maintenance of the crypt, and thus on 'incorporation': 'Incorporation is never finished' and also 'never finishes anything *off*' (Derrida 1986: xxi).

We can also trace in Michel Foucault this double movement of something that is never closed even when, and precisely because, it closes itself off. Foucault is not generally associated with deconstruction, especially now that his early work up to *The Order of Things* (1966) is neglected in favour of a later biopolitical corpus that eschews any reference to literature or psychoanalysis (Rajan 2002: 142–98). Yet in 1963, well before Starobinski or Abraham and Torok, he published a book on the early twentieth-century writer

Raymond Roussel's 'textual machines': his obsession with anagrams, homonyms, portmanteau words and catachreses, an entire writing system that moves purely at the level of the signifier, even as it 'indicates' something beyond this tissue of words. Roussel is part of the literary corpus that has since been used to unpack the 'mad' side of his contemporary Saussure, the limit where structuralism turns on itself and becomes anti-science and *délire*. Lacan calls this *délire* '*lalangue*', a chaotic fore-language, which is the very opposite of the *langue* that a more public Saussure uses to ground *parole* (Lecercle 1985: 2–11, 18–23). But unlike others who see Roussel as inventing a (post-)structuralist *nouveau roman* or opening up a Deleuzian creative schizophrenia (Robbe-Grillet 1965: 79–87; Deleuze 1990: 84–5), Foucault's study is a cryptonymy that adds a whole level of Gothic affect to Roussel's writing system through the accompanying images he foregrounds. Thus, in his posthumous *How I Wrote Certain of My Texts* (1935), Roussel offers his own key to his work through the 'process', a mechanical writing programme, void of affect and imagery, which functions purely at the level of the signifier, through puns, homonyms and, above all, the anagram as the fantasy of a secret and total meaning. But Foucault begins with Roussel's death behind a door 'locked on the inside', making 'the process' a double crypt: 'a key which is itself locked up, a cipher which deciphers and yet is encoded' (Foucault 1986: 4–5). His analysis is populated by figures of labyrinths, 'automaton corpses', the 'enclosed sun', the 'solar void' and the title of one of Roussel's novels, *La Doublure* (both a lining and a doubling). It is also punctuated by references to Roussel's missed encounters with the analysts Ludwig Binswanger and Pierre Janet (Foucault 1986: 155, 162–4). Framing Roussel's magic word(s) through his death, Foucault thus opens his language games into the black hole of the Thing (as deployed by Lacan, Žižek, Kristeva and others). He unravels them into their negative, disclosing 'the imprint of a pathological nervous system' on this 'language about language' (Foucault 1986: 159, 166).

Foucault's *Raymond Roussel* remained untranslated until 1986, when it was posthumously retitled *Death and the Labyrinth*, referring to its chapter on the minotaur lurking at the heart of the labyrinth of language, which figures the 'duplication of life in death' that haunts all signification (Foucault 1986: 86). The return of this book that had been locked away was then accompanied by an interview (1983) in which Foucault describes it as his 'secret affair. You know, he was my love for several summers' (1986: 185). Given his other secret, his imminent death from AIDS, and the fact that Roussel was probably homosexual but deeply closeted, the book forms a crypt in Foucault's own corpus. For Foucault curiously insisted it be published on the same day as *The Birth of the Clinic*, a quite different and less private work. Superficially, *The Birth of the Clinic* resembles later genealogies such as *Discipline and Punish: The Birth of the Prison* (1975). It deals with the medical gaze in the context of clinical institutions; indeed, in its 1972 revision, it makes a fetish of avoiding any 'excess of the signifier over the signified', wanting to reduce 'the voluminous mass of language' to a 'discourse' that is simply 'the fact of its ... appearance' (Foucault 1973: xvi–xvii; 1986: 16). As such it aims at the 'clarity' that Foucault, writing on Flaubert's *The Temptation of Saint Anthony* in 'Fantasia of the Library' (1967), had seen as achievable only through the 'conflagration' of a 'primary discourse' that remains 'suspended' over Flaubert's work as a 'temptation' constantly to be 'repress[ed]' (Foucault 1977: 88). Yet despite the seeming distance between the sociology of medicine and a literature 'folded back upon the enigma of its own origin' (Foucault 1970: 300), *The Birth* is linked by secret passages to *Death and the Labyrinth*: topically (because of Roussel's encounters with doctors) and because at *The Birth*'s end Foucault turns the 'brightness' of the medical 'gaze' back into 'the abyss beneath illness', evoking Nietzsche's *The Birth of Tragedy* and the death of God and turning fleetingly to an underworld populated by Rilke, Sade and Hölderlin's Empedocles standing on the edge of Etna (Foucault 1973: 195–9). In his essays from 1963 to 1967 on Blanchot, Roussel, Bataille and others, Foucault repeatedly uses the word 'murmuring', borrowed from Blanchot, to suggest a subtle haunting by echoes and traces that 'murmur' in its interstices as the very essence of 'literature' (Foucault 1977: 60). Literature in this sense is also a style of reading, and, by bringing it to a book such as *The Birth*, we can see the institutions and procedures through which medical consciousness circulates as similar to the signifiers through which Roussel's 'process' moves, an uneasiness that indicates the duplication of life in death.

Together with the posthumous interview, these twin texts suggest how Foucault too wrote his texts on 'multilevels of secrecy' (Foucault 1986: 7). After *The Archeology of Knowledge* (1969), Foucault would turn to being a public intellectual, giving up the 'world populated' by 'ancient ... spirits' which he had inhabited in these early essays and which we also see in the haunted and hauntingly poetic prose of *The Order of Things*. In a conflagration of his own archive, he would begin what he attributes to Flaubert: 'an "education" in the prose of the modern world' (Foucault 1977: 87). Foucault's later work is not deconstructive, but together *Death* and *The Birth* enact an auto-deconstruction of the human sciences by literature. However, what this deconstruction *is* constitutes an unresolved and continuing issue. On the one hand, we could see the relationship between *The Birth* and *Death* as that which Foucault describes in *The Order of Things* between 'the cogito and the unthought', a relation requiring the 'articulation of thought on everything' which, though insuperably 'exterior', is still 'not foreign to thought' (1970: 324). In this formulation, which does not embrace the death of the subject but insists on a 'modern' form of the 'cogito' (Rajan 2002: 187–8), Foucault uses the word 'unthought' and not 'unconscious'. He makes the haunting of the *cogito* of intellectual history and the social sciences by the unthought of literature into a deconstruction that is reflective and productive, thus also making a bold claim for the wider social relevance of a deconstruction that has literature as its lining. On the other hand, Foucault's conception of literature is powerfully influenced by Blanchot, who associates it with night, death and solitude. From this perspective, the labyrinth of signs that conceals Roussel's death discloses literature as the place of what de Man calls 'the zero'. The zero, to which I will return later, is the complete cancellation of meaning. In order to avoid this groundlessness, we see it as 'a *one*', a 'something', and give it a 'name'. But as de Man writes, evoking Beckett, 'the zero is actually nameless, "innommable"' and incapable of being 'reinscribed in a system of intelligibility'. Deconstruction's charge, in this second scenario, is to disclose any discourse with a content, for instance a genealogy of the clinic, as substituting something for nothing, making the zero appear 'in the guise of a *one*' (de Man 1996: 59–61).

Unlike Foucault, who turns from this madness to sociological positivities, Derrida tried to keep a place for deconstruction, but often at the cost of a certain sublimation, notably in his abandonment of his close focus on language as the process of death at work in signs. De Man's last work is quite different. The essays collected in *The Rhetoric of Romanticism*, including 'Autobiography as De-Facement' and 'Shelley Disfigured' (both 1979), return repeatedly to moments of hanging or drowning, particularly in Romantic literature – the primal scene of both deconstruction and the Gothic. They are also fascinated by terms such as disfiguration and defacement that seem deliberately caught in the impossibility of sublimating their materiality into a figural reference. But de Man's Gothicism is as much a missed encounter as the late Derrida's lack of it, since these cryptic enclaves index something undigested in his 'linguistics of literariness' (de Man 1986: 11). Neil Hertz analyses de Man's 'lurid figures' as the scene of an extreme tension between his technical analyses of rhetoric and their often 'melodramatic' subtexts (Hertz 1989: 82): 'les mots sous les mots' in Starobinski's gloss on anagrams, a work important for late de Man. If anyone had sought to make a technology out of the linguistic turn and its 'rigour', it was de Man in *Allegories of Reading*. In chiasmic formulations such as 'the rhetorization of grammar' and the 'grammatization of rhetoric', in that book's rare foray into popular culture through Archie Bunker (de Man 1979: 15), de Man tries to schematise, in the concept of an aporia or impassable path, what he later calls the 'uncontrollable power of the letter as inscription' (de Man 1986: 37). He sees language as an inhuman 'machine' that produces a vertiginous 'set of aberrations all linked to the positional power of language'. As a result, even 'death' is abstracted into being no more than 'the displaced name for a linguistic predicament' (de Man 1984: 81).

At the same time, a machine has a logic and 'program'; it is 'systematic in its performance', though 'arbitrary in its principle, like a grammar' (de Man 1979: 268, 298). Hence de Man takes a perverse pleasure in describing this 'mad science' (see Rajan 2002: 46–54). Yet as Hertz argues, the undead metaphors of disfigurement and defacement that haunt de Man's corpus convey a 'pathos of uncertain agency' in which a phantom 'subject is conjured up', who is ambiguously victim and perpetrator of this catastrophe: is de Man 'the killer' or only 'the discoverer of the corpse?' (Hertz 1989: 86). Of particular note is the late de Man's growing interest in tropes such as *prosopopeia*, anthropomorphism and catachresis, figures that he *makes* lurid by 'outing' their structures of incorporation. As he writes, almost in the mode of a horror film, *prosopopoeia*, the giving of a face, 'implies that the original face can be missing or nonexistent'. Catachresis, if viewed as an undead metaphor (the *leg* of a table or the *face* of a mountain), is a 'monstrous' figure that abuses metaphor by confusing substances, and thus 'dismember[s] the texture of reality and reassemble[s] it in the most capricious of ways' (de Man 1996: 44). These surrealisations of classical tropes open up a death of meaning in language which de Man in 'Hypogram and Inscription' (1981) gathers into the discovery of the anagram as a form of anti-matter (de Man 1996: 44). The anagram was an explosive moment in French theory: it does not behave like a sign, since it is not semantically readable, but is pure sense as non-sense (Milner 1990: 209–17). According to de Man it is 'an underlying word or proper name' that is broken up and disseminated throughout the text in a 'coded dispersal' (de Man 1986: 36). For Baudrillard, the linguistics of the anagram produced an 'ex-termination' of terms, a 'disintegration' that can return them 'to an inorganic, *ungebunden* state . . . to utopia, as opposed to the articulate and constructive topics of Eros' (Baudrillard 1993: 236, 149). But for de Man the anagram – or the para- or hypogram, but always with 'the suffix *gram* (letter) rather than *phone* (sound)', which connects it to Derrida's *Of Grammatology* (1967) – is a glimpse into 'terror', since the 'key word is the proper name in all its originary integrity' and the 'laws for its dispersal . . . are not phenomenally nor even mathematically perceivable'. Evoking a patient of Freud, de Man compares this traumatic disintegration of the proper name 'into discrete parts and groups', into non-semantic sense, pure sense as non-sense, to 'the worst phantasms of dismemberment' in Schreber's *Denkwürdigkeiten eines Nervenkranken* (de Man 1986: 36–7).

Like the anagram itself, de Man's lurid figures do not work through this terror but incorporate it, in Abraham and Torok's sense of ingesting something that has not been digested. De Man keeps the madness of language in the cells of his corpus, caulked and padded by what Gasché calls an 'apathetic formalism' (Gasché 1998: 3–5, 112). But his final essays are deeply 'archiviolithic', to use Derrida's term in *Archive Fever* for a 'death drive' or 'aggression drive' that 'destroy[s]' and 'effac[es]' what it is constructing, obliterating its own traces in the process (Derrida 1995: 10–11). *Archive Fever*'s opening pages constitute the late Derrida's most de Manian text, though the rest of the text gets sidetracked into an esoteric engagement with the Jewish thinker Yerushalmi. These initial pages return to Derrida's own earlier 'Freud and the Scene of Writing' (1966), on the mystic writing-pad as a form of 'representation abandoned to itself', and to the notion, surely seminal for de Man, of the '*machine*' as 'death and finitude *within* the psyche' (Derrida 1978: 228). The archiviolithic or 'anarchival' destroys, from within, the 'archontic' process of giving materials a place in a museum or canon. This latter power of '*consignation*', which coordinates texts in a 'single corpus' without any 'secret' or 'partition', marks 'the passage from the private to the public' (Derrida 1995: 2–3, 10). But for Derrida the archontic proves self-subverting, as the exhaustive 'deposit[ing]' of materials exhausts the capacity to remember, obliterating the archive whose excess then produces a contradictory energy in which the materials 'burned' and forgotten by their conservation feverishly return from repression (1995: 3, 11–12, 19).

Arguably the de Man whom Derrida forgets in his *Memoires for Paul de Man* (1988) returns in *Archive Fever* through the archontic process of mourning, in the underground connection between this text and 'Shelley Disfigured'. For de Man's essay on Shelley's last poem, *The Triumph of Life*, is about this very question of monumentalisation and how to 'dispose of' Shelley's corpus in the wake of his drowning (de Man 1984: 120). *The Triumph*, for de Man, compulsively obliterates its own traces and the traces of its reading, enacting what Derrida later calls the 'radical effacement ... of that which can never be reduced to mnēmē or anamnēsis' (Derrida 1995: 11). Moreover, Shelley's 'defaced body' becomes a catachresis for the poem, as the body, 'burned' for sanitary reasons after Shelley drowned, is incorporated 'in the margin of the last manuscript page' as 'an inseparable part' of the poem (de Man 1984: 120–1), thus dispersing and dismembering the author's proper name within a badly mutilated manuscript that is itself self-obliterating.

De Man's last essays, which he did not himself assemble as books, bring forward an 'archiviolithic force that leaves nothing of its own behind' (Derrida 1995: 11). There is no archive *fever* in them, except in 'Shelley Disfigured', whose close reading of a single text involves the essay's destruction-drive in a scene of reading in which the poem cannot help but return as both *eros* and *thanatos* (see Rajan 1990: 323–53). This destruction-drive is why, even though de Man's followers, like Derrida's, often want to protect his legacy, Cohen offers the 'site of "de Man" as one particular troubled *cipher*'. So instead of reverting to de Man's rhetoric of tropes, he suggests that we approach the figure (de Man) 'already ghosting itself in the late texts', as an 'event and anomaly – an algorithm rather than a precise set of idioms and preoccupations' (Cohen 1998: 32, 42; 2012a).

As Cohen sees him, de Man provides 'toxic assets' for a future very different from Derrida's qualified messianism (Cohen 2012b: 107). De Man's work, unbound from its systemisation by some of his followers, becomes, to evoke Žižek, the Real or 'leftover' or 'excess' of Derrida's attempts to put deconstruction into the symbolic order (Žižek 1989: 191). Lee Edelman's disfiguration of the 'reproductive futurism' of a society that figures itself through the child is one example of this toxic legacy. His deconstruction of how the liberal left finds 'reassurance' in the 'queer' because it 'seem[s] to give a name to what, as Real [in the Lacanian sense], remains unnameable' draws on de Man's insight into how the zero 'appears in the guise of a *one*' (Edelman 2004: 3, 26; de Man 1996: 60). Another example is Cohen's own analytical work, which uses the often Gothic Alfred Hitchcock as the uncanny other of 'cultural studies' to expose the 'phantom at the centre of all reference systems' that rely on '*mimetic-humanism*' (Cohen 1998: 6, 14). In Cohen's two volumes on Hitchcock, *Cryptonomies* (2005), the Gothic, like the queer for Edelman, is another trope for the zero, which can also be described in Žižekian terms as a 'hole, a gap' in 'the middle of the symbolic order', a negativity that is 'revers[ed] into the Positive' (Žižek 1989: 191; 1997: 294) when we give the uncanny incorporation of trauma at the level of the signifier in a film such as *The Birds* (1963) a mimetic content. To disturb this mimesis, Cohen describes Hitchcock's 'writing systems' in ways that recall Foucault's description of Roussel's textual machines, the circulation of meaning through a chain of hollowed-out signifiers that we began by seeing as characteristic of the Gothic. Cohen's account of Hitchcock's de-totalised corpus is indeed profoundly Gothic, as he builds his analysis around 'secret agents', giving an uncanny agency to anagrams, '"secret" visual elements, graphic riddles, letteration, and cryptonomies that traverse all of [Hitchcock's] works' so as to 'sabotage' the 'perceptual grid' and 'rewire its memory system' (Cohen 2005: I, xi). Between de Man and Cohen, the machine has become more than just a metaphor through the increasing dominance of cybernetic systems: it intimates a trauma that enters theory through Kittler's account – influenced by 'Freud and the Scene of Writing' – of how Nietzsche suffered the worst phantasms of dismemberment through the typewriter (Kittler 1990: 178–96). Had Freud known them, these *Aufschreibensysteme*,[3] as Derrida notes, would have transformed not just the '*secondary recording*' and 'printing' of psychoanalysis but its very notions of the unconscious, 'its very *events*' (Derrida 1995: 16). For Cohen, combining Kittler and Lacan with de Man, these inscription or '*ex*scription' systems make cinema the site of 'mnemonic relays' anterior to representation, which form an unconscious external to the self, like the crypt: a circuitry that alters 'the hard disk' of our consciousness (Cohen 1998: 17, 204; 2001: 117). De Manian deconstruction's Gothic reanimation of the machine as an autonomic nervous system can be set against the current techno-euphoria among posthumanists influenced by Deleuze and Guattari's theories of machinic assemblages. Continuing in this darker vein, and using de Man Gothically against Derrida as a kind of avenging spirit, Cohen has recently argued, with reference to 'ecocatastrophic' phenomena such as war and climate change, that de Man 'formulates a pre-emptively suicidal war machine [. . .] more suited to 21st century problematics than the social and historical urgencies of the 1990s' that led to his abjection (Cohen 2012b: 108), those liberal urgencies to which Derrida responded in *Memoires for Paul de Man*.

Derrida's anxiety over this 'algorithm' surfaces in his curious placing of de Man alongside 'nuclear waste' (Derrida 1989: 808), while using the more proper apparatus of mourning in *Memoires* to restore the proper name de Man. 'Biodegradables' let themselves be de- and re-composed but, Derrida says, there are 'artefacts' that 'resist degradation', that are so 'singular' that they cannot be 'assimilated', like 'nuclear waste', like the zero of de Man's work (1989: 824–8, 845). If de Man's lurid figures lay waste to the archive with an unprocessed ruthlessness, the equally lurid figure of nuclear waste abjects on to de Man what is in some sense the charge and problem of deconstruction. For this waste that is not biodegradable recalls Foucault's figure of the 'precious ashes', the 'black unmalleable coal' that a conflagration of the archive cannot eliminate (Foucault 1977: 88). Can deconstruction be affirmative or is it tasked with disclosing an unusable negativity to which no other literary ontology has been sensitive? Does this ruthless negativity in de Man – a Nietzschean *destruktion* rather than a more Kantian and critical deconstruction – miss the complex commerce between the materiality of language and the discourse of ideas, using the former to freeze the latter in a radical intransitivity? Or do we avoid something by reintegrating deconstruction's toxic assets into a dialogue between the cogito and the unthought? These issues continue to trouble deconstruction, as evident recently in the work of Catherine Malabou, with which I now propose to conclude.

Drawing on neuroscience and regenerative medicine, Malabou effects a radical change of terrain in deconstruction by adapting the 'scheme' of 'writing' to that of brain plasticity as a medium of '*inscription*' that similarly exceeds our control (Malabou 2007: 36). In *What Should We Do With Our Brain?* (2004), she considers this plasticity in a social register. But elsewhere she reflects on the plasticity of philosophical texts, as she revisits her first book, *The Future of Hegel* (1996), to ask how a text (for her always a philosophical text) can 'return' from its deconstruction, like the salamander, different but without scars (Malabou 2007: 29–34). In both cases, Malabou uses the neural turn, whose traumatic traces we see in Kittler and Cohen, to theorise an affirmative deconstruction.

Yet in *The New Wounded* (2007) and *Ontology of the Accident* (2009), confronting old age and Alzheimer's, Malabou describes a 'senseless' power of modification, an 'event' or 'accident' that results in placing another person inside the focal person but unrecognisable to him or her. Ontologically these metamorphoses resemble the worst phantasms of the Gothic in which the human changes into something bordering on the inhuman, as in the *Strange Case of Dr Jekyll and Mr Hyde* or *Dracula*. But the style of what we might call the 'everyday Gothic' of these two books is quite different, closer to the neuro-determinism of nineteenth-century naturalism. Malabou uses the word 'effraction' to describe this 'brute accident' or 'wound without hermeneutic future', which blocks psychoanalysis, remaining forever 'exterior to the interior' and 'constitutively unassimilable' (Malabou 2012: 5–8). Although Malabou was Derrida's student and shows no familiarity with de Man, her 'destructive plasticity' (2012: xv) is closer to de Man's uncontrollable power of the letter as inscription than to anything in the late Derrida. Her account of the 'accident' that suddenly makes the normality of ageing into something random and horrific resembles de Man's deconstruction of narrative in 'Shelley Disfigured', where he writes that 'nothing ... ever happens in relation' to anything else but only as a 'random event' that cannot be integrated into a historical sequence (de Man 1984: 122). Are the two forms of plasticity complementary, responding to different situations, or does destructive plasticity displace its adaptive counterpart?[4] As a 'dark precursor' of deconstruction,[5] the Gothic is that vault that refuses ever to fully release into critical enlightenment what remains most cryptic and scandalous in deconstruction.

Notes

1. This is Schmitt's critique of Romanticism for treating the world as an 'occasion' and 'opportunity' for its own 'productivity' without finally committing to anything (Schmitt 1986: 17–19, 85).
2. Abraham and Torok refer to 'Ulalume' (1994: 118), but since Poe was much better known in France than other Gothic authors writing in English, we can assume a familiarity with his short stories.
3. Given the 1985 date of *Aufschreibesystem* (the original title of the book, meaning 'systems of inscription' and not 'discourse networks'), Kittler would have known 'Freud and the Scene of Writing' but not *Archive Fever* or much of de Man's work.
4. I asked Malabou this question (conversation, February 2015), and she opted for the second answer, but the chronology of her work shows that the two options remain entangled.
5. Deleuze suggests that the 'infantile series' is the 'dark precursor' of the 'adult', but not in any way that makes the latter the maturity of the former. Rather, 'there are torsions and drifts, that only the embryo can sustain: an adult would be torn apart by them' (Deleuze 1994: 119–24).

References

Abraham, Nicholas, and Maria Torok (1986) [1976], *The Wolf-Man's Magic Word: A Cryptonymy*, trans. Nicholas Rand, Minneapolis: University of Minnesota Press.

Abraham, Nicholas, and Maria Torok (1994) [1987], *The Shell and the Kernel: Renewals of Psychoanalysis, Volume 1*, ed. and trans. Nicholas Rand, Chicago: University of Chicago Press.

Baudrillard, Jean (1993) [1976], *Symbolic Exchange and Death*, trans. Iain Hamilton Grant, London: Sage.

Blanchot, Maurice (1982) [1955], *The Space of Literature*, trans. Ann Smock, Lincoln: University of Nebraska Press.

Castricano, Jodey (2001), *Cryptomimesis: The Gothic and Jacques Derrida's Ghost-Writing*. Montreal: McGill-Queen's University Press.

Cohen, Tom (1998), *Ideology and Inscription: "Cultural Studies" After Benjamin, de Man, and Bakhtin*, Cambridge: Cambridge University Press.

Cohen, Tom (2001), 'Political Thrillers: Hitchcock, de Man, and Secret Agency in the "Aesthetic State"', in Tom Cohen, Barbara Cohen, J. Hillis Miller and Andrzej Warminski (eds), *Material Events: Paul de Man and the Afterlife of Theory*, Minneapolis: University of Minnesota Press, pp. 114–52.

Cohen, Tom (2005), *Hitchcock's Cryptonomies*, 2 vols, Minneapolis: University of Minnesota Press.

Cohen, Tom (2012a), 'Interview', 5 November, http://noise-admiration.blogspot.ca/2012/11/the-interview-22012-tom- (accessed 2 July 2016).

Cohen, Tom (2012b), 'Toxic Assets: de Man's Remains and the Ecocatastrophic Imaginary (an American Fable)', in Tom Cohen, Claire Colebrook and J. Hillis Miller (eds), *Theory and the Disappearing Future: On de Man, on Benjamin*, London: Routledge, pp. 89–129.

Deleuze, Gilles (1990) [1969], *The Logic of Sense*, trans. Mark Lester, ed. Constantin Boundas, London: Athlone Press.

Deleuze, Gilles (1994) [1968], *Difference and Repetition*, trans. Paul Patton, New York: Columbia University Press.

de Man, Paul (1979), *Allegories of Reading: Figural Language in Rousseau, Nietzsche, Rilke, and Proust*, New Haven, CT: Yale University Press.

de Man, Paul (1984), *The Rhetoric of Romanticism*, New York: Columbia University Press.

de Man, Paul (1986), *The Resistance to Theory*, Minneapolis: University of Minnesota Press.

de Man, Paul (1996), *Aesthetic Ideology*, ed. Andrzej Warminski, Minneapolis: University of Minnesota Press.

Derrida, Jacques (1973) [1967–8], *Speech and Phenomena and Other Essays*, trans. David Allison, Evanston: Northwestern University Press.

Derrida, Jacques (1978) [1966], 'Freud and the Scene of Writing', in *Writing and Difference*, trans. Alan Bass, Chicago: University of Chicago Press, pp. 196–231.

Derrida, Jacques (1986) [1976], 'Fors: The Anglish Words of Nicolas Abraham and Maria Torok', trans. Barbara Johnson, in Nicholas Abraham and Maria Torok, *The Wolf-Man's Magic Word: A Cryptonymy*, trans. Nicholas Rand, Minneapolis: University of Minnesota Press, pp. xi–xlviii.
Derrida, Jacques (1989), 'Biodegradables: Seven Diary Fragments', trans. Peggy Kamuf, *Critical Inquiry*, 15.4: 812–73.
Derrida, Jacques (1994) [1993], *Specters of Marx: The State of the Debt, the Work of Mourning, and the New International*, trans. Peggy Kamuf, New York: Routledge.
Derrida, Jacques (1995), *Archive Fever: A Freudian Impression*, trans. Eric Prenowitz, Chicago: University of Chicago Press.
Derrida, Jacques (2002) [1996], '"Dead Man Running": Salut, Salut', in *Negotiations: Interventions and Interviews, 1971–2001*, trans. Elizabeth Rottenberg, Stanford: Stanford University Press, pp. 257–92.
Edelman, Lee (2004), *No Future: Queer Theory and the Death Drive*, Durham, NC: Duke University Press.
Foucault, Michel (1970) [1966], *The Order of Things: An Archaeology of the Human Sciences*, New York: Vintage.
Foucault, Michel (1973) [1963, rev. 1972], *The Birth of the Clinic: An Archaeology of Medical Perception*, trans. A. M. Sheridan, London: Routledge.
Foucault, Michel (1977), *Language, Counter-memory, Practice: Selected Essays and Interviews*, trans. Donald F. Bouchard and Sherry Simon, Ithaca: Cornell University Press.
Foucault, Michel (1986) [1963], *Death and the Labyrinth: The World of Raymond Roussel*, trans. Charles Ruas, Berkeley: University of California Press.
Freud, Sigmund (1955) [1920], *Beyond the Pleasure Principle*, in the *Complete Psychological Works*, ed. and trans. James Strachey, London: Hogarth Press, XVIII, pp. 7–64.
Gasché, Rodolphe (1998), *The Wild Card of Reading: On Paul de Man*, Cambridge, MA: Harvard University Press.
Guillory, John (1993), *Cultural Capital: The Problem of Literary Canon Formation*, Chicago: University of Chicago Press.
Hegel, G. W. F. (1970), *Aesthetics: Lectures in Fine Art*, trans. T. M. Knox, 2 vols, Oxford: Clarendon Press.
Hertz, Neil (1989), 'Lurid Figures', in Lindsay Waters and Wlad Godzich (eds), *Reading de Man Reading*, Minneapolis: University of Minnesota Press, pp. 82–104.
Hogle, Jerrold E. (1994), 'The Ghost of the Counterfeit in the Genesis of the Gothic', in Allan Lloyd Smith and Victor Sage (eds), *Gothick Origins and Innovations*, Amsterdam: Rodopi, pp. 23–33.
Hogle, Jerrold E. (1998), '*Frankenstein* as Neo-Gothic: From the Ghost of the Counterfeit to the Monster of Abjection', in Tilottama Rajan and Julia Wright (eds), *Romanticism, History and the Possibilities of Genre*, Cambridge: Cambridge University Press, pp. 176–210.

Kittler, Friedrich (1990) [1985], *Discourse Networks 1800/1900*, trans. Michael Metteer, Stanford: Stanford University Press

Lecercle, Jean-Jacques (1985), *Philosophy Through the Looking-Glass: Language, Nonsense, Desire*, La Salle, IL: Open Court.

Lee, Sophia (2000) [1783–5], *The Recess; or, A Tale of Other Times*, ed. April Aliston, Louisville, KY: University of Kentucky Press.

Lotringer, Sylvère (1973), 'The Game of the Name', *Diacritics*, 3.2: 2–9.

Malabou, Catherine (2007), 'Again: "The wounds of the Spirit heal and leave no scars behind"', *Mosaic*, 40.2: 27–38.

Malabou, Catherine (2012) [2007], *The New Wounded: From Neurosis to Brain Damage*, trans. Steven Miller, New York: Fordham University Press.

McQuillan, Martin (2012), *Deconstruction Without Derrida*, London: Continuum.

Milner, Jean-Claude (1990) [1978], *For the Love of Language*, trans. Ann Banfield, Basingstoke: Macmillan.

Rajan, Tilottama (1990), *The Supplement of Reading: Figures of Understanding in Romantic Theory and Practice*, Ithaca: Cornell University Press.

Rajan, Tilottama (2002), *Deconstruction and the Remainders of Phenomenology: Sartre, Derrida, Foucault, Baudrillard*, Stanford: Stanford University Press.

Rajan, Tilottama (2012), 'Romanticism and the Unfinished Project of Deconstruction', *European Romantic Review*, 23: 293–303.

Rajan, Tilottama (2015), 'The Gothic Matrix: Shelley between the Symbolic and Romantic', in David Brookshire (ed.), *Percy Shelley and the Delimitation of the Gothic*, College Park, MD: Romantic Circles Praxis, http://www.rc.umd.edu/praxis/gothic_shelley (accessed 4 October 2018).

Rajan, Tilottama (2017), 'Sophia Lee's Baroque Narratology: *The Recess* and the (Dis)simulation of the Real', in Sandra Heinen and Katharina Rennhak (eds), *Narratives of Romanticism*, Trier: Wissenschaftlicher Verlag, pp. 123–35.

Rand, Nicholas (1986), 'Translator's Introduction', in Nicholas Abraham and Maria Torok, *The Wolf-Man's Magic Word: A Cryptonymy*, trans. Nicholas Rand, Minneapolis: University of Minnesota Press, pp. li–lxix.

Robbe-Grillet, Alain (1965) [1963], *For a New Novel: Essays on Fiction*, trans. Richard Howard, New York: Grove Press.

Schmitt, Carl (1986) [1919], *Political Romanticism*, trans. Guy Oakes, Cambridge, MA: MIT Press.

Sedgwick, Eve Kosofsky (1986) [1980], *The Coherence of Gothic Conventions*, New York: Methuen.

Silverman, Hugh (2007), 'Response-abilities for Legacies: Jacques, *on vous suit à travers vos textes*', *Mosaic*, 40.2: 297–306.

Starobinski, Jean (1979) [1971], *Words Upon Words: The Anagrams of Ferdinand de Saussure*, trans. Olivia Emmett, New Haven, CT: Yale University Press.

Wang, Orrin (2011), 'Gothic Theory', in Orrin Wang, *Romantic Sobriety: Sensation, Revolution, Commodification, History*, Baltimore: Johns Hopkins University Press, pp. 138–57.
Žižek, Slavoj (1989), *The Sublime Object of Ideology*, London: Verso.
Žižek, Slavoj (1997), *The Plague of Fantasies*, London: Verso.

Chapter 13

Dark Materialism: Gothic Objects, Commodities and Things
Fred Botting

Disorder of Things

Gothic fictions are traversed by darkly material disturbances, traces of unformed things operating beyond the reach of reason, rule and sense. Going bump in the night, making skin crawl or hairs stand on end, these things undo the laws of the known world, out of place, out of time and out of nature. In Horace Walpole's *The Castle of Otranto* (1764), a huge helmet falls from nowhere to crush the estate's unlawful heir on his wedding day (Walpole 1996: 18). Too large at times, things of terror and horror also assume much smaller form: plague narratives such as Mary Shelley's *The Last Man* (1826) or Edgar Allan Poe's 'The Masque of the Red Death' (1842) manifest malign, non-human and microscopic powers of (monstrous) nature. Ghosts manifest little substance. Things evince too much materiality. Victor Frankenstein, assembling a creature from dead limbs and organs, almost collapses in horror at the sight of animated and excess physicality (Shelley 1968: 57). Solid bodies disintegrate yet remain animate: in Poe's 'The Tell-Tale Heart' (1843) an eviscerated organ continues to beat loudly; in 'The Facts in the Case of M. Valdemar' (1845) a swollen, blackened tongue speaks from beyond the grave. Bodies dissolve: released from mesmeric stasis, M. Valdemar rapidly decomposes into a putrid 'liquid mass' (Poe 1986: 359). Arthur Machen's 'The Novel of the White Powder' (1895) ends with a body, 'neither liquid nor solid', oozing and bubbling in terminal dissolution (Machen 1977: 233). Even buildings defy the laws of nature, crashing in ruins without identifiable cause, manifesting strange animations on and in walls, or contravening the laws of physics (Walpole 1996; Poe 1986: 138–57; Gilman 1992; Jackson 2005; Danielewski 2001). Everyday objects, too, are malevolently animated against humanity (James 1987: 292).

Towards the end of the nineteenth century, such entities proliferate. Fears of cultural degeneration appear among malformed, criminal and atavistic bodies. Science meets mysticism, glimpsing 'the unthinkable gulf' between worlds of matter and spirit to disclose horrible forces 'at the heart of things' (Machen 2005: 185, 225). Pagan legends materialise as things from 'outer Darkness', slimy, slug-like, slavering horrors (Benson 1992: 229, 238). Dr Moreau's vivisectionist experiments confound species identity with 'Things' that question the priority of humanity (Wells 1946: 62). William Hope Hodgson's *The Night Land* describes strange, horrid, monstrous, creeping and evil things on almost every page (2008: 9, 11, 36, 78, 88, 109). Things that 'cannot be', these 'Ab-human' invaders from horrifying dimensions, materialise and threaten the human species (Hodgson 2008: 10, 12). H. P. Lovecraft's fiction sees a proliferation of things on the doorstep or in the moonlight, 'pinkish', 'accursed', 'flaming', 'nameless' things (2008: 669, 684, 695, 520, 750). Arguing that 'accelerated taxonomical activity' in the nineteenth century produced paradigm disorder, Kelly Hurley identifies a range of corporeal forms that challenge conventional notions of solid and inert materiality (Hurley 1996: 26). Things become fluid, slimy and revolting, like the protoplasm considered by T. J. Huxley to be the basis of life (Hurley 1996: 32). 'Things', 'rent from within by their own heterogeneity', are signs of 'chaotic fluctability' and a materialism without transcendent anchor, reality or meaning (Hurley 1996: 9). 'Gothic materialism' discloses bodies as partial and plural categories rather than definite objects, a body of multiple effects and affects existing outside the determination of objectivity (Fisher 2011: 241).

In the late eighteenth century, two astronomer-mathematicians independently inferred the existence of 'dark bodies'. The first, John Michell, in the course of a paper delivered to the Royal Society in 1784, proposed that a star with a radius 500 times larger than the diameter of the sun would have a gravitational field stronger than the speed of light so that 'all light emitted from such a body would be made to return towards it, by its own proper gravity' (Michell 1784: 42). Considering the implications of observing stellar objects that allow 'no information from light', he notes that, without data from the senses, calculation and better tools will be needed to study 'non-luminous bodies' more effectively (Michell 1784: 50–4). For Pierre-Simon Laplace, in his *System of the World* (1798), dark stellar bodies posed a challenge to explaining the physical laws of the universe. In the recording of planetary orbits, there are stars whose motions do not conform to predictions based on their brightness or distance from other bodies (Laplace 1798: 422–4). Laplace calculates that a star of sufficient magnitude and density could produce gravitational forces powerful enough to inhibit the emission of light, going on to speculate that there may be many large, invisible stellar bodies throughout the universe, bodies he calls '*corps obscurs*' (1798: 424). Dark bodies have considerable gothic resonance. In 'Eureka' (1848), Poe's scientific romance, '*non-luminous stars*' are described as 'suns whose existence we determine through the movements of others, but whose luminosity is not sufficient to impress us' (Poe 1904: 84). The ability to deduce presence from an absence that itself provides an alternate mode of information is not so far from the method of detection employed by Poe's Dupin or the mode of 'proof' advanced in unmasking public performances of automata (Poe 1986: 330–49; 1967: 97–122). Poe's 'tale' also pursues a new theory of matter that '*exists* only as attraction and repulsion', a polarisation of atomic particles calibrating gravitation and electricity to body/matter and soul/spirit (Poe 1904: 34–5). It reaches a striking conclusion: given the universe's tendency to return to a state of 'objectless unity', matter's existence is temporary. When things return to the universal oneness that is nothing, there will be 'matter no more' (1904: 144–5).

In a period of rational and empirical enquiry, obscure bodies disclose a peculiar darkness in Enlightenment knowledge, one that is not the negative or absence of light but harbours an active, material (non-)presence. Developments in natural science, too, involve obscure bodies: monsters do not exist simply as negatives enabling classifications of species but also disclose a 'ceaseless background murmur' that both undermines and enables taxonomic distinctions (Foucault 1970: 54–6). Baseless bases, black holes, as it were, puncture modern discourse from within. They also evince wider disturbances of dark, insubordinate energies and entities called 'base matter': neither homogeneous, organised nor discrete, its 'contradictory materialism' opposes the 'physicist's mechanical and rational materialism' (Hollier 1998: 64); base matter as 'an *active* principle having its own essential autonomous existence as darkness (which would not be simply the absence of light but the monstrous *archontes* revealed by this absence)' (Bataille 1997: 162). Not simply negative (which would already place it within a system of hierarchies and distinctions), it lies 'outside myself and the idea', remains 'external and foreign to ideal human aspirations' and refuses 'to allow itself to be reduced to the great ontological machines resulting from these aspirations' (Bataille 1997: 163). Many types of 'materialism' are, from this perspective, considered idealist, since they are forms of thought that tie 'dead matter' to 'a conventional hierarchy of diverse facts' (Bataille 1995: 58). To view planetary bodies as discrete stellar objects occludes the material dynamism of a universe seen as a 'whirling explosion' of stellar prodigality and generosity: the life-giving light of a Sun contradicts a reductively terrestrial perspective in which life is nothing more than object and expression of human 'avidity' and 'unquenchable greed' (Bataille 1986: 75–8). Base matter refuses isolation: an effect of 'non-logical difference', it is 'neither a transcendental signified nor an ultimate referent, neither the final reality (the basis of things) nor the controlling idea'. It cannot be 'subsumed by theory' nor 'submitted to the categories of reason': 'matter is insubordinate' (Hollier 1989: 135).

As insubordination, base matter destabilises any system of understanding, whether idealist or materialist, theoretical or practical. Disclosing the absence of any final ground (Hollier's 'ultimate referent') or any presiding idea ('transcendental signified'), it shows all structures, whether cultural, scientific, philosophical or linguistic, to be incomplete, constituted and confounded by a negativity in excess of the antitheses articulating subject and object, idea and thing, spirit and matter: base matter is not (not something, not nothing, just not). Theory, knowledge and meaning founder. Collapse is held at bay by means of the limit-figures called Things: registers of obscure destabilisation, Things and, conversely, spectres acknowledge the systemic frailties that admit too much – or too little – formless matter. Excluded from yet intrinsic to any system's functioning, Things exhibit a particular and necessary asystematicity haunting any theory: deconstructive 'aporia' and *différance*, psychoanalytic objects (*a*) and abjection, schizoanalytical '*anomals*' signal unruly traversals of atheological, ateleological and atheoretical energies.

Things, the plugs and holes on and through which base matter may be temporarily focused and filtered, remain apart and different from unformed base material. The argument that follows tracks their immaterial appearance as spectres, ghosts and phantoms in the historical materialism of Karl Marx and goes on to identify – as monstrous automata and vampires – an over-materialisation associated with surplus value. Spectres disturb the reality sought by dialectical materialism: immaterial and all-too real instantiations of the commodity form, in Jacques Derrida's reading of *Capital*'s spectres, disclose both the dematerialisations activated by economic transformation and the frustrations attendant on any critical attempt to restore a rational and human sense of social reality. In one direction, solid things seem to evaporate in phantasmal, spectral shapes. The other track, however, sees the excessively material incarnations of capital as monstrous machine and voracious vampire. Here Marxism's revolutionary impulse is aligned with insubordinate base materialist energies. Giving up the attempt to recover social realities that have been lost or occulted by the commodity-form, Marx's metaphors push monstrosity to its limit to frame capital's exploitation of all bodies and values in terms of the utmost horror. The effect of this critical destruction-creation (making space for an as yet unavailable human and social reality) is to entangle Gothic figures fully and contradictorily in the work of commodification and fetish: they sustain, in their difference and in the limits they mark, the (ideological) 'reality' that circulates as an effect of the commerce of ghosts and spectres at the same time as they acknowledge the phantasmal character of lived, modern 'reality'. They become the fantasy objects that occlude the fantasy form in which reality is lived. Negative and avowedly unreal, Gothic figures do not overturn the modern reality of capital's empire of things, making no claim to present another world nor radically displacing this one: they provide the shadow that alludes to its substance. Gothic forms and fictions remain aligned with commodities and capitalist production, as the final section, on Alasdair Gray's *Poor Things*, argues.

Base Marxism

Base matter undermines any idea that things, human life included, are ultimately reducible to discrete and useful objects. It contests economic practices in which accumulation makes the overriding demand that 'productive forces produce only new productive force' (Bataille 1986: 78). Instead, it activates unruly materialism, 'a crude liberation of human life from the imprisonment and masked pathology of ethics, an appeal to all that is offensive, indestructible, and even despicable, to all that overthrows, perverts, and ridicules spirit' (Bataille 1985: 32). In an essay attacking Surrealism's radical gestures as 'pretentious idealistic aberrations', Bataille calls upon the materialist 'Old Mole' (a figure Marx uses to describe the unpredictable patterns of political struggle): 'revolution hollows out chambers of decomposed soil repugnant to the delicate noses of the utopians'; it 'begins in the bowels of the earth, as in the materialist bowels of proletarians' (Bataille 1985: 32, 35). Base Marxism emerges in this trenchant refusal of idealism: 'by excavating the fetid ditch of bourgeois culture, perhaps we will see open up in the depths of the earth immense and even sinister caves where force and human liberty will establish themselves, sheltered from the call to order of heaven that today demands the most imbecilic elevation of any new spirit' (Bataille 1985: 43). Matter robustly refuses spirit, dismissing any system of thought that is a 'servile idealism to the extent that it is not immediately based on psychological or social facts, instead of on artificially isolated physical phenomena' (Bataille 1995: 58). Just as Marxism interrogates the way that commodities, when fetishised, construct an objectivity and sense of value that effaces the social relations of the labour process, so Bataille's critique of the idealism informing 'artificially isolated' things looks to materialist 'social facts'. In line with Marxism's interrogation of commodities, base materialism refuses idealist mystifications, but importantly, without recourse to a pre-formed sense of reality.

Base matter also revises the inversion characterising a Marxist approach to things. For Marx, capitalism evinces 'the rule of things over man, of dead labour over the living, the product over the producer' (Marx 1976: 990). It is an inverted order that may be rectified. Though recognising the 'unreserved surrender to *things*' demanded by capital and sharing Marx's aim to 'free the world of *things*', Bataille proposes a strategy that involves 'going to the limit of the possibilities implied by *things*': rather than denouncing the dominance of things over humans, it requires 'the movement that reduces man to the condition of *things*' be taken to its 'ultimate consequences' so that current hierarchies are overturned and exhausted. Only then, when things are reduced 'to the condition of man', when, that is, the idealism sustaining an (inverted) hierarchy of things over humans is expended, can humans achieve 'the free disposition' of themselves (Bataille 1988: 135–6). A dual strategy emerges, countering surplus with excess and disrupting the spectral realm of commodities with unruly energies: it challenges acquiescence to prevailing bourgeois values, forms and (un)realities and activates unproductive and insubordinate energies against imperatives of accumulation.

Numerous phantoms, spectres and monsters gather in the reality dominated by commodity-forms. A commodity should be a 'trivial thing and easily understood', but it turns out to be 'a very queer thing, abounding in metaphysical subtleties and theological niceties' (Marx 1976: 163). Reality, too: shaped by the ideas of a ruling class (ideology), it involves 'false conceptions' and 'phantoms' that, having escaped human brains, dominate the world. Liberating people from the 'yoke' of 'chimeras', 'dogmas', 'imaginary beings' requires the transformation of the 'phantoms' of consciousness and the 'material life-process' that informs them (Marx and Engels 1970: 37, 47).

Dialectical analysis aims to exorcise this 'phantasmaterialism' but becomes entangled in the very metaphors that it uses for clarification and criticism: optical analogies (such as the way in which an inverted image of a physical object appears real on the retina compared to the false reality perceived under capitalism) imply that an objective situation existing beyond the eye can be reinstituted (Marx 1976: 165). As Sarah Kofman observes, these optical metaphors assume that inverting the inversion will secure a return to original meaning and 'given' reality. However, Marx's analysis of commodity-effects discloses a simple thing, a wooden table, as being 'swept up in vertigo, having lost its grounding, drunk': 'the table dances. It turns' (Kofman 1997: 3). Neither given, nor readily recuperable beyond ideological artifice, reality is 'a world already transformed enchanted', 'the reflection of a reflection, the phantasm of a phantasm'. Material processes shaping consciousness are, from the start, caught up in ideological 'darkness, evil and terror': not even science can 'dissipate ideological phantasmagoria' (Kofman 1997: 11, 17–18). Simple demystification is ineffective. Instead, the 'labour of transformation' provided by critique is required (Kofman 1997: 19).

Instability dominates analyses of value and the commodity: distinctions of use- or exchange-value do not delineate strict divisions but manifest value's impermanence, a 'passing form' changing in respect of the costs of commodities and variations in price and regulated by an 'eternal form' (money) also subject to alterations in patterns of exchange and driven by a restless pursuit of surplus. As capital, money is only viable when producing profit (Marx 1973: 646–7). Stable realities and value-systems evaporate amid productive flux, allowing no return to usefulness outside the net of exchange-value. Commodities change 'into something transcendent' and exist 'in relation to all other commodities' rather than being tied to human and social needs. Marx's exemplary commodity, a table, 'stands on its head, and evolves out of its wooden brain, grotesque ideas', turning 'a definite social relation between men' into 'the fantastic form of a relation between things' (Marx 1976: 163–4). Derrida's account of Marx's spectres notes how dancing, turning, wooden brains produce a theatre of sensuous, sensible and supersensible animated Things assuming many material and immaterial forms. It transforms the world of being and things in themselves – ontology – into the 'spooking' of a less substantial 'hauntology' (Derrida 1994: 150–1).

While spectres and phantoms emphasise fantastic and unreal effects of commodification, monsters give form to capital's less visible effects and agencies that are driven from two locations: directly embodied as the mechanism central to manufacturing and, more abstractly and obscurely, as the agency of accumulation. Industry's interconnecting and automation of discrete machines demonstrates how capital 'constitutes itself a vast automaton' driven 'by a self-acting prime mover': the automaton, materialising capital, is endowed with 'consciousness and will', 'animated by the drive to reduce to a minimum the resistance offered by men, the obstinate, yet elastic human behaviour' (Marx 1976: 502, 526–7). A 'mechanical monster' possessing 'demonic power', it usurps working minds and bodies, reducing the need for skills and physical strength, exhausting nervous systems and rendering the content of labour meaningless. Workers are trained out of 'desultory' human habits and forced to 'identify themselves with the unvarying regularity of the complex automaton' (1976: 503, 548–9). Consciousness is divided: production creates the conditions for a new subject (a 'collective worker'), but, since agency is given to the 'mechanical monster', capital decomposes labour into the 'conscious organs' of 'the unconscious organs of the automaton' (1976: 544). Another inversion occurs: the 'technical and palpable reality' of production employs the worker, displaying how capital operates as 'dead labour' which dominates and soaks up living labour power (1976: 548). The phrase connects the mechanical monster of technical dehumanisation to another image of capital: the vampire.

Vampire Materialism

Production is both 'labour process' and 'capital's process of valorization' (Marx 1976: 548). The latter – capital's 'sole driving force' – demands ceaseless extraction of surplus value (1976: 342). Profit is not to be spent uselessly but, in the interests of continued accumulation, returned to production in order to create more surplus value. Surplus, inherent in but external to the inexhaustible process of accumulation, drives and destabilises everything. Abstract, impersonal and relentless, it is inhuman and voracious: 'capital is dead labour, which vampire-like, lives only by sucking living labour and lives the more the more labour it sucks' (1976: 342). 'Dead' is synonymous with 'static': whether invested in machines or buildings (the result of prior labour), capital only profits by extracting surplus value (Osborne 2005: 96). The bloody vampire metaphor at the core of production also presides over the entire system. The sucking of lifeblood depicts how capital sustains value and duration (Marx 1973: 646); underpins the forced freedom of wage slavery (Marx 1976: 416); and signals work's callous squandering of human blood, flesh, nerves and brain (Marx 1981: 182). In extending the working day, it again sucks on living labour, children's blood too; in money form, it 'comes dripping from head to toe, from every pore, with blood and dirt' (Marx 1974: 79; 1976: 926). The pattern is reiterated: blood, life, flesh, labour are objects of a voracious, abstracted yet very real consumption by something not really a thing. Without the figure of the vampire, capital's surplus drive is difficult to imagine.

The vampire remains a curious metaphor to be employed in a serious critical work. Wondering whether Marx's spectres are merely remnants of 'medieval illusions and fantasies' dispelled by modernity, or bogeymen thrown up to scare children, Chris Baldick argues that they are 'more than a decorative trick of style': they constitute meaningful attempts to explain the effects of a haunting that is not so much of the past but registers the strange effects of capital itself (Baldick 1987: 121). 'Gothic Marx', a writer prone to 'mixing his metaphors' in negative juxtapositions of feudal images and modern forms, uses 'a gothic literary imaginary' to visualise capital 'secretly possessed by a series of pre-modern forms' while actually revealing them to be effects of present contradictions: fetishism, thrown up and then thrown back by modernity, exemplifies the 'arbitrary materialism' discarded by Marx but does not revive animistic beliefs, denoting instead a new mode of 'social *idealism*' derived from exchange-value (Osborne 2005: 16–17, 19). Fetishism inverts colonialist projections of primitivism: demonising other cultural investments in the power of objects, it enables a 'disavowal' of things by the subjects of European capital so that they can enter the transcendent realm of market value (Stallybrass 1998: 184–6). As projection, fetishism turns commodity capitalism into a 'religion' invested in 'non-sensuous desire' and reproducing itself in processes of occultation and substitution: here money circulates like metaphor, concealing social materiality and substituting commodities in its place (McNally 2011: 122, 120). As a metaphor entangled in productions of reality and value, the vampire is no idle decoration. Eschewing populist associations of usury and anti-Semitism and liberal fears of sexual difference, Marx's metaphor negotiates the 'dual character' of commodities and labour, rousing the living and shedding the weight of the dead (whether dead labour or dead, feudal forms). Its twofold function demonstrates the operations of capital and warns against it (Neocleous 2003: 684).

As a figure of demonstration and caution, the vampire reactivates an older function of monstrosity in a new context: reiterating dual forms of value and dual (trivial–transcendent) forms of commodities, its twofold dynamic traverses living and dead labour and fantastic and material conditions. Duality extends to the use of a figure from popular horror. Odd and obtrusive, vampire metaphors draw attention to artifice by foregoing stylistic smoothness and foregrounding incomplete substitution, refusing, against commodity fetishism, to occult social and productive processes. A metaphor of surplus addresses the way capital 'invisibilizes its own monstrous formation' (McNally 2011: 114). It gives form to something that is barely perceptible but has real effects (without furnishing it with a substance, timelessness or value); suggests extensive, mysterious powers (without dignifying or deifying them); fractures processes of substitution-exchange by which reality and value are transformed (rather than naturalising a fantastic-real world); and turns a figure of surplus into critical excess. The vampire's condensations of different clusters of connotation maintain a series of unresolved negations: not rational, not sensible, not human, not social, not spiritual, not moral, not natural, not real, not animal, not machine. Though echoing Enlightenment oppositions (reason–superstition, nature–culture, spirit–matter, modern–primitive), the vampire metaphor eschews conventional structure: reason, for instance, assumes a sane, if inhuman, economic logic, just as the transcendent value or supernatural power of surplus is not sacred or moral but systematic and monetary. The oscillations and alterations of negation continue: not social, the vampire's individualism counters human autonomy and agency, particularly that of a collective subject; not generous, it maintains a calculating, cold and predatory appetite untouched by interests or values apart from its own; unproductive, it depends on the work of others, disallowing social bonds or useless expenditure or pleasure; unnatural, it assumes diverse species forms and reproduces through blood, disease and death; insubstantial, it thrives only in relations which it consumes; unreal, without history, existence or objectivity, a flux of commodities and values, its fantastic form has material effects. Its negations conjure up a callous, asocial and inhuman form, maintaining critical distance without coalescing into position, affirmation or substance. Behind the metaphor lies nothing but un-life, un-reality, fantastic materialisations. Incomplete, the vampire figure does not crystallise as metaphor proper: reflecting no pre-existent reality or value, instituting no final substitution, it leaves matters open to contestation, critical reading and collective transformation. Without ground and solidity, the vampire retains only the spectral objectivity of the commodity: sever its headless surplus, pierce its automated heart, and there is only dust. Irreducible to anything but

Thing, tangled condensation and conjuration of antinomies, polarisations and oppositions, 'matterphor' without solid form, finality or fixity. Too much, it also marks an empty locus, a figure divesting history, content and meaning, surplus matter and voided materiality at once.

Surplus Materialism

Marx enjoyed horror fiction (Neocleous 2003: 673). Reading preferences aside, horror metaphors display an additional surplus: affect. Horror involves repulsion, recoil, nausea, abhorrence, disgust, revulsion (but not yet revolution). Marx's vampire is never a figure of identification or attraction but sustains an implacably negative relation: surplus value's vampiric associations signal another excess: the intense, unproductive, uncontrollable and destructive connotations of capital describe the inhuman demands of accumulation and inscribe an overwhelming human reaction. Surplus value involves a mode of extreme pleasure, a pleasure to the point of horror, called 'surplus *jouissance*' ('*plus-de-jouir*') (Lacan 1998: 80). Combining a sense of 'more' (more effort, more gratification, more spending of energies) and 'no-more' (things have become unbearable), the double gesture registers both the demand and exhaustion of excess. *Jouissance* pertains to bodily, sexual and material intensities associated with a reality (the 'Real') beyond ordinary representation and encountered as breakdown, shock, trauma and orgasm. Integral to and outside everyday reality, it sustains and derails normal functions – sexuality, for example, enabling both reproduction and ecstatic abandonment. Ultimately unproductive, it has to be moderated by law, articulated at the limit of more-no-more by the 'Thing' (Lacan 1998: 3). Lacan's Thing lies at an 'unbearable' limit, an 'outer extremity of pleasure' (Lacan 1992: 80). Beyond representation and reason, the Thing is both strange and familiar, an otherness and gap that, in horror, threatens utter dissolution (1992: 54, 71). Yet it also provides the occasion for law (the Symbolic) to reassert itself and serves as a site for the projection of imaginary figures that assuage more pervasive anxieties (1992: 43, 84). Locus of disturbance, occlusion and projection, the Thing evinces a curious and surplus materiality notable in the circulation of spectres and monstrosities and in anamorphotic visual disturbances (Lacan 1977: 92).

Mr Hyde and Dracula are exemplary Things. The former's physical deformities coalesce projections of degenerate monstrosity and derail bourgeois habits of perception: Enfield notes a wrongness and 'feeling of deformity' which eludes description; Utterson apprehends an 'impression of deformity without any nameable malformation'; Lanyon observes an 'odd subjective disturbance' occasioned by proximity, something both 'abnormal and misbegotten' and 'seizing, surprising and revolting' (Stevenson 1979: 34, 40, 77–8). Partially visualised, he is experienced rather than seen in a moral-affective reaction correlated to disrupted perception: an anamorphotic blur denaturing reality. Dracula, too, is a Thing condensing anxieties and disturbing normal perceptions. 'Thing', 'him' and 'it', the vampire confounds and exceeds species categories: 'this Thing is not human – not even beast' (Stoker 1998: 109, 293). Likewise, the vampirised Lucy Westenra, voracious of appetite and distinctly non-maternal, shatters all the codes used to maintain Victorian femininity. Killed, buried and then returned undead, Lucy becomes 'nightmare', a 'carnal', 'unspiritual', a 'devilish mockery' of her former 'sweet purity': a 'foul Thing'. As Thing, she is also the occasion for a restoration of values. The group of men who conduct the task in her tomb in the dead of night do so furnished with holy instruments, incantations and righteousness. Arthur, her husband-to-be and widower-to-become, hammers a stake through white flesh and into her heart: she writhes; utters 'a hideous, blood-curdling screech'; fangs bite her own mouth until 'crimson foam' bubbles; body quivers, contorts, blood spurting from a pierced heart. All the while, Arthur's arms rise and fall, 'driving deeper and deeper'. Excess body fluid and sexual violence contrast with justifications of 'mercy' and 'high duty' supporting her return to the sweetness and 'holy calm' of a beautiful and properly feminine – and dead – object (Stoker 1998: 272–7). Symbolic and religious modes employ and suppress excess in the name of value and spirit. The violence is legitimate and symbolic (a marriage and funeral service at once) and too much, consuming all parties in its intensity. Both sides enjoy bodily tremors, blood and tears: Lucy screams, writhes, spits; Arthur sweats, cries, grows pale. Surplus *jouissance* excites and exhausts them both, her monstrous excess exorcised by his extreme expenditure, her voracious energy, endlessly calling for more, met by his sanctioned but horrifying force (legitimate but too much), a gesture of excess exorcising unbearable excess.

Interrelations of law and excess deploy violence to exhaust violence, throwing everything into disarray in order to restore things to their place. The trouble in Stoker's novel, associated with concerns about unbridled materialism, degeneration and regression, is that all demarcations ordering social reality have been disturbed: things flow across borders, bodies transmute, values evaporate. Any sense of proper, naturalised and unified reality is upset. Aberrant and excessive flows of sexual energy are not the only concern. Lucy embodies female sexual abandon. Her counterpart, Mina, displays the intelligence and skill-set (her typewriting and secretarial work notably) that suggest the economic potential and threat of the 'New Woman' (Wicke 1992). Cut Dracula and he bleeds notes and coinage. Like movements of desire and appetite, money flows across borders, between and beyond social codes, roles and bodies, unregulated by moral values or human, cultural interests. Money has a hypnotic allure, reproducing itself unnaturally and sustaining itself by exhausting human life. Though figured as aristocratic, savage and alien, the antithesis and excess of a bourgeois culture that cannot live without it, capital's vampire cannot be easily excised. Dracula also evinces bourgeois characteristics: without servants (they are unproductive labour), he savours neither violence nor blood (it is necessary and used carefully), is 'a saver, an ascetic, an upholder of the Protestant Ethic', and has an incorporeal body that, 'sensibly supersensible', compares to the commodity-form. His appetite, 'impelled towards a continuous growth', exemplifies accumulation (Moretti 1982: 72–3). Dracula embodies the monopoly form of capital as it emerged at the end of the nineteenth century. Threatening the balance previously associated with free trade and individual liberty in the market, the significance of monopoly capital explains the vampire's aristocratic associations and why new US money, in the shape of Quincey, must die at the end (Moretti 1982: 75). Conjunctions of aristocratic and bourgeois features affirm, in horror, Dracula's excess: as a figure of surplus the vampire manifests a thoroughly inhuman, amoral imperative; as a fetishised image of the commodity-form, it signals a phantasmatic – and very real – disturbance in the system of values structuring realities of economic circulation.

Poor Things

The vampire of capital is a fabrication, but no less effective for that. Giving form to what is abstract and obscure, its unreality imitates commodity substitution, its horror anchoring fetish-effects in the production of a sense of materiality. Consumer society only delivers semblants and only circulates 'an imitation surplus *jouissance*' (Lacan 1998: 81). Semblants, Gothic forms and figures function as capital's shadow, offering images of the effective unreality of commodity fetishism rather than naturalising an idea of universal stability or solidity. Rarely, if at all, do they locate a space outside capital's sway. Gothic monsters and phantoms tell a parallel story of commodification, ideology and power: in affirming unreality (as fancy, superstition, madness, hallucination), their horror enables a return to and naturalisation of a world framed in bourgeois terms. Realism and reality, also haunted, are similarly effects of fictional stagings of differential oscillation (of fancy–probability, propriety–vice, romance–reason).

In the eighteenth century, novels and romances circulated as commodities in an expanding popular and feminised market characterised in terms of questionable tastes and propriety and threatening older hierarchies and paternal virtues (Lovell 1987; Williams 1970). Fictions, as cautionary endorsements and readerly escapism, tested female virtue while testifying to its economic necessity in a contemporary marriage market, sexual purity being correlated directly with commodity value (Clery 1995: 122). In Ann Radcliffe's novels, moral and economic values almost embrace: nowhere, amid her fiction's copious lessons, does any heroine display as much fortitude as Emily St Aubert in *The Mysteries of Udolpho*, when, alone, unprotected and threatened with imminent death, she defies the pressure to sign away the economic independence of her inheritance (Radcliffe 1980: 381). Metaphorical and economic movements see spectral forms intimate an order in and beyond market forces: like the gigantic objects that herald providential intervention in *The Castle of Otranto*, an 'invisible hand' ensures good measure (Adriopolous 1999). A world materialised by way of spectral economic virtues and values, however, does not necessarily advance human interests: the interrelation of use- and exchange-value sketches a prototypical Gothic world in which character is not so much a synthesis of singular human traits but an aggregation of commodity features leaving self somewhat shadowy and insubstantial, a hollow – and interchangeable – figure (Henderson 1994: 229–30). Even people, as exchange-value comes to encompass nature and reality, do not escape the domination of the commodity but remain things in the realm of things, objects of exchange and commerce.

Alasdair Gray's *Poor Things* (1992) interrogates capital's empire of things, probing the extent of the commodity's grip on bodies, selves, communities and places. While its main narratives unfold in Glasgow during the industrial revolution, it opens in the 1970s, replaying the trope of the discovered manuscript and playing out a framing dialogue between a novelist and a local historian as to the veracity (or not) of the story. The discovered text, reprinted in facsimile form with grotesque illustrations, makes explicit reference to the canon of Gothic fiction. Written by a shy doctor in the city, it is a fantastic tale of monstrous creation, relating the recovery and reanimation of the body of a pregnant woman drowned in the River Clyde. Though brain-dead, the mother is brought back to life by the transplantation of her baby's cerebral organ. Her new life, enlightened education and subsequent adventures relate a story of female emancipation, her humanity and reason unclouded by contemporary mores. Her existence – one person made up of two – questions the basis of bourgeois individualism; her education and experience challenges Victorian sexual, moral, class and racial prejudice; her vitality exceeds male fantasy. Undermining prevailing patriarchal and imperialist assumptions, her fantastic existence and actions disclose the artificiality of the morality and reality that tries to contain (and, in the shape of her first Victorian husband, own) her. In that guise, like many others in the novel, she is one of the impoverished entities to which the novel's title alludes. Things pervade the novel: a city of manufacturing and trade, Glasgow reeks with the smoke of industrial production and the steam of the ships and trains that distribute goods; a city of knowledge and power, it is inhabited by lawyers, doctors and scientists able to organise and regulate a world of objects (including the bodies of patients). Industrial fabrication extends from the production of material and physical objects, from the shaping of reality, to less obviously material things. Chapter titles extend manufacturing to persons, characters, identities: 'Making Me', 'Making Godwin Baxter', 'Making Bella Baxter'. The heroine, a woman's body with a child's brain, not only manifests the extent to which constructions of bodies and identities are affected by education, science and politics, but pursues and challenges how these constructions of value, meaning and prejudice are materialised and circulated.

The novel's attention to sexual commodification is paralleled by political and economic considerations: objectifying systems of power impoverishing female existence are part of a commercial and industrial culture that thrives by perpetuating conditions of unnecessary deprivation, from bad housing to poor sanitation, malnourishment and ill-health. The final part of the novel (aside from a closing section of genuine and fabricated critical and historical notes) takes a very different form and tone as it rebuts the claims of the previous tale. A posthumous letter offering a realist account of the events already rendered in fantastic form, it sternly corrects earlier Gothic flights of fancy. Its writer, a female doctor, socialist and widow of the facsimile's fabricator, debunks its sad fantasies of femininity with a plausible, but no less wonderful, account of a woman's struggle to receive medical training and qualifications in late nineteenth-century Glasgow. It goes on to trace her subsequent professional and political achievements in ameliorating the conditions of poverty in that city. Dismissing the impoverished male fantasy of her husband's manuscript as a waste of money (its production cost would have been 'enough to feed, clothe and educate twelve orphans for a year'), she expounds a strong critical reading of the entire fictional canon on which it draws: Gothic writing, a symptom of the callous commercial culture which nurtured it, 'positively stinks all that was morbid in that most morbid of centuries' (Gray 1992: 251, 272). An extensive literary catalogue is accompanied by a list of Victorian Gothic buildings, materialisations of the same cultural fantasy that inspires fiction: styles of fabrication and construction to be dismissed as 'sham-gothic', they warrant criticism for the way they, like the commodity fetish, present a gloomy, haunted and fantastic materiality that occludes the real and terrible conditions of industrial exploitation suffered by so many people: 'their useless over-ornamentation was paid for out of needlessly high profits squeezed from the stunted lives of children, women and men working more than twelve hours a day, six days a week in NEEDLESSLY filthy factories' (Gray 1992: 275). The expenditure of time, energy and money on such hideous fabrications is reprehensible in its wilful neglect of social welfare, good housing, clean water and decent education. 'Sham-gothic' is not an idle term but actualises a distraction from social realities by materialising Gothic commodities. And it turns human beings into 'poor things'.

Narrative juxtaposition seems to achieve an unequivocal critique of Gothic fabrications. Linking buildings such as the Scott Monument and the Houses of Parliament to fictions such as *Jekyll and Hyde* and *Dracula* foregrounds a widespread materialisation of fantastic forms (including the 'Victorian values' of hard work, thrift, prudence): stones and slate as well as words and images are scrutinised as fantasy forms supporting a world dominated by fetish-things obscuring social reality and feeding on impoverished and objectified labouring bodies. In the epistolary criticism of the ideological limitations of patriarchal fantasy, 'poor things' addresses the conditions engendered by Victorian culture and condemns the poverty of (the idea of) bourgeois materialism and its unashamed preference for fantastic things. However, the choice the novel seems to offer (a polarisation of Gothic patriarchal bourgeois fantasy against socialist-feminist humane reality) is not so easily sustained, given the postmodernised trope of the discovered manuscript that frames the two accounts. Offering no resolution, its playful and reflexive gestures pose the question of fiction and history, not in terms of a stable, interdependently defined system in which distinctions of fantasy and reality, truth and falsity are securely fixed, but as a constructive process in which things, persons and realities are made and remade.

While formally more credible and politically more sympathetic, the socialist, humane realism of the epistolary account recognises its place in a world overwhelmed by commodities and fantasy. A choice between positions and narratives, already staged amid the fabricated distinctions and fantastic materialisations composing Victorian reality, is further entangled in the frames of a novel all too aware of the postmodern resonances of its contemporary contextualisation. The attention to and interplay of forms and things (commodity fetishism in particular) suggests another approach: to select one or other position as outlined in the book would involve readerly absorption – a mode of textual fetishism – and assume the objective reference of the writing, thus requiring an identification with a fantastic form of reality (uncritically, passively taking prescribed codes for granted, recognising already-naturalised distinctions and accepting given meaning without question). The framing and juxtaposition of two formally very different renditions of female struggle and emancipation, both emphasising processes of making, however, invites readers to assume an active role in the labour of determining and producing meaning. Reading occurs in material contexts. Even in private it remains a social and political process. And it can be dialogic rather than fetishistic if it takes place in acknowledgement of material conditions beyond the covers of a book rather than being absorbed by fantastic-real stories. Here things continue to move, darkly and otherwise, between object-print and Thing-text, not stabilising any particular arrangement of signification, any particular order of things, but making materialism a matter of productive and critical social processes.

References

Adriopolous, Stefan (1999), 'The Invisible Hand: Supernatural Agency in Political Economy and the Gothic Novel', *English Literary History*, 66: 739–58.

Baldick, Chris (1987), *In Frankenstein's Shadow: Myth Monstrosity and Nineteenth-Century Writing*, Oxford: Clarendon Press.
Bataille, Georges (1985), 'The "Old Mole" and the Prefix *Sur* in the Words *Surhomme* [Superman] and *Surrealist*', in *Visions of Excess: Selected Writings, 1927–1939*, ed. Allan Stoekl, Minneapolis: University of Minnesota Press, pp. 32–45.
Bataille, Georges (1986), 'Celestial Bodies', trans. Annette Michelson, *October*, 36: 75–8.
Bataille, Georges (1988), *The Accursed Share, Vol. I*, trans. Robert Hurley, New York: Zone Books.
Bataille, Georges (1995), 'Materialism', in Robert Lebel and Isabelle Waldberg (eds), *Encyclopedia Acephalica*, London: Atlas Press, p. 58.
Bataille, Georges (1997), 'Base Materialism and Gnosticism', in Fred Botting and Scott Wilson (eds), *The Bataille Reader*, Oxford: Blackwell, pp. 160–4.
Benson, E. F. (1992) [1920], 'Negotium Perambulans', in *The Collected Ghost Stories*, ed. Richard Dalby, London: Robinson Publishing, pp. 227–38.
Clery, E. J. (1995), *The Rise of Supernatural Fiction 1762–1800*, Cambridge: Cambridge University Press.
Danielewski, Mark Z. (2001), *House of Leaves*, London: Doubleday.
Derrida, Jacques (1994) [1993], *Specters of Marx: The State of the Debt, the Work of Mourning and the New International*, trans. Peggy Kamuf, London: Routledge.
Fisher, Mark (2011), 'Gothic Materialism', *Pli*, 12: 230–44.
Foucault, Michel (1970) [1963], *The Order of Things: An Archaeology of the Human Sciences*, London: Tavistock
Gilman, Charlotte Perkins (1992) [1892], 'The Yellow Wall-Paper', in Chris Baldick (ed.), *The Oxford Book of Gothic Tales*, Oxford: Oxford University Press, pp. 249–63.
Gray, Alasdair (1992), *Poor Things*, London: Bloomsbury.
Henderson, Andrea (1994), '"An Embarrassing Subject": Use and Exchange Value in Early Gothic Characterisations', in Mary Favret and Nicola J. Watson (eds), *At the Limits of Romanticism*, Bloomington: Indiana University Press, pp. 225–45.
Hodgson, William Hope (2008) [1912], *The Night Land*, New York: Grendel Hall Press.
Hollier, Denis (1989), *Against Architecture*, trans. Betsy Wing, Cambridge, MA: MIT Press.
Hollier, Denis (1998), 'The Dualist Materialism of Georges Bataille', in Fred Botting and Scott Wilson (eds), *Bataille: A Critical Reader*, Oxford: Blackwell, pp. 59–73.
Hurley, Kelly (1996), *The Gothic Body*, Cambridge: Cambridge University Press.
Jackson, Shirley (2005) [1959], *The Haunting of Hill House*, Harmondsworth: Penguin.

James, M. R. (1987), *Casting the Runes and other Ghost Stories*, ed. Michael Cox, Oxford: Oxford University Press.
Kofman, Sarah (1997), *Camera Obscura of Ideology*, trans. Will Straw, London: Athlone.
Lacan, Jacques (1977), *The Four Fundamental Concepts of Psychoanalysis*, trans. Alan Sheridan, Harmondsworth: Penguin.
Lacan, Jacques (1992), *The Ethics of Psychoanalysis*, trans. Dennis Porter, London: Routledge.
Lacan, Jacques (1998), *Encore*, trans. Bruce Fink, London: Routledge.
Lacan, Jacques (2014), *Anxiety*, trans. A. R. Price, Cambridge: Polity.
Laplace, Pierre-Simon (1798), *Exposition du Systême du Monde*, 2nd edn, Paris: Duprat.
Lovecraft, H. P. (2008), *The Complete Fiction*, ed. S. T. Joshi, New York: Barnes and Noble.
Lovell, Terry (1987), *Consuming Fiction*, London: Verso.
Machen, Arthur (1977) [1895], 'The Novel of the White Powder', in Charles Fowkes (ed.), *The Best Ghost Stories*, London: Hamlyn, pp. 224–37.
Machen, Arthur (2005) [1894], 'The Great God Pan', in Roger Luckhurst (ed.), *Late Victorian Gothic Tales*, Oxford: Oxford University Press, pp. 183–233.
Marx, Karl (1973), *Grundrisse*, trans. Martin Nicolaus, Harmondsworth: Penguin.
Marx, Karl (1974), *The First International and After*, ed. David Fernbach, Harmondsworth: Penguin.
Marx, Karl (1976) [1867], *Capital*, Vol. I, trans. Ben Fowkes, Harmondsworth: Penguin.
Marx, Karl (1981) [1867], *Capital*, Vol. III, trans. David Fernbach, Harmondsworth: Penguin.
Marx, Karl, and Friedrich Engels (1970), *The German Ideology*, ed. C. J. Arthur, London: Lawrence and Wishart.
McNally, David (2011), *Monsters of the Market*, Leiden and Boston: Brill.
Michell, John (1784), 'On the Means of Discovering the Distance, Magnitude, &c. of the Fixed Stars', *Philosophical Transactions of the Royal Society of London*, 74: 35–57.
Moretti, Franco (1982), 'The Dialectic of Fear', *New Left Review*, 136: 67–85.
Neocleous, Mark (2003), 'The Political Economy of the Dead: Marx's Vampires', *History of Political Thought*, 24.4: 668–84.
Osborne, Peter (2005), *How to Read Marx*, New York: Norton.
Poe, Edgar Allan (1904) [1848], 'Eureka', in *The Works of Edgar Allan Poe*, Vol. IX, London: Fuch and Wagnells.
Poe, Edgar Allan (1967), *Bizarre and Arabesque*, ed. Kay Dick, London: Panther.
Poe, Edgar Allan (1986), *The Fall of the House of Usher and Other Writings*, ed. David Galloway, Harmondsworth: Penguin.

Radcliffe, Ann (1980) [1794], *The Mysteries of Udolpho*, ed. Bonamy Dobrée, Oxford: Oxford University Press.

Shelley, Mary (1968) [1818], *Frankenstein*, ed. M. K. Joseph, Oxford: Oxford University Press.

Stallybrass, Peter (1998), 'Marx's Coat', in Patricia Spyer (ed.), *Border Fetishisms*, London and New York: Routledge.

Stevenson, Robert Louis (1979) [1886], *The Strange Case of Dr Jekyll and Mr Hyde and Other Stories*, ed. Jenni Calder, Harmondsworth: Penguin.

Stoker, Bram (1998) [1897], *Dracula*, ed. Maurice Hindle, Harmondsworth: Penguin.

Walpole, Horace (1996) [1764], *The Castle of Otranto*, ed. E. J. Clery, Oxford: Oxford University Press.

Wells, H. G. (1946) [1896], *The Island of Dr Moreau*, Harmondsworth: Penguin.

Wicke, Jennifer (1992), 'Vampiric Typewriting: *Dracula* and its Media', *English Literary History*, 59: 467–93.

Williams, Ioan (ed.) (1970), *Novel and Romance: A Documentary Record 1700–1800*, London: Routledge & Kegan Paul.

Chapter 14

Thinking the Thing: The Outer Reaches of Knowledge in Lovecraft and Deleuze

Anna Powell

Affects are [. . .] nonhuman becomings. (Deleuze and Guattari 1994: 168)

H. P. Lovecraft's Things are both physically abject and ineffably Other. 'The Thing on the Doorstep' (1937) assaults the senses and the mind as its monstrous appearance and foul stench make the narrator faint, twice, when he 'saw and smelled what cluttered up the threshold where the warm air had struck it' (Lovecraft 2008: 647). In 'The Dunwich Horror' (1929), the alien otherness of 'the thing itself' – known as Wilbur Whateley – overwhelms perception, being impossible to visualise 'by anyone whose ideas of aspect and contour are too closely bound up with the common life-forms of this planet and of the three known dimensions' (Lovecraft 2008: 279). Lovecraft distances his own kind of 'weird tale' from cruder Gothic stage machinery, as 'something more than secret murder, bloody bones, or a sheeted form clanking chains according to rule' (Lovecraft 1927: 1). Instead, he seeks to create a 'certain atmosphere of breathless and unexplainable dread of outer, unknown forces' (1927: 1). This 'dramatisation of a rigorous philosophy' is at once sensory and speculative (Luckhurst 2013: xxi). It is this inexplicable disturbance of the 'natural' order that attracted radical philosopher Gilles Deleuze to Lovecraft's fiction, despite its deeply reactionary politics and repellent racism. This chapter therefore proposes to place Lovecraft's paranoid Gothic in dialogue with the life-affirming optimism of Deleuze, both alone and with Félix Guattari (hereafter DG when I refer to their co-authored works or concepts), to help us begin to grasp both their and Lovecraft's unthinkable things and their affects.

Deleuze's theory and Lovecraft's vision are linked by an engagement with affect that casts light on them both. The philosopher Henri

Bergson, who influenced Deleuze, considers affect as a qualitative response to stimuli via the 'intensive vibration' of a 'motor tendency in a sensory nerve' (Bergson 1991: 55–6). Receptive organs, in this scheme, both refract and absorb affective images (Deleuze 1992: 65–6). Rejecting the conservative dynamics of Sigmund Freud's Oedipal unconscious, Deleuze extends this notion into a psychic 'plane of immanence' where shifting 'constellations of affects' form 'intensive maps' of becoming (Deleuze 1998c: 64). Affect thus pre-exists individual subject-formation and is trans-personal, yet it retains singularities, specific and distinct traits such as those generated by literary style.

Hence Lovecraft's highly affective yet elusive images have potential to elucidate DG's theoretical process and vice versa. Lovecraft's Gothic tales presage particular concepts that DG later theorise, and the latter can be used in turn to explore Lovecraft's mysterious fictional effects, especially when they help to single out the terrifying 'Thing or Entity' as an 'Outsider' figure (Deleuze 2002: 42). Lovecraft's blend of physical and metaphysical and 'aura of strange, awesome mutation' (Lovecraft 2008: 399) is congruent with DG's wider perspective on transformation and becoming. DG's process of 'schizoanalysis', after all, aims to replace psychoanalysis by mobilising non-subjective affects to produce new becomings. These theorists contend that schizoanalysis counters the 'archaeology' of the familial unconscious, by making the psyche an 'orphan', an auto-productive tool for reimagining subjectivity, art and politics (Deleuze and Guattari 2004: 371). Schizoanalysis thus operates between philosophy and art, concept and affect. One way it can melt boundaries between self and world is through intense engagement with artworks (see Buchanan and Collins 2014).

Deleuze both references specific art forms and conceptualises art as a broader affective force that combines culturally shared signifiers with 'nonsign states' of affect (Deleuze and Guattari 1988: 21). This complex enables us to adapt his work on one medium to the processes of another, as well as to explore the wider applicability of affect. Lovecraft's contagious prose, in turn, impresses rather than expresses feelings, since its affects operate as a multiplicity that exceeds language and representation. They make us 'richer in ideas and the more pregnant with sensations and emotions' as we share the affective impulse with him (Bergson 1971: 18). My case studies here include 'The Dunwich Horror', 'The Dreams in the Witch House' (1933) and 'From Beyond' (1934) (all in Lovecraft 2008). These tales extend from more familiar Gothic devices to unthinkable terror as sensory descriptions reach out to the 'beyond' of affect.

Many of Lovecraft's themes and aesthetic strategies arise from the intense affects and cognitive challenge of the thing-world. To help us get at these as they dialogue with DG, then, we need to begin with the theoretical antecedents to DG's interest in such affective things.

Thinking About the Thing

Immanuel Kant draws a 'necessary distinction between things as objects of experience and things as they are in themselves' (*das Ding an sich*) (Kant 2017: 3). He defines these as *phenomena* and *noumena* and notes 'our unavoidable ignorance' of the latter and 'the necessary limitation of our theoretical cognition to mere phenomena' (2017: 3). Sigmund Freud later adapts this distinction to psychic topography, though his model of unconscious drives undermines Kant's ultimate valorisation of Reason. In 'The Unconscious' (1915), Freud observes that conscious ideas of an object are split into 'the idea of the word (verbal idea) and the idea of the thing (concrete idea)' (Freud 1963: 147). For Freud, the unconscious idea of the object is 'that of the thing alone' (1963: 147). In his reworking of Freud, Jacques Lacan further extends Kant's view that *das Ding* remains elusive, being 'the true secret' (Lacan 1999: 46), the primordial Other outside language as 'the beyond-of-the-signified' (1999: 54). The void opened up by the inaccessible *das Ding* actually constitutes human subjectivity, by ensuring that 'the subject keeps its distance and is constituted by primary affect, prior to any repression' (1999: 54). Lacan contends that both art and religion are produced by responses to the unrepresentable but ominously threatening otherness of *das Ding* (1999: 130). As Slavoj Žižek comments, Lacan's '*das Ding* is the absolute void, the lethal abyss which swallows the subject' whereas any symbolic object of a subject's desire (Lacan's *objet petit a*) 'designates that which remains of the Thing after it has undergone the process of symbolization' (Žižek 1997: 81).

Although Lacan's influence on DG is clear (he trained Guattari), the Thing of the psychoanalytical establishment diverges fundamentally from DG's radical schizoanalysis. DG do not make the Other constitute the subject, neither do they endorse Lacan's view of the human condition as an alienated questing of desire to fill a primal lack. They contend instead that affect dissolves psychic boundaries to develop new links and possibilities. In this connection, they cite the nature-defying illusions of Lovecraft's fictional 'outsideness' via affects that are 'no longer feelings or affections; they go beyond the strength of those who undergo them' (Deleuze and Guattari 1994: 164). Such images effectively produce total and pure difference for a human 'self' encountering them, exposing subjectivity as only one possible level in the flux of pre-personal desires and potential connections.

DG's approach can usefully be compared to that of Graham Harman, who fits Lovecraft's 'things' into his project of object-oriented ontology. His detailed close readings of the tales demonstrate philosophical disjunctions between consciousness and world. For Harman, Lovecraft's things are 'locked in impossible tension with the crippled descriptive powers of language' and thus 'display unbearable seismic torsion with their own qualities' (Harman 2012: 27). He identifies two 'axes' of gaps in Lovecraft's descriptions. The first is 'horizontal' literary 'cubism', in which Lovecraft's claim that 'the thing cannot be described' is contradicted by the adjectival overload of a 'gluttonous excess of surfaces and aspects of the thing' (2012: 25). Lovecraft's second '"vertical" or allusive' axis opens up a different gap 'between an ungraspable thing and the vaguely relevant descriptions' of an impossible reality (2012: 24). For Harman, this involves 'splitting a thing off as a dark, brooding unit in distinction from its palpable qualities' (2012: 34).

Yet Harman's philosophical use of Lovecraft sidelines both affect and the Gothic. As Geoffrey Weinstock reminds us, Lovecraft presents 'mysterious objects that exceed their intended purposes and, through their interactions with human characters, become drenched with affect and supersaturated with psychic investment' (Weinstock 2016: 65). Harman's irreducible aporia between mind and matter differs fundamentally from Deleuze's assertion that consciousness is actually 'embodied in matter' (Deleuze 1992: 4). For Deleuze, after Leibniz, the fullness of the universe (*plenum*) denies any such emptiness (Deleuze 1993). Rather than Harman's disjunction between mind and things, Deleuze reveals the vital process of flux and change operant *across and between* them. Harman's reading of Lovecraft's things remains grounded in 'pure' analytical philosophy, whereas DG use such impossible and unnameable entities as transformations produced when singularities intersect.

For DG, the fluctuating border between world and thing is an affective interval filled with creative becomings that undermine typological norms. The Lovecraftian Anomalous is a disruptive thing that catalyses systemic change, being 'always at the frontier, on the border of a band or a multiplicity; it is part of the latter, but it is already making it pass into another multiplicity, it makes it become, it traces a line-between' (Deleuze 2002: 43). Anomalous entities tax thought and shatter epistemological categories: self and other, inside and out, earth and cosmos, clock time and duration. For DG, Lovecraft's

'Outsider' has philosophical potency as 'the Thing, which arrives and passes at the edge, which is linear yet multiple' (1988: 245). Lovecraft's tales combine the affective energy of Gothic with the epistemology of radical physics and metaphysics. Their 'mixed plane' force-field is an ideal medium for anomalous becomings. Lovecraft's tales often leave behind an uneasy sense that the Anomalous lives on. At the end of 'The Colour Out of Space' (1927), a small particle of extraterrestrial aerolite remains to blight the grey wasteland that 'creeps an inch a year' (Lovecraft 2008: 188). Long after we stop reading such a tale, in fact, particles of affect continue to undermine consensual responses to the world. Both Deleuze and Lovecraft explore the outer reaches of knowledge where meaning breaks down, but the bewildered mind is compelled to go further by the senses and feelings. Lovecraft's entities exceed the scope of analytical logic to affect consciousness quite materially.

Lovecraft's fiction and DG's theory overlap in their assemblage of Gothic aesthetics, corporeal affect and metaphysical dynamics. Yet DG scholar Patricia MacCormack eschews Lovecraft's self-identification with the Gothic tradition, asserting that he 'shrugs off the fetters of Gothic writing and creates the hybrid, folklore-physics systems through which becomings occur' (MacCormack 2010: 9). Lovecraft and the Baroque are often aligned, both by critics and the writer himself, who did apply the term to his own style (Lovecraft 1998: 378). Deleuze shares Lovecraft's interest in the historical Baroque, despite his very different philosophical and political perspective. MacCormack applies Deleuze's study of the Baroque fold (Deleuze 1993) to illuminate the plasticity of Lovecraft's hybrid becomings via his manipulation of perspective, form and perception in both stylistic and thematic terms. MacCormack's own ecosophical ethics see a Baroque Lovecraft challenging anthropocene dominance in the interests of general ecological survival.

Despite her Baroque inflection, however, MacCormack's reading retains its own Gothic ambivalence as she admits to 'both wonder and horror' (2010: 17) and 'an excitation that is also a dread' in facing Lovecraft's mythos (MacCormack 2010: 210). She offers a thorough study of 'Through the Gates of the Silver Key' (1934), admired by DG for its 'infinite multiplicity' and subjective dissolution (1988: 405). This metaphysical romance tale lacks focus on the thing and minimises physical horror, so I will not detail it here. Yet Deleuze's interest in the transformative potential of Lovecraft's 'powerful oeuvre' is arguably located within a broader interest in the Gothic mode (1988: 399).

Indeed, while we concede the prominence of the Baroque in Deleuze, his overtly Gothic references remain potently suggestive. DG mobilise the Gothic mix of physical and metaphysical when they include werewolves and vampires as transformative becomings of man (Deleuze and Guattari 1988: 275). Elsewhere, Deleuze finds a dynamic 'spirituality of the body' expressed in the Northern Gothic architectural line (Deleuze 2003: 34). The mode's more covert influence also runs a kind of unacknowledged 'Gothic line' through his film philosophy. Rather than discussing Gothic elements in Terence Fisher's film *The Brides of Dracula* (1960), however, Deleuze finds it a stimulus to philosophical thought (Deleuze 1992: 112), and Mario Bava's surreal Italian Gothic is read by Deleuze as an 'impulse-image' (1992: 50). F. W. Murnau's seminal vampire film *Nosferatu* (1922) stages the metaphysical struggle of light and darkness (noted in Deleuze 1992: 101) via its diegetic 'space of virtual conjunction, grasped as pure locus of the possible' (Deleuze 1992: 109). This is manifest on the 'tactile' plane as 'textural intensity rather than spatial extensity' (1992: 109). Deleuze's view of the Lovecraftian entity as 'terror, but also great joy' (Deleuze 2002: 6) recalls Edmund Burke's ambivalent sublime, in which astonishment joins terror to sweep us away with an 'irresistible force' not without pleasure (Burke 2014: 1).

Like DG's theories, Lovecraft's 'weird tales' shift paradigms via multiplicity and becoming. In their own ways, each explores the 'limited and fragmentary nature' of perception when encountering 'the outside abyss of unthinkable galaxies & unplumbed dimensions' (Lovecraft 1998: 294). By relocating horror and terror to extraterrestrial agendas and life forms, Lovecraft's fiction offers an unusual kind of philosophy that challenges humanity's status. If reason fails us, we need other ways to breach the unthinkable, and he offers us corporeal bodies as flesh-in-process. The human can undergo biotechnological modifications, like Akeley, reduced to a brain in a canister for interplanetary travel in 'The Whisperer in Darkness' (1931). The embodied mind is similarly modified by literary technologies acting as a Deleuzian body-without-organs (BwO). A BwO is a kind of inorganic doppelgänger, a cluster of forces in an 'intensive, anarchist body that consists solely of poles, zones, thresholds and gradients' and a dynamic model of affect (Deleuze 1998b: 131).

Denying depth and psychic interiority as we usually think of them, DG insist upon art's immanence, as a 'being in sensation and nothing else: it exists in itself' distinct from codes of signification (1988: 164). In cinema, for example, the 'intensive' close-up face is an 'unextended' affection-image that leans away from subjective representation and 'suspends individuation' (Deleuze 1992: 103). Affective intensities are experienced when sensory and cognitive images enter the raw transitional processes of the BwO. In Lovecraft's prose, flat characterisation and stereotyping achieve a comparable effect by sidelining subjective 'personality' in favour of the affective thing.

Yet the map of affective crossings between DG's philosophy and Lovecraft's fiction is marked by fundamental disjunctions. Lovecraft is nostalgic for an idealised past as a refuge from, and refutation of, modern life, whereas the political affirmation of DG looks to a post-capitalist future and an internationalist 'people to come' (Deleuze 1989: 221). Lovecraft is socially aloof and misanthropic, with elitist fantasies of superiority, whereas DG seek to dissolve bourgeois individualism and develop the communal bonding of extended groups. DG assert the social nature of desire and anti-capitalist micropolitics, but the conservative, sometimes fascistic Lovecraft abominates the social melting pot of urban America. One crucial split between DG and Lovecraft can be demonstrated by a consideration of alien 'things'.

For Lacan, *das Ding* is 'by its very nature alien, *Fremde*' (Lacan 1999: 22), while Lovecraft's Great Old Ones deploy their alien multiplicity in a project to overrun and recolonise the cosmos. DG suggest that 'multiplicities are defined by the outside' (Deleuze and Guattari 1988: 9); the Old Ones emanate from beyond the edges of the known universe, carrying heterogeneity with them like an infectious virus. In Lovecraft, a Gothicised racism sometimes rears its ugly head via his paranoid application of negative affects to the multiplicity of supposed 'alien' cultures in the USA. The heterogeneous population of the 'polyglot abyss' that Lovecraft feared in 'The Horror at Red Hook' (Lovecraft 2008: 149) is abjected as 'a hopeless tangle and enigma; Syrian, Spanish, Italian, and negro elements impinging upon one another [in] a babel of sound and filth [producing] strange cries' (2008: 151). The diabolical rites performed by a nominally Yazidi group of dehumanised 'creatures' are uncovered by the 'charnel odour' exuded by the decaying corpses of sacrificed children from other ethnic groups (2008: 160). Lovecraft's eugenicist thinking also extends to those 'repellently decadent' northern Europeans, who, in New England backwater communities, 'form a race by themselves, with the well-defined mental and physical stigmata of degeneracy and inbreeding' ('The Dunwich Horror', 2008: 266). In Lovecraft's paranoid fantasies, both types of 'degenerate' have an evil propensity for black magic and monstrous congress with subterranean mutants or interplanetary aliens. As Jed Mayer argues, 'the mingling of horror and recognition' in Lovecraft's 'alien' encounters is 'vitally shaped [by] the fear of hybridity and miscegenation' (Mayer 2016: 119).

Such paranoia is completely antithetical to DG, who warn us to beware of 'microfascisms just waiting to crystallise [. . .] in even the most deterritorialised lines of flight' (Deleuze and Guattari 1988: 10). When Lovecraft's deterritorialised affects are sucked into the 'black holes' of actual horrors such as racism, DG's theory can help us address the operations of such 'fascist concretions' in art, ourselves and the world (1988: 10). DG identify three types of BwO: cancerous, empty and full (1988: 163). These types may become confused if 'the strata spawn their own BwOs, totalitarian and fascist, terrifying caricatures of the plane of consistency' where becoming is frozen into catatonia (1988: 163). The cancerous BwO replicates homogeneous 'cells', for example in the racist insistence that one ethnic type should dominate all others (1988: 163). In order to combat such entropy, art's desiring-machines must be 'plugged in to other collective machines' to 'connect, conjugate, continue' in social engagement (1988: 161). When Lovecraft objectifies others as abject things, he destroys the vital potential of aesthetic affects to become 'tools for blazing life-lines' (1988: 187).

Imaging Affect: Opsigns, Tactisigns, Sonsigns and Olsigns

To help us explore Lovecraft's affects, Deleuze's insights into cinematic images can be repurposed and adapted to literature. Film's affection-images, as 'pure singular qualities or potentialities' that exceed representation for Deleuze, can elucidate how Lovecraft's style affects us in non-signifying ways (Deleuze 1992: 102). In *Cinema 2*, Deleuze offers a typology of affection-images: opsigns (imaged vision), tactisigns (imaged touch) and sonsigns (imaged sound). Chiaroscuro lighting and extreme close-ups in German Expressionist film, for example, enhance our responses to narrative content. In *Pandora's Box* (directed by G. W. Pabst, 1929), 'emotions (terror) optical sensations (brightness)' are virtual 'power-qualities' actualised in the complex affect of compassion when Pandora (Louise Brooks) is murdered by Jack the Ripper (Deleuze 1992: 102). The 'tactile optical function' of Jack's gleaming dagger in close-up engages the haptic combination of vision and touch (Deleuze 2003: 151). Without the intermediary visual or sonic 'cues' of cinema to mediate tactile-optical or sonorous perception, literary techniques such as imagery and prose rhythms isolate and empower particular affects, extending the brain's field of operations and stimulating fresh thoughts.

Lovecraftian Gothic intrigues by just such techniques that both stimulate and conceal. Detailed descriptions of sense impressions abound, but, like images of aliens, monsters and other anomalies, they remain teasingly incomplete, inviting more. In 'The Colour Out of Space', Mrs Gardner is possessed by alien affects, 'things in the air which she could not describe. In her ravings, there was not a single specific noun, but only verbs and pronouns. Things moved and changed and fluttered, and ears tingled to impulses which were not wholly sounds' (Lovecraft 2008: 176). MacCormack argues that Lovecraft deploys 'the inexpressible, unnameable and inconceivable' to stimulate speculation about human limits (MacCormack 2016: 203). Although Lovecraft's language operates tangentially in relation to the thing, it still intensifies our affective encounter with it through sensuous description that resists standard signification. His experimental use of asignifying sound reaches its climax in alien language, which recalls the glossolalic utterance of ecstatic states. In 'The Shadow over Innsmouth' (1936), Old Zadok 'speaks in tongues' when initiated into the Dagon cult: '"Iä! Iä! Cthulu fhtagn! Ph'nglui mglw'nafh Cthulu R'lyeh wgah-nagl fhtagn" [he] was fast lapsing into stark raving' (Lovecraft 2008: 530). In just this way, DG evoke an asignifying BwO which utters non-linguistic and non-phonetic 'gasps and cries that are sheer unarticulated blocks of sound' that replace meaning with pure affect (Deleuze and Guattari 2004: 8).

For the Gothic musicologist Isabella van Elferen, Lovecraft's style performs 'ontological veiling' via the unimaginable qualities of cosmic sound (van Elferen 2016: 88). His character Eric Zann's cello evokes extraterrestrial 'dread of vague wonder and brooding mystery' until its harmonics shift from enchantment to intolerable discord (Lovecraft 2008: 61). Van Elferen's detailed sonic reading contends that Lovecraft 'spawns metaphysical as well as materialist being' (van Elferen 2016: 93). Yet sublimity rebounds into terror and horror, as in the sounds of 'cacodaemoniacal ghastliness' made by ghoulish instruments of grave-robbed bones in Lovecraft's 'The Hound' (1924) (Lovecraft 2008: 82). Van Elferen characterises the Old Ones' speech as an 'alien buzziness' (van Elferen 2016: 81). In 'The Whisperer in Darkness', Akeley records *the other voice* of the 'god' Nyarlathotep (Lovecraft 2008: 313) which recalls 'the drone of some loathsome, gigantic insect [with] singularities of timbre, range and overtones' beyond the human (Lovecraft 2008: 313–14). Van Elferen contends that Lovecraft's 'paradoxical materialism', which 'weirdly combines ontology with phenomenology', diverges sharply from Harman's materialist ontology, which eschews metaphysics (van Elferen 2016: 79). Lovecraft deploys hypnotic repetitions and intensive sounds in the ritualised crossing between planes (van Elferen 2016: 83), for example in the 'ceaseless, half-mental calling from underground' and the chanting of the demonic 'hymn' '"Cthulu fhtagn"' ('The Call of Cthulu', Lovecraft 2008: 216). Alien 'music of the spheres', generated by the invasive forces of the cosmos, is channelled by human emissaries to inveigle the unwary.

Van Elferen therefore locates Lovecraft in the Gothic sublime. For her, 'music-as-liturgy' is 'the melopoetic vehicle for transcendence, for a temporary dissolution of the subjectivity' and thus affords only short-term alterity (van Elferen 2016: 84). She regards cosmic sound as an ineffable event 'as material as it is immaterial', especially in the 'hyper-cacaphonic' passages (2016: 91). Her conclusion leaves Lovecraft's acoustics at the uncertain, semi-metaphysical border of 'paradoxical materialism' (2016: 93). Similarly, yet differently also, Deleuze's 'dark vitalism', in Ben Woodard's suggestive term, moves between physical and metaphysical with fluid ease on other planes than object-oriented ontology or the temporary altered states of the sublime (Woodard 2012: 11).

While indeed employing terrifying sights and sounds, Lovecraft evokes the potent tactile impact of phenomena in ways comparable to the 'intensive sensation' of Deleuze's haptic 'tactisign' (Deleuze 1989: 12). Such sensory encounters can induce synaesthesia, as when Nahum Gardner's horrible destruction by alien forces is overheard as 'a most detestable sticky noise as of some fiendish and unclean species of suction' in an onomatopoeic condensation of sound and touch (Lovecraft 2008: 180). MacCormack indicates that such a 'quality of luminescence and bubbling of ooze that is threatening as affect and not as act' operates in Deleuze-Guattarian 'sensation-compounds' when disgusting sensory images multiply to increase revulsion (MacCormack 2010: 9). Although Deleuze does not consider the affects of smell, Lovecraft often includes them. Adding to Deleuze's categories, I propose calling such olfactory images *olsigns*.

A Loathsome Foetor: 'The Dunwich Horror'

The most malodorous of Lovecraft's tales, 'The Dunwich Horror' is an often repetitive barrage of sensory anomalies. Tactisigns and olsigns vie with opsigns and sonsigns to evoke the indescribable otherness of the Whateley brood. Lovecraft overwhelms us with sliding similes in the elusive 'octopus, centipede, spider kind o' thing [with] a haff-shaped man's face on top of it', the affective pile of human degeneration and inhuman abjection that is Wilbur Whateley's 'pure blood' alien twin (Lovecraft 2008: 297). The onomatopoeic audio accompaniment to the strange goings-on in the boarded-up Whateley farmhouse features subterranean rumblings, 'surging, lapping sounds' (2008: 281) and 'the daemoniac piping of late whippoorwills' (2008: 284). Wilbur's twin intones such 'deep, cracked, raucous vocal sounds [that] the vocal organs of man can yield not such acoustic perversions' (2008: 295). The entity also makes 'a kind o' mushy sound, like a elephant puffin' an' treadin'' (2008: 291). Wilbur's noxious 'demon brother' repeatedly assaults the nostrils with an 'unwonted stench' that 'smells like thunder' (2008: 281), leaves 'a distant, undefinable foetor' behind (2008: 283), and returns bringing 'a touch of ineffable foetor to the heavy night air' (2008: 290). The scale of Dunwich olsigns ranges from the 'faint, malign odour' (2008: 265) of the village streets and the general lack of 'olfactory immaculateness' in local homes and sheds (2008: 271) to the 'indescribable stench' of the *denouément*'s 'lethal foetor that seemed about to asphyxiate them' (2008: 296).

Death reveals the full extent of Wilbur's own hybridity, as a 'teratologically fabulous' thing lying in 'a foetid pool of greenish-yellow ichor and tarry stickiness', yet, despite such perceptible features, he remains ultimately 'unthinkable' (2008: 279). Wilbur's anatomical anomalies include 'a score of long greenish-grey tentacles with red sucking mouths' protruding limply from his abdomen and 'saurian limbs' terminating in 'ridgy-veined pads that were neither hooves nor claws' (2008: 279). Colour opsigns join tactisigns in a sickening synaesthetic assemblage to produce

> a yellowish appearance which alternated with a sickly greyish-white in the spaces between the purple rings [and] foetid greenish-yellow ichor which trickled along the painted floor beyond the radius of the stickiness. (2008: 279)

The noxious Whateley stench disperses, and the tar-like residue of horribly dispatched locals dries up, but the vegetation on Sentinel Hill remains 'queer and unholy' (2008: 296). From these physically close yet cognitively distant stimuli, we move towards the unthinkable outer cosmos and the thoughts it nevertheless compels.

Things from beyond Space and Time: 'The Dreams in the Witch House'

'The Dreams in the Witch House' combines more familiar Gothic affection-images with the terrifying opsigns of geometric abstractions. This tale presents a becoming-schizo, in DG's sense, as sinister occult forces conspire to turn the mind's analytical capacities against themselves. Mathematics student Walter Gilman, seduced by the lure of forbidden knowledge, 'sells his soul to the Devil' for 'dreams' in the Arkham Witch House that dazzle reason with visions of unknown terror and beauty. Old and new forms of Gothic trap him in a sardonic pincer movement:

> non-Euclidean calculus and quantum physics are enough to stretch any brain; and when one mixes them with folk-lore [and] a strange background of multi-dimensional reality behind the ghoulish hints of the Gothic tales [. . .] one can hardly expect to be wholly free of mental tension. (Lovecraft 2008: 358–9)

This description is also apposite to Lovecraft's own generic hybrid, the weird tale.

Lovecraft reveals a predilection for uncanny part objects, things with an occulted life of their own. Here they include the strangely angled corner of Gilman's room and the utter anomalies of the dreams themselves. Gilman is assaulted by sourceless sonsigns, from rat-like scrabbling to a 'monstrous burst of Walpurgis rhythm in whose cosmic timbre would be concentrated all the primal, ultimate space-time seethings which lie behind the mass spheres of matter' (2008: 380). Such 'almost unendurable cacophony' breaches sonic laws to access and intimate the previously unheard and unthought (2008: 361). Lovecraft rejects the 'puerile symbolism' of Freud's sexualised reading of unconscious fantasies ('Beyond the Wall of Sleep' [1923]; Lovecraft 2017: 1). DG, as we have seen, likewise seek to replace the imploded Oedipal unconscious with the socially extended, affective desiring-machine of schizoanalysis, and Lovecraft has anticipated them.

DG also repurpose Melanie Klein's theory of ambivalent part-objects. For her, the suckling infant projects phantasmatic compensation for lost unity with the mother. Splitting the breast into over-invested 'good' and sadistically rejected 'bad' part-objects, the infant develops 'strong feelings of omnipotence' to offset the loss (Klein 1988: 2). For DG, Klein aimed 'to water down oedipus, to miniaturise it, to find it everywhere' (Deleuze and Guattari 2004: 48). Yet if her model of ambivalence is repudiated, part-objects can do other valuable work. Rather than being Klein's phantasms of a maternal dyad, DG's partial objects become 'different or really-distinct things, distinct "beings"' (2004: 356). Relocated to a machinic unconscious, raw partial objects are 'dispersed working parts of a machine that is itself dispersed' (2004: 356). Viewed this way, Lovecraft's improbable things can also be considered as part-objects, liminal forces neither inside nor out. They interact with the reader's embodied consciousness as 'intensive principles' of fluctuating desire in a force-field of literary affect (Deleuze and Guattari 1988: 165). For Lovecraft's things and their human receptors, 'forms become contingent, organs are no longer anything more than intensities that are produced, flows, thresholds and gradients' (1988: 164). Magical transformations occur when 'an intensive trait starts working for itself, a hallucinatory perception, synaesthesia, perverse mutation, or play of images shakes loose and challenges the hegemony of the signifier' (1988: 16). Freed from an organised body by the indefinite article, Lovecraft's 'intensive traits' express the pure 'intensive difference' of an abstract desiring machine (1988: 164). So how do such fictional part-objects engineer radical desire?

Lovecraft's affective things both generate ideas and give concepts material form. Like Deleuze, Lovecraft was intrigued by relativist physics and non-Euclidian mathematics, incorporating Albert Einstein and Bernhard Riemann in his fictional search for occult knowledge. His hybrid Gothic thus spawned anomalous modern imagery that would extend the genre in new directions. The sorcerous operation of non-subjective desire is strikingly expressed in Gilman's visions of living geometric figures in 'The Dreams in the Witch House' (Lovecraft 2008: 362). Lovecraft's style here moves between sensory immediacy and a 'pure abstract figural dimension ("abstract" in the sense of abstract painting)' (Deleuze and Guattari 2004: 385). Gilman's encounters with physically manifest abstractions begin in his room, the former dwelling of the 'witch', Keziah Mason, and of Brown Jenkin, her rat/human familiar. Gilman wants to uncover what gave 'a mediocre woman of the Seventeenth Century an insight into mathematical depths perhaps beyond the utmost modern delvings of Planck, Heisenberg, Einstein, and de Sitter' (Lovecraft 2008: 359). The room's corner has a 'queerly irregular shape' with walls slanting inward and downward (2008: 360). Gilman becomes 'absorbed' by the occult 'mathematical significance' of these 'odd angles' which enabled Keziah's journeys through 'unplumbed voids' to anomalous space and time (2008: 360). Gilman's obsession triggers 'a touch of brain-fever' and the onset of awesome dreams (2008: 360).

Gilman's dreams even enable travel in the 'twilight abysses' of the fourth dimension (2008: 369), a kind of Deleuzian plane of consistency with strange opsigns: 'titan prisms, labyrinths, cube-and-plain clusters, and quasi-buildings' that tax speculative thought (2008: 366). These 'organic entities' move in mysterious ways (2008: 362). Gilman speculates that some of them are 'projections' of humans and other Earth-life, but his mind is unhinged by attempts to analyse the properties of extraterrestrial entities. Two of these 'things' attach themselves to him, 'congeries of iridescent, prolately spheroidal bubbles and a very much smaller polyhedron of unknown colours and rapidly shifting surface angles' (2008: 366). In a later dream, Gilman experiences the fascination of 'becoming imperceptible' like certain 'semi-entities', 'wisps of milky, barely luminous mist in this farther void of ultimate blackness' (2008: 373). Yet these becomings lack autonomy, being directed by the sinister alien 'god' Nyarlathotep 'along the alien curves and spirals of some ethereal vortex [to] the thin monotonous piping of an unseen flute' (2008: 373).

Gilman's most convincing dream unfolds in the 'endless, cyclopean city' of another planet (2008: 370). He is astounded by pavement tiles with 'bizarre-angled shapes ... based on some unearthly symmetry whose laws he could not comprehend' (2008: 369). Here he accidentally knocks a 'spiky thing' off an ornate balustrade (2008: 371). Sensorial opsigns and tactisigns make the dream extrude into everyday reality, as the waking Gilman is shocked to find the anomalous figure in his room, 'the ridged, barrel-shaped centre, the thin, radiating arms, the knobs at each end, and the flat, slightly outward-curving starfish arms spreading from those knobs – all were there' (2008: 371). When scientifically tested, the object's metal alloys lie outside the periodic table (2008: 375). As the occult threat increases, other dreams undermine their oneiric status with physical markers. Gilman once awakes with puncture marks on his wrist and another time with perforated eardrums. For Deleuze, following Bergson, every artwork has actual and virtual elements, being 'the actualisable relation with other sets, and the virtual relation with the whole' that opens into duration (Deleuze 1992: 18). Deleuze's crystal image figures the 'coalescence' and interchange of actual and virtual (Deleuze 1989: 68). When an image is reflected as a virtual double of itself, it has 'assumed independence and passed into the actual' (Deleuze 1989: 68). For Lovecraft's Gilman, just in this way, the virtual and the actual have inconceivably changed places as things actualise their terrifying potential.

Gilman's 'dreams' have a further real effect, enhancing his mathematical abilities to astound fellow students by displaying an 'intuitive knack for Riemannian Equations' and 'comprehension of fourth-dimensional and other problems' (Lovecraft 2008: 363). He demonstrates knowledge of 'freakish curvatures in space, and of Theoretical points of approach [to] tentatively conceived cosmic units beyond the whole Einsteinian space-time continuum' (2008: 363). Gilman's preternatural brilliance follows the Faustian Gothic route to the point of generic punishment for unseemly curiosity. In a hallucinatory occult climax, Keziah and Jenkin inveigle him to seal his contract with their diabolical master, the Black Man, by child sacrifice, but he rebels. In a horrible literalisation of Gilman's metaphorical longing for the unattainable, his roommate finds him dead, with 'a tunnel through his body – something had eaten his heart out' (2008: 383). Years later, workmen demolishing the Witch House unearth several 'utterly inexplicable objects' as an alien memorandum (2008: 385). To think further in between Lovecraft's Gothic and Deleuze's philosophy through affect, I will now visit the laboratory of another obsessive 'mad scientist'.

Into the Interstice: 'From Beyond'

The spirit of Shelley's Frankenstein haunts the laboratory of Crawford Tillinghast in 'From Beyond', where his infernal perception-machine glows with a 'sickly, sinister, violet luminosity' (Lovecraft 2008: 389). Like other mad scientists, Tillinghast justifies his lust to exceed 'infinitely narrow' human limitations. He asserts that underdeveloped human perceptions conceal 'the boundlessly complex cosmos' from us and that we compare badly to other, superior beings who, 'with a wider, stronger, or different range of senses [might] see and study whole worlds of matter, energy, and life which lie close at hand' (2008: 388). His invention generates waves of energy that stimulate the pineal gland to reveal 'strange, inaccessible worlds', vitalising 'unrecognised sense-organs that exist in us as atrophied or rudimentary vestiges' to reveal astounding 'vistas unknown to man' (2008: 388). This tale thus overtly operates between the sensuous and the ineffable.

Tillinghast consequently persuades his friend to experience impressions from 'beyond'. The narrator's psychedelic visions induce fear that he would 'dissolve or in some way lose the solid form' to become imperceptible (2008: 390). Processing this 'kaleidoscopic [. . .] jumble of sights, sounds, and unidentified sense-impressions' demands extended sensory capacities (2008: 390). The narrator's perception of 'confused pictures' and 'huge animate things' drifting through his 'supposedly solid body' are perceived clearly by Tillinghast's 'better trained senses' and 'preternatural eye' (2008: 391). When the narrator himself gains 'augmented sight' of the unbearable excess of things, he realises that 'of all the space unoccupied by familiar material objects not one particle was vacant. Indescribable shapes both alive and otherwise were mixed in disgusting disarray, and close to every known thing were whole worlds of alien, unknown entities' (2008: 391). Lovecraft's vertiginous haptic kaleidoscope is a kind of Deleuzian interstice of becoming. By means of Lovecraft's 'radical calling into question of the image', 'the interval is set free, the interstice becomes irreducible and stands on its own' (Deleuze 1989: 180, 277). Here, like Lovecraft's narrator, we slide between mind and body, flesh and spirit, feeling and thought, as our subjectivity becomes dispersed into the terror and joy of the Gothic Event.

The affective interval thus draws on 'the power of the outside' to spawn both concepts and feelings (Deleuze 1989: 175). Entities on this shifting plane include magnified molecules or larval creatures in 'loathsome profusion' (Lovecraft 2008: 391). The 'great inky, jellyish monstrosities which flabbily quivered in harmony with the vibrations from the machine' are only partially manifest (2008: 391). These 'semi-fluid' hybrids, which pass 'through one another and through what we know as solids', possess 'malignant purpose', having already dematerialised Tillinghast's servants (2008: 391). The machine's electronic magnifier has revealed unbearable 'things that float and flop about you and through you every moment of your life [. . .] creatures that form what men call the pure air and the blue sky' (2008: 391). The narrator is horrified at the hubris of his deranged friend, who asks, 'in breaking down the barrier; have I not shown you worlds that no other living men have seen?' (2008: 391). The satanic Tillinghast, whose 'eyes were pits of flame', claims to have vanquished scientific and philosophical problems of time, magnitude, form and matter, having 'seen beyond the bounds of infinity and drawn down daemons from the stars' and boasting that 'Space belongs to me' (2008: 392). In a dramatisation of schizoanalytical operations between planes, this tale's affects pull us away from familiar ground into the turbulence of what Deleuze calls the 'interstitial'. Deleuzian multiplicities are determined by 'the between' in any set of inseparable relations (Deleuze 2002: viii). The process of becoming has 'neither beginning nor end, origin nor destination, it is always in the middle' (Deleuze and Guattari 1988: 263). DG's figure of the interstice was borrowed from set theory to develop their fundamental concept of 'between' via 'the method of AND "then this then that"' (Deleuze 1989: 180). The interstice is a fissure 'between two actions, between two affections, between two perceptions, between two visual images, between two sound images, between the sound and the visual: make the indiscernible, that is, the frontier, visible' (1989: 180).

There is certainly a wide fissure between the antitheses of DG and Lovecraft, who remain polarised in important psychological and political ways. Though their lines of flight intertwine, they do not intersect, but keep a necessary distance. DG choose to work with particular techniques in the 'minor literature' of Lovecraft and others by 'a sort of groping experimentation' that transmutes anomalous affects into new possibilities. They remain vigilant about the dangers of 'measures that are not very respectable, rational, or reasonable [which] belong to the order of dreams, of pathological processes, esoteric experiences' (Deleuze and Guattari 1994: 41). To stretch poles of thought, feeling and practice further apart or closer together is staking out a 'small plot of new land' for becoming interstitial (Deleuze and Guattari 1988: 161). In this experiment, deviant Gothic joins deviant theory, compelling us to 'follow the witch's flight' like Gilman and enter the living interval where unthinkable Things become things as yet unfelt and unthought (Deleuze and Guattari 1994: 41).

References

Bergson, Henri (1971) [1889], *Time and Free Will: An Essay on the Immediate Data of Consciousness*, trans. F. L. Pogson, London: Allen and Unwin.

Bergson, Henri (1991) [1896], *Matter and Memory*, trans. Nancy Margaret Paul and W. Scott Palmer, New York: Zone Books.

Buchanan, Ian, and Lorna Collins (2014), *Schizoanalysis and Visual Art*, London: Bloomsbury.

Burke, Edmund (2014) [1757], *A Philosophical Inquiry into the Origin of our Ideas of the Sublime and Beautiful*, https://ebooks.adelaide.edu.au/b/burke/edmund/sublime/part2.html (accessed 13 July 2017).

Deleuze, Gilles (1989), *Cinema 2: The Time-Image*, trans. H. Tomlinson and R. Galeta, London: Athlone.

Deleuze, Gilles (1992), *Cinema 1: The Movement-Image*, trans. H. Tomlinson and B. Habberjam, Minneapolis: University of Minnesota Press.

Deleuze, Gilles (1993), *The Fold: Leibniz and the Baroque*, trans. Tom Conley, Minneapolis: University of Minnesota Press.

Deleuze, Gilles (1998a), 'Literature and Life', in *Essays Critical and Clinical*, trans. Daniel W. Smith and Michael A. Greco, London: Verso, pp. 1–7.

Deleuze, Gilles (1998b), 'To Have Done with Judgement', in *Essays Critical and Clinical*, trans. Daniel W. Smith and Michael A. Greco, London: Verso, pp. 126–36.

Deleuze, Gilles (1998c), 'What Children Say', in *Essays Critical and Clinical*, trans. Daniel W. Smith and Michael A. Greco, London: Verso, pp. 61–8.

Deleuze, Gilles (2002), 'Dead Psychoanalysis: Analyse', in Gilles Deleuze and Claire Parnet, *Dialogues II*, trans H. Tomlinson and B. Habberjam, London: Athlone, pp. 77–124.

Deleuze, Gilles (2003), *Francis Bacon: The Logic of Sensation*, trans. Daniel W. Smith, London: Continuum.

Deleuze, Gilles, and Félix Guattari (1988), *A Thousand Plateaus: Capitalism and Schizophrenia*, trans. Brian Massumi, London: Athlone.

Deleuze, Gilles, and Félix Guattari (1994), *What is Philosophy?*, trans. G. Burchill and H. Tomlinson, London: Verso.

Deleuze, Gilles, and Félix Guattari (2004) [1972], *Anti-Oedipus: Capitalism and Schizophrenia*, trans. Robert Hurley, Mark Seem and Helen R. Lane, London: Continuum.

Freud, Sigmund (1963) [1915], 'The Unconscious', in *General Psychological Theory: Papers on Metapsychology*, ed. Philip Rieff, New York: Macmillan, https://www.sas.upenn.edu/~cavitch/pdf-library/Freud_Unconscious.pdf (accessed 6 July 2017).

Harman, Graham (2012), *Weird Realism: Lovecraft and Philosophy*, Washington, DC: Zero Books.

Kant, Immanuel (2017) [1787], Preface, *The Critique of Pure Reason*, 2nd edn, trans. J. M. D. Meiklejohn, https://www.gutenberg.org/files/4280/4280-h/4280-h.htm (accessed 12 June 2017).

Klein, Melanie (1988), *Envy and Gratitude and Other Works: 1946–1965*, London: Virago.

Lacan, Jacques (1999), *The Seminar of Jacques Lacan, Book VII: The Ethics of Psychoanalysis*, trans. Dennis Porter, ed. Jacques-Alain Miller, New York: Norton.

Lovecraft, H. P. (1927), 'Supernatural Horror in Literature', https://www.gutenberg.net.au/ebooks06/0601181h.html (accessed 24 May 2017).

Lovecraft, H. P. (1998), *Selected Letters III (1929–1931)*, ed. August Derleth and Donald Wandrei, Sauk City, WI: Arkham House.

Lovecraft, H. P. (2008), *Necronomicon: The Best Weird Tales of H. P. Lovecraft*, ed. Stephen Jones, London: Gollancz.

Lovecraft, H. P. (2017) [1923], 'Beyond the Wall of Sleep', http://www.hplovecraft.com/writings/texts/fiction/bws.aspx (accessed 10 August 2017).

Luckhurst, Roger (2013), 'Introduction', in *H. P. Lovecraft: The Classic Horror Stories*, Oxford: Oxford University Press.

MacCormack, Patricia (2010), 'Lovecraft through Deleuzio-Guattarian Gates', *Postmodern Culture*, 20.2, http://www.pomoculture.org/past-issues/volume-20-number-2-january-2010/ (accessed 9 April 2017).

MacCormack, Patricia (2016), 'Lovecraft's Cosmic Ethics', in Carl Sederholm and Jeffrey Weinstock (eds), *The Age of Lovecraft*, Minneapolis: University of Minnesota Press, pp. 199–214.

Mayer, Jed (2016), 'Race, Species and Others: H. P. Lovecraft and the Animal', in Carl Sederholm and Jeffrey Weinstock (eds), *The Age of Lovecraft*, Minneapolis: University of Minnesota Press, pp. 117–32.

Van Elferen, Isabella (2016), 'Hyper-cacophony: Lovecraft, Speculative Realism, and Sonic Materialism', in Carl H. Sederholm and Jeffrey Weinstock (eds), *The Age of Lovecraft,* Minneapolis: University of Minnesota Press, pp. 79–96.
Weinstock, Jeffrey (2016), 'Lovecraft's Things: Sinister Souvenirs from Other Worlds', in Carl H. Sederholm and Jeffrey Weinstock (eds), *The Age of Lovecraft*, Minneapolis: University of Minnesota Press, pp. 62–78.
Woodard, Ben (2012), *Slime Dynamics: Generation, Mutation and the Creep of Life*, Washington, DC: Zero Books.
Žižek, Slavoj (1997), *The Plague of Fantasies*, London: Verso.

Filmography

The Brides of Dracula, dir. Terence Fisher, Hammer Studios, 1960.
Nosferatu, dir. F. W. Murnau, Prana Film, 1924.
Pandora's Box, dir. G. W. Pabst, Süd-Film, 1929.

Chapter 15

Gothic and the Question of Ethics: Otherness, Alterity, Violence

Dale Townshend

It is during a particularly tense scene in Horace Walpole's *The Castle of Otranto* (1764) that Frederic, Marquis of Vicenza, is brought unexpectedly into confrontation with a dark, hooded figure that he encounters kneeling at the altar in the castle's Oratory. As it turns slowly towards him, the form exposes its face to reveal 'the fleshless jaws and empty sockets of a skeleton, wrapt in a hermit's cowl' (Walpole 2014: 97–8). Startled and disarmed, Frederic falls prostrate upon the ground, yet this moment in the narrative turns out to be nothing less than epiphanic. Abjured by the ghastly spectral face 'To forget Matilda!', the Marquis summarily ends his participation in Manfred's last-ditch attempt at securing his illegitimate rule of Otranto through coercing his daughter Matilda into a loveless alliance with Frederic and marrying Frederic's daughter, Isabella, himself (Walpole 2014: 98). In narrative terms alone, it would seem that Frederic's encounter with a ghostly visage serves a positive if not strictly 'ethical' function.

In the Preface to the second, revised edition of the fiction that was first published as *The Champion of Virtue* in 1777, Clara Reeve deemed the graphic nature of this and other scenes in Walpole's narrative to be inimical to 'the work of imagination', arguing that the 'machinery' that it employed was so 'violent' and 'improbable' and it 'pall[ed] upon the mind' and 'destroyed' the effect that it was 'intended to excite' (Reeve 2003: 3). Consequently, she attempted to remedy these extremes in her own staging of the supernatural in *The Old English Baron* (1778), particularly when the ghost of the murdered Arthur Lovel returns to the haunted apartments on the eastern side of Lovel Castle. Reflecting on the visions that had troubled him when he elected to spend the night in these rooms, the hero Edmund notes that the strange oneiric figure – later to be revealed as the ghost of his murdered father – 'was dressed in complete armour', though tellingly, he recalls, with 'his helmet down' (Reeve 2003: 38). This is Reeve's pointed reworking not only of the graphically exposed face of the spectral skeleton in *Otranto*, but also of those lines in Shakespeare's *Hamlet* in which Horatio claims to have glimpsed beneath the lifted visor of his helmet the exposed and vulnerable countenance of the ghost:

> *Hamlet*: Then saw you not his face.
> *Horatio*: O yes, my lord, he wore his beaver up.
> *Hamlet*: What looked he? Frowningly?
> *Horatio*: A countenance more
>   In sorrow than in anger. (I.ii.226–9; Shakespeare 2008: 1706)

When, in marked contrast to this scene, Edmund's ghostly father reappears before Markham and Wenlock later on in the narrative, he is again described as being dressed 'in compleat [*sic*] armour' (Reeve 2003: 68), that is, without any intimation of a visible face. Denied the powers of speech possessed by both Old King Hamlet and Walpole's spectral skeleton, this ghost can do nothing but mime and gesture with its hands (Reeve 2003: 68). Thus does Reeve attempt to curb Walpole's excesses, imposing silence on her ghost and decorously screening off its face with the helmet's drawn-down visor.

For Walter Scott, though, this change amounted to nothing less than a violent reduction of the ghost's excessive, ultimately unfathomable nature to the 'ordinary rules of humanity', an unfortunate 'fettering' of the realm of shadows to the world of reason and probability (Scott 1825: II, 165). A more responsible treatment of the supernatural, he claimed, might reside in the writer's respect for the ghost's fundamental alterity, a commitment to invoking in fiction no spirit 'whom he is not capable of endowing with manners and language corresponding to their supernatural character' (1825: II, 166–7). Guilty of more than just aesthetic failure, Reeve, for Scott, had subjected the absolute Other to an unspeakable act of violence by returning the spectre of Walpole's 'Gothic Story' to the world of 'ordinary fiction' and revealing no more of Lord Lovel's ghost than was absolutely necessary (1825: II, 168).

This textual exchange between Walpole, Radcliffe and Scott draws sharply into focus my concerns in this essay: alterity, the field of absolute otherness as it is expressed in Gothic through the face, and the various ways in which this is negotiated, both responsibly (or 'ethically') and violently, in a selection of Gothic fictions and films from the eighteenth century to the present day. Of course, it is nothing new to claim that Gothic is the writing of the Other, and critics, albeit often without specific theoretical coordinates, have frequently invoked the category in order to account for and describe the revenants, monsters, freaks, aliens, wanderers, strangers and outsiders that traverse the Gothic mode. In this essay, however, I wish to approach the notion of otherness in a theoretically specific fashion. As I begin by arguing, the Gothic preoccupation with the face of the Other – that strange and unsettling face of the ghostly skeleton that is glimpsed in *Otranto* but carefully occluded in *The Old English Baron* – shares certain affinities with Emmanuel Levinas's account of alterity, absolute otherness, responsibility and the ethics of the face-to-face encounter in *Time and the Other* (1947) and *Totality and Infinity* (1961). Consequently, it is through Levinas's revisionist phenomenology, I claim, that we might begin to think through the ethics of the Gothic mode, particularly in its characteristic concern with the faces of ghostly, villainous or monstrous Others that, irrespective of their moral make-up, defy all attempts at rational decoding and assimilation, totalisation and control. Levinas, however, only takes us so far, for as I show by way of conclusion, the Gothic, far from thematising the terms of a simple and problem-free ethical relation, already seems to have thought through many of the problems, complications and paradoxes of the ethical position latterly explored by Jacques Derrida, especially in his work on hospitality, itself a way of ethically approaching the field of absolute otherness that is deeply indebted to Levinas's own. Derrida, in other words, retrospectively outlines an ethical programme that has already been 'theorised' in the Gothic: in both, if one is to enter into an ethical relationship with the Other at all, it is through a relationship that is founded upon an irresolvable aporia, a non-dialectical double bind in which one remains caught between inescapable violence, on the one hand, and fundamental impossibility, on the other.

As Levinas accounts for it, the face of the Other is, first and foremost, the face of the 'other person' [*autrui*], the visage or the countenance of the other human person with which the 'I' or the 'me', the 'self' of human subjectivity and everyday social existence, is brought into contact at the moment of that self's formation as such. This, indeed, is one of the implications of Levinas's frequently rehearsed claim that ethics is 'first philosophy': the encounter with the Other is the primary, even primordial, ground upon which language and discourse, human subjectivity and social interaction in general are based. That is, in the pre-conceptual, pre-linguistic realm of the 'there is' [*il y a*] – that dark, anonymous, chaotic and vertiginous field of 'existence' that is, as yet, lacking in beings or 'existents' – the human subject (or 'existent') is constituted as such in relation to an Other during a moment of 'hypostasis' (Levinas 1987: 43–51). Far from being an active agent in this process, the subject always adopts in relation to the Other a thoroughly passive role: he is delivered from the nameless 'horror' of the 'there is' only through the Other's presence, setting in place an attitude of obligation and 'pure passivity' that will characterise his relationship with otherness from this moment onwards (Levinas 1987: 80). In this sense, the face of the Other might be said to be both primordial and determinative, a manifestation of what Levinas refers to as the 'an-archic', a primaeval force – or non-force, for the Other never actively resists – that is simultaneously disruptive and constitutive of human subjectivity. Here, Levinas's departure from psychoanalytic accounts of subject-formation is salient: in the beginning, for Levinas, was not the Word or the Lacanian symbol, but the dark, pre-conceptual and pre-linguistic presence of a strange and unfathomable Other. Similarly, the face of the Other that so plagues and 'haunts' the subject is not, for Levinas, the face of the paternal *imago* – the psychoanalytic term for the representation of the father, real or imagined, that structures much psychic life – but a genderless, non-paternal Other whose structuring effects are, in a sense, far more fundamental.

Key to Levinas's notion of the Other is the emphasis that he places upon the Other's ultimate unknowability, an inflection that differentiates his approach from the phenomenology of Edmund Husserl and Martin Heidegger. The Other, he asserts, is 'wholly Other' [*tout Autre*], by nature, unknowable, inscrutable and incomprehensible, beyond the grasp and remit of both ontology ('being') and epistemology ('knowledge'), and perhaps even of philosophy itself. More than an object to be understood and rationally conceptualised, the Levinasian Other is absolutely 'other to' – in the sense of being radically different from – the subject of conscious perception and always occupies in relation to the ego or 'I' a position of radical exteriority. For this reason alone, the Other is always more than the subject's alter ego, the mirror-like replication of the narcissistic 'me' in the place of the 'you': 'The Other as Other is not only an alter ego: the Other is what I myself am not. The Other is this, not because of the Other's character, or physiognomy, or psychology, but because of the Other's very alterity' (Levinas 1987: 83). For the same reason, the Other can never be reduced to, or accommodated within, a relational system of difference, for difference, even the apparently vast differences between two discrete species, always takes its place within 'the community of a genus' (Levinas 1999: 194). Its realm, by contrast, is that of the infinite, with infinity being juxtaposed in

Levinas's thought with the totalising order of 'the same', the principle according to which the everyday world of labour, 'nourishment' and 'enjoyment' is organised.

As its name implies, 'totality' for Levinas is barely distinguishable from 'totalitarianism': founded upon objectification, abstraction and reduction, totality refuses to accommodate the Other, but strives instead to return alterity to the order of the same through gross acts of violence. It is in this sense that Reeve's subjection of the ghost of *Otranto* to the rules of 'probability' might be thought of as a violent and 'totalising' gesture. To the unifying order of the same, however, the Other offers the promise of escape, a route into the infinite and the transcendent that, in itself, marks 'the overflowing of objectifying thought' (Levinas 1999: 28) – precisely the richly imaginative counter-objectifying potential with which Walpole's spectral visage, in Scott's estimation, had been imbued. The 'gleam of exteriority or of transcendence', Levinas movingly writes, is to be glimpsed 'in the face of the Other', gratifying in this respect what he figures as the deep, metaphysical, human 'desire' for an encounter with the field of absolute alterity (Levinas 1999: 24, 196). For the eighteenth century, this congress with the infinitely Other marked the place of sublimity: like the sublime object, the Other affords the subject a moment of respite from the selfhood to which he is otherwise tightly 'enchained', countering the stultifying realm of totalisation with a glimpse of infinity (Levinas 1987: 55–6). It is for this reason, among others, that the Levinasian Other is, in itself, profoundly ethical, a reconceptualisation of the Platonic 'Good' that always remains wholly in excess of the metaphysical categories of Being attendant upon it.

Incapable of being grasped, understood or possessed as such, the infinite Other marks the field of unfathomable mystery, and expresses or represents these attributes – insofar as it is answerable to notions of 'expression' and 'representation' at all – in and through the figure of the face: the face, Levinas claims, is 'this exceptional presentation of self by self' (Levinas 1999: 202). To be sure, though, this is not the visage or countenance that habitually presents itself to the world of ordinary visual and tactile sensory perception, but the face as it embodies the Other's fundamental alterity, the face, that is, as the expression of the Other in all its excessive, uncontained and uncontainable otherness:

> The face is present in its refusal to be contained. In this sense it cannot be comprehended, that is, encompassed. It is neither seen nor touched – for in visual or tactile sensation the identity of the I envelops the alterity of the object, which becomes precisely a content. (Levinas 1999: 194)

As this indicates, the face of the Other is never recognisable as a familiar countenance, nor ever reducible to a set of distinctive features that constitute an identifiable sense of 'character'. Instead, the face is 'de-ontic' insofar as its expression always exceeds the processes of identification and recognition. Put differently, the face *is* the expressive non-substance of the Other rather than a secondary and external means of representing it.

Nonetheless, when the subject is brought into confrontation with it – a moment of encounter that Levinas refers to as an 'epiphany', though without that term's connotations of the holy and the numinous (Levinas 1999: 194) – the face of the Other articulates both a petition and a demand, imploring the subject with the Mosaic injunction 'Thou shalt not commit murder' and imposing upon him the requirement that he assume in relation to it an attitude of absolute responsibility. For its stance, Levinas claims, is one of abject misery, vulnerability and destitution: 'nude' and 'hungry' by default, the face of the Other solicits us with a call to which we cannot remain deaf (1999: 200). Instead, the Other's face arouses the subject's 'goodness', calling him or her to a responsibility without limits, an obligation without end. Far from presenting the self with the terms of a reciprocal agreement, the face of the Other calls into place relations that are unequal and asymmetrical in the extreme: addressing the subject as if from on high, the Other's face requires of him or her a responsibility to infinity without the possibility of a return, requiring this not only for the Other's own acts, but for the acts of the countless Others that the subject is always yet to encounter. Ethics, Levinas claims, requires that the subject extend towards the Other a welcoming form of 'hospitality', albeit a hospitality in which the rules of reciprocity and exchange no longer pertain (1999: 27). It is for this reason that the Other brings human subjectivity itself fundamentally into question, 'paralysing' it with his demands and sinking the subject's freedom and self-determination in an anterior, unelected sense of obligation and responsibility (1999: 207). Levinasian ethics, then, resides not in the careful subscription to the terms laid out in a metanarrative of 'The Good', but only in the small, contingent, often counter-intuitive and invariably singular acts of responsibility to which an encounter with the Other's face calls us: the face-to-face encounter, he writes, is 'pure sincerity' (1999: 202). Thus, more than offering a point of entry or 'gateway' to the ethical world, the face of the Other is, in itself, ethical non-substance and ground itself: to have glimpsed it in its nakedness and destitution is already to have entered into the ethical relation.

And yet, if the world of ordinary existence is to continue to function at all, it is imperative that the face of the Other, with all its petitions and demands, be temporarily screened off, at least until that epiphanic moment in which the subject encounters the absolute Other in the face-to-face relation. As Levinas explains, if, in day-to-day interaction, the relationship with the other person 'involves more than relationships with mystery', it is because one has, out of necessity, 'accosted' the Other, covering over the Other's 'solitude and fundamental alterity' by drawing over and across it what he evocatively describes as a 'veil of decency' (Levinas 1987). As psychoanalytic readings have long taught us, the Gothic, at its most characteristic, is given over to exposing that disturbing uncanny and abject material that otherwise exists beneath the bar of cultural proscription, from incestuous sexuality to seeping bodily fluids, degenerative and antisocial drives and impulses to nightmarish versions of the past. This tendency to reveal that which should have remained hidden is no less apparent in the Gothic in relation to the face, for, well beyond the example from *The Castle of Otranto*, the mode routinely draws aside the veil of decency so as to bring its readers into a close and intimate confrontation with the face of absolute alterity.

Ann Radcliffe's most memorable villains, to be sure, express their moral, sexual and economic alterity to the subjects of bourgeois modernity in and through their unreadable countenances. For Emily St Aubert in *The Mysteries of Udolpho* (1794), the countenance of Signor Montoni has something deeply puzzling about it: while it seems superficially 'handsome', and appears to express the 'quickness' of his mental perceptions, it is governed by a force of dissimulation that replaces spontaneous reflection with studied, artificial poses (Radcliffe 1998: 122). The face of the Gothic villain remains for the heroine always fundamentally unreadable, strange, sublimely obscure and Other. Emily's impulses towards admiring Montoni's attractiveness are thus strongly checked and complicated by 'a degree of fear she knew not exactly wherefore' (1998: 122). Much the same pertains to the face of Father Schedoni in *The Italian* (1797), the description of which is indebted to the strange, unreadable countenance of the Armenian in the 1795 English translation of Friedrich Schiller's *The Ghost-Seer; or, Apparitionist* (1787–9). When Schedoni's cowl is retracted, it reveals a countenance that, in its singularity, eludes the generalising functions of linguistic description: 'There was something in his physiognomy extremely singular, and that can not easily be defined' (Radcliffe 1968: 35). His is a visage that refuses to remain fixed, mercurially shifting from 'gloom and austerity' to 'a countenance entirely different', a face that withstands all attempts at formulation and visual recognition by effortlessly adapting itself to the tempers and passions of those around it (Radcliffe 1968: 35). The Other always resists the subject's attempt to know, understand and contain it, characteristics that make its presence always much more redoubtable than that of a psychoanalytic paternal *imago*.

Writing against the critical tendency to apply psychological metaphors of depth, Eve Kosofsky Sedgwick has argued that the countenances that we encounter in these and other early Gothic fictions are notable for their celebration of surface and superficiality (Sedgwick 1981). This is certainly true of some Gothic countenances, such as the face of the anonymous cleric that, when it appears in Lorenzo's dream in the opening sections of Matthew Lewis's *The Monk* (1796), has inscribed upon it in 'legible characters' the words 'Pride! Lust! Inhumanity!' (Lewis 2004: 55). While this is an accurate foreshadowing of the actions of Lewis's eponymous monk, the face of Ambrosio himself, when it first presents itself, remains, like the character that it expresses, obstinately indecipherable: though his aquiline nose, large, sparkling eyes and dark brows make his features 'uncommonly handsome', there remains 'a certain severity in his look and manner that inspired universal awe, and few could sustain the glance of his eye, at once fiery and penetrating' (2004: 47–8). More acutely, other sections of Lewis's narrative seem intent upon confounding the ordinary processes of facial recognition and identification, not least of all in the Bleeding Nun episode, a scene that is as much indebted to the exposed face of the spectral lover in Gottfried August Bürger's *Lenore* (1774) as it is to the bare countenances of the ghosts in *Hamlet* and *Otranto*. 'What a sight presented itself to my startled eyes!', observes Raymond, as the ghostly nun slowly lifts her veil in order to reveal to him the face of absolute alterity: 'I beheld before me an animated corse. Her countenance was long and haggard; her cheeks and lips were bloodless; the paleness of death was spread over her features; and her eye-balls, fixed stedfastly [*sic*] upon me, were lusterless and hollow' (2004: 155).

Nineteenth-century Gothic writing is heir to this tradition, characteristically making of the face, countenance or visage the site of absolute alterity. Mary Shelley's account of the visual appearance of her creature in *Frankenstein; or, The Modern Prometheus* (1818, 1831) is notoriously sparse, and even in those instances in which a description is offered, his face seems to elude the grasp of language altogether. Though the individual features of his 'shrivelled complexion' might be enumerated – the 'watery' and 'dull yellow eye', 'yellow skin', 'dun white sockets', hair of 'lustrous black', 'teeth of a pearly whiteness' and 'straight black lips' (Shelley 1980: 57) – these never accrete into a recognisable visage, just as his individual body parts, though selected by Victor for their attractiveness, never amount to anything approaching beauty. His face is, at once, more *and* less than the sum of its parts, exceeding and overflowing its composite features even as it disappears into the unnamed and unnameable spaces between them. We gauge the sheer extent of the creature's alterity primarily by the effect that his face has on those whom he encounters, from Victor's own initial revulsion, through the horror of Felix, Safie and Agatha, the terror of the infant William and the fear of the other villagers, to the disgust of Robert Walton: 'Never did I behold a vision so horrible as his face, of such loathsome yet appalling hideousness' (1980: 218–19). As absolute Other, however, his is a face that does not necessarily need to be seen in order to function as an effective means of ethical petition: even as it exceeds language and vision, the Other's face, Levinas claims, is nonetheless able to 'speak', thereby 'inviting' the subject into an ethical relation that is 'incommensurate' with established modes of power (Levinas 1999: 198). It is this that the creature momentarily achieves in the darkness afforded him by Monsieur De Lacey's blindness, the interactions between the two being some of many instances in the narrative during which the human subject is brought into a face-to-face encounter with the Other and made subject to the Other's ethical plea and command: 'Do not kill me, but adopt in relation to me an attitude of absolute responsibility.' Like many before him, Walton cannot remain mute to the creature's supplication, but is instead thrown back upon himself in order to ponder over the extent of his responsibility: 'I shut my eyes involuntarily', he records 'and endeavoured to recollect what were my duties with regard to this destroyer' (Shelley 1980: 219). Daunted by the magnitude of his obligation, however, Walton ultimately elects to ignore it, choosing to veil the Other's face with a superficial concern for decency, decorum and socially determined ideals of beauty: 'I dared not again raise my eyes to his face', he confesses, 'there was something so scaring and unearthly in his ugliness' (1980: 219).

It is in the midst of a scene of carnivalesque festivity in Edgar Allan Poe's 'The Masque of the Red Death' (1842) that Death, the Levinasian figure of radical alterity *par excellence*, makes its presence felt, eventually unmasking itself to reveal a perplexing ontological vacuum in the place usually occupied by the face: in a reworking of both *Hamlet* and *Otranto*, Poe's revellers gasp in 'unutterable horror' upon discovering that 'the grave cerements and corpse-like mask, which they handled with so violent a rudeness' is 'untenanted by any tangible form' (Poe 1986: 101). Beyond the category of Heideggerian *Dasein*, the Levinasian Other is ghostly, insubstantial, a non-phenomenal object, much like the blank, spectral face of Jacob Marley that haunts Ebenezer Scrooge in Charles Dickens's *A Christmas Carol* (1843). Through such figures as Heathcliff and Mr Rochester in the middle of the century, the otherness of the Other's face continues to vex, but it is in the well-known fictions of the Victorian *fin de siècle* that its destabilising presence becomes especially pronounced. Mr Utterson in Robert Louis Stevenson's *Strange Case of Dr Jekyll and Mr Hyde* (1886) soon becomes obsessed with seeing a face that, in its singularity, refuses to yield to the totalising and unifying functions of vision, language and representation itself:

> And still the figure had no face by which he might know it; even in his dreams, it had no face, or one that baffled him and melted before his eyes; and thus it was that here sprang up and grew apace in the lawyer's mind a singularly strong, almost an inordinate, curiosity to behold the features of the real Mr Hyde. (Stevenson 1989: 16)

Even once his desire to see the face of Hyde has been gratified, Utterson is no closer to clearing up the 'mystery' of the Other for which the face serves as the most singular expression (Stevenson 1989: 17). Although aspects of Hyde's strange physiognomy are reliable expressions of the savage, criminal and animalistic nature that lies within, his sheer alterity throws the laws of physiognomy, phrenology and taxonomic classification into disarray. For this reason, too, Hyde, though apparently related to Jekyll through a differential relation of doubling, is always more than the doctor's alter ego. The picture of Dorian Gray in Oscar Wilde's 1891 novella of that name fulfils much the same function, mobilising in the portrait's continuously shifting face an otherness that goes well beyond the differential relations of Gothic doubling. Indeed, it is his radical alterity to Jekyll's sense of self that ignites Jekyll's desire for Hyde in the first place: 'Even as good shone upon the countenance of the one, evil was written broadly and plainly on the face of the other [. . .] And yet when I looked upon that ugly idol in the glass, I was conscious of no repugnance, rather of a leap of welcome' (1989: 63). Under the threat of death, Jekyll chooses to offer hospitality to the absolute Other, an Other that, rupturing the ego, initially promises for him the possibility of infinity and transcendence.

As Jonathan Harker in Bram Stoker's *Dracula* (1897) is the first to observe, vampirism is, first and foremost, a condition of the face, the radical otherness of the Other 'marking' itself on the Count's singular physiognomy: the aquiline nose and arched nostrils, the lofty domed forehead, the arrangement of the hair, the eyebrows 'almost meeting over the nose', and the mouth, 'fixed and rather cruel-looking, with peculiarly sharp white teeth' that protrude over the ruddy, full lips (Stoker 1998: 48). Subsequently, by the light that falls from his lantern, Van Helsing is able to read on Lucy Westenra's countenance the sign of her vampiric becoming, noticing that 'the lips were crimson with fresh blood, and that the stream had trickled over her chin and stained the purity of her lawn death-robe' (1998: 249); later, when Mina Harker begins vampirically to mutate, Dr Seward records Van Helsing as observing that '"I can see the characteristics of the vampire coming in her face. It is now but very, very slight; but it is to be seen if we have eyes to notice without to prejudge"' (1998: 363). Otherness in Gothic is primarily a matter of the face, the established conventions of the mode often serving to defamiliarise the 'other person' [*autrui*] by turning his or her countenance into something unknowable, unreadable and ineluctably Other.

Hence examples of radical alterity in and of the face proliferate through Gothic texts of the twentieth and twenty-first centuries. Professor Parkins, the protagonist of M. R. James's '"Oh, Whistle, and I'll Come to You, My Lad"' (1904), who unwittingly conjures up a supernatural entity in his room at the Globe Inn, recalls very little of the encounter except that it had 'a horrible, an intensely horrible, face of *crumpled linen*': 'What expression he read upon it he could not or would not tell, but that the fear of it went nigh to maddening him is certain' (James 2013: 92). As in 'The Masque of the Red Death', the Other lacks all substantial and phenomenal presence, bringing language and subjectivity itself to a point of crisis. Through allusions to the weird countenances in *Otranto*, *Frankenstein* and Poe, the eyes and face of the eponymous Erik in Gaston Leroux's *The Phantom of the Opera* (1910) are described as 'two big black holes' in 'a dead man's skull', his skin, 'which is stretched across his bones like a drumhead', not 'white' but 'a nasty yellow', and his nose disturbingly 'absent' (Leroux 1995: 9). As ever, the Other exceeds Being, language and the processes of everyday comprehension.

The face of the Other in all its primal 'nakedness' remains a staple feature of the Gothic when the mode takes that great technological leap from the page to the screen at the beginning of the twentieth century: the deranged face of John Barrymore's Mr Hyde in John S.

Robertson's *Dr Jekyll and Mr Hyde* (1920); the imploring and pitiful face of the vampiric Max Schreck in F. W. Murnau's *Nosferatu* (1922); Lon Chaney's unmasked skeletal face in Rupert Julian's *The Phantom of the Opera* (1925); the exposed, upward-turned face of Boris Karloff's creature in James Whale's *Frankenstein* (1931); the face of Mrs Bates that subtly superimposes itself over Norman's countenance towards the end of Alfred Hitchcock's *Psycho* (1960); and the face of the little girl Anne Stewart that metamorphoses beneath the wedding veil into that of an old woman in Alejandro Amenábar's *The Others* (2001). As these shifting, ultimately unfixable faces in Hitchcock and Amenábar indicate, the Other in horror film often resists the visual representations of cinema itself, a technique that is replayed in the constantly changing face of the vampire in Francis Ford Coppola's *Bram Stoker's Dracula* (1992). And although it is denied the powers of language and sound in several of these early examples, it is through its exposed countenance that the Other of cinema nonetheless continues to 'speak', articulating its cries in the muteness of the cinematic face-shot or close-up. As the example of Leroux's Erik suggests, however, the face of the Other in modern and contemporary Gothic is often masked, shielded or screened, such as in the transplanted, emotionless face of Christiane in Georges Franju's *Les yeux sans visage* (1960); the mask of dead human skin worn by Leatherface in Tobe Hooper's *The Texas Chainsaw Massacre* (1974) and its subsequent remakes; the expressionless mask of Michael Myers in the *Halloween* franchise (1978–2009); the protective hockey mask of Jason Voorhees in the *Friday the 13th* films (1980–2009); the generic mask of Ghostface in the *Scream* series (1996–2011); and the various masked disguises worn by Jigsaw and his acolytes in the *Saw* franchise (2004–17). In the Slasher genre, the face that lies behind the killer's mask is often revealed during a moment of climactic conflict, such as when Jason, in a scene towards the end of *Friday the 13th, Part VIII*, removes his mask to expose his face to the gang of Manhattan youths who are taunting and threatening him (Conrich 2010: 180–1). Here, the film replays the figuring of the unrepresentable face in *Frankenstein*, for although the revelation of the exposed countenance occurs offscreen, the intense reactions of those who see it in its nakedness tell the viewer something of its import: shaken, unnerved and overcome, the gang flees in fear, horror and disgust.

Horror and terror, dread, fear and angst: this moment in *Friday the 13th* throws into relief a concern that has run implicitly throughout this argument and one that threatens to expose the limits of the applicability of Levinas's ethical schema to a reading of the Gothic. In each of the examples above, the encounter with the Other's face is inseparable from the Gothic's generation of its most characteristic psychological and emotional affects. In Gothic, we might say, the encounter with the face of absolute otherness marks the advent of absolute anxiety, discomfort and fear. Yet if there is one thing upon which Levinas, via a reworking of Søren Kierkegaard, is insistent, it is that the 'presence of the face' does *not* 'overwhelm' the subject as a 'numinous essence arousing fear and trembling' (Levinas 1999: 215). Levinas's later 'Substitution' (1968), a short but important essay that was written after *Totality and Infinity* and subsequently reworked into *Otherwise than Being*, represents one of his few concessions to the sheer discomfort of the subject's approach upon alterity. Here, and more so than in the earlier work, the identity of the 'I' is said to be challenged and put seriously into question by the encounter with alterity, its 'ipseity' – Levinas's term for sovereignty and self-mastery, to which I shall return below – in some senses already a 'hostage' to the Other that makes of it a demand for absolute responsibility (Levinas 1996: 90). If the 'I' is already a substitution for the anonymous Other in the field of the 'there is' [*il y a*], its relationship with the Other, Levinas claims, will always be characterised by obsession, accusation and persecution (Levinas 1996: 88–94). Ethics starts to assume a far more unsettling undertone. Levinas's ethical relation is not without moments of terror, since it draws the subject into an encounter with the 'horror' of the 'there is' [*il y a*] out of which it originally arose (Marder 2008), that void-like state of anonymity and non-being that threatens its very existence. Even so, the discomfort of the ethical relation never really approaches the intense reactions provoked by the Gothic, a mode in which the fear of the Other's face is deliberately harnessed to provoke recoil, retreat and flight rather than ethical acts of kindness and responsibility.

No doubt this is because, as the above discussion has shown, the faces of the Gothic seldom resemble the examples of absolute otherness to which Levinas continuously returns – 'the weak' and 'the poor' of *Time and the Other* (Levinas 1987: 83) or the 'stranger, the widow, and the orphan' of *Totality and Infinity* (Levinas 1999: 215). Derived from Exodus, Deuteronomy, Isaiah and other Hebrew scriptures, these Others are defenceless, friendless and abject, and each lacking in vital points of social protection, anchorage and support. While the outsiders, strangers and aliens of the Gothic are often similarly figures of extreme solitude and isolation, their countenances, to invert Horatio's description of the face of Old Hamlet, conventionally speak more in 'anger' than in 'sorrow'. In ways that exceed Levinas's account of the discomfort of the encounter with the Other in 'Substitution', the Gothic Other adopts in relation to the subject an attitude of persecution, its face more threatening than threatened, its red, glowing, basilisk-like eyes more a mark of preternatural agency than the pitiful expression of the Other's fundamental destitution. Again, though, Levinas insists on something quite different: if the Other resists me at all, this is not a resistance that is expressed violently and negatively, but rather an ethical resistance that resides in the Other's refusal to submit to my powers of totalisation and control. The Other presents itself 'without opposing me as obstacle or enemy' (Levinas 1999: 215), but always slips away from any attempt at exerting power over it. But so long as the Gothic Other is construed as the enemy, the epiphany of its face serves as a passionate incitement to kill. As Stoker's *Dracula* clearly demonstrates, this moment often involves the methodological infliction of violence upon the Other's face, its singular and most sensitive aspect. Wishing to destroy the 'mocking smile on the bloated face' that drives Jonathan Harker almost mad, he seizes a nearby shovel, 'and lifting it high, struck, with the edge downward, at the hateful face' (Stoker 1998: 84). Like Clara Reeve and countless Gothic writers ever since, Stoker contrives to draw absolute alterity back into the totalising order of the same. Again, the Gothic could not be further from Levinas's insistence upon the non-violence of the ethical position, a relation, he claims, that 'is maintained without violence', and always established 'in peace' with the Other's absolute alterity (Levinas 1999: 197).

Undoubtedly, there remain moments in Gothic when the Other is not construed as the persecuting enemy, and, consequently, moments when its face, exposed in all its desolation, hunger and nakedness, evokes a far less violent response. The gentle, partly feminised and strangely beautiful face of the monster in James Whale's *Frankenstein* is one such example, as are those poignant scenes when the mask-wearing slashers of horror film are themselves revealed to be the victims of unbearable violence, abuse and pain. In the tradition of Wes Craven's Freddy Krueger or Thomas Harris's Hannibal Lecter, the villain's facial covering often hides a face of absolute authenticity and vulnerability, a face that, in the past, has been brutally disfigured by violence and the controlled infliction of torture. Equally, moments of ethical response might be elicited by the imploring faces of Tod Browning's *Freaks* (1932), by the pitiful, hungry countenance and staring eyes of Murnau's Count Orlok, by the misunderstood vampiric outsiders of Anne Rice, or, for that matter, by the werewolves and sparkling vampires that populate the pages of contemporary YA Gothic fiction. As critics have frequently pointed out, the monster becomes an object of pity in much modern Gothic cultural production. But, as Levinas reminds us, so long as these moments of sympathetic identification are founded upon the assumption of a universal humanism, a narcissistic recognition of aspects of the 'self' in the 'other person', all that is ever achieved is a violent reduction of the Other to the totalising order of the same. An ethical relationship with otherness, he writes, 'is not an idyllic and harmonious relationship of communion, or a sympathy through which we put ourselves in the other's place' (Levinas 1987: 76). Sympathy for the Gothic Other, then, turns out to be strangely indistinguishable from the violent forms of actual and symbolic murder with which these narratives often end – the dismemberment and obliteration of the monster or the expulsion and exorcism of the ghost. Despite their mutual preoccupations with absolute alterity, Levinas's ethical schema and the Gothic aesthetic seem drawn in vastly divergent directions.

Levinasian theory is certainly not without potential solutions to these problems. The moment of epiphany, Levinas claims, presents the subject with a choice: to let the Other live or to kill it, to heed the Other's call for a responsibility without limits or to destroy and annihilate it. To an extent, though, the choice is a false one, its outcome largely irrelevant, for to have glimpsed the face of the Other is already to have entered into an ethical relationship with absolute alterity. As I have suggested, the face of the Other is ethical non-substance itself, offering a welcome breach in the objectifying and totalising world of labour, nourishment and enjoyment and providing the subject with a sublime glimpse of infinity at the very moment of its apprehension. Although, in Gothic, the subject is often manipulated into rejecting or killing the Other, he or she, in acknowledging its face, has already responded ethically to it. Perhaps, in this respect, the draw of Gothic is fundamentally an ethical one. Furthermore, Levinas maintains that, in that very moment in which my power to kill realises itself, the Other has already escaped me (Levinas 1999: 201). It is in this sense that the Other is ultimately indestructible, always exceeding 'the point of the sword or the revolver's bullet' (Levinas 1999: 199), a claim that, again, might go some way towards accounting for the persistence of the Gothic and the perennial return therein of the Other's masked or exposed face.

Still, to insist in this manner upon the ethical functions of the Gothic face might well be to impose upon the mode a theoretical paradigm to which it is least suited. Instead, and by way of conclusion, it might be more fruitful to approach the question of Gothic ethics from a different, yet related, perspective. In its heightened awareness of the violence by which all relations to the Other are beset, and in its articulation of the terror that accompanies the ethical relation, the Gothic seems already to have thought through some of the irresolvable paradoxes attendant upon ethics that the work of Jacques Derrida has brought to the fore, from his earliest engagements with Levinasian thought in *Writing and Difference* (1967), through to his later writings on spectrality, otherness and the ethics of hospitality in *Specters of Marx* (1993; trans. 1994), *Adieu to Emmanuel Levinas* (1999), *Of Hospitality* (1997; trans. 2000) and a number of other essays. This is not the place to elaborate upon Derrida's ethics of hospitality in any detail, and I shall restrict these remarks to the two major points of difference between Levinas and the Gothic that I have explored above: the ubiquity of violence in the Gothic aesthetic and the problems that horror, terror and other Gothic responses pose for the constitutive and foundational 'peacefulness' of Levinas's ethical relation. First, for Derrida, the encounter with the absolute Other is never entirely free of violence, a point that he initially made in 'Violence and Metaphysics: An Essay on the Thought of Emmanuel Levinas' (1967; trans. 1978). Shining the blinding light of metaphysical reason into the Other's sensitive eyes, Levinas in this essay becomes the perpetrator of a violence as intense as that inflicted by Stoker's Crew of Light. When, in his work on hospitality, the later Derrida places a Levinasian conceptualisation of otherness at the heart of his own ethical programme – for even in Levinas's *Totality and Infinity*, Derrida reminds us, the 'first philosophy' that is ethics is fundamentally a matter of hospitality towards the absolute Other – these preoccupations with the inevitability of violence become more acute. In the realm of what Derrida refers to as 'ordinary' or 'everyday' hospitality, hospitality, that is, as it is commonly understood, the subject invites the Other across a border, boundary or threshold into his home, territory or nation, in the fashion of Immanuel Kant's account of the grounds of the political peace of the nation-state in *Perpetual Peace: A Philosophical Sketch* (1795) (Derrida 2000b). Violence, however, mars the purity of hospitable intentions from the outset. Since ordinary hospitality is, by definition, limited – in logistical terms alone, it is never possible to admit or offer hospitality to simply everyone – the Other and, indeed, the Other of the Other and the infinite line of Others behind it, can only ever fall foul of the sovereign power of exclusion.

Moreover, addressed in a language that is, of necessity, alien to him, the foreigner as Other can only ever be violently objectified in the name and identity that even the most well-meaning of hosts imposes upon him. Hostility is already at work within hospitable relations, a claim that Derrida foregrounds through the coining of the neologism 'hostipitality' (Derrida 2000a: 3). The scene of ordinary hospitality has always already been invaded by the hostility of the enemy; to take a 'step' in the direction of hospitality is also to cancel out the terms of its existence. In consistently representing the violence in which the relation to the Other is steeped – the violence that the subject heaps upon the Other, but also the violence that the Other itself inflicts – Gothic has already begun to articulate this Derridean problematic.

But if a Kantian ordinary hospitality towards the Other for Derrida marks violence's persistent return, the Levinasian realm of 'radical', 'unconditional' or 'absolute' hospitality is barely a suitable alternative. This order of hospitality, Derrida contends, is inevitably the realm of the spectral, for it is the 'absence of determinable properties, of concrete predicates, of empirical visibility' in Levinas's conceptualisation of alterity that gives to the Other's face 'a spectral aura' (Derrida 1999a: 111). Consequently, 'There would be no hospitality', Derrida writes, 'without the chance of spectrality' (Derrida 1999a: 111–12). As these metaphors of ghostliness suggest, the offer of absolute hospitality that Levinas extends towards the Other is, for Derrida, fundamentally impossible. Although 'ipseity' is necessary to the act of hospitality – in order to serve as the Other's host, Derrida reasons, I have to be master of both my self and my home – the sovereignty of the host within the realm of absolute hospitality can be neither guaranteed nor permanently sustained. Hosts can be held hostage, guests may conceivably turn malevolent, and the distinction between guest and host is anything but absolute – a lesson that Sheridan Le Fanu's *Carmilla* (1871–2), among numerous other Gothic fictions, appears already to have worked out. Yet to set in place a process of pre-selection is already to have precluded the possibility of Levinas's ethical schema altogether. For if one is to say 'yes' to the uninvited visitor, if one is, indeed, 'to let oneself be swept by the coming of the wholly other' in the ways that Levinas advocates, one has to lay oneself open to the possibility of a profound discomfort (Derrida 2002: 361). Amplifying by considerable degrees the discomfort of the ethical relation that Levinas had theorised in 'Substitution', Derrida articulates the horror and terror of ethics that the Gothic mode has been aware of from the start – and witnessed in Frederic's encounter with the face of absolute alterity in *The Castle of Otranto*. Unconditional hospitality towards the Other, Derrida writes, is 'terrible' and 'unbearable' insofar as it breaks with the relations of reciprocity, suspends the host's powers of identification and unsettles his powers of mastery (Derrida 1999b: 70). More than this, absolute hospitality hovers always on the cusp of horror and terror since, in refusing to discriminate between those who are and those who are not to be admitted, it always includes the possibility of entertaining a guest who is demonic in nature (Derrida 1999b: 71). As it so frequently does in the Gothic, the ghostly Other might well take the form of a malevolent spirit, yet if absolute hospitality is to be 'absolute' in any meaningful sense at all, it must remain open to the possibility of entertaining pure evil. This is a possibility of which the Gothic has always been all too aware: be it in the form of a villain, a monster, a vampire or a ghost, the Other, when it comes, often does so with malevolent intent, aiming to threaten, to persecute and to destroy. And yet, if the ethical relation is to be achieved, this is a risk to which we have to remain permanently exposed. Caught between violence, on the one hand, and impossibility, on the other, the Gothic aesthetic stumbles cautiously on, violently cancelling out the possibility of pure ethics in each ethical step of hospitality that it takes. The only constant that remains is the absolute alterity that drives the ethical relation, the otherness of the Other as it is expressed in Gothic in and through the figure of the unsettling face.

References

Conrich, Ian (2010), 'The *Friday the 13th* Films and the Cultural Function of a Modern Grand Guignol', in Ian Conrich (ed.), *Horror Zone: The Cultural Experience of Contemporary Horror Cinema*, London: I. B. Taurus, pp. 173–90.

Derrida, Jacques (1999a), *Adieu to Emmanuel Levinas*, trans. Pascale-Anne Brault and Michael Naas, Stanford: Stanford University Press.

Derrida, Jacques (1999b), 'Hospitality, Justice and Responsibility: A Dialogue with Jacques Derrida', in Richard Kearney and Mark Dooley (eds), *Questioning Ethics: Contemporary Debates in Philosophy*, London: Routledge, pp. 65–83.

Derrida, Jacques (2000a), 'Hostipitality', trans. Barry Stocker and Forbes Morlock, *Angelaki*, 5.3: 3–18.

Derrida, Jacques (2000b), *Of Hospitality: Anne Dufourmantelle Invites Jacques Derrida to Respond*, trans. Rachel Bowlby, Stanford: Stanford University Press.

Derrida, Jacques (2002), 'Hostipitality: Session of January 8, 1997', in Jacques Derrida, *Acts of Religion*, ed. Gil Anidjar, New York: Routledge, pp. 358–420.
James, M. R. (2013), *Collected Ghost Stories*, ed. Darryl Jones, Oxford: Oxford University Press.
Leroux, Gaston (1995) [1910], *The Phantom of the Opera*, trans. Mireille Ribière, London: Penguin.
Levinas, Emmanuel (1987), *Time and the Other, and Additional Essays*, trans. Richard A. Cohen, Pittsburgh: Duquesne University Press.
Levinas, Emmanuel (1996), 'Substitution', in Simon Critchley and Robert Bernasconi (eds), *Emmanuel Levinas: Basic Philosophical Writings*, Bloomington: Indiana University Press, pp. 79–95.
Levinas, Emmanuel (1999) [1961], *Totality and Infinity: An Essay on Exteriority*, trans. Alphonso Lingus, Pittsburgh: Duquesne University Press.
Lewis, Matthew Gregory (2004) [1796], *The Monk*, ed. D. L. Macdonald and Kathleen Scherf, Peterborough, ON: Broadview Press.
Marder, Michael (2008), 'Terror of the Ethical: On Levinas's *Il y a*', *Postmodern Culture*, 18.2, doi:10.1353/pmc.0.0014 (accessed 20 November 2017).
Poe, Edgar Allan (1986) [1845], *Tales of Mystery and Imagination*, London: Octopus Books.
Radcliffe, Ann (1968) [1797], *The Italian*, ed. Frederick Garber, Oxford: Oxford University Press.
Radcliffe, Ann (1998) [1794], *The Mysteries of Udolpho*, ed. Bonamy Dobrée and Terry Castle, Oxford: Oxford University Press.
Reeve, Clara (2003) [1778], *The Old English Baron*, ed. James Trainer and James Watt, Oxford: Oxford University Press.
Scott, Walter (1825), *Lives of the Novelists*, 2 vols, Philadelphia: H. C. Carey, I. Lea et al.
Sedgwick, Eve Kosofsky (1981), 'The Character in the Veil: Imagery of the Surface in the Gothic Novel', *PMLA*, 96.2: 255–70.
Shakespeare, William (2008), *The Norton Shakespeare*, 2nd edn, ed. Stephen Greenblatt, Walter Cohen et al., New York: Norton.
Shelley, Mary (1980) [1818, 1831], *Frankenstein; or, The Modern Prometheus*, ed. M. K. Joseph, Oxford: Oxford University Press.
Stevenson, Robert Louis (1989) [1886], *Dr Jekyll and Mr Hyde and Weir of Hermiston*, ed. Emma Letley, Oxford: Oxford University Press.
Stoker, Bram (1998) [1897], *Dracula*, ed. Glennis Byron, Peterborough, ON: Broadview Press.
Walpole, Horace (2014) [1764], *The Castle of Otranto*, ed. Nick Groom, Oxford: Oxford University Press.

Part VI

The Gothic–Theory Relationship in Retrospect and Prospect

Chapter 16

On the Threshold of Gothic: A Reflection
David Punter

In 1980 I published a book called *The Literature of Terror: A History of Gothic Fictions from 1765 to the Present Day*. It was inspired by a mixture of fascination and disappointment: fascination with early Gothic fictions and their later supernatural avatars, and disappointment with their then current critical treatment, which was mostly purely bibliographical or weirdly celebratory, or both (see Summers 1938; Varma 1966). Substantial parts of my own book were, in fact, largely descriptive; but I also attempted to move towards what I then conceived of as the 'theoretical'.

In doing so, I made most use of Freud and Marx, of psychoanalysis and the notion of unconscious desire, and of class and economic structure. When I updated the book in 1996, I added some reflections both on more recent developments in psychoanalytic thinking and on the then current sociopolitical situation, but, even so, the resulting analyses over time have come, of course, to seem crude: the realm of theory has moved on – or, it might be better to say, has become problematised, first with the advent of the cultural moment in the West known as 'high theory', with which the names of Gayatri Chakravorty Spivak, Edward Said and Homi Bhabha are indissolubly associated, and then with the apparent demise of this moment as the cultural assumptions that they so effectively destabilised have proved even more unstable and challenging to any false universalisms (see, e.g., Spivak 1996; Said 1978; Bhabha 1994).

Relevant here has been what we might call the increasing 'spectralisation' of theory: the recurrence of supernatural figures across the terrains of previously assumed materialisms, as in Derrida's 'spectres of Marx' (Derrida 1994), and ideas of the structure of the psyche, as in Abraham and Torok's formulations of the phantom and the crypt (Abraham and Torok 1994). This, obviously, is a series of developments that I could not have anticipated in 1980; but more importantly, what I did not anticipate was the extraordinary mobility of the Gothic. By this I do not only mean the whole set of phenomena we have come to refer to as 'global Gothic' (see Byron 2013), but also the remarkable ability of Gothic to modify and develop in order to address different *topoi* and societal emphases. I suppose I could have anticipated this: after all, from the very beginning – whatever the 'beginning' of Gothic might have been – it has demonstrated an exceptional agility in taking up and providing sidelights on issues not only of class and the psyche, but also of race, gender and, perhaps encompassing all of these, of the definition and limits of the human.

It has come to seem to me that what links all these matters together – and what therefore in turn might provide a beginning of an answer to that vexed, perhaps increasingly vexed, question, 'What is the Gothic?' – has to do with thresholds, with liminality. And therefore this essay will explore a series of those thresholds – thresholds within fictions, but which also always have a bearing on our theoretical consideration of what it means to be human and what, in turn, it might mean to cross, or indeed to linger upon, those thresholds.

What is equally important here, too, is to break that question away from its apparent essentialism. For the question of what it means to be human, although it might appear universalist, is in fact subject to all manner of difference: difference of historical time; difference of geographical space; difference of philosophical outlook. So a better question than 'What is the Gothic?' might be 'What is the Gothic now?', and that would apply, *mutatis mutandis*, to all the major Gothic tropes – the monster, the vampire, the ghost: phantoms now are not, as it were, what they once were, but are subject to mutation. The zombie apocalypse is being constantly remade, and Frankenstein's creature's status as, for example, a refugee is ever renewed in the light of changing world conditions, as we might be reminded by the recent novel *Frankenstein in Baghdad* (2014) (Saadawi 2018).

Yet behind, or within, these questions of difference there might still lie a connecting thread, and it would be the issue of modernity, and modernity has its own faces of Janus. On the one hand, as it replaces the forms regarded as 'traditional', it seeks to erect an unassailable stability – city planning, the skyscraper, the indestructible robot – while on the other it promulgates, then falls prey to, all manner of uncertainties – Heisenberg's so-called 'principle', ethical relativisation, ghosts in the machine. Surplus profit, as Marx said, cannot go on forever; repression, as Freud said, will breed its own returns.

Twisted Sisters

There are no witches. There never have been witches. Yet there have always been witches. Witches are all around us. The witch is a figure of fear, a figure of desire. The witch may achieve supremacy; the witch may be finally abjected. Witches are (despite the Witch-King of Angmar) women. Women are witches. Witches are woken women; wikka is awoken in the flames of wicker; women are burnt; witches fly above the fires; witches are the spirits of fire and must be returned whence they came; otherwise ... Witches are white, witches are black; witches gather herbs, witches gather poisons; witches save villages, witches destroy crops. And so, witches are a challenge to history: where historians yearn to tell us a story – and more so, to have us believe it – witches come to tell us that the story is not told, not rightly told. It might be said that, in some ways surprisingly, the witch has not been a prominent Gothic figure (despite William Harrison Ainsworth, John Buchan and others, oddly mostly men [see Ainsworth 1849; Buchan 1927]), but I want here to say a little about Jeanette Winterson's *The Daylight Gate* (2012) as a novel that is also an implicit work of theory.

The story concerns a group of women (and these are indeed the Lancashire witches, the witches of Pendle) who find themselves caught on a painful cusp of power and powerlessness; in the extremity of their despair, even though they know (or think) that they are not witches at all, they decide that maybe it would be good to claim that they are – not necessarily for human (patriarchal) eyes and ears, but in case their plight might indeed come to the attention of some god, some demon or other, who might come to their assistance. Nobody comes to their assistance, though, not even John Dee or Edward Kelley, those famous figures of magical power whose fate appears, at least at times, intricately entwined with their own. But the argument, the theoretical argument, if you like, that surrounds their story is about three things: it is about (obviously) gender; it is about class; and it is about the control of history. And in these three arenas, the role of the supernatural figure of the witch becomes, as it were, focused – as if it were a burning eye, perhaps shone through the daylight gate, that starts the conflagration – wherein the apparently supernatural, the substance of the Gothic phantasmic, becomes all too material, but material, as it were, only at the moment of its own destruction.

This destruction, through fire, is designed to leave no trace of its transgression; yet it is this very threshold that Winterson explores, describes, memorialises, and it is here that we find, through the smoke, the traces of theory, specifically of a historicism that will allow the remnants of a shattered, abjected past to rise against the spoils of the victor. 'Already . . . they will have burned her body. Already she is gone' (Winterson 2012: 223). But that is not, of course, so: her body, the body of the witch, has not gone at all; instead it is preserved – here, in this book, but also in the underlying documentation, the documentation that continues to tell the documented lies, the contested records that have been integral to Gothic since its (forged) beginnings – so that we may say that Gothic emerges as the challenger to all the biased histories that have proceeded since our fears began the long, slow process of unmaking that started (perhaps) with the destruction of the great library of Alexandria and continues to struggle to tell another story, a different story, a story under erasure.

Hence it could be contended, I now think, that the effort of Gothic to tell a 'different' story comes further into its own the more we recognise that history is only, really, documentation, and, simultaneously, that most if not all documentation is forged. Where Gothic, however, might have a truly distinctive role to play in this gradual exposure of the falsity of history is in its continuing interplay between the 'serious' (whatever that impossible word means) and the playful: after all, Walpole was only mucking about, wasn't he? Or was he making a substantial, if displaced, contribution to Whig supremacism at his time?

The Monster

Gothic transgresses boundaries; Gothic reminds us of the uncertainties of history. In 1927, apparently, a Russian called Ilya Ivanovich Ivanov conducted a macabre series of experiments, in what was then French Guinea, designed to produce an ape/human hybrid. He did not succeed, but whether he was stopped because of general revulsion or because he ran out of money may be a moot point. Gothic deals in the production of the monster; it deals in how far the human body in particular might be malleable, and thus it anticipates the ongoing practice of cyborgisation, as it has done since at least H. G. Wells's *The Island of Doctor Moreau* (1896) and the idea of the transcending 'bath of burning pain' (Wells 1896: 76).

The obvious figures here are the body-artists Orlan and Stelarc (see Smith 2011), although Orlan has reminded us, in some of her incarnations, of her own origins in Elsa Lanchester's portrayal of the (misnamed) bride of Frankenstein, and so the Gothic web is tightened. It is appropriate to think of Frankenstein's 'creature', and not only what this vastly influential trope 'meant' in 1818, but what it has come to signify since. The sheer number of recent 'treatments' of *Frankenstein* – novels, films, video games – is remarkable, after all, and it presumably has its roots in one of the central ambiguities of Mary Shelley's text: namely, to what extent do our sympathies lie with Victor, to what extent with the creature? Across this terrain, a vast set of possibilities opens out, but what it has at its heart is a contestation over where the 'human' lies: in the 'scientism' of Victor, in the uncontrollable passions of the creature.

Of course, ongoing arguments about nature and nurture can be invoked here: I would prefer to invoke more recent and politically potent issues about the role and fate of the refugee. Beginning from Julia Kristeva, how do we theorise refugee status, incursion, nationalist resistance (see Kristeva 1991)? One way we do it, of course, is through language: immigrants, we sometimes say, should have a language test, for only if they speak 'our' language can they savour the delights of 'our' political system. The creature in Shelley's novel is sublimely articulate, far more so than Victor; in many of the early films he was mute; in more recent novels he has found a voice again. What does this trajectory mean? Well, it might be thinkable through Jean Laplanche's ideas of the enigma and the message, which have gained a little more traction in recent years, unpalatable as they may be: unpalatable because what Laplanche suggests is that what is hidden from the developing child (the creature is a developing child) is not some set of Lacanian secrets held by the parents but actually an ongoing enigma which the parents themselves do not understand – or, at least, about which they are not capable of speech (see Laplanche 1989).

And so ignorance goes on perpetuating itself down the line – and here we can again circle back to the 'original Gothic' and its obsession with non-articulable secrets: as Gothic has explored the vexing question of the 'explained' and the 'unexplained' supernatural, so has psychology, and especially child psychology, continued to develop an apparatus for communication in realms that might otherwise appear truly 'monstrous'. Everything to a small child is 'supernatural'; everything is natural. Everything is assumed; nothing is explicable. Infancy is a Gothic condition.

But I have been referring to the 'creature', and that is because I believe that what we have in *Frankenstein*, as is being increasingly revealed, is not a monster at all, but a process of monster-isation. Consider China Miéville:

> your monsters are only legitimate to the extent that they 'really mean' something else. I spend a lot of time arguing for [the] literalism of [the] fantastic, rather than its reduction to allegory. Metaphor is inevitable but it escapes our intent, so we should relax about it. Our monsters are about themselves, and they can get on with being about all sorts of other stuff too, but if we want them to be primarily that, and don't enjoy their monstrousness, they're dead and nothing. (VanderMeer 2012)

Miéville goes on to talk about Helen Oyeyemi, Vilém Flusser, D. K. Broster, E. F. Benson, Marion Fox, Jane Gaskell, Philip Challinor, Neil Bell and so on; but his main point is that the monster is a monster, and our academic attempts to metaphorise are unwelcome and indeed reductive to the imagination; a true theory of the monster is a theory that is true to the monster, that respects it in all of its discordant parts. Thus has Gothic shown the way towards the monster as a monsterisation of the ordinary, a display (a 'showing') of the terminally non- (or ab-) human.

The Zombie Apocalypse

Max Brooks's *World War Z* (2006) is an exciting book, and it was made into a truly terrible film. The reason for this distinction is that the book respects and encapsulates a variety of local responses to the zombie apocalypse, while the film focalises this through a single narrator/celebrity. What does the zombie represent, what does it materialise, what does it metastasise? As we deal in this decade with the ongoing flood of zombies, the answers come thick and fast: the zombie is the ultimate consumer; the zombie is the subject of inexplicable capitalist practices; the zombie is the 'perfect stranger'; the zombie is the acme of libertarianism; the zombie is the key to survival; the zombie is the answer to the problem of the family. Or perhaps the zombie is the sign of the 'philosophical apocalypse':

> What is the philosophical apocalypse? It is the inability of secular philosophy to keep up with the discoveries of science and cosmology – the lack of philosophy and cultural theory that attempts to provide a meaningful and unifying narrative for humanity in the vast and ancient universe. (Vacker 2013: 159–60)

'What is left to fill the void', so Barry Vacker claims, is 'tribalism and theism, particularly the rise of creationism and fundamentalism and the increasing attacks on science, evolution, cosmology, and the Enlightenment project.' To these we might even add the equally increasing attacks on any kind of 'expertise', such that the gross ignorance of the zombie becomes an avatar of our own wider condition, a Gothic condition of the living dead, in which we spacewalk our way to doom: 'the zombie is the unthinking human reborn, a body without a mind, stalking and devouring brains on the planet it hopes to rule in a cosmos it fears and does not understand nor care to understand' (Vacker 2013: 176).

I find this argument a persuasive account of our current obsession with the zombie, and it touches at all points on the relation between Gothic and 'theory'. Theory, we may assume, involves the attempt to discover a 'larger plan'; the zombie comes to suggest – forcefully – to us that there is no larger plan, that instead there is random death. The zombie comes also to remind us that our dream of individuation is just that, a fantasy: behind, or below, the dream lies a further layer in which we are all just the same, exemplars of drives that are not specifically human, drives towards survival at whatever cost. And what better way to ensure that nothing disturbs this anti-aesthetic than to devour the brain? We thus come again to the question of the threshold, of that which both transgresses and secures our notion of the human. We have come a long way – zombies have come a long way – from George Romero to the gay porno cinema of Bruce LaBruce; from beleaguered humans to a type of necropolitics where it is the humans themselves – blinkered, prejudiced, tied to outmoded ways of relating – that prove the obstacle to the evolution of a new way of life, a way of life based on libertarian *jouissance*.

Gothic, we often say, is about history; and so it is. But it has also come to be about the future, about the various trajectories along which we might see ourselves evolving. It has not always been the case that Gothic has told an anti-Enlightenment story; an opposition to reason does not always or necessarily imply a total discarding of reason. But zombie theory would form a new twist on an age-old story: that the monster is the new form of the self, that monster-isation is the inevitable correlate of growing up, that we all grow up twisted, bent out of the true, whatever that forgotten 'true' might have been.

The Outlaw

To think about growing up is inevitably to think about adolescence, and this shift takes us perhaps to the major arena in which theory and Gothic seem at the moment to consort, which is, to put it simply, in the high school. It seems to me that the major concern of contemporary vampire fiction is with the outlaw, and specifically with the 'outlaw group' – although of course this might not be as new as it may seem.

We can go back to the moment in Stoker's *Dracula* where the unfortunate Harker realises that the Count cannot do his dire work alone. Instead he has to rely on a group, an outlaw group – in this case the gypsies. It is the gypsies who thwart Harker's escape from imprisonment; it is they who supply his letter to Dracula; in other words, it is they who interrupt the chain of address, who intercept the possibility of a direct message. They are the 'outlaw'; but they are also a mode of 'indirection'. They stand (in) for a threshold over which none shall pass; but they do all this by virtue of their own status as representative of that which is not authorised, and thus they also reprise the Gothic theme of that account, or transmission of an account, which has no authority.

Again we find ourselves in the terrain of theory strung between authority and the local. Here is, I think, an interesting, if off-the-cuff, remark by Slavoj Žižek, which has its own relation to the Gothic:

> Hollywood knows everything. It's obsessed with dystopias, like in *Elysium* or *The Hunger Games*. I really think this is one of our quite possible futures. Young people today should prepare for a big catastrophe, but engage in well thought out, local everyday struggles, and not escape into moralism. (Forster 2016)

Is there any authority to be found in the local? Let us look again at the Gothic. The Gothic began (again that troublesome word 'began', but we have to start from somewhere) from the local: from specific sets of conjunctures, political, national, cultural – and, of course, architectural, literary and so on. And then it became – it has become – an 'assemblage' in the full meaning ascribed by Deleuze and Guattari; but the question then becomes, what does this have do with transgression, how does this always threatening domestication of the Gothic (which was also always, in a different sense, a domestic genre) turn us, as it were, on the threshold, encourage us to look in rather than out?

There is the need for a group, after all: a group of vampires. Anne Rice, Poppy Z. Brite, the film *Only Lovers Left Alive* (2013) – the list could go on. The question would be whether and to what extent these 'new' groups – vegetarian vampires, vegan vampires, eco-conscious vampires – constitute something truly transgressive or replicas of the existent. As theory moves forward, it is possible to suppose that it increasingly uncovers the impossibility of dissent, the number of ways in which apparent dislocation in fact barely masks a less than fully thought acquiescence: when we think we are most athwart (and, according to one set of arguments, that might be in adolescence) we are most ripe for the lure of conformity.

So where might 'theory' lie? In the ideas we might like to see promulgated by a 'philosophical' elite, or in the apparently more successful ideas brought forward and instantiated by the advertisers and sellers? What Judith Williamson demonstrated so many years ago about the codification of advertising (Williamson 1978) needs, of course, to be updated, but the updating is neither difficult nor surprising. Google, Facebook and Apple have designs on our minds; they openly wish to redesign our brains and neural circuits. They wish, too, to usurp the role of prophet: they wish to predict the text. Gothic, of course, has been here before: Gothic has always, in a sense, predicted the text; yet the text has never emerged, Primavera-like, dripping from the well of truth. It has instead been contaminated, engendered by its prohibited ancestors, aware – at least up to a point – of the always disputed provenance of text, family, heritage, kinship, childhood – adolescence. To become a creature of total prediction would be to evade what we might call 'the Gothic of the random' (M. R. James's unmotivated ghosts) and at the same time to fall prey to the endless web of determination that conditions so many Gothic protagonists . . .

Haunted

It is not entirely clear to me where to go from here in terms of Gothic and theory, and so I shall turn to ignorance, always the best defence. Among the many things I did not properly understand in 1980, when I wrote *The Literature of Terror*, was to what extent people – individuals and whole peoples – could be ghosted. I am thinking – now – of men, and occasionally women, returning from wars, frequently not of their making (and here I cannot avoid mentioning the magnificent novels of Pat Barker, any more than I can refrain from saying that all of this is the stuff of the revenant, and has thus been the weird nutrition of the Gothic for centuries as it has tried to negotiate impossible, unthinkable memories or memorialisations). But I am also thinking of women (and more rarely men) whose entire lives and cultures have collapsed, or dissolved, in the face of wars fought for reasons beyond usual imagining – but usually, of course, for those very resources which will, in fact, increasingly dry up as the wealth of the planet is steadily drained into the north and west.

Let us, however, consider what the relations might be between this kind of ghosting – of whole communities, whole peoples whose marks are now seen only as erasing tracks in the desert – and the processes of ghosting that have been the province of Gothic down the ages. We could – and I shall in a moment – look at Toni Morrison, whose work is emblematic of this conjuncture; but let us pause to re-examine the relationship between Gothic and theory. The word 'theory' in English has its origins in 'a looking at, viewing, contemplation, speculation'; yet in this respect it is rarely adequate, as Thomas Browne noted in what we might consider to be a proto-Gothic context in 1643: 'Nor can I thinke I have the true Theory of death when I contemplate a skull, or behold a Skeleton with those vulgar imaginations it casts upon us' (*OED*). So much, then, for Yorick, but William Harvey, writing ten years later, is even more severe: 'All their theory and contemplation (which they count Science) represents nothing but waking mens dreams, and sick mens phrensies [*sic*]' (*OED*). In both cases, theory is haunted: by the always removed promise of the Real, by the actuality of death, by the possibility of awaking from a dream of scientific order.

A recent book called *Snuff: Real Death and Screen Media* (2016) may be a case in point, for it turns out that it has no topic: that is to say, it deals in the liminal possibility that death might have occurred during the making of one or more 'snuff movies', but has finally to admit that this is an impossible question to answer, for the scenario has always already moved into the past, and besides, it has been occluded behind the 'ghastly of the Real': images of terrorist beheadings, of murdered Syrian civilians, of the convulsions of Death Row. None of our Gothic imaginings can do more than rehearse the Real, but they can, of course, foreshadow it, emblematise it, 'produce' it on a darkly lit inner stage.

Then there is the killing of a baby and the terror of slavery in Toni Morrison's *Beloved* (1987):

> They forgot her like a bad dream. After they made up their tales, shaped and decorated them, those that saw her that day on the porch quickly and deliberately forgot her. It took longer for those who had spoken to her, lived with her, fallen in love with her, to forget, until they realised they couldn't remember or repeat a single thing she said, and began to believe that, other than what they themselves were thinking, she hadn't said anything at all. So, in the end, they forgot her too. (Morrison 1987: 274)

The conjuring of terror is also the forgetting of terror, because terror cannot fit into, cannot be accounted for by, theory. Literary theory is, I think, on a cusp: it will have increasingly to account for the ephemeral, that which is nowhere written down, that which is simply locked into the machine and discarded, sometimes at random moments. We have a dim memory that somewhere, at some time, we discovered this or that on the web, in the net; but it has already gone. It remains in only a Gothic way: as a haunting.

Snuff

I want to return to snuff – to the irreducible but non-reproducible moment of death. In *The Literature of Terror*, I mentioned, in quite different contexts, J. G. Ballard's novel *The Atrocity Exhibition* (1970) and Michael Powell's film *Peeping Tom* (1960). The former concerns a varied but obsessive scenario of car crashes, celebrity death, penetrative wound sex; the second the showing of damage and death on camera. *Peeping Tom* is concerned with the instillation and recording of terminal fear; *The Atrocity Exhibition* seems to record a world where fear, like every other affect, has become obsolete. But both of these works, it now seems to me, have to do with the exploration of the threshold, with that realm – the 'fatal bourn' of course comes to mind – from which it is, or might become, impossible to return. In Jeremias Gotthelf's *The Black Spider* (1842), the situation is vividly emblematised in the shape of a spider which is buried in the lintel of a house, and – through one of those frequent errors committed by Gothic protagonists who, presumably, are not aware that they are in a Gothic story – is brought back to a vicious life when the lintel is removed.

Yet it is difficult to see that there is anything beyond this threshold, and here is where the question of theory arises again. As I write, I hear of the death of the great physicist Stephen Hawking, who was in large measure responsible for the discovery of 'dark matter'. But that, of course, is not to put matters in the correct light: it would be better, if cumbersome, to say that what he discovered was the current in-discoverability of dark matter. We know, it seems, that it is there, but we know that only through deductions from its impact on other things – exactly as Abraham and Torok claim that we know of the existence of the psychic 'crypt' because of the imprints, the patterns it leaves on what appear to be our waking lives. Gothic has always claimed, in one way or another, that those waking lives are but a small part of our experience, one that we choose to valorise because then we shall be able to remain less unsettled, less as though we are, in fact, refugees in our own world. We know – or think we know – that the dungeons of the Inquisition are there, that the tortures of the pit and the pendulum cannot be removed from our memories and prophecies, but we have to get on with life anyway, through a continual process of forgetting.

Gothic has thus predicted the limits of the bodily. I have just read Kameron Hurley's *God's War* (2011). It is set in a fantasy of an Islamicised future, and it opens with a comment about how our protagonist has just 'sold her womb'. I found this initially a shock tactic, but then I found myself reflecting on how easily replaceable some of our body parts have become, as well as on the processes of surrogacy that do imply the sale, or hire, of organs. To go back to Orlan, the body is no longer the unassailable fortress of our earlier imaginings: on the contrary, it is haunted by possibilities of change, violent or otherwise. What Gothic films such as *Les yeux sans visage* (1960) predicted has now come to pass.

At the same time, the emphasis on the imbrication between Gothic and forgery so keenly analysed by Jerrold Hogle is now all around: 'Nothing is true, everything is permitted.' A key development here, I think, is the fate of the 'signature': that signatures can be forged we have always known, and that fact has been the historical source of a plethora of Gothic faked wills and inheritances, but the new twist is that a 'signature' need not be a signature at all, merely a typed representation of one. Similarly with the photograph: thoroughly photoshopped, rendered the epitome of the inauthentic, how long will it be before the law catches up and reduces photographic evidence to its new status as just one type of falsifiable evidence among so many others?

Abjection

Sarah Kane's notorious play *Blasted* (1995) might be a 'gratuitous welter of carnage, cannibalism . . . and other atrocities' (Cross 1995), including faecal obsession, rape, fatal illness and various kinds of mental torture. Or it might be a well-organised piece of Gothic drama:

> For the audience the impossibility of determining who is victim, perpetrator or bystander becomes almost unbearable, as does simultaneously, on the level of content, Ian's state of existence, which is again mirrored

in the final collapse of form. Once more we can see how well content and form are married in Kane's play and that her dramatic work is far from displaying a random assortment of horrific actions. (Ablett 2014: 14)

What it certainly is *is* blasphemous, and the point about the inner dialectic of blasphemy is well made by Sarah Ablett when she quotes St John's Gospel:

I say unto you, except ye eat the flesh of the Son of man, and drink his blood, ye have no life in you. Whoso eateth my flesh, and drinketh my blood, hath eternal life; and I will raise him up at the last day. For my flesh is meat indeed, and my blood is drink indeed. He that eateth my flesh and drinketh my blood, dwelleth in me, and I in him. (Ablett 2014: 16)

Blasphemy, transgression, the liminal. Much of the Gothic has traditionally offended against God, whether it be through the figure of the criminal monk in Lewis or Maturin or in the image of human usurpation of divine right in Wells or Richard Marsh. One question would be: how are we to achieve equivalents of these modes of transgression in an increasingly secular universe? But behind this would lie another question, which is whether we are living in an increasingly secular universe at all.

Kristeva, in *Powers of Horror: An Essay on Abjection* (1980), made one of the worst predictions of recent times when she applauded the fact that, as she saw it, there would be no more religious wars; we could now alternatively say that we are living our lives in the context of the longest and bloodiest religious war ever known. It was also Kristeva, of course, who gave us the term 'abjection', to cover all manner of throwings-off and throwings-down, the denial of fault in the (national, cultural, individual) self, accompanied by a resituating of blame in the Other. Kane's play, it seems to me, emblematises where we seem more recently to have go to in examining the theoretical processes of abjection: it throws up a net of fault and blame, endlessly reticulating and complicating our responses to the othering of the Other. This is no longer a black-and-white world where domination and submission can be simply assigned; instead the 'Gothic condition' has come to encompass and envelop the action, so that individuals themselves are no longer the central point. When the neo-Jungian James Hillman said many years ago that the one thing that all our dreams have in common is that they take place in a 'darkened world' (Hillman 1979), he was speaking not only of visual affect, nor of moral uncertainty, but also of a Gothic darkening in the almost literal sense of an absence of enlightenment.

Gothic speaks everywhere of the dangers of barbarity, of the fragility of the threshold that must be crossed if, as Yeats put it, civilisation is not to sink. Yet we might ask again, what is this 'Gothic' of which we speak – or rather, what has it become? It is a remnant of the past; a reminder of the insufficiency of reason; a sign of the omnipresence of death; a cavalcade of half-eroded symbols and tropes of the supernatural; a colonising endeavour to suborn the ghost tales and ancestral rites of 'othered' cultures; a set of expressionist gestures of Promethean defiance; a catalogue of body horrors; a celebratory terror of the sufferings of the flesh . . . All these and more, no doubt. What is it that is thrown under the threshold, to act as a warning, as a prophylactic, as a talisman that will – eventually – rescue us from pain? And what will happen if what is held in the Gothic world were ever to seep out into the real?

The Techno-monster

Actually this is mostly rhetorical flourish: the monstrous Real is all too present, and it slips and slides among the stage props that we regard as the material world. We might consider, for example, the case of Slender Man. Slender Man is a 'creepypasta' internet meme dating from 2009, its (or his) stated purpose being 'to formulate something whose motivations can barely be comprehended, and [to cause] unease and terror in a general population' (Robinson 2016). How is Slender Man Gothic? In the most obvious sense, he is a figure of fear, and especially of fear among children, whom he menaces and threatens to abduct. But, more importantly, he has no origin, or rather his origin only proliferates and becomes more and more complex as various additions to the oeuvre provide him with background, fictional ancestors, a body of past texts in which traces of him can be found. This is one example of a new textuality, largely freed from authorial control or even influence: if Roland Barthes was ever right about the impending 'death of the author', then we have here a sublime instance. But what we have here also is a slippery, unreliable text, one in which it would be impossible to distinguish the authentic from the counterfeit, one in which such terms have indeed ceased to have any reliable meaning.

Slender Man is not alone, he is not the only meme out there, but he does seem to represent a beginning, and it is surely interesting now to reflect back again on the complex relations between Gothic and beginnings. It is conventional to say that Gothic has no beginnings; we cannot simply look back to the Dark Ages, or to medieval architecture, or to *The Castle of Otranto*, and say that the Gothic began there: all of this is interwoven, constantly recapitulated, a non-linear history. Yet at the same time Gothic points us towards the imbrication between the supernatural and beginnings, or innovations, most particularly and obviously in the beginnings of that scary phantasmagoria that we now know as cinema, in which so many of the very first films were made of Gothic stories, and for obvious reasons: if film itself were supernatural, or to be seen to have a supernatural effect, what better content than *Frankenstein*, or *Dracula*, or *Jekyll and Hyde*?

Mutatis mutandis: if the medium is to be haunted from the beginning, if modernity is always to be shadowed by its vanishingly slender other, what better trope than a figure that catches up in itself our own best hopes, our own worst fears? Our own hopes in that Slender Man is, almost literally, 'untraceable': in a world increasingly patrolled by quasi-total surveillance, a vast extension of the theoretical world of the panopticon, what better wish-fulfilment could there be than a body that is not a body, a body that has presence but no extension, the shape of the human without distinguishing features? Our fears may be that if we can, in fantasy, achieve this invisibility, this curiously resounding quietude, then who is to say what returning others have not come back, returned from the dead, from that 'huge and birdless silence' of which Philip Larkin speaks, in the same condition, and might not even now be perpetrating the foulest of crimes on our loved ones?

The anonymous text; the bodiless horror; the partially glimpsed face in the crowd; the emerging conflict between ill-informed democracy and an attempt to return to a quasi-eugenic privileging of the educated (the clerisy): the metonymic chain continues. We know of Slender Man, but we know little or nothing of other similar figures, slipping and sliding among the pages (the textuality) of the dark web, these new monsters which, we fear, are already contaminating the daylight world, suggesting to us the inevitability of the most repressive of actions and political processes. And so an image from Freud returns, even amid the turn to neuropsychology: the image of the night-time patrol, the ego – oddly mindless – keeping guard, a 'cemetery guard' as Derrida put it, maintaining, or attempting to maintain, responsibility for a threshold over which none shall pass – except that we know that the boundaries have already been breached, that the monsters cannot be kept securely locked away, instead they are around the corner, behind our backs, emerging fully fledged from our dark imaginings.

Conclusion

Gothic, we might say, is in part a literature, a culture of 'things' – things that recur, things that refuse to stay in place, things that appear to have a life of their own (as in Lovecraft or in Freud's crocodiles). And one of the contemporary theoretical turns that appears to consolidate the role of Gothic as progenitor and emblem is object-oriented ontology, also known as speculative realism. Without going into detail about what this philosophical school might signify, it is worth saying that its deity, its object of reverence, has oddly enough turned out to be H. P. Lovecraft himself – that same Lovecraft whom Miéville venerates as the harbinger of the non-human, tentacular Other and who also appears in the pre-credit list of Slender Man.

These 'things' appear to be known, unknown, half-known; I suspect that in their way they are cognate with dark matter. We know them by their impress, their embrace, their enwrapping, all that is conveyed by the silent guardian in M. R. James's masterpiece, 'The Treasure of Abbot Thomas' (1904). And so, at the same time, we do not know them at all; they have no 'presence'. We live in a world of increasing knowledge; but at the same time, and by the same token, we live in a world of increasing ignorance. There are too many 'things' (whether physical or mental) for us to 'know'; we suffer from a radical reduction of communicable or intelligible understanding. The Age of Enlightenment vs. the Dark Ages – Gothic has historically been strung (out) between the two. Recent attempts to theorise our current condition (I am thinking here particularly of Giorgio Agamben, Gianni Vattimo, Paul Virilio, but of course these names, like Slender Man, have already slid behind the screens) have focused upon reductions of ornamented (Gothic) man to bare necessities. But the attempt has not been entirely successful: the body and the mind heave themselves up from the dark sea already encrusted, revenants from 'full fathom five' – modernity cannot so easily (or at all) win a victory. The towers of futurity will continue to blaze, but in both senses: as a beacon and as a living death.

So how does the Gothic, that almost expressly outmoded form, constrained by history and geography, continue to resonate with theory? One way is through the dialectic of the local and the universal, which is almost over-neatly summarised in the notion of haunting. Haunting is absolutely local – we all have, so the legend goes, our 'haunts', our neighbourhoods, our repeated patterns of activity. Yet haunting is ubiquitous: wherever we go, however we try to shake off our preoccupations, abject them on to whatever passing Other takes our fancy, we remain haunted, unable to remain unaware of all that shadows what we are. Another way is through Gothic's resolute attention to the extremes – in all manner of ways, some more melodramatic than others, but particularly through the extremes of the physical (bodily, material) and the supernatural (psychic, ectoplasmic). This is why, it seems to me, I am no more able now than I was in 1980 to say, 'This is Gothic': there is too much mobility, but now that mobility around the limits of the human is greater than before.

Or perhaps it isn't; perhaps it is more that it exists now on a set of different planes. We might consider the extraordinary majesty of Edward Young's depiction of the human plight in *Night Thoughts* (1742–5), strung between the 'animal' and the divine, and set alongside it the equally compelling plight of M. John Harrison's characters in his extraordinary, theory-laden trilogy, where the essential confrontation is between his strange, narcissistic, addicted protagonists and what can be known only as a 'singularity', an endless 'event horizon'. Since I wrote *The Literature of Terror*, everything, of course, has changed. The nature of Gothic has changed; so too, although I have made no attempt to take cognisance of it here because space prohibits, has the nature of Gothic criticism, which has developed and proliferated into a field which, in my opinion, constitutes a theoretical trajectory and critique all of its own. I have no idea (any more than did Lovecraft, or Miéville, or the lamented Sarah Kane) where any of this will go next; but my hope is that amid the flood of creativity and creative criticism, there will be *jouissance* amid the deadlights, as there are undoubtedly deadlights amid the *jouissance*.

References

Ablett, Sarah (2014), 'Approaching Abjection in Sarah Kane's *Blasted*', *Performance Research*, 19.1: 63–71.

Abraham, Nicolas, and Maria Torok (1994), *The Shell and the Kernel: Renewals of Psychoanalysis*, trans. Nicholas Rand, Chicago: University of Chicago Press.

Ainsworth, William Harrison (1849), *The Lancashire Witches*, London: Henry Colburn.
Bhabha, Homi K. (1994), *The Location of Culture*, London: Routledge.
Brooks, Max (2006), *World War Z*, New York: Crown.
Buchan, John (1927), *Witch Wood*, London: Hodder & Stoughton.
Byron, Glennis (ed.) (2013), *Globalgothic*, Manchester: Manchester University Press.
Cross, John (1995), review of Sarah Kane's *Blasted*, *Sunday Telegraph*, 22 January.
Derrida, Jacques (1994), *Specters of Marx: The State of the Debt, the Work of Mourning and the New International*, trans. Peggy Kamuf, London: Routledge.
Forster, Katie (2016), interview with Slavoj Žižek, *The Guardian*, 10 December.
Gotthelf, Jeremias (2013) [1842], *The Black Spider*, trans. Susan Bernofsky, New York: New York Review.
Hillman, James (1979), *The Dream and the Underworld*, New York: Harper & Row.
Hurley, Kameron (2011), *God's War*, New York: Night Shade Books.
Jackson, Neil, Shaun Kimber, Johnny Walker and Thomas Joseph Watson (2016), *Snuff: Real Death and Screen Media*, London: Bloomsbury.
James, M. R. (1904), 'The Treasure of Abbot Thomas', in *Ghost Stories of an Antiquary*, London: Edward Arnold.
Kane, Sarah (2001) [1995], *Blasted*, in *Complete Plays*, London: Methuen.
Kristeva, Julia (1982) [1980], *Powers of Horror: An Essay on Abjection*, trans. Leon S. Roudiez, New York: Columbia University Press.
Kristeva, Julia (1991), *Strangers to Ourselves*, trans. Leon S. Roudiez, New York: Columbia University Press.
Laplanche, Jean (1989), *New Foundations for Psychoanalysis*, trans. David Macey, London: Wiley-Blackwell.
Morrison, Toni (1987), *Beloved*, London: Chatto & Windus.
Robinson, Joanna (2016), 'American Horror Story and Slender Man', *Vanity Fair*, 28 January.
Saadawi, Ahmed (2018) [2014], *Frankenstein in Baghdad*, trans. Jonathan Wright, London: Oneworld Publications.
Said, Edward (1978), *Orientalism*, New York: Pantheon Books.
Smith, Kathy (2011), 'Abject Bodies: Beckett, Orlan, Stelarc and the Politics of Contemporary Performance', *Performance Research*, 12.1: 66–76.
Spivak, Gayatri Chakravorty (1996), *The Spivak Reader*, ed. Donna Landry and Gerald MacLean, London: Routledge.
Summers, Montague (1938), *The Gothic Quest: A History of the Gothic Novel*, London: Fortune Press.
Vacker, Barry (2013), 'Space Junk and the Second Event: The Cosmic Meaning of the Zombie Apocalypse', in Murali Balaji (ed.), *Thinking Dead: What the Zombie Apocalypse Means*, Lanham, MD: Lexington.

VanderMeer, Jeff (2012), 'China Miéville and Monsters: "Unsatisfy me, frustrate me, I beg you"', *Weird Fiction Review*, 20 March, http://weird-fictionreview.com/2012/03/china-mieville-and-monsters-unsatisfy-me-frustrate-me-i-beg-you/ (accessed 5 October 2018).
Varma, Devendra P. (1966), *The Gothic Flame*, New York: Russell & Russell.
Wells, H. G. (1896), *The Island of Doctor Moreau*, London: William Heinemann.
Williamson, Judith (1978), *Decoding Advertisements: Ideology and Meaning in Advertising*, London: Marion Boyars.
Winterson, Jeanette (2012), *The Daylight Gate*, London: Arrow Books.

Notes on Contributors

Fred Botting is Professor of English Literature at Kingston University, London, where he teaches literary theory, genre, contemporary writing and Gothic fiction. He has written extensively on theory and Gothic writing. Among his numerous publications are *Making Monstrous: Frankenstein, Criticism, Theory* (1991), the *Gothic* volume in Routledge's New Critical Idiom series (1996), *Sex Machines and Navels: Fiction, Fantasy, and History in the Future Present* (1999) and *Limits of Horror: Technologies, Bodies, Gothic* (2008). He has also been honoured with the Distinguished Scholar Award by the International Association for the Fantastic in the Arts.

Elisabeth Bronfen is Full Professor of English and American Studies at the University of Zurich, Switzerland, and, since 2007, Global Distinguished Professor at New York University. She has written widely in the areas of gender studies, psychoanalysis, film, cultural theory, the Gothic and visual culture. Her many book publications include *Home in Hollywood: The Imaginary Geography of Cinema* (2004), *Specters of War: Hollywood's Engagement with Military Conflict* (Rutgers University Press, 2012), *Night Passages: Philosophy, Literature, and Film* (Columbia University Press, 2013) and *Mad Men, Death, and the American Dream* (Diaphanes/Chicago University Press, 2016).

Steven Bruhm is Professor Emeritus and formerly Robert and Ruth Lumsden Professor of English at the University of Western Ontario in London, Ontario. He is the author of *Gothic Bodies: The Politics of Pain in Romantic Fiction* (1994), *Reflecting Narcissus: A Queer Aesthetic* (2000) and numerous articles on the contemporary gothic, queer theory and dance. He is the former managing editor of *Horror Studies* and past president of the International Gothic Association, as well as a member of the advisory boards for *Gothic Studies*,

Manchester University Press's International Gothic Series and the University of Wales Press's Horror Studies series.

David Collings is Professor of English at Bowdoin College in the USA, where he contributes to programmes in Environmental Studies and Gender, Sexuality and Women's Studies. He is the author of *Wordsworthian Errancies: The Poetics of Cultural Dismemberment* (Johns Hopkins University Press, 1994), *Monstrous Society: Reciprocity, Discipline, and the Political Uncanny, c. 1780–1848* (Bucknell University Press, 2009), *Stolen Future, Broken Present: The Human Significance of Climate Change* (Open Humanities Press, 2014) and *Disastrous Subjectivities: Romanticism, Modernity, and the Real* (forthcoming). With Jacques Khalip, he has edited a special issue on *Romanticism and Disaster* (2012) and, with Michael O'Rourke, another on *Queer Romanticisms* (2004–5).

George E. Haggerty is Distinguished Professor Emeritus at the University of California, Riverside, and specialises in eighteenth-century English Literature and Queer Studies. His books include *Gothic Fiction/Gothic Form* (1989), *Unnatural Affections: Women and Fiction in the Later Eighteenth Century* (1998), *Men in Love: Masculinity and Sexuality in the Eighteenth Century* (1999), *Queer Gothic* (2006) and *Horace Walpole's Letters: Masculinity and Friendship in the Eighteenth Century* (2011). In addition, he has co-edited *Professions of Desire: Lesbian and Gay Studies in Literature* for the Modern Language Association (1995) and *The Blackwell Companion to LGBT/Q Studies* (2007). He has also published a wide range of essays in such journals as *Eighteenth-Century Studies*, *Eighteenth-Century Fiction*, *The Eighteenth Century: Theory & Interpretation*, *Genders*, *Novel* and *SEL* and in various collections and anthologies. His most recent book is *Queer Friendship: Male Intimacy in the English Literary Tradition* (Cambridge University Press, 2018).

Anya Heise-von der Lippe is Assistant Lecturer with the Chair of Anglophone Literatures at the University of Tübingen. Her research focuses on the parallels between monstrous corporeality and monstrous textuality, as well as other forms of non-normative corporeality in Gothic and horror texts. She has been teaching English literature and cultural studies for several years, frequently focusing on the Gothic and monstrous, posthumans, post-apocalyptic, dystopian and cyberpunk fiction, as well as new forms of textuality such as hypertext and graphic novels. Recent publications include *Posthuman Gothic* (University of Wales Press, 2017) and *Literaturwissenschaften in der Krise* (co-edited with Russell West-Pavlov) (Tübingen: Narr, 2018).

Jerrold E. Hogle is Professor Emeritus of English and University Distinguished Professor at the University of Arizona. A former president of the International Gothic Association and Guggenheim and Mellon Fellow for research – as well as the 2013 winner of the Distinguished Scholar Award of the Keats-Shelley Association of America – he has published widely on Romantic literature, literary and cultural theory, and the Gothic in many different forms. His books include *Shelley's Process* (Oxford University Press, 1988), *The Undergrounds of The Phantom of the Opera* (Palgrave, 2002), and both *The Cambridge Companion to Gothic Fiction* (2002) and its recent successor, *The Cambridge Companion to the Modern Gothic* (2014). He has also written the history of theory chapters in *The Cambridge Companion to British Romanticism* (2nd edn, 2010), *Teaching the Gothic* for the Palgrave Teaching the New English Series (2006) and *A Companion to American Gothic* for the Blackwell Companions to Literature and Culture (2013).

Robert Miles is Professor of English at the University of Victoria in Western Canada. A past president of the International Gothic Association and former editor in chief of the journal *Gothic Studies*, he is the author of such major volumes on the Gothic as *Gothic Writing 1750–1820: A Genealogy* (1993), *Ann Radcliffe: The Great Enchantress* (1995) and *Romantic Misfits* (2008), among many other books, essays and edited collections. His current interests include Jane Austen and the history of conspiracy fiction.

Anna Powell has retired from her post as Reader in English and Film at Manchester Metropolitan University to become an Honorary Research Fellow there. She is the author of *Deleuze and Horror Film* (2005), *Deleuze, Altered States and Film* (2007) and co-editor of *Teaching the Gothic* (2006). She continues to publish articles and chapters on Deleuze and Gothic film and literature, its affects and effects. Among her recent research topics are Jan Svankmajer's Poe films, Gothic children in *The Shining* and H. P. Lovecraft. She is a member of the editorial boards of *Deleuze Studies* and *Dark Arts* and founder of *A/V*, the online journal for Deleuze-related studies. As well as working as a visiting lecturer and running public study groups, she enjoys creative writing.

David Punter is Professor of English at the University of Bristol. He is a poet, writer and academic, and has published extensively on topics including the Gothic, romantic literature, contemporary writing, literary theory, metaphor and modernity. His published books include *The Literature of Terror: A History of Gothic Fictions from 1765 to the Present Day* (1980), *The Hidden Script: Writing and the Unconscious* (1985), *The Romantic Unconscious: A Study in Narcissism and Patriarchy* (1989), *Gothic Pathologies: The Text, the Body and the Law* (1998), *Writing the Passions* (2000), *Postcolonial Imaginings: Fictions of a New World Order* (2000), *The Influence of Postmodernism on Contemporary Writing: An Interdisciplinary Study* (2005), *Metaphor* (2007), *Modernity* (2007), *Rapture: Literature, Addiction, Secrecy* (2009) and *The Literature of Pity* (2014). His newest book is *The Gothic Condition: Terror, History, Psyche* (2016) in the Gothic Literary Studies series from the University of Wales Press.

Tilottama Rajan is Canada Research Chair and Distinguished University Professor at the University of Western Ontario, as well as former director of its Centre for Theory and Criticism and founder of the North American Society for the Study of Romanticism (NASSR). She is the author of *Dark Interpreter: The Discourse of Romanticism* (Cornell University Press, 1980), *The Supplement of Reading: Figures of Understanding in Romantic Theory and Practice* (Cornell University Press, 1990), *Deconstruction and the Remainders of Phenomenology: Sartre, Derrida, Foucault, Baudrillard* (Stanford University Press, 2002) and *Romantic Narrative: Shelley, Hays, Godwin, Wollstonecraft* (Johns Hopkins University Press, 2010). She is also the author of a hundred articles, has edited Mary Shelley's *Valperga* and William Godwin's *Mandeville* (Broadview, 1998 and 2015), and has co-edited five collections of essays.

Alison Rudd received her PhD from the University of Northampton in 2007. Her monograph, *Postcolonial Gothic Fictions from the Caribbean, Canada, Australia and New Zealand*, was published in 2010 and was nominated for the Allan Lloyd Smith Memorial Prize awarded by the International Gothic Association for the best book of the year on a Gothic subject. She currently works for the Quality Enhancement Team at the University of the West of England in Bristol.

Catherine Spooner is Professor of Literature and Culture at Lancaster University. She has published widely on Gothic in literature, film and popular culture, both in monographs (*Fashioning Gothic Bodies* [2004] and *Contemporary Gothic* [2006]) and in co-edited collections (*The Routledge Companion to Gothic* [with Emma McEvoy, 2006],

Monstrous Media/Spectral Subjects: Imaging Gothic from the Nineteenth Century to the Present [with Fred Botting, 2015] and *Return to Twin Peaks: New Approaches to Materiality, Theory and Genre on Television* [with Jeffrey A. Weinstock, 2015]). She has also served as co-president of the International Gothic Association. Her latest book is *Post-Millennial Gothic: Comedy, Romance and the Rise of Happy Gothic*, published in 2017.

Dale Townshend is Professor of Gothic Literature at Manchester Metropolitan University. His recent publications include *Ann Radcliffe, Romanticism and the Gothic* (with Angela Wright, 2014), *The Gothic World* (with Glennis Byron, 2014), *Terror and Wonder: The Gothic Imagination* (2014), *Romantic Gothic: An Edinburgh Companion* (with Angela Wright, 2016) and *Writing Britain's Ruins* (with Michael Carter and Peter N. Lindfield, 2017). His new monograph, *Gothic Antiquity: History, Romance, and the Architectural Imagination, 1760–1840*, will be published in late 2019.

Maisha Wester is Associate Professor in African-American and African Diaspora Studies at Indiana University. She is the author of *African American Gothic: Screams from Shadowed Places* (2012) and co-editor of the collection *Twenty-First-Century Gothic* (forthcoming 2019). She is also the author of numerous articles and essays, including 'Gothic and the Politics of Race' in *The Cambridge Companion to the Gothic* (2014), 'Text as Gothic Murder Machine' in *Technologies of the Gothic in Literature and Culture* (2015) and 'Torture Porn and Uneasy Feminisms' in *Dread of Difference: Gender and the Horror Film* (2015). Working in both Gothic literary studies and horror film studies, she specialises in the racial and gender discourses of the Gothic, specifically focusing on the ways marginalised Others have critiqued and appropriated the Gothic genre and tropes.

Index

References to notes are indicated by n.

abjection, 74–5, 77, 80, 83, 108–14, 119–20
  and feminism, 130
  and Punter, 312–14
  and queer theory, 153–4
Aborigines, 74, 76–84, 85n6
Abraham, Nicholas, 224–6, 311
  The Shell and the Kernel, 224
  The Wolf-Man's Magic Word, 224, 226
advertising, 309
affect, 260–4, 265–6
African-Americans, 13, 54, 56–7
Aiken, John, 'On the Pleasure Derived from the Objects of Terror; with Sir Bertrand, A Fragment', 2
alien things, 266
alterity *see* the Other
America *see* United States of America
American Mary (film), 142
Amityville Horror, The (film), 92
anagrams, 224, 225, 226–7, 230–1
anasemic reading, 224–5
anthropomorphism, 230
Arbus, Diane, 135
Aristotle, 39, 40
  Poetics, 2, 36–7
artificial intelligence, 189
astronomy, 241–3

Atwood, Margaret, *The Handmaid's Tale*, 9
Austen, Jane, 37
Australia, 71, 73–4, 76–84

Bakhtin, Mikhail, 11
Baldick, Chris, 137, 139, 248
Ballard, J. G., *The Atrocity Exhibition*, 311
Banks, Iain, *The Wasp Factory*, 10
barbarism, 139–44
Barker, Pat, 309
Barnes, Djuna, *Nightwood*, 135
Baroque, 264
base matter, 242–4, 245
Bataille, Georges, 242–3, 244–5
Baudrillard, Jean, 117–18, 197, 206
  Simulacra and Simulations, 184
Bava, Mario, 265
Beattie, James, 139
Bergson, Henri, 260–1
Bhabha, Homi, 73, 301
Binswanger, Ludwig, 227
biomediated body, 186–7, 189–90, 196–7
Birds, The (film), 233
Birkhead, Edith, *The Tale of Terror*, 5
birth, 109–11, 112
Bjelland, Kat, 141

'Black Cat, The' (Poe), 13
Black Mirror (TV series), 183–4
Blake, William, 33–4
Blanchot, Maurice, 228, 229
   The Space of Literature, 220
blasphemy, 313
Blatty, William Peter, *The Exorcist*, 92, 96, 101–4, 105–6
bodies, 91–3, 96–7, 97–9, 100, 312
   and biomediated, 186–7, 189–90, 196–7
   and sexuality, 204, 205
   and technology, 191–4
   and without-organs (BwO), 265–6, 267
   and women, 132, 135, 136
Botting, Fred, 130–1
Braidotti, Rosi, 136, 182–3, 184
Bram Stoker's Dracula (film), 290
Braun, Johann Leopold, 102
Brides of Dracula, The (film), 265
British Empire, 80–1
Brontë, Charlotte *see Jane Eyre*
Brontë, Emily, *Wuthering Heights*, 138–9, 140, 141
Brooks, Max, *World War Z*, 306
Brown, Charles Brockden, 34–5
   Edgar Huntly, 3–4, 13
   Memoirs of Carwin the Biloquist, 48–9
   Wieland; or, the Transformation, 44, 45–9
Brown, Rebecca, *The Terrible Girls*, 11
Browne, Thomas, 310
Bürger, Gottfried August, *Lenore*, 286
burial, 206, 207
Burke, Edmund, 3, 19, 34, 35, 41–2, 265
   Philosophical Enquiry on the Sublime and Beautiful, 2, 120–1, 152
   and symbolic exchange, 206, 207

Butler, Judith, *The Psychic Life of Power*, 155, 158
Butler, Octavia, 190
Byron, George Gordon, Lord, 149, 213
   Manfred, 95

Caleb Williams (Godwin), 40, 41–2, 44
Canada, 72, 73, 75–6
capitalism, 6–7, 38, 243–9, 252–3
Carter, Angela, 133
   'The Bloody Chamber', 9
Castle of Otranto, The (Walpole), 1, 2, 10, 11–12, 15, 21, 167
   and dark materials, 240
   and economics, 253
   and Gothic, 114–17, 118–20
   and the Other, 22, 279–80, 283, 286, 296
   and queer theory, 150–1
   and spectres, 122–3
   and sublime, 121–2
catachresis, 230, 232
Cavell, Stanley, 167
childhood, 141, 305
chivalry, 35, 41–2
Christensen, Jerome, 37–8
cinema *see* film
class, 36, 117–19, 301, 302
Clery, E. J., 118–19
Clough, Patricia, 186–7
Coetzee, J. M., *Waiting for the Barbarians*, 12
Cohen, Jeffrey Jerome, 136–7
Cohen, Tom, 221–2, 232–3
   Cryptonomies, 233
Cole, Rev William, 147, 148
Coleridge, Samuel Taylor, 4
Collins, Felicity, 83
colonialism, 12–13, 64–5, 71–2, 79–80, 134; *see also* postcolonialism
commodities, 244, 245, 246, 248–9, 252–3

communism, 17
Conrad, Joseph. *Heart of Darkness*, 12
counterfeits, 117–18, 119, 120
Cronenberg, David, 15
cryptonymy, 224, 225–6, 227, 301
culture, 209–12
Curtis, John, *The Shipwreck of the Stirling Castle*, 82
Cyber-Gothic, 184
cyberspace, 15, 25
'Cyborg Manifesto, The' (Haraway), 136–7, 138, 185, 190

Dacre, Charlotte, *Zofloya, or The Moor*, 95, 157–8, 212
Danielewski, Mark Z., *House of Leaves*, 17, 21, 186
dark materialism, 240–1, 311
Darwin, Charles, 6
Davis, Therese, 83
De Beauvoir, Simone, *The Second Sex*, 131–2
De Man, Paul, 220, 221–2, 224, 229–32, 233–4
    Allegories of Reading, 230
    The Rhetoric of Romanticism, 229–30
    'Shelley Disfigured', 221, 229, 232
De Sade, Marquis, 207
    Justine, 133
death, 120–1, 311–12
    and film, 167–8
    and queer theory, 150
    and symbolic exchange, 206, 207
    see also burial; ghosts
deconstruction, 220–3, 224, 226–7, 228–35
Del Toro, Guillermo, 22–3
Deleuze, Gilles, 20, 21, 26, 260–1
    Cinema 2, 267
    and Lovecraft, 262–6, 267, 269, 271–2, 273, 275–6

demonic possession, 91–6, 99–106, 158
Derrida, Jacques, 16, 17, 21, 25–6, 186
    Adieu to Emmanuel Levinas, 294
    Archive Fever, 231–2
    and deconstruction, 221, 222, 224–5, 226, 229–30, 233–4
    and ethics, 281, 294–6
    'Fors', 224, 225
    and Marx, 243, 246
    Memoires for Paul de Man, 231, 233–4
    Of Grammatology, 231
    Of Hospitality, 22, 294
    Specters of Marx, 26, 220, 294
    Writing and Difference, 294
desire, 21
Devil, the, 96–8; *see also* demonic possession
Devils, The (film), 93
Dickens, Charles, *A Christmas Carol*, 288
Dinesen, Isak, 135
Doctor Wooreddy's Prescription for Enduring the Ending of the World (Mudrooroo), 76–7, 78, 80, 84
doppelgängers, 100
double, the, 169–70
Dr Jekyll and Mr Hyde (film), 289–90
Dracula (Stoker), 12, 13, 56, 92
    and abjection, 113
    and extimate figure, 212
    and face, 289
    and metamorphoses, 235
    and Mudrooroo, 79, 80–1
    and the Other, 292
    and outlaw, 308
    and religion, 215–16
    and Thing, 250–2
dreams, 96–7, 147–50, 272–3
'Dreams in the Witch House, The' (Lovecraft), 261–2, 270–4

Dryden, John, *The Conquest of Granada*, 139
Du Bois, W. E. B., 54
Du Maurier, Daphne, *Rebecca*, 18
'Dunwich Horror, The' (Lovecraft), 260, 261–2, 269–70
Dyer, Richard, 67
 Matter of Images, A, 65

economics, 184–5, 253; *see also* capitalism
Edelman, Lee, 221, 232
 No Future, 150
Edgar Huntly (Brown), 3–4, 13
Edwards, Justin D., 72
Einstein, Albert, 272, 273
Eliot, T. S., 5, 135
Ellison, Ralph, 65
 Invisible Man (Ellison), 54–5, 66–7
empire *see* British Empire
Engelstein, Stefani, 187
English Civil War, 50
Englishness, 57–9, 63, 64–5
Enlightenment, the, 34, 46, 47, 93–4, 98–9, 105
 and darkness, 242
 and feminism, 130–1, 134
 and Illuminati, 48–9
escape, 131–3, 135
ethics, 279–82, 284, 291, 293–6
exorcism, 92, 93, 101, 102, 104
Exorcist, The (Blatty), 92, 96, 101–4, 105–6
extimate agent, 212

faces, 286–93
Faerie Queene, The (Spenser), 2
Faflak, Joel, 98, 99, 100, 101
Fanon, Frantz, *Black Skin, White Masks*, 55, 59–60
fantasmata (erotic dreams), 96, 97
Faust (Goethe), 95
feminism, 8–10, 25, 129–38, 141–2

fetishism, 148, 248, 252–3
Fiedler, Leslie, 7
Fielding, Henry, 1
film, 14, 15, 22–3, 25, 165–71
 and Deleuze, 267
 and faces, 292–3
 and Hitchcock, 171–80, 232–3
 and the Other, 289–91
 and women, 142
Flaubert, Gustave, *The Temptation of Saint Anthony*, 228
Foucault, Michel, 34, 36, 38–9, 224
 Archeology of Knowledge, 228
 The Birth of the Clinic, 228–9
 Death and the Labyrinth, 226–9
 and the Devil, 97–8, 99, 103
 The Order of Things, 228, 229
 Raymond Roussel, 226–9
Frankenstein (film), 14, 290, 292
Frankenstein; or, The Modern Prometheus (Shelley), 9, 13, 15, 56, 223
 and abjection, 108–9, 110–11, 112–13, 119
 and aesthetics, 193–4
 and authorship, 187–8
 and dark materials, 240
 and feminism, 135, 136, 137–8
 and the Other, 22
 and queer theory, 158–60
 and race, 67
 and science, 182, 185
 and treatments, 302, 305–6
 and visual appearance, 286–7
Frankenstein in Baghdad (Saadawi), 302
Fraser, Eliza, 82–3, 85n4
freaks, 135, 138
Freaks (film), 292
Freccero, Carla, 157, 159
French Revolution, 206, 213
Freud, Sigmund, 5–6, 7, 25, 214, 216
 and bodies, 91–3, 100
 The Ego and the Id, 155

and Haizmann, 102
Interpretation of Dreams, 6
and introjection, 42, 43
On Narcissism, 100
and possession, 93–5
and subconscious, 114
and transference, 104, 105
and uncanny, 72–3, 109, 169–70
and unconscious, 225, 262
and Wolf-Man, 224
Friday the 13th (film series), 290–1
Fukuyama, Francis, 37–8

Gelder, Ken, 73–4
gender, 10–11, 25, 189–91, 302; *see also* women
genealogy, 34–5, 38–43, 48, 49–51
Genet, Jean, 18
ghosts, 16, 115–16, 204–5, 302, 309–11
  and alterity, 279–80
  and film, 166, 176–7
  and postcolonialism, 74
  and race, 64
  and symbolic exchange, 213–14
Gibson, William, *Neuromancer*, 15, 193
Gilbert, Sandra, *The Madwoman in the Attic*, 132
Gilmore, Jane, 141–2
Gilpin, William, 3
Ginger Snaps (film), 142
'Girl Who Was Plugged In, The' (Tiptree), 184, 185, 186, 188–9, 190–8
Goddu, Teresa, 55–6
Godwin, William, 34–5, 36–8, 39–43, 50–1
  and Brown, 44
  Caleb Williams, 40, 41–2, 44
  An Enquiry Concerning Political Justice, 48
  Mandeville, 49–51
  'On History and Romance', 39

Goethe, Johann Wolfgang von, *Faust*, 95
Gothic
  and abjection, 108–11, 113–14
  and Aborigines, 78–9, 84
  and barbarism, 139–41
  and bodies, 91–3, 105–6
  and colonialism, 12–13
  and dark materials, 240–1
  and deconstruction, 220–3
  and feminism, 8–10, 129–35
  and film, 165–80
  and genealogy, 34–5, 42–3, 48
  and Lovecraft, 260, 261, 264–5, 268–9, 270–1
  and materialism, 255–6
  and 'matrix', 223–4
  and the Other, 22–3, 291–4, 296
  and postcolonialism, 71–2, 75–6
  and psychoanalysis, 17–20, 216–17
  and Punter, 301–17
  and queer theory, 10–11, 150–1
  and race, 53–69
  and structuralism, 16–17
  and symbolic exchange, 206, 208–9, 211, 213–14
  and technology, 14–16, 185, 187
  and theory, 1–8, 11–12, 23–7, 185–6
  and unconscious, 103
  and Walpole, 114–17, 118–20
Goths, 139–40
Gotthelf, Jeremias, *The Black Spider*, 311
Gray, Alisdair *see Poor Things*
Greenblatt, Stephen, 11
Guattari, Félix, 20, 260, 261
  and Lovecraft, 262–6, 267, 271–2, 276
Gubar, Susan, *The Madwoman in the Attic*, 132

Haitian Revolution, 56, 58
Haizmann, Christoph, 92, 93–6, 101, 102
Halberstam, Judith, 55–6
   The Queer Art of Failure, 153–4
Hall, Stuart, 71–2
Halloween (film series), 290
Hamlet (Shakespeare), 3, 6, 117–18, 280, 286
Haraway, Donna
   'The Cyborg Manifesto', 136–7, 138, 185, 190
   Staying With the Trouble, 144
Harman, Graham, 263
Harrison, M. John, 317
Harvey, William, 310
Hawthorne, Nathaniel, 35
   House of the Seven Gables, 13
   'The Minister's Black Veil', 54
Hayles, N. Katherine, 189–90, 193
Hébert, Anne, *Kamouraska*, 75
Hegel, Georg Wilhelm, 223–4
Heidegger, Martin, 282
Herder, Johann Gottfried, 34
high culture, 4, 11–12
Hillman, James, 313–14
Hippocrates, 98
historical romance, 39–43
history *see* genealogy; New Historicism
Hitchcock, Alfred, 171–80, 232–3
Hobsbawm, Eric, 35
Hodgson, William Hope, *The Night Land*, 241
Hoeveler, Diane Long, *Gothic Feminism*, 133–4
Hoffman, E. T. A., 'The Sandman', 5–6
Hogg, James, *The Private Memoirs and Confessions of a Justified Sinner*, 99–101, 212
honour codes, 35
Hopkinson, Nalo, *Brown Girl in the Ring*, 76
horror, 250

hospitality, 294–6
humanity, 182–3, 302
Hurd, Richard, *Letters on Chivalry and Romance*, 1–2
Hurley, Kameron, *God's War*, 312
Hurley, Kelly, 241
Husserl, Edmund, 282

Illuminati, 48–9
immigrants, 58–9
imprisonment, 131–3, 135
incorporation, 225–6
indigenous peoples, 71, 72, 74, 75; *see also* Aborigines
Inside Out (film), 151
interstice, 274–5
introjection, 42, 43
Invisible Man (Ellison), 54–5, 66–7
ipseity, 291, 295
Italian, The (Radcliffe), 152, 154–5, 156, 285
Ivanhoe (Scott), 39, 42
Ivanov, Ilya Ivanovich, 304

Jackson, Neil, *Snuff: Real Death and Screen Media*, 310
Jackson, Shelley, *Patchwork Girl*, 137
Jacobs, Jane M., 73–4
James, M. R.
   'Oh, Whistle, and I'll Come to You, My Lad', 289
   'The Treasure of Abbot Thomas', 316
Jane Eyre (Brontë), 9, 12, 132, 133, 134
   and savagery, 140, 142–3
Janet, Pierre, 227
Jennifer's Body (film), 142
Johnson, Colin *see* Mudrooroo

Kane, Sarah, *Blasted*, 312–13
Kant, Immanuel, 18–19, 262
   Perpetual Peace: A Philosophical Sketch, 294

Kenan, Randall, 10–11
  A Visitation of Spirits, 10–11
King, Stephen, *Shining, The*, 7–8
Kittler, Friedrich, 221, 233
Klein, Melanie, 271–2
Knudsen, Eva Rask, 78
Kofman, Sarah, 246
Kristeva, Julia, 17–18, 19, 305, 313
  and abjection, 109–14, 120, 122–3, 153
  Powers of Horror, 55, 74–5, 108, 109, 114
  Strangers to Ourselves, 111–12

Lacan, Jacques, 18, 20, 104, 111
  and *das Ding*, 250, 262, 266
language, 221–2, 225, 227, 229–31, 268, 305
Laplace, Pierre-Simon, *System of the World*, 241–2
Laplanche, Jean, 305
Lawn, Jennifer, 74
Le Fanu, Sheridan, *Carmilla*, 295
Lee, Sophia, 223
  The Recess, 223
Leroux, Gaston, *The Phantom of the Opera*, 12, 113, 289
Lesnik-Oberstein, Karin, 141
Levin, Ira, *Rosemary's Baby*, 97
Levinas, Emmanuel, 21–2, 26, 221, 294, 295
  Existence and Existents, 220
  and the Other, 281–5, 287, 288, 293
  Otherwise than Being, 291–2
  Time and the Other, 281, 291
  Totality and Infinity, 22, 281–3, 291
Lewis, Matthew *see The Monk*
Lloyd Smith, Allan, 16–17
Locke, John, 97, 98–9, 116
  Essay Concerning Human Understanding, 114–15
lost children, 83–4, 85n5

Love, Courtney, 141
Lovecraft, H. P., 6, 26, 241, 260–7, 316
  'The Call of Cthulu' 269
  'The Colour Out of Space', 264, 268
  'The Dreams in the Witch House', 261–2, 270–4
  'The Dunwich Horror', 260, 261–2, 269–70
  'From Beyond', 261–2, 274–6
  'The Horror at Red Hook', 266
  'The Hound', 268
  'The Shadow over Innsmouth', 268–9
  'The Thing on the Doorstep', 260
  'Through the Gates of the Silver Key', 264
  'The Whisperer in Darkness', 265, 268
low culture, 4, 5, 11–12
lucid possession, 96

Mabo and Others v. Queensland, 74
Macaulay, Thomas Babington, 148
MacCormack, Patricia, 264, 268, 269
McCullers, Carson, 135
McGahan, Andrew, *The White Earth* (McGahan), 12
Machen, Arthur, 'The Novel of the White Powder', 240
machine, the, 233
machine of society, 39–40
Mad Men (TV series), 165–7
Malabou, Catherine
  The Future of Hegel, 234
  The New Wounded, 234–5
  Ontology of the Accident, 234–5
  What Should We Do With Our Brain?, 234
Malchow, H. L., 55–6, 57
Malleus maleficarum (Institoris/Sprenger), 97

Marx, Karl, 34, 243–4, 247–8, 250
Marxism, 6–7, 11, 17, 36, 244–7
masculinity, 10
Master of the Ghost Dreaming series (Mudrooroo), 76–84
materialism, 244–52
mathematics, 272, 273
Maturin, Charles, *Melmouth the Wanderer*, 95
Mauss, Marcel, 206
medical gaze, 228
medievalism, 35
Méliès, Georges, 14
Melville, Herman, 35
   Pierre; or, the Ambiguities, 43–4
Michell, John, 241
Miéville, China, 306
Mighall, Robert, 139
Mittelholzer, Edgar, 53–4
   My Bones and My Flute, 67–8
modernity, 117–18, 302
Moers, Ellen, 9
   Literary Women, 130, 135, 138–9
Monk, The (Lewis), 4, 95, 97, 286
   and queer theory, 156–7, 158
   and supernatural, 204–6
   and symbolic exchange, 210–13, 214–15
monsters, 135–8, 186, 246–7, 302, 304–6, 314–16
Mootoo, Shani, *He Drown She in the Sea*, 73
Moravec, Hans, 192, 193
Morrison, Toni, 65, 134
   Beloved, 13, 310–11
   Playing in the Dark, 13, 54, 56–7
Moth Diaries, The (film), 142
Mudrooroo, 76–84
multiculturalism, 72
Muñoz, José Estabon, *Cruising Utopia: The Then and There of Queer Futurity*, 155–6, 160

Munro, Alice, 75
Mysteries of Udolpho, The (Radcliffe), 8, 152–3, 203–6, 209–10, 253, 285

Nancy, Jean-Luc, 221
narrative, 194–7
Native Americans, 3–4, 13
Native Son (Wright), 13, 60, 65, 67
Neuromancer (Gibson), 15, 193
New Historicism, 11–12, 17, 33–4, 35–8
New Zealand, 71, 75
Newman, Judie, 72
Nietzsche, Friedrich, 34, 38, 42
   The Birth of Tragedy, 228
Nosferatu (film), 265, 290
novels, 1, 37
nuclear waste, 234

Oesterreich, T. K., 95–6
olsigns, 267, 269, 270
opera, 14
opsigns, 267, 269, 270, 272–3
oral culture, 45, 47
Orlan, 304–5
Other, the, 22–3, 26, 111, 279–89, 291–4
   and Derrida, 294–6
   and film, 289–91
Others, The (film), 290
outlaws, 307–9
Oyeyemi, Helen, 53–4
   and barbarism, 142–4
   White is for Witching, 57–9, 61–3, 64–5, 68–9, 142–4

Paine, Thomas, 207
Pandora's Box (film), 267
part-objects, 271–2
past, the, 165–8, 208–11
Pearson, Wendy, 79, 81, 84
Peeping Tom (film), 311
Penny Dreadful (TV series), 137

Perry, Phyllis Alesia, 53–4
  Stigmata, 64
Petry, Ann, 54
  The Street, 60–1, 65–6
Phantom of the Opera, The (film), 290
Phantom of the Opera, The (Leroux), 12, 113, 289
Phillips, Julie, 188–9
Philosophical Enquiry on the Sublime and Beautiful (Burke), 2, 120–1, 152
philosophy, 37
phobogenic object, 55
Pierce, Peter, 83
Plath, Sylvia, 135
Poe, Edgar Allan, 4–5
  'The Cask of Amontillado', 226
  'Eureka', 242
  'The Facts in the Case of M. Valdemar', 240
  'The Fall of the House of Usher', 113
  'The Masque of the Red Death', 240, 287–8
  'The Premature Burial', 226
  'The Raven', 13
  'The Tell-Tale Heart', 240
Poor Things (Gray), 20, 137, 244, 253–6
Possessed (TV movie), 92
possession, 91–6, 99–106
post-structuralism, 16–21, 25–6
postcolonialism, 12, 25, 71–2
  and abjection, 74–5
  and location, 75–6
  and race, 63–4
  and uncanny, 72–4
  and vampires, 80–1
posthumanism, 185
Powell, Enoch, 64–5
Price, Uvedale, 3
priests, 104–5
print culture, 45, 47

prosopopeia, 230
psyche, 301, 302
Psycho (film), 22, 179–80, 290
psychoanalysis, 5–6, 7, 17–20, 25
  and anasemic reading, 224–5
  and incorporation, 225–6
  and possession, 92, 93–5
  and symbolic exchange, 216–17
  and unconscious, 103
Punter, David, 72, 301–17
  The Literature of Terror: A History of Gothic Fictions from 1765 to the Present Day, 8, 26–7, 301
  Postcolonial Imaginings, 75

queer theory, 10–11, 25, 147–9, 150–1, 153–60

race, 2, 13, 25, 53–69, 302
  and barbarism, 143–4
  and Lovecraft, 266–7
Radcliffe, Ann, 8, 34, 94, 209–10, 253
  and alterity, 285–6
  The Italian, 152, 154–5, 156, 285
  'On the Supernatural in Poetry', 3
  and queer theory, 151–5, 156
  Romance of the Forest, 213
  and supernatural, 203–6, 226
  and symbolic exchange, 213
  see also The Mysteries of Udolpho
Real, the, 18–20
Rebecca (Du Maurier), 18
Rebecca (film), 174–7
reconciliation, 82–3
Reeve, Clara, 283
  The Old English Baron, 3, 279–80
  The Progress of Romance, 3
refugees, 302, 305

religion, 7, 46, 47, 48–9, 92
   and blasphemy, 313
   and the Devil, 97, 98
   and genre, 114
   and priests, 104–5
   and symbolic exchange, 214–16
revolutionism, 208
Rhys, Jean, *Wide Sargasso Sea*, 12, 142–3
Richards, I. A., 5
Richardson, Samuel, 1
Riemann, Bernhard, 272, 273
Ring, The (film), 186
Riot Grrrl, 141
Robinson, Eden, 75
   Monkey Beach, 12
Robinson, George Augustus, 77, 79
Roiphe, Katie, 141
romance, 1, 3, 34, 208–9
Roussel, Raymond, 227–8, 229
   How I Wrote Certain of My Texts, 227
Rushdie, Salman, *Midnight's Children*, 12
Russ, Joanna, 188, 190
Russell, Ray, *The Case Against Satan*, 92, 103, 104–5
Russo, Mary, 129

Said, Edward, 301
   Orientalism, 12
Sartre, Jean-Paul, 220
Saussure, Ferdinand de, 16, 225, 226, 227
savagery, 138–9, 140–4
Schaffer, Kay, 82
Scheckter, John, 83
Schiller, Friedrich, *The Ghost-Seer; or, Apparitionist*, 34, 285–6
schizoanalysis, 261
science, 182
science fiction, 15, 185

Scott, Sir Walter, 34, 35, 36–7, 38–9, 280, 283
   Ivanhoe, 39, 42
   'On Romance', 4
   Waverley, 39, 42
Scream (film series), 290
secrecy, 222–3, 228
Sedgwick, Eve Kosofsky, 286
sexuality, 10, 25, 97
   and the body, 204, 205
   and race, 56, 57
   see also queer theory
Shakespeare, William, 14, 35–6
   Hamlet, 3, 6, 117–18, 280, 286
   Macbeth, 3
Shape of Water, The (film), 22–3
Sheldon, Alice, 188–9
Shelley, Mary, 34, 149–50
   The Last Man, 240
   see also Frankenstein
Shelley, Percy Bysshe, 149, 232
   The Daemon of the World, 99
   St Irvyne, 223
   The Triumph of Life, 232
Showalter, Elaine, 8–9
signifiers, 16–18, 20–1, 117, 119, 222–3
slavery, 56–7, 64, 67–8, 134, 310
Slender Man, 314–15
Smollett, Tobias, 1
social relations, 207–8
sonambulism, 95–6, 100
sonsigns, 267, 269
sound, 268–70
spectres, 16–17, 115–16, 122–3, 220, 301
   and commodities, 245–6
   and dematerialism, 243
   and film, 168–9
Spenser, Edmund, *The Faerie Queene*, 2
Spillers, Hortense, 53
Spivak, Gayatri, 134, 136, 140, 301
Starobinski, Jean, 225, 226, 230
Stelarc, 304

Stephenson, Craig E., 95, 96
Stoker, Bram *see Dracula* (Stoker)
Stowe, Harriet Beecher, *Uncle Tom's Cabin*, 13
Strange Case of Dr Jekyll and Mr Hyde (Stevenson), 12, 56, 113, 235
  and face, 288
  and Thing, 250–1
structuralism, 16–17
sublime, 2, 3, 19, 120–2, 152–3
supernatural, 1, 3, 94, 203–6
surplus materialism, 250–2
Suspicion (film), 177–9
symbolic art, 223–4
symbolic exchange, 205–17

tactisigns, 267, 269, 270, 273
technology, 14–16, 182–5, 186–7, 189–98, 314–16
terror, 2, 3, 5, 310–11
Texas Chainsaw Massacre, The (film), 290
Things, 243, 245, 250–2, 254, 262–7
  and Lovecraft, 260, 261
thresholds, 302, 311
Tillyard, E. M. W., *The Elizabethan World Picture*, 35–6
Tiptree, James
  'The Girl Who Was Plugged In', 184, 185, 186, 188–9, 190–8
  'The Women Men Don't See', 188
Todorov, Tzvetan, *The Fantastic*, 16
Torok, Maria, 224–6, 311
  The Shell and the Kernel, 224
  The Wolf-Man's Magic Word, 224, 226
traditionalism, 208
tranced grief, 43–4, 48

trauma, 40–1, 42–3, 48, 49–50, 73
Turcotte, Gerry, 79, 81, 82, 83
Turing, Alan, 189

uncanny, the, 72–4, 80, 83–4, 100, 169–70
  and film, 178–80
  and Freud, 109
  and Lovecraft, 271
  and symbolic exchange, 213–14
Uncanny, The (Freud), 5–6, 100
unconscious, 43, 44, 103, 225, 262
unhomely (*unheimlich*), 73, 100, 169, 214
United States of America, 3–5, 7, 13, 44–9
  and race, 54, 56–7, 66–7
universality, 40
Ursuline nuns, 92, 93

Vacker, Barry, 306–7
vampires, 79–82, 83, 84, 215, 293, 302
  and faces, 289
  and materialism, 247–50
  and outlaws, 308–9
Van Elferen, Isabella, 268–9
veiling, 54–5
Vertigo (film), 171–4
victim feminism, 133, 150–3
Videodrome (film), 15
violence, 40–1, 43, 44, 129, 210
  and the Other, 292, 294, 295

Walpole, Horace, 3, 4, 14, 122–3, 147–9, 151; *see also The Castle of Otranto*
Wandering Jew, 214–15
war, 309–10
Watt, James, 208–9
Weinstock, Geoffrey, 263
Weir, Johann, *Cinq livres de l'imposture et tromperie des diables*, 97

Wells, H. G., *The Island of Doctor Moreau*, 304
Whateley, Richard, 37
White is for Witching (Oyeyemi), 57–9, 61–3, 64–5, 68–9, 142–4
whiteness, 64–9
Wilde, Oscar, 288
Williams, Anne, 111, 123
Wilson, Janet, 75
Winterson, Jeanette, *The Daylight Gate*, 303–4
Wisker, Gina, 63
witches, 303–4
Wolfe, Cary, 182, 183
Wollstonecraft, Mary, 134
  Maria, or The Wrongs of Woman, 131
  A Vindication of the Rights of Woman 131
women, 8–9, 81–2, 187–8, 254–5, 256
  and abjection, 111
  and cyborgs, 193–4
  and savagery, 138–9, 140–4
  and sexuality, 204, 205
  and victimisation, 150–3
  and war, 309–10
  and witches, 303–4
  see also feminism
Wright, Richard, *Native Son*, 13, 60, 65, 67
Writing from the Fringe (Mudrooroo), 78
Wuthering Heights (Brontë), 138–9, 140, 141

xenophobia, 56

Yeux sans visage, Les (film), 290, 312
Young, Edward, *Night Thoughts*, 317
Young, Robert, 71

zero, the, 229, 233
Žižek, Slavoj, 119–20, 222, 233, 262, 308
  The Sublime Object of Ideology, 112
Zofloya, or The Moor (Dacre), 95, 157–8, 212
zombies, 302, 306–7

EU representative:
Easy Access System Europe
Mustamäe tee 50, 10621 Tallinn, Estonia
Gpsr.requests@easproject.com

www.ingramcontent.com/pod-product-compliance
Lightning Source LLC
Chambersburg PA
CBHW070745020526
44116CB00032B/1982